Tattoo Bible

BOOK TWO

BY

SUPERIOR TATTOO

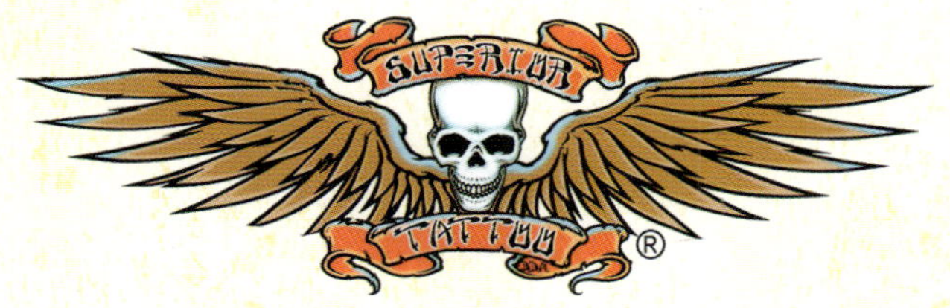

Published by:

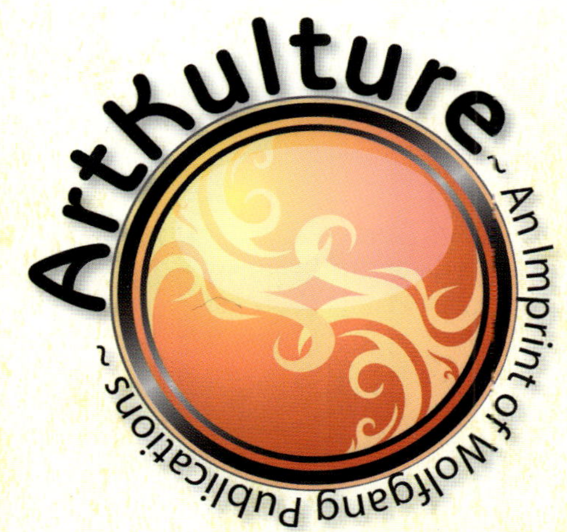

PO Box 223
Stillwater, MN 55082
www.wolfpub.com
www.artkulture.com

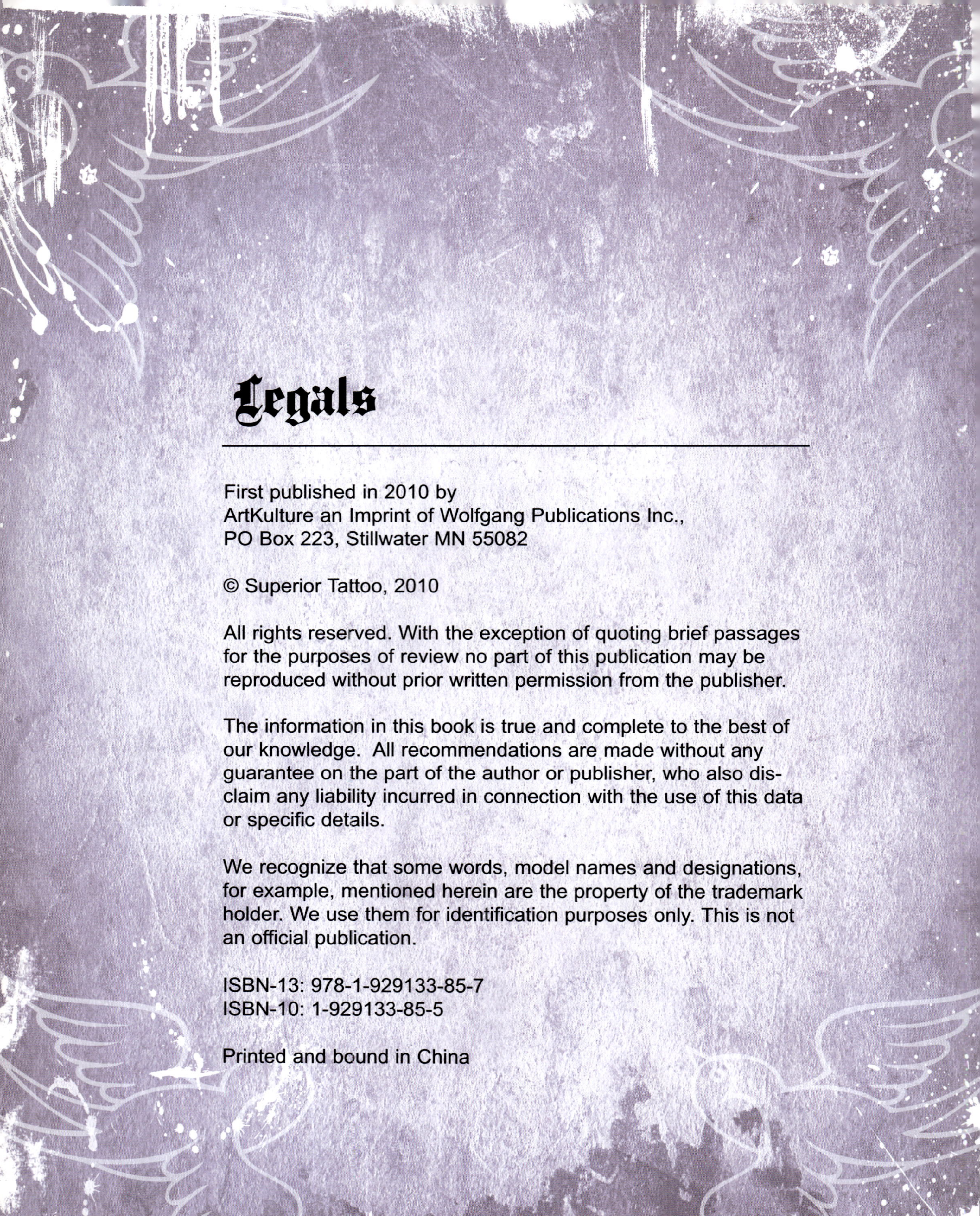

Legals

First published in 2010 by
ArtKulture an Imprint of Wolfgang Publications Inc.,
PO Box 223, Stillwater MN 55082

The information in this book is true and complete to the best of our knowledge. All recommendations are made without any guarantee on the part of the author or publisher, who also disclaim any liability incurred in connection with the use of this data or specific details.

We recognize that some words, model names and designations, for example, mentioned herein are the property of the trademark holder. We use them for identification purposes only. This is not an official publication.

ISBN-13: 978-1-929133-85-7
ISBN-10: 1-929133-85-5

Printed and bound in China

Acknowledgements

Superior Tattoo Equipment, Inc. would like to thank many of the same people as Book One. This includes the artists of course, as without them it would just be a bunch of blank pages. Additional thanks to Karen Bachler, Crystal Simeister, Tom Kaczor, and Jim Watson at Superior Tattoo Equipment for their time spent in design, selection, scanning, and artwork setup. I also wish to thank Timothy Remus of Wolfgang Publications for his agreement to use full-bleed pages throughout the book. For those that don't know, full-bleed allows the art to flow right off the edge of the page instead of being reduced in size to accommodate a border. As you will see when you view the book, this artwork needs to fill the entire page. Please visit Superiortattoo.com for all your tattoo needs. The artists that contributed to this book include:

Chris Bailey
Jeff Bartels
William "Inkee" Blanchard
Danny Boy
Hollis Cantrell
Doni Castello
Edward Chambers
Brandon Chavez
Aaron Coleman
Andre Davis
Katelyn Eileen
Elordi
Michael Fitts
Marina Holguin
Wes Humpston
Pat Jones
Kevin LeBlanc
Nicole McCord
Danny Most
Tom Nickels
Nate Powers
Prakash
Radical Ron
Screamin' Mimi
Bob Sims
Spider
Stoneface
Lisa Van Pelt
Jim Watson
Wish
Darren Yeisley
Zaya
Joe Zuniga

Introduction

Tattoo Bible - Book Two has full page images from your favorite artists or soon will be. It really is the best of the best, formatted to give you every detail of their work. Some of the pages took many many hours to draw, using pencils, prisma-color pencils, paint, and even a couple that were done with ball point pen. See if you can decide which ones they are. This book has been designed to provide imaginative ideas for the perfect tattoo, we think it's a resource that can be found nowhere else. Let us know your thoughts on future categories you would like to see in upcoming books by dropping us a note at: sales@superiortattoo.com

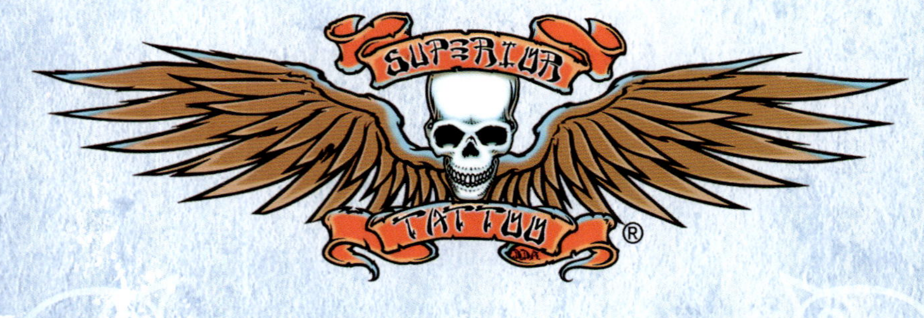

From the Publisher, Book Two

There seem to be two things that tattoo enthusiasts can't get enough of: tattoos, and images of tattoos. Tattoo Bible - Book One was so well received that we asked Martin and the staff at Superior Tattoo to go back into their archives and do it one more time. Thus you hold in your hands a new collection of high quality flash from one of the world's largest purveyors of tattoo equipment.

Whether you're looking for traditional American art, or something with a more Oriental orientation, Book Two contains 144 pages of art from Superior Tattoo. Art you can use right off the page, art you can massage into the design of your dreams, art you can use as a catalyst to create something totally different.

When we agreed to do Book One, I did so with some trepidation. I'm a dyed in the wool control freak. Allowing another company to not only contribute to, but essentially design, a book for us set off a whole series of alarm bells. As I reported, however, that first experience was smooth and completely stress free. And once again, Martin and his crew have provided us with high quality images, in a format that fits our groove. Whenever I fly, people ask, "How was the trip?" And generally I reply, "Great, no lumps, no bumps, on time and no scary parts." Dealing with Superior is much the same; no lumps, no bumps, everything on time, and there are never any scary parts where I begin to wonder about the partnership.

Timothy Remus

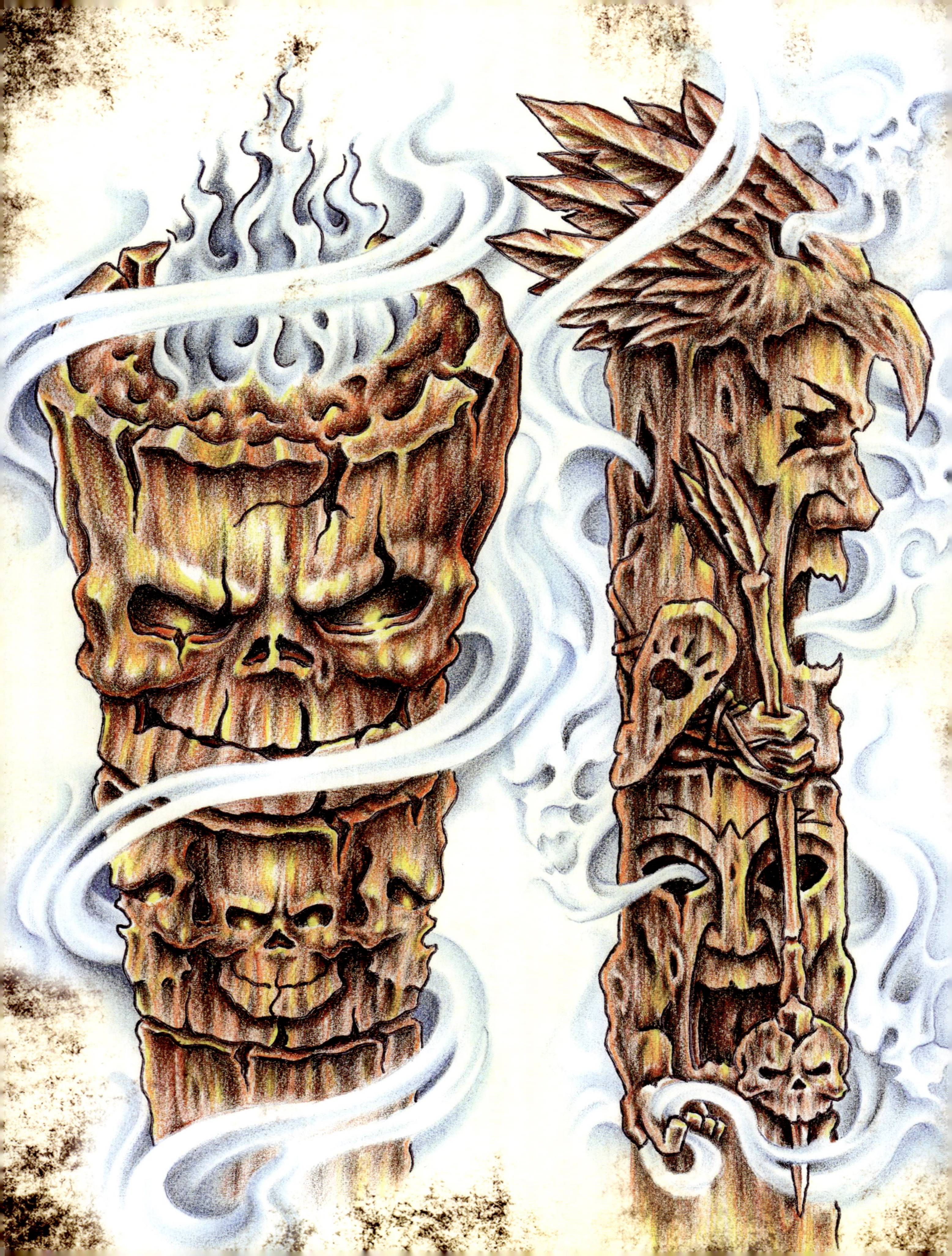

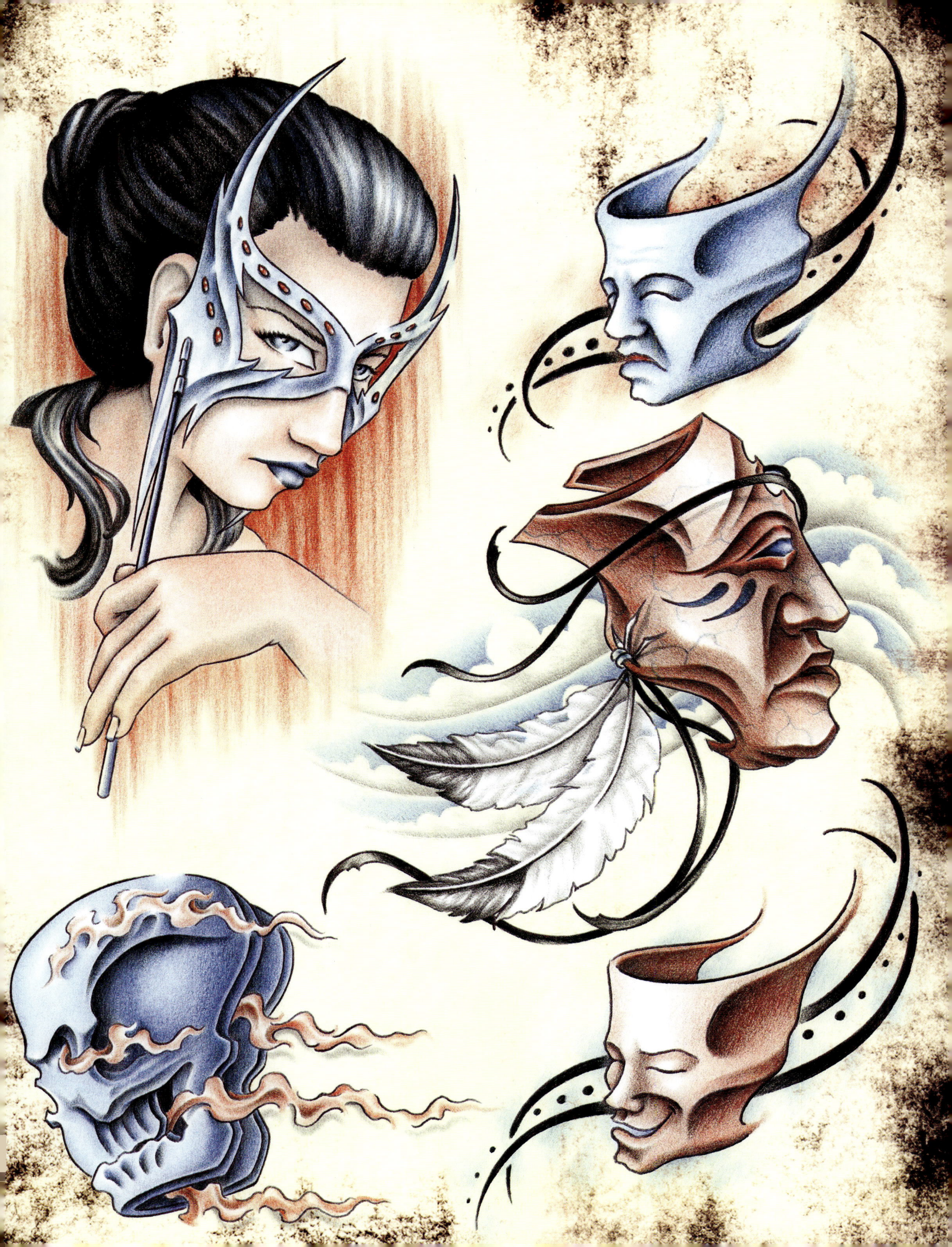

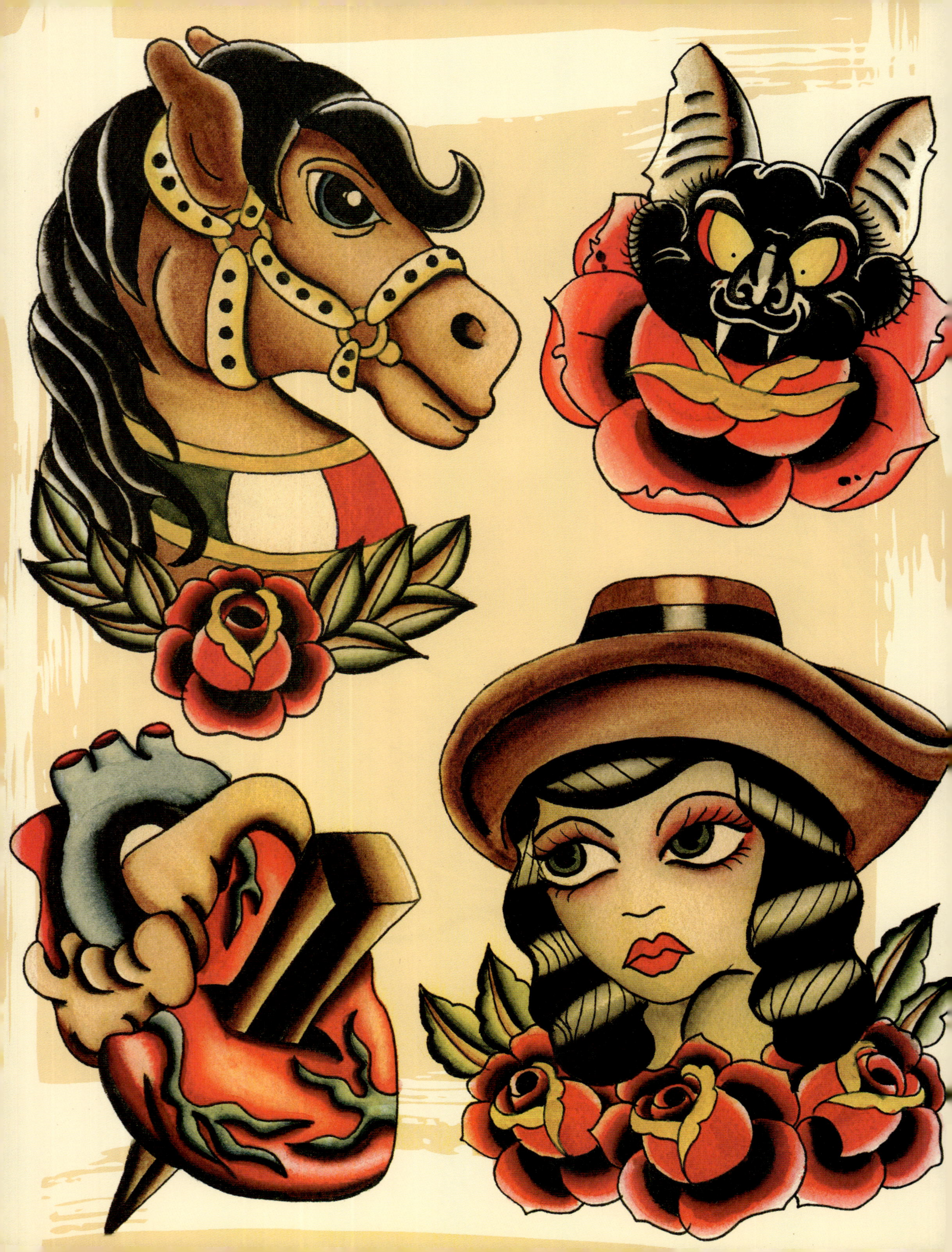

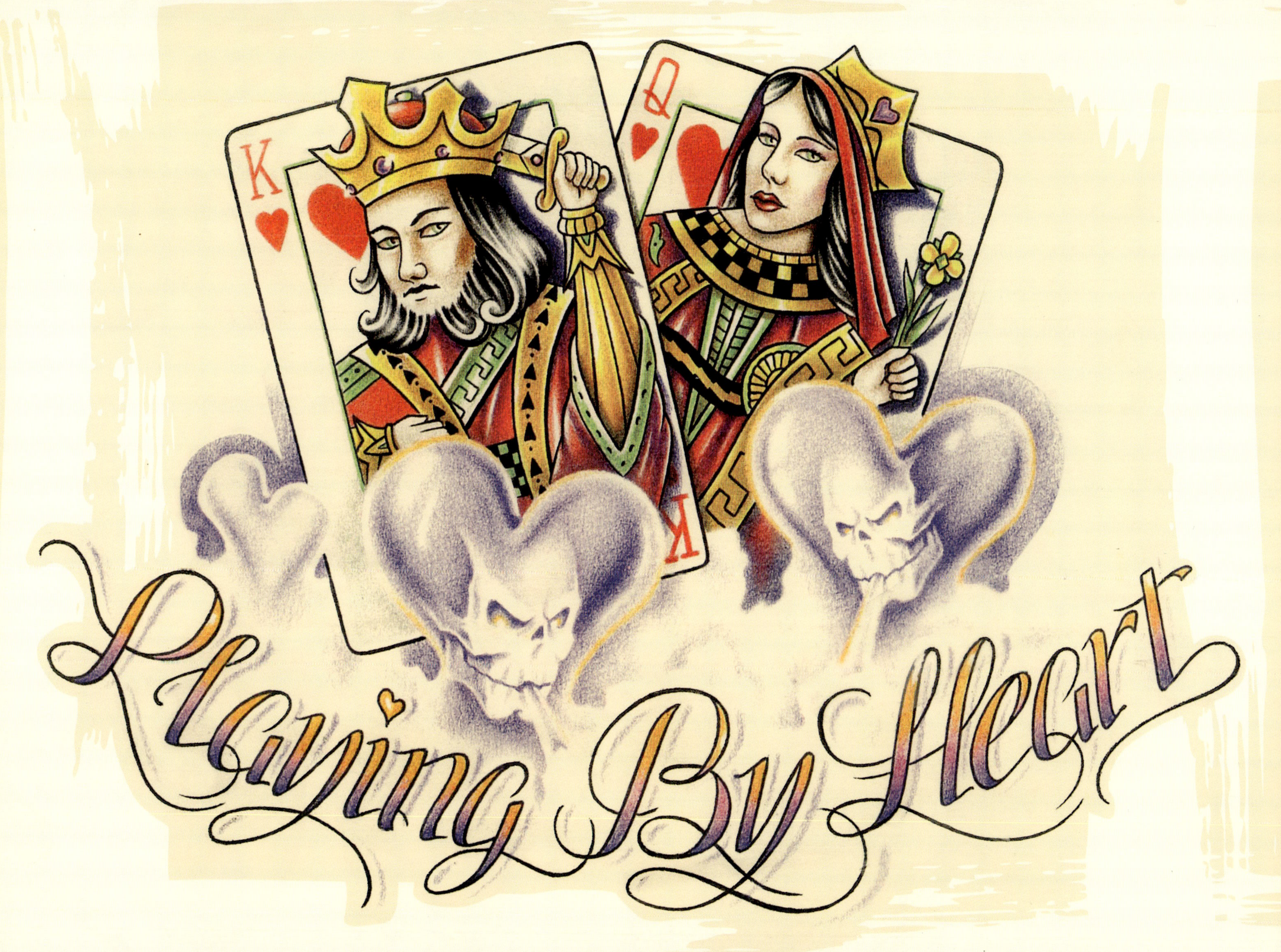
Playing By Heart

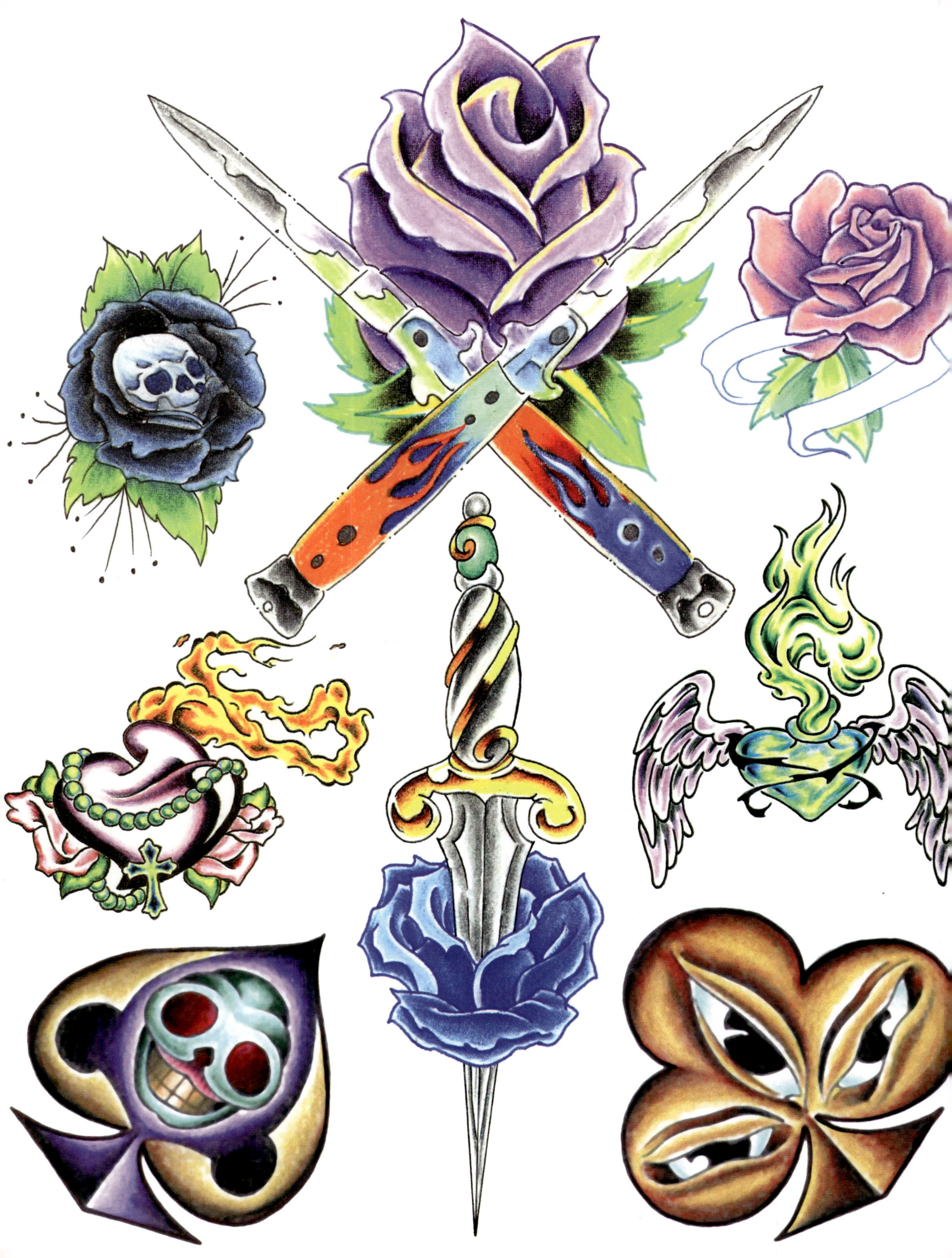

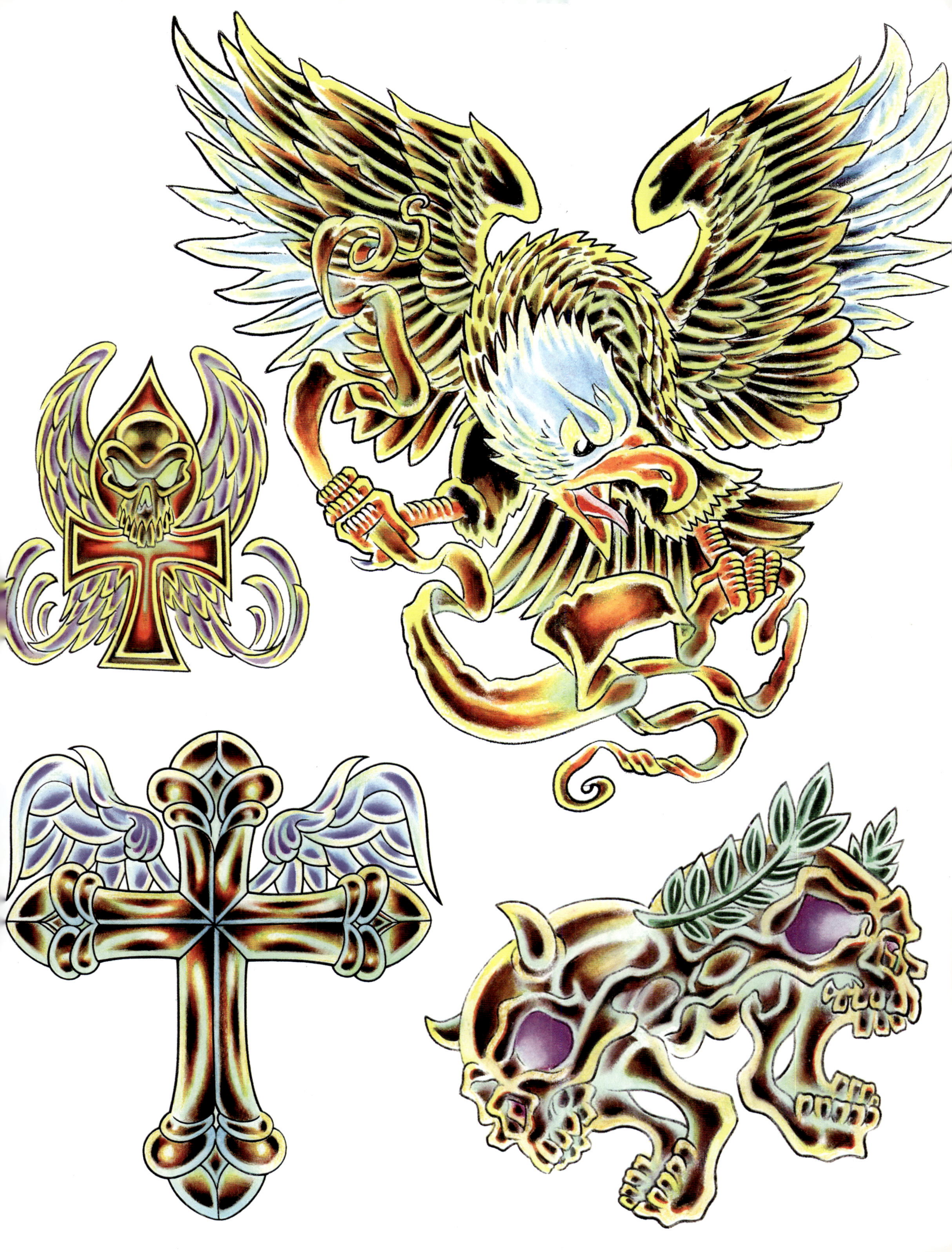

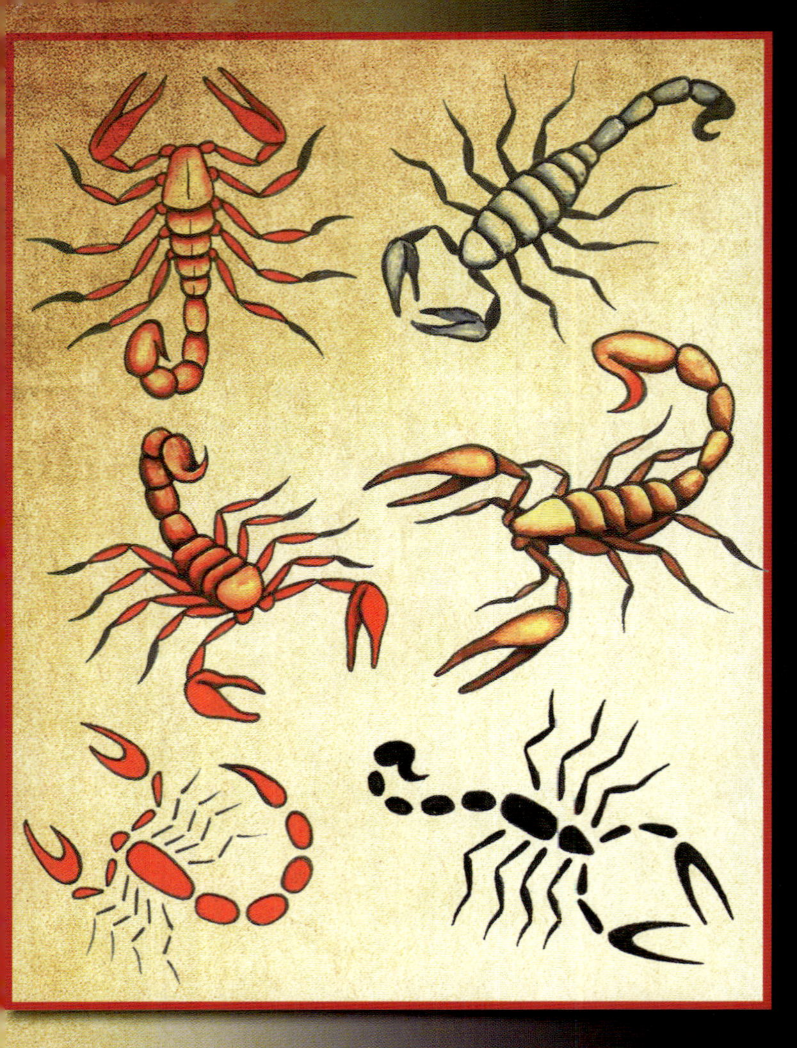
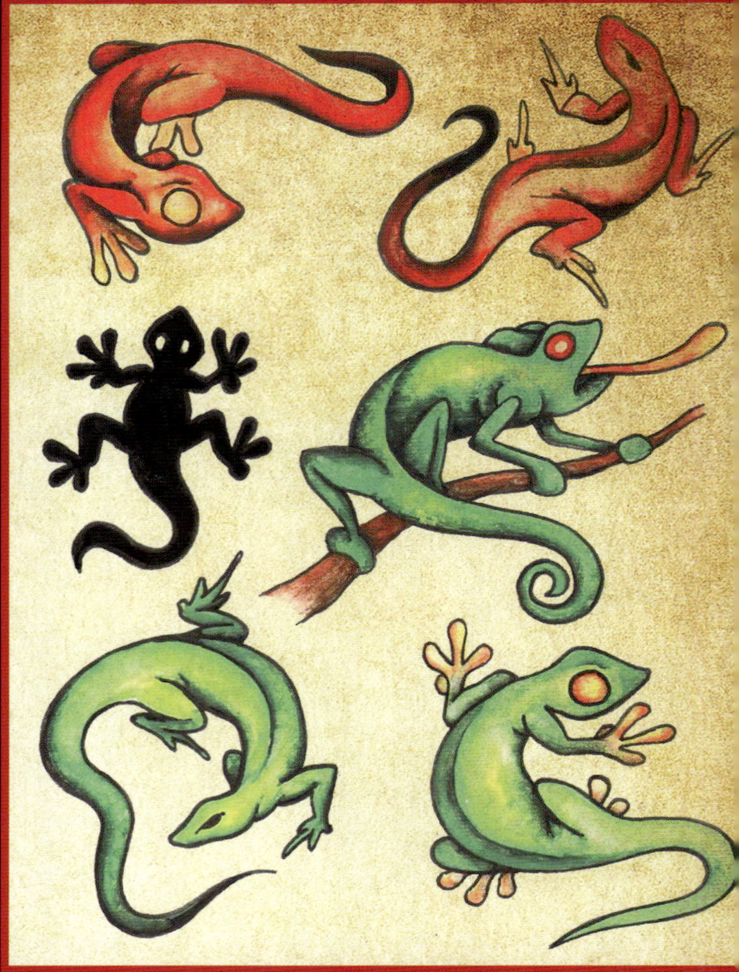
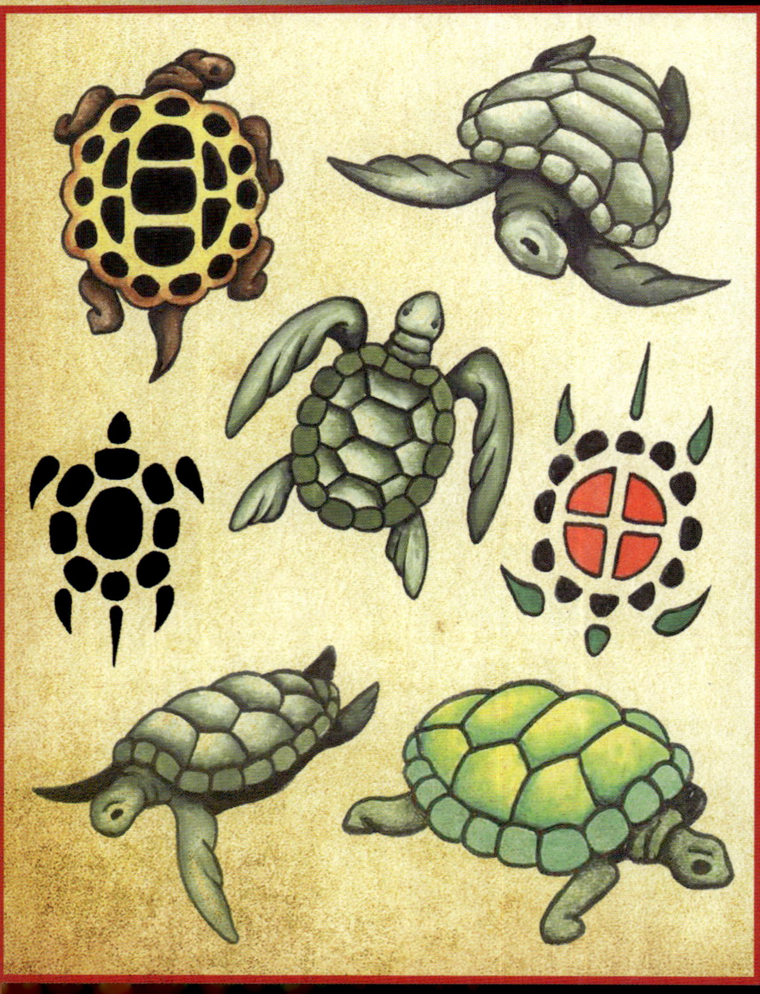
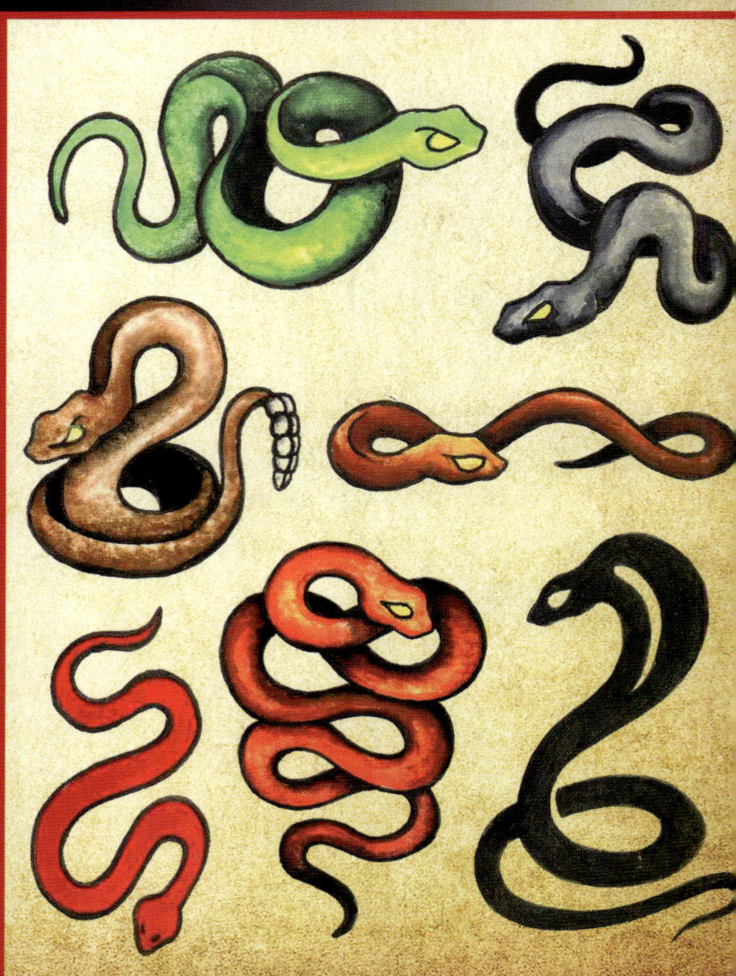

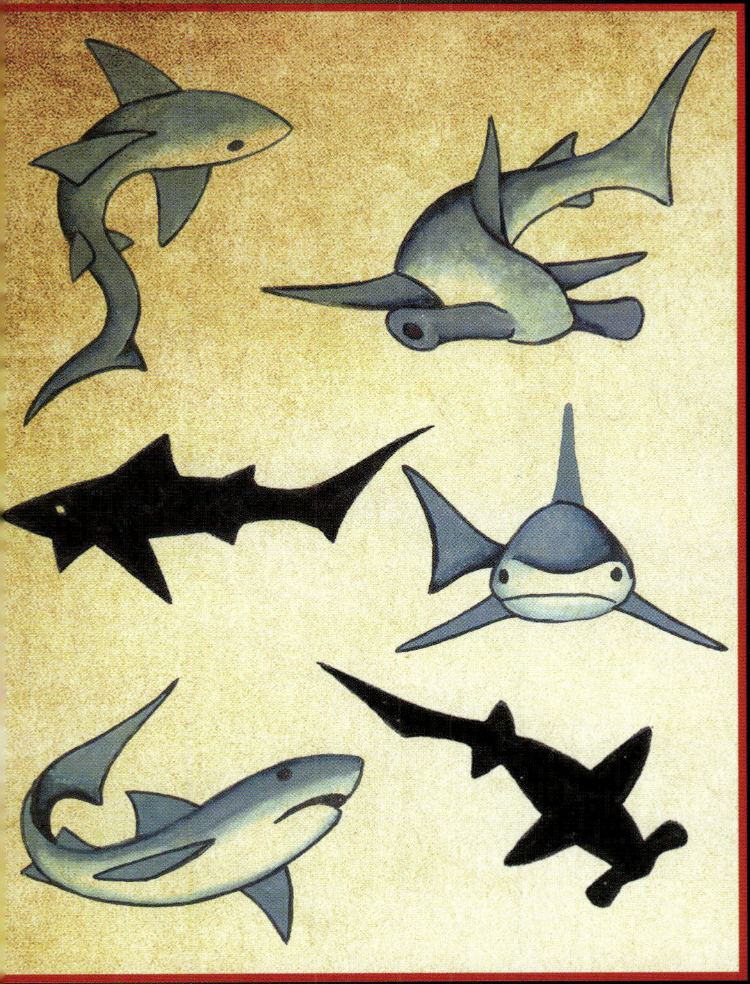

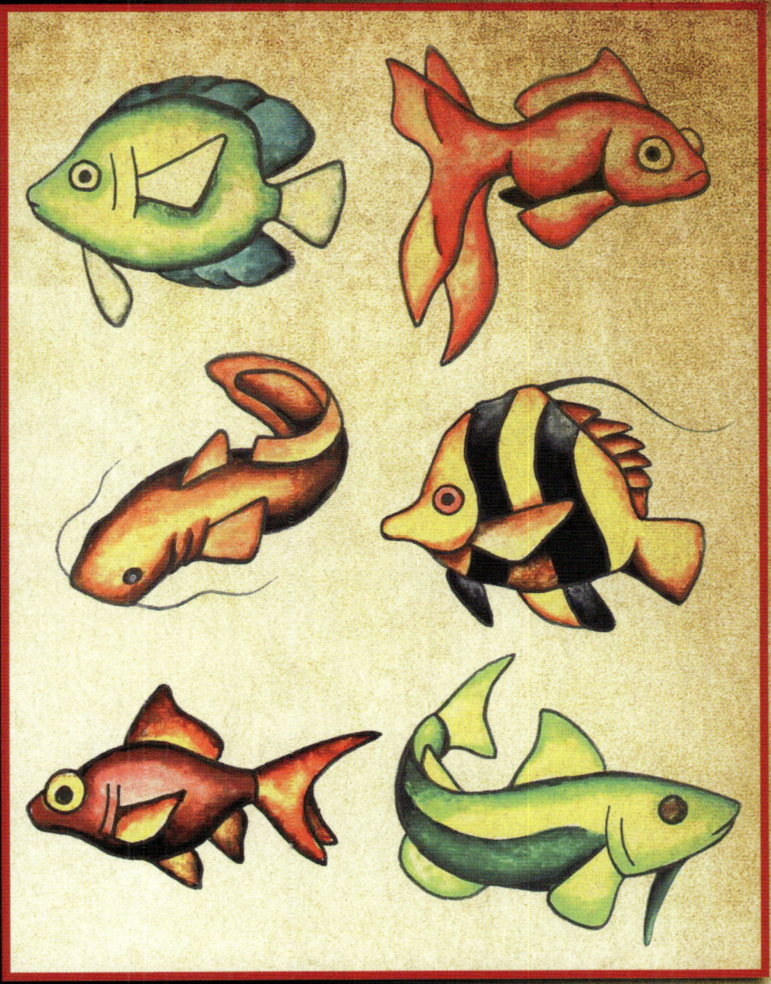

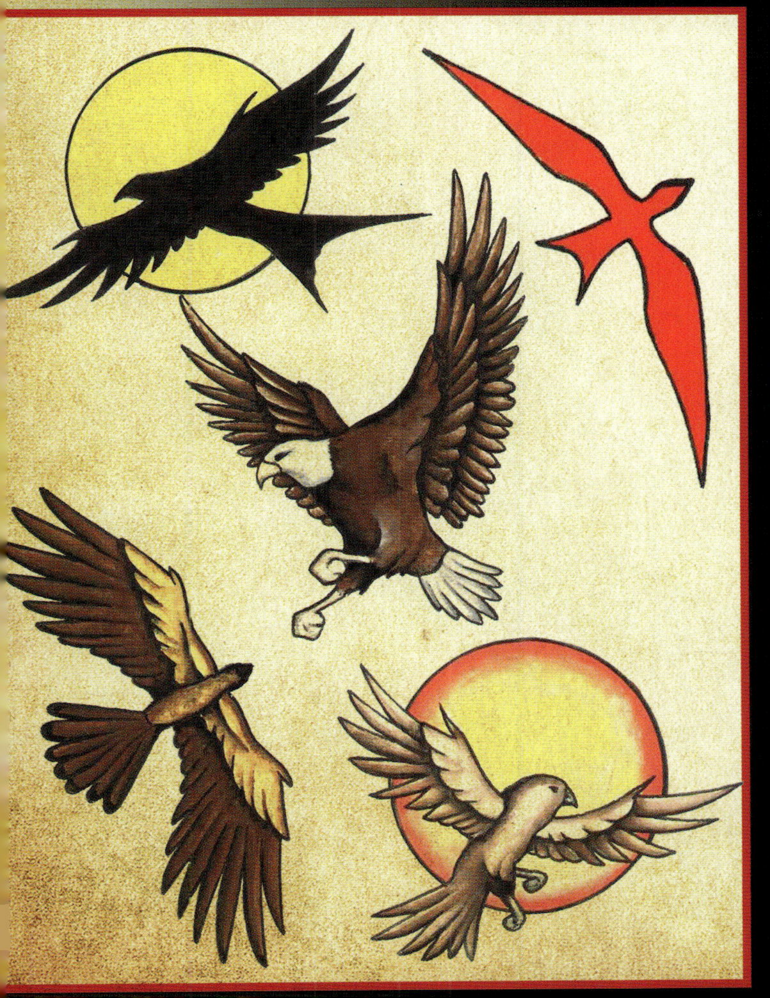
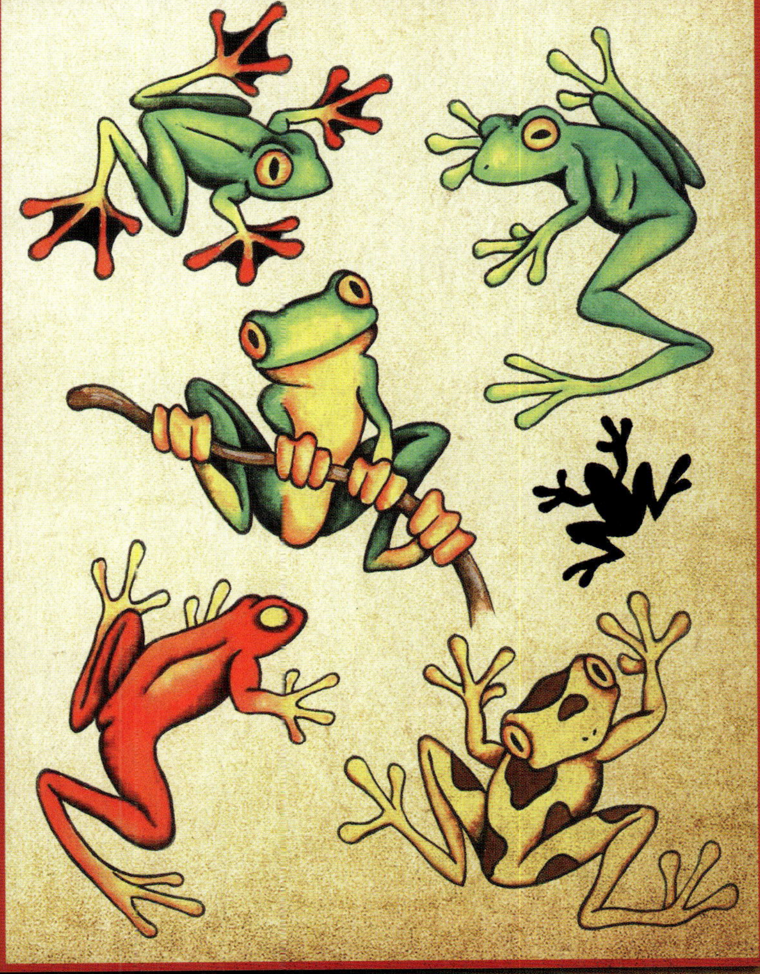

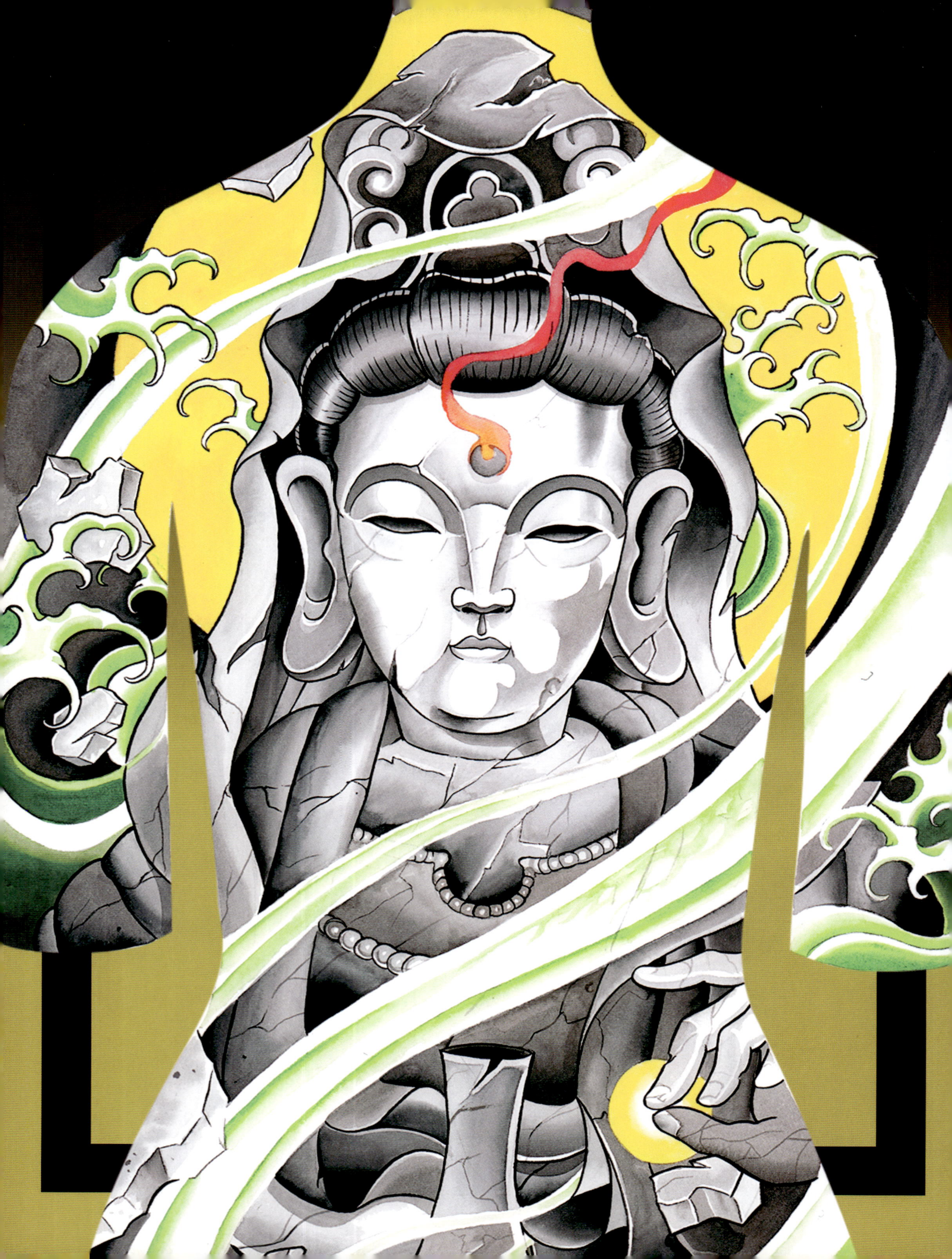

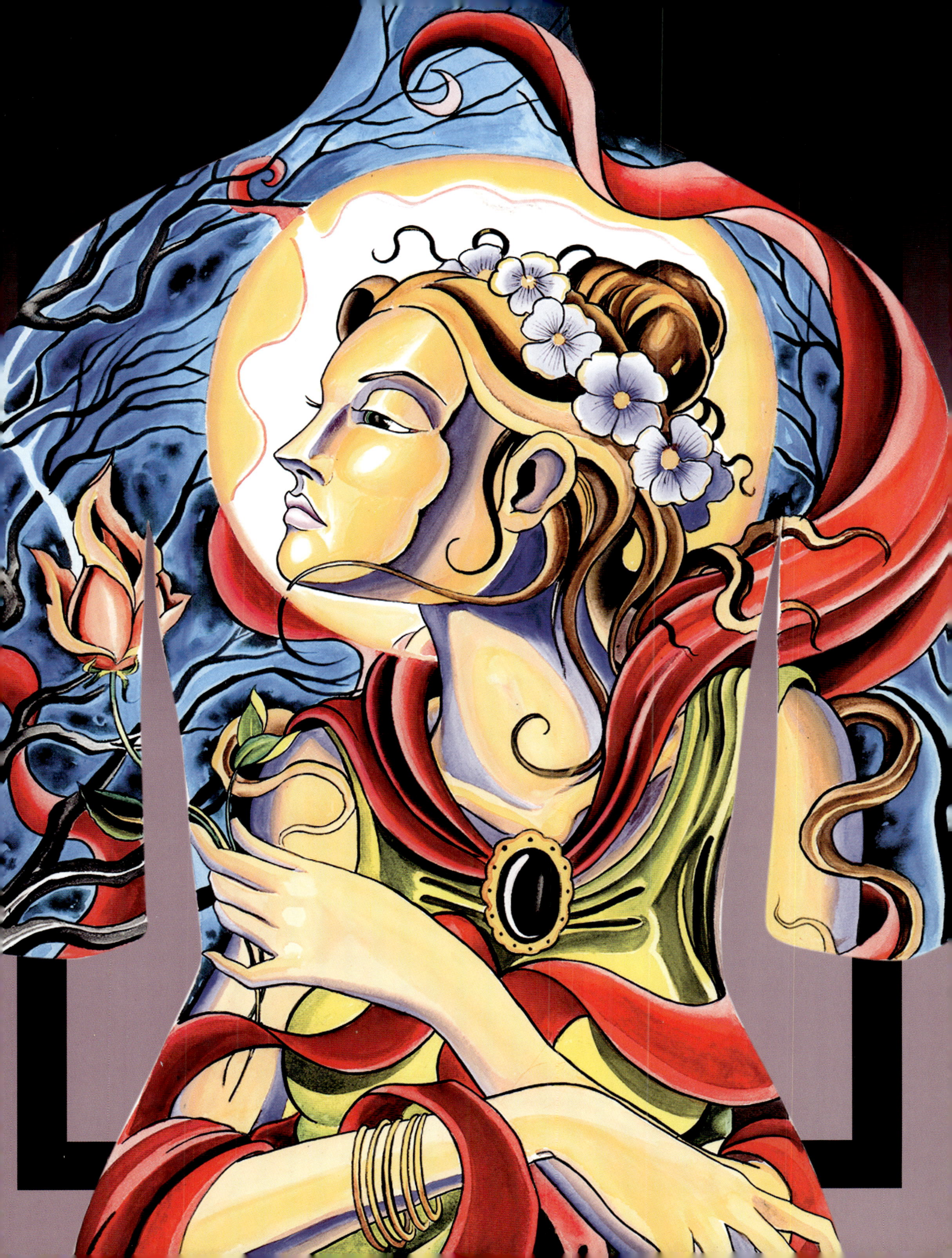

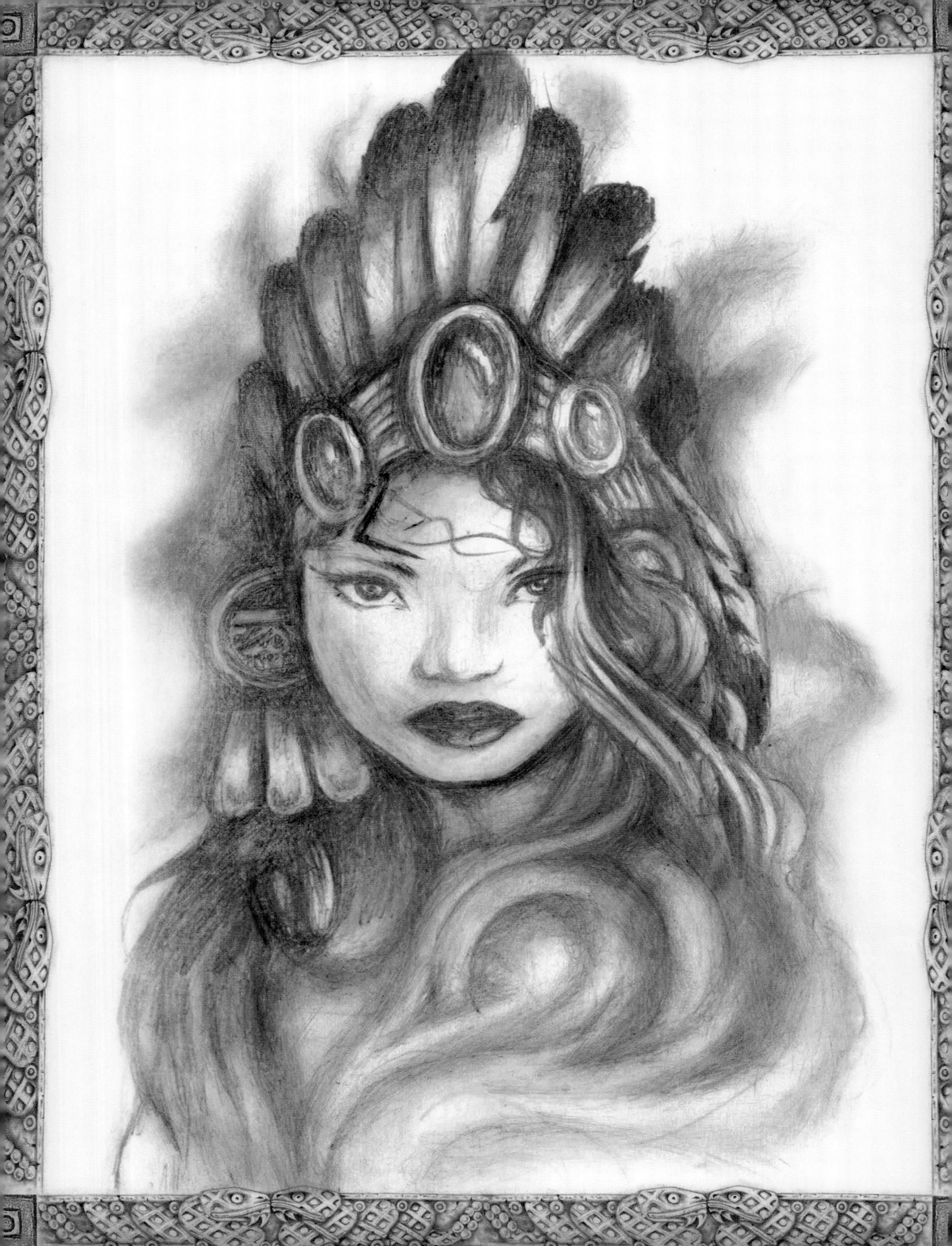

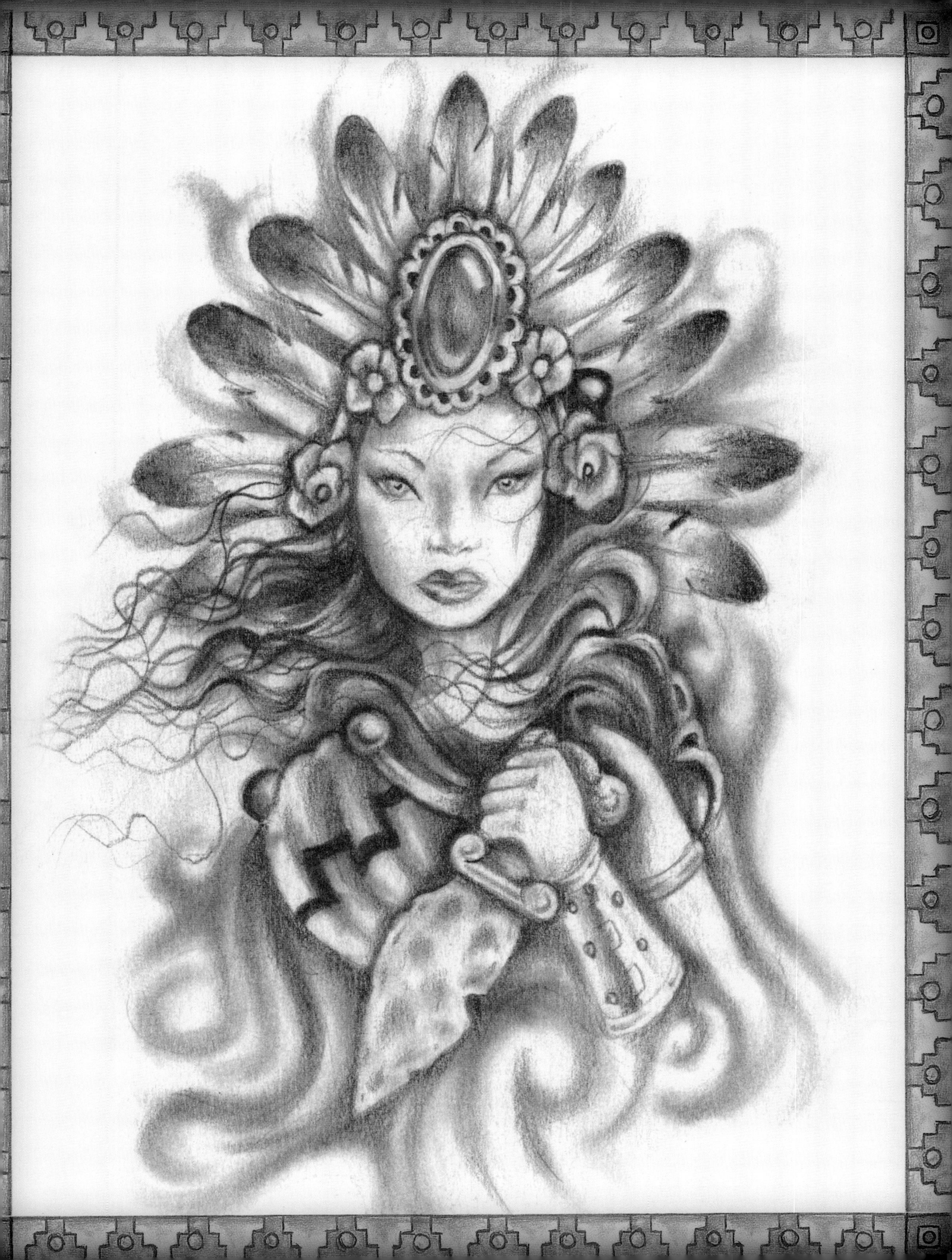

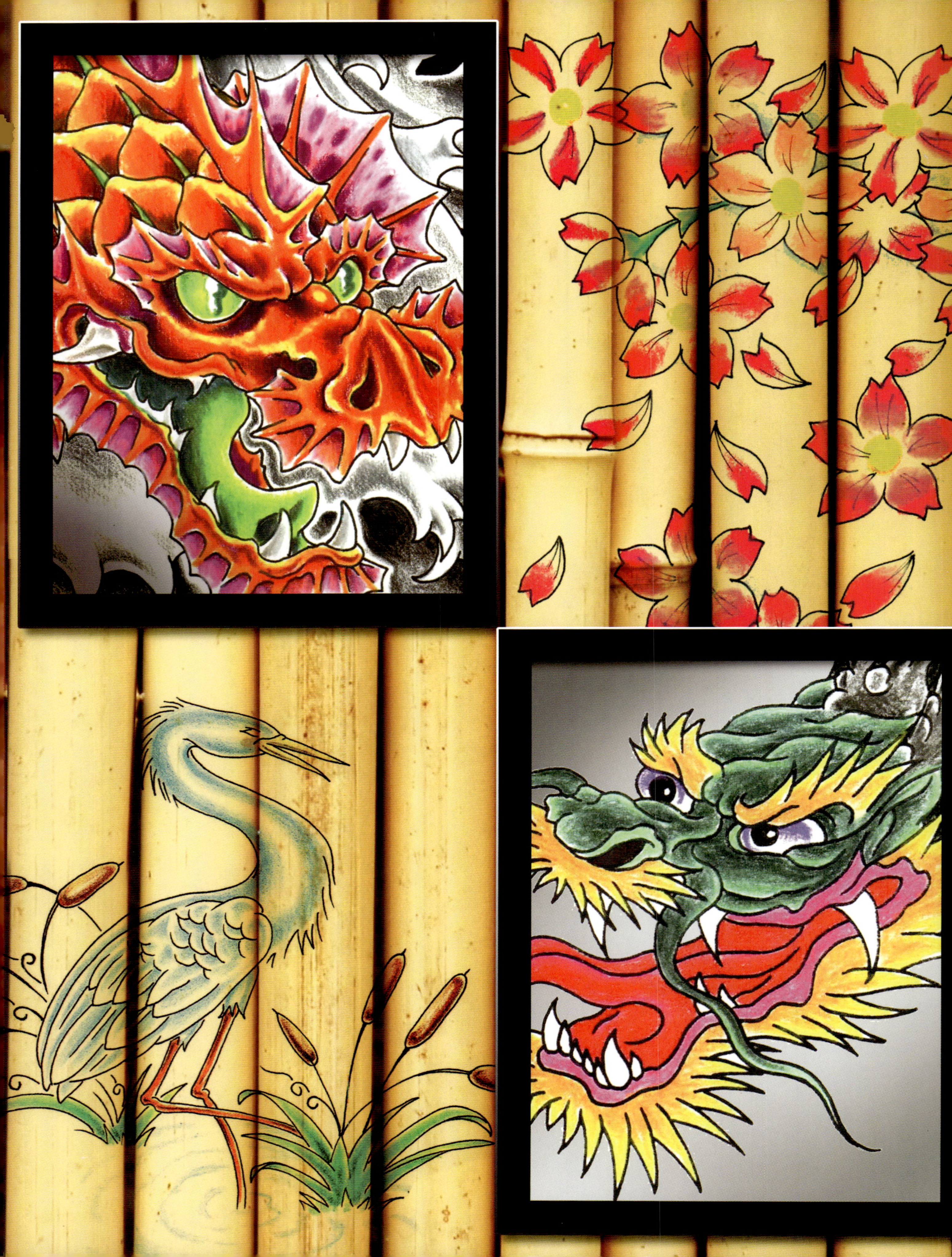

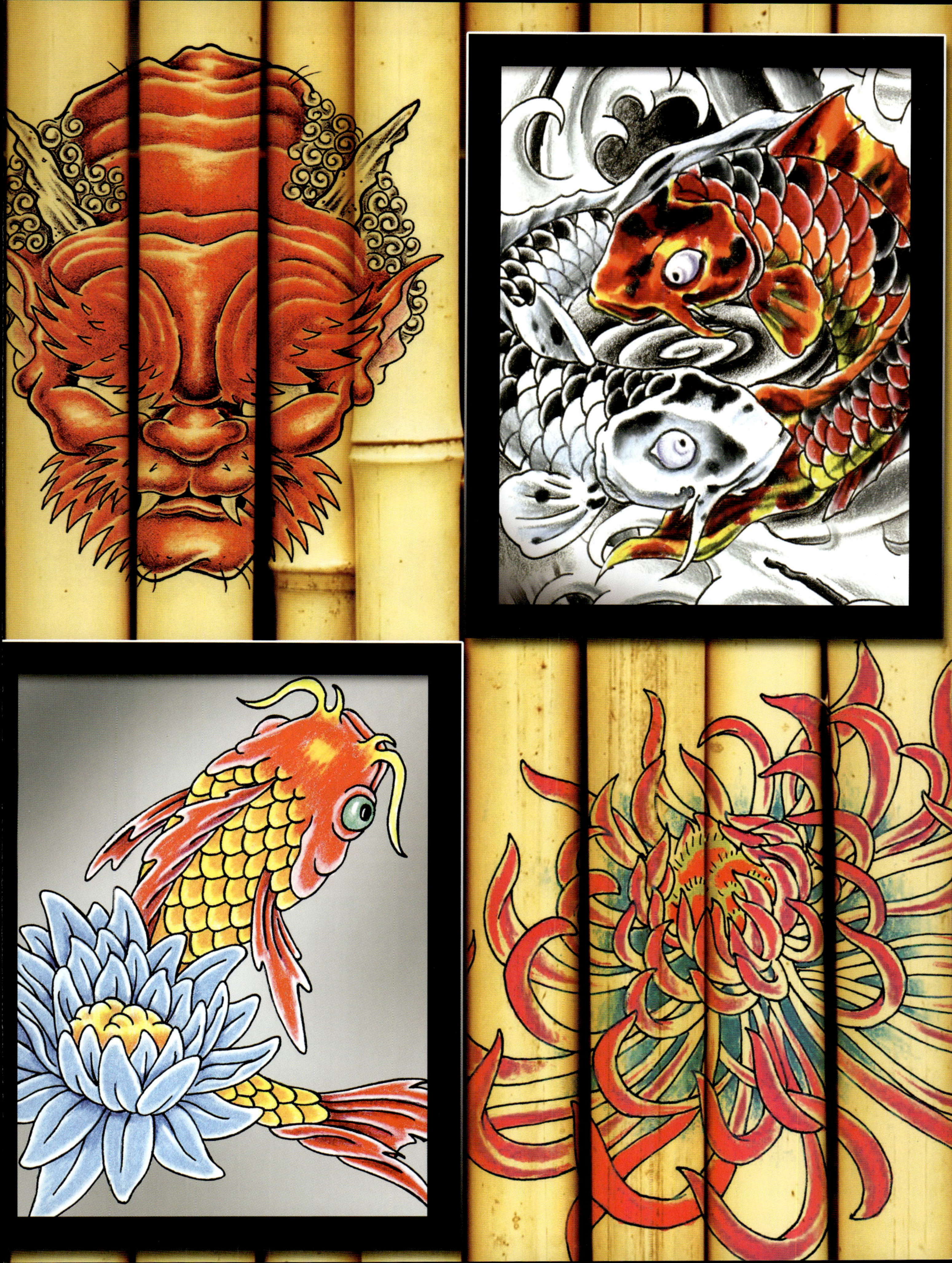

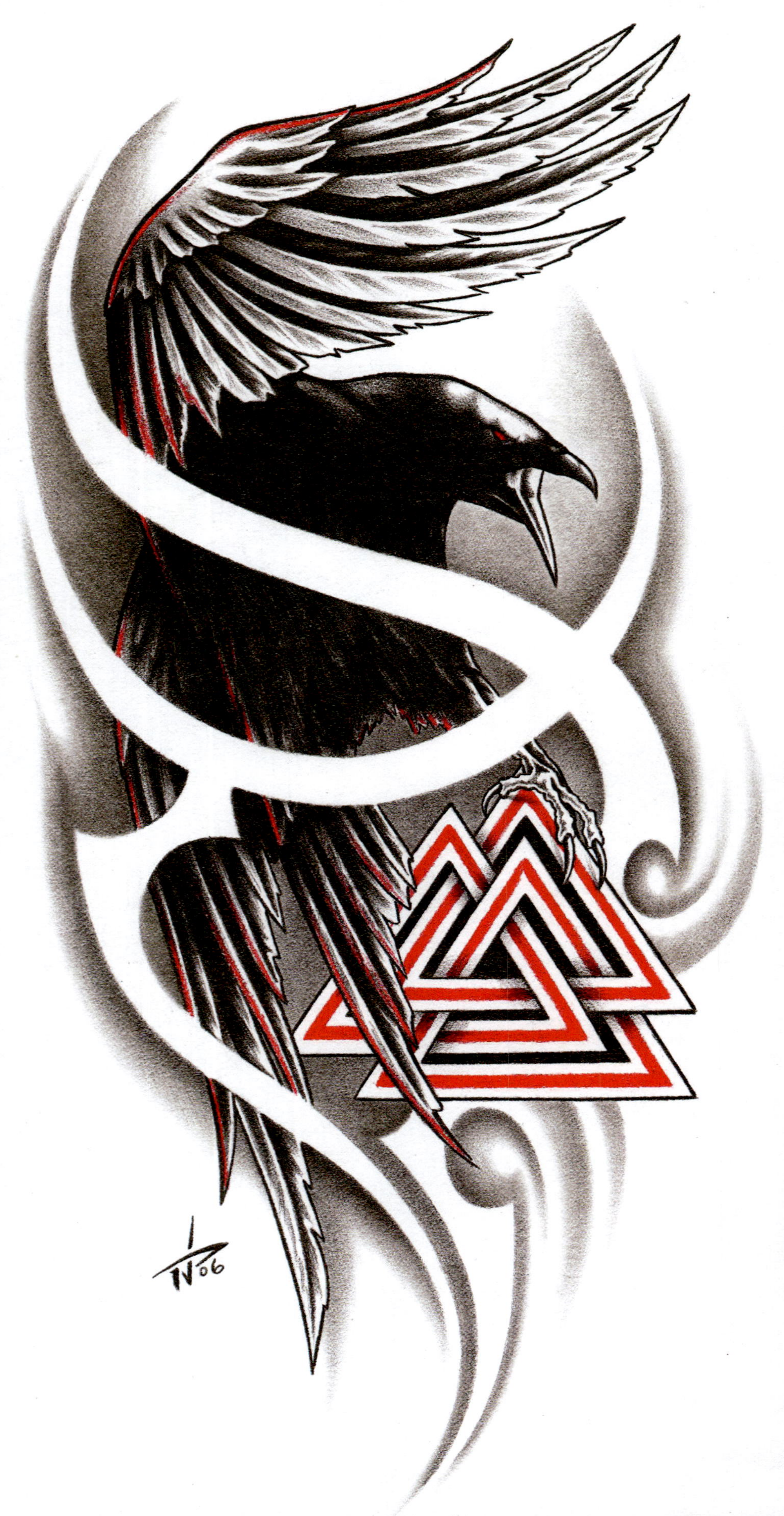

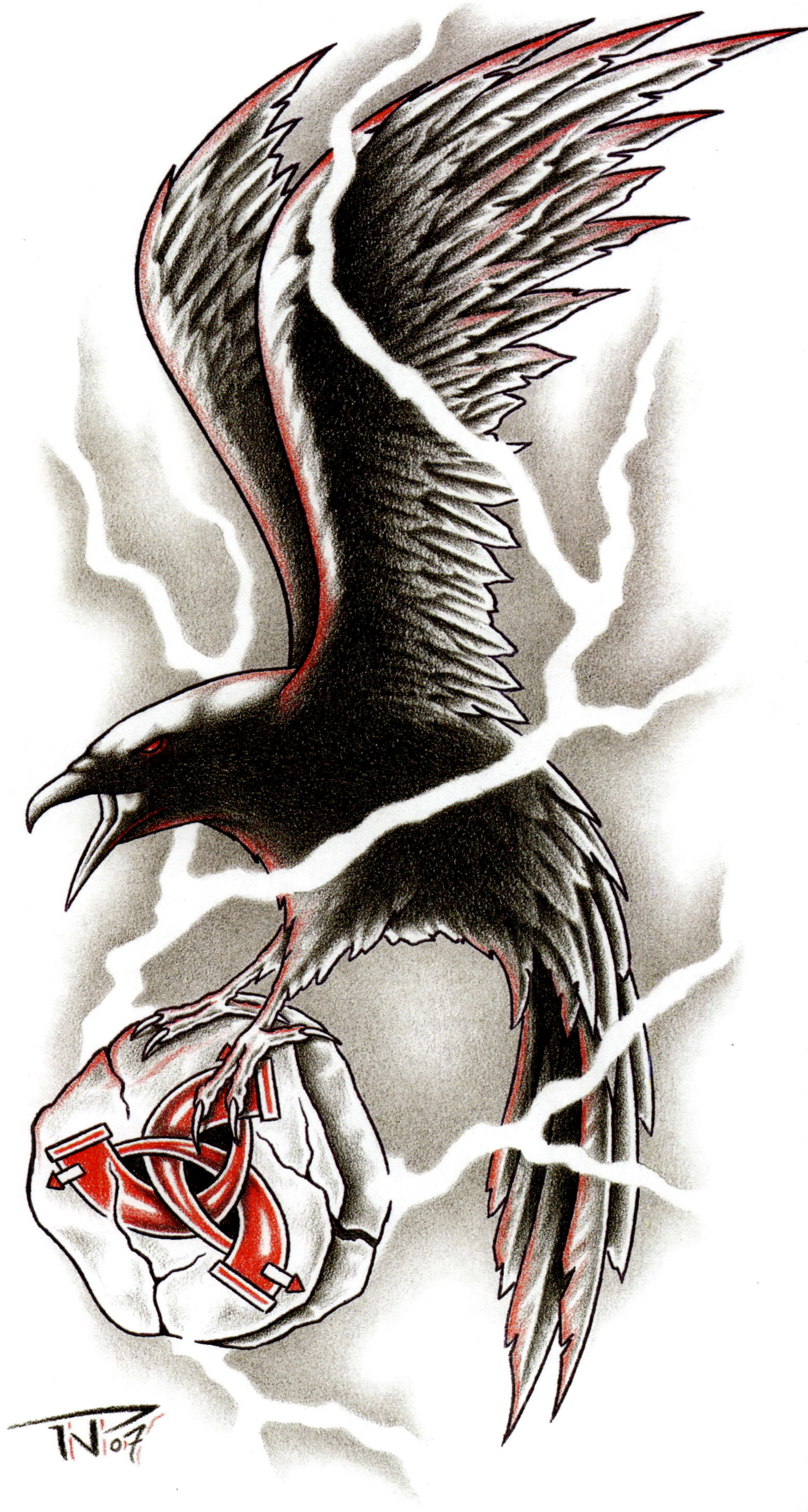
TN'07

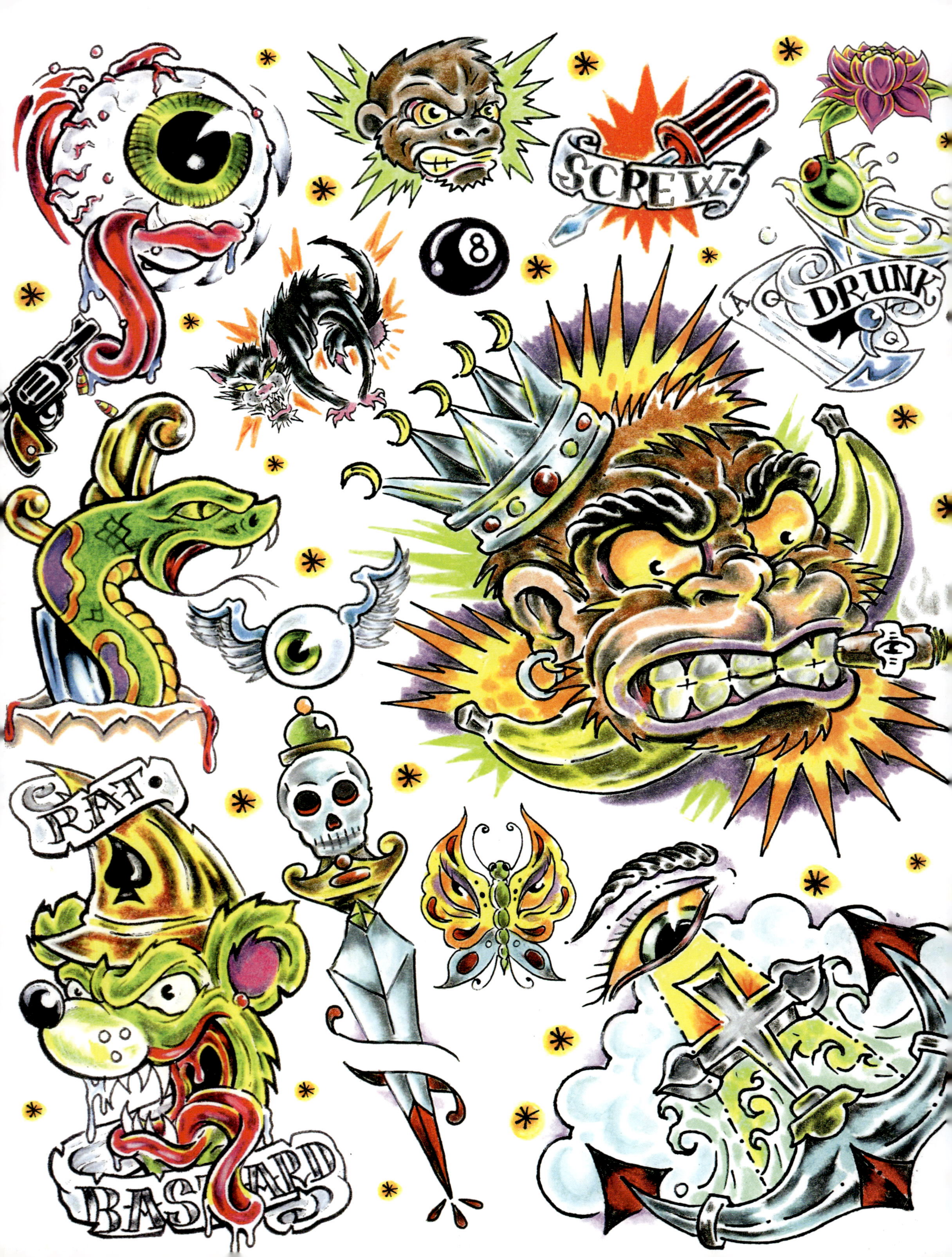
SCREW!
DRUNK
RAT
BASTARD

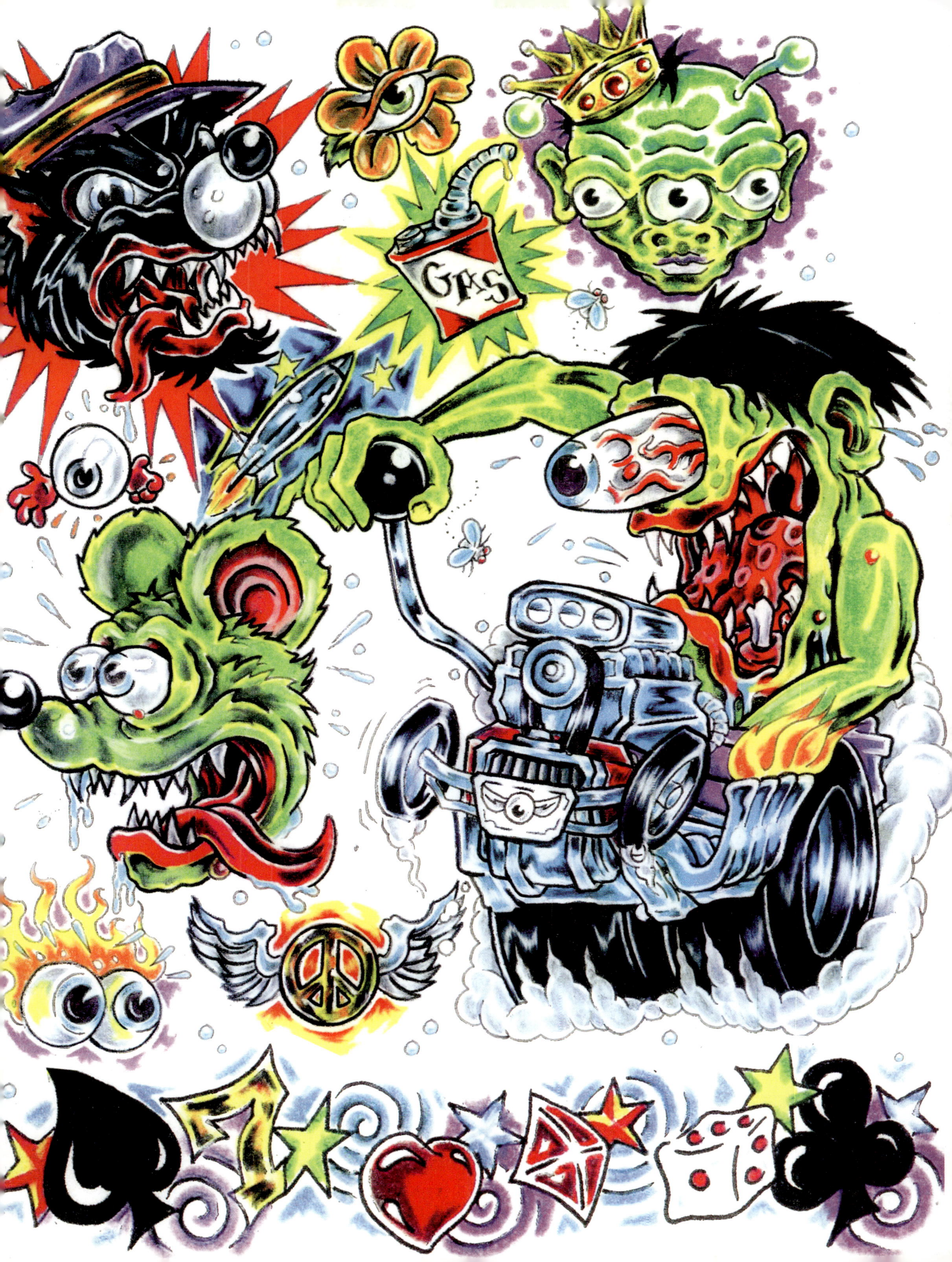
GAS

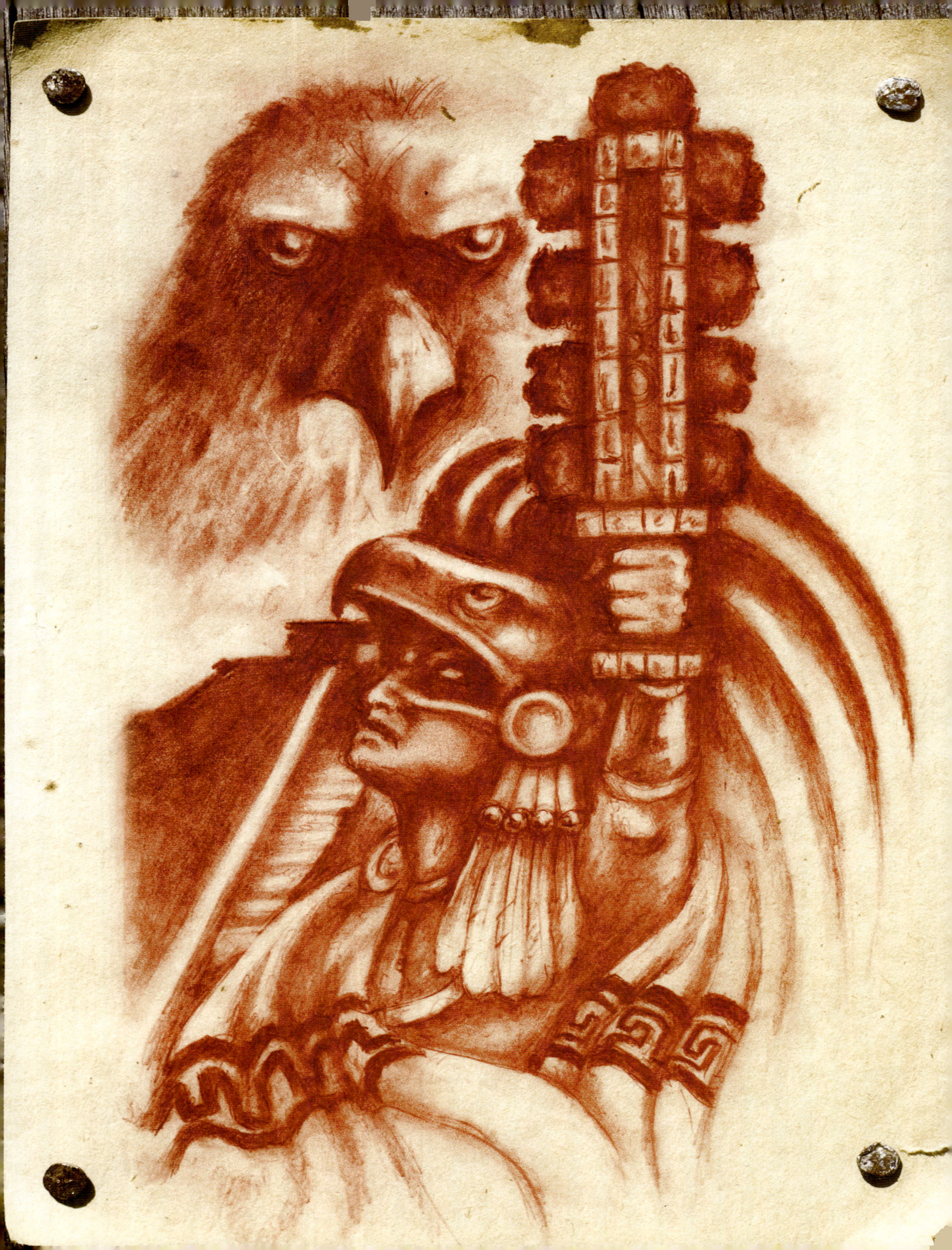

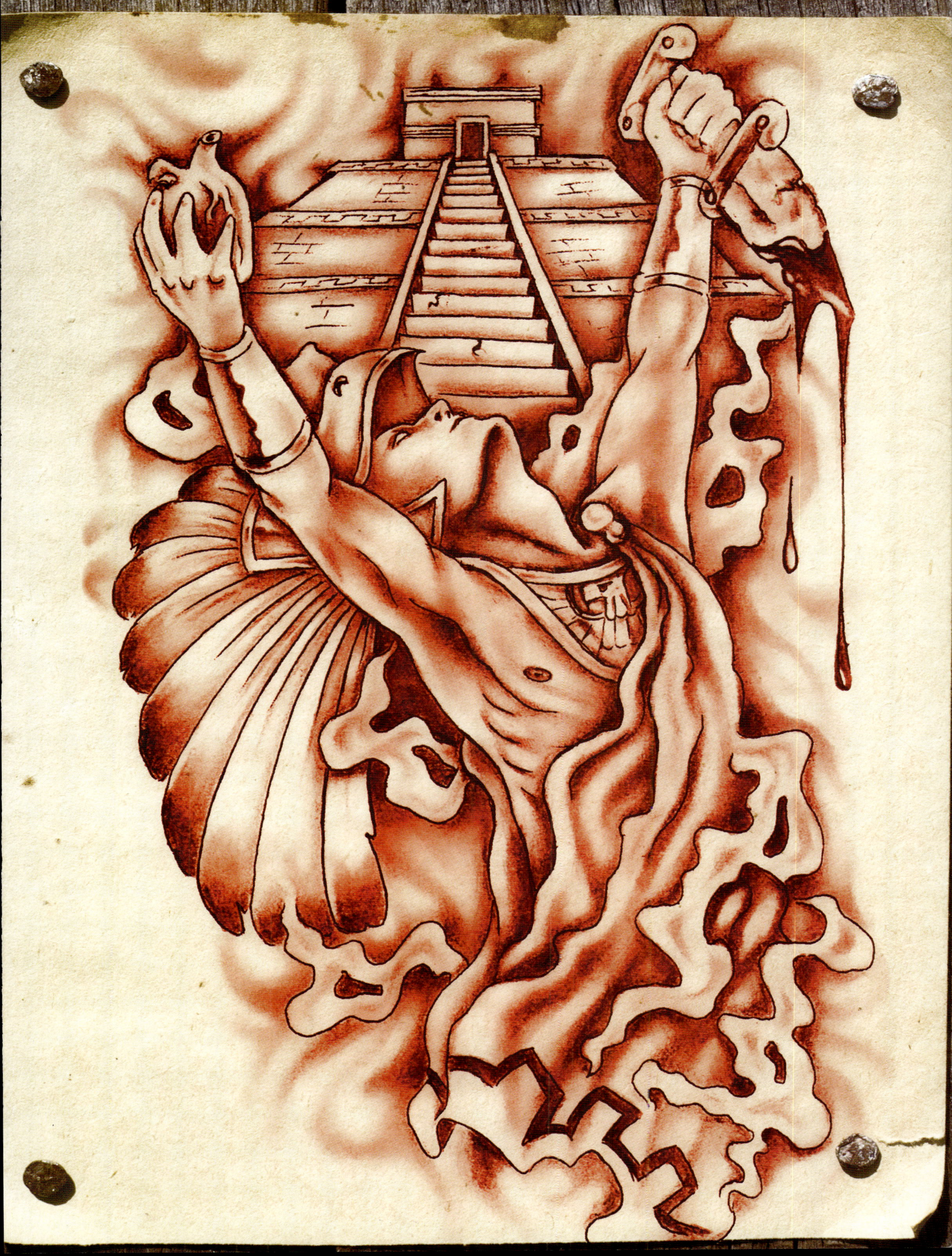

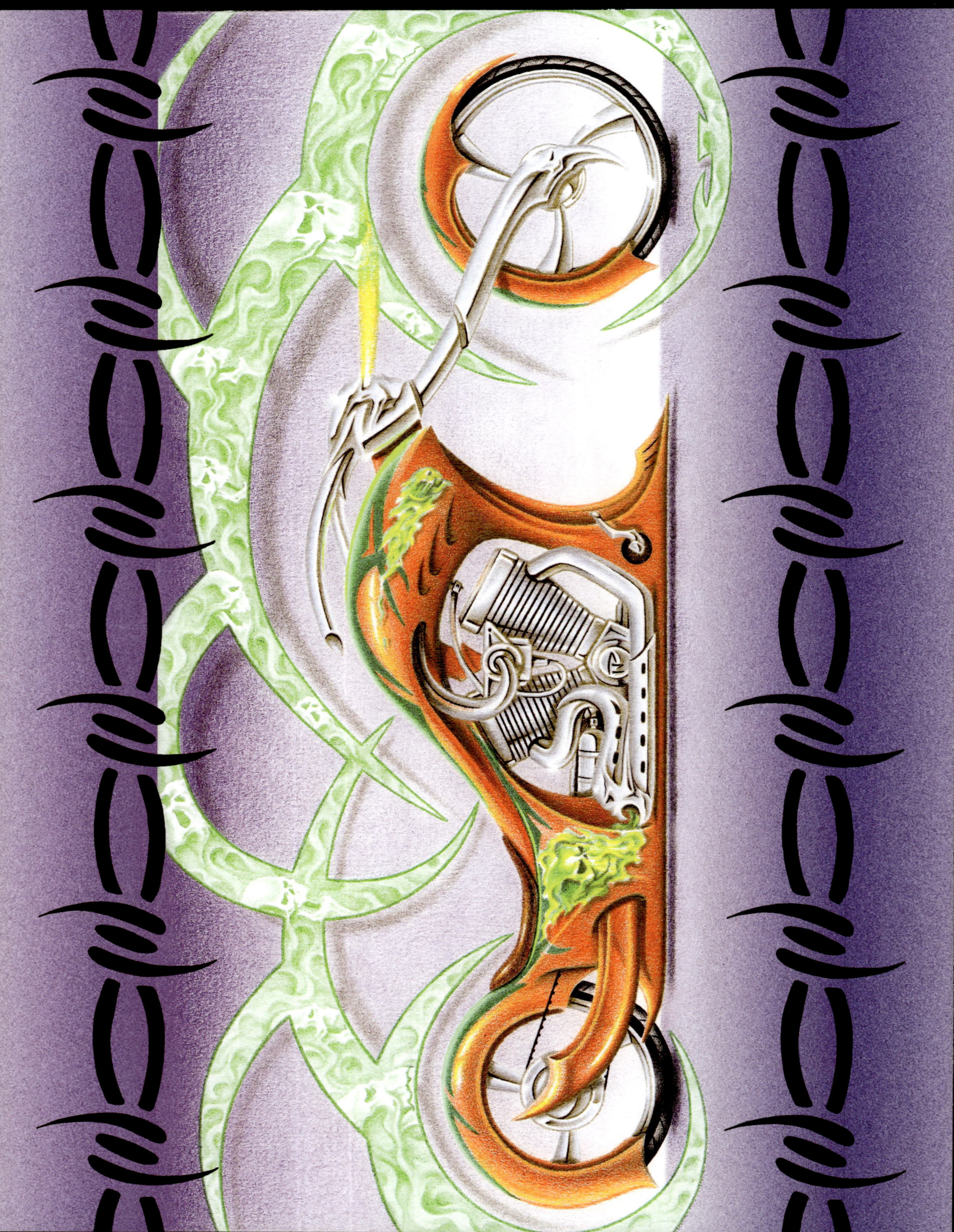

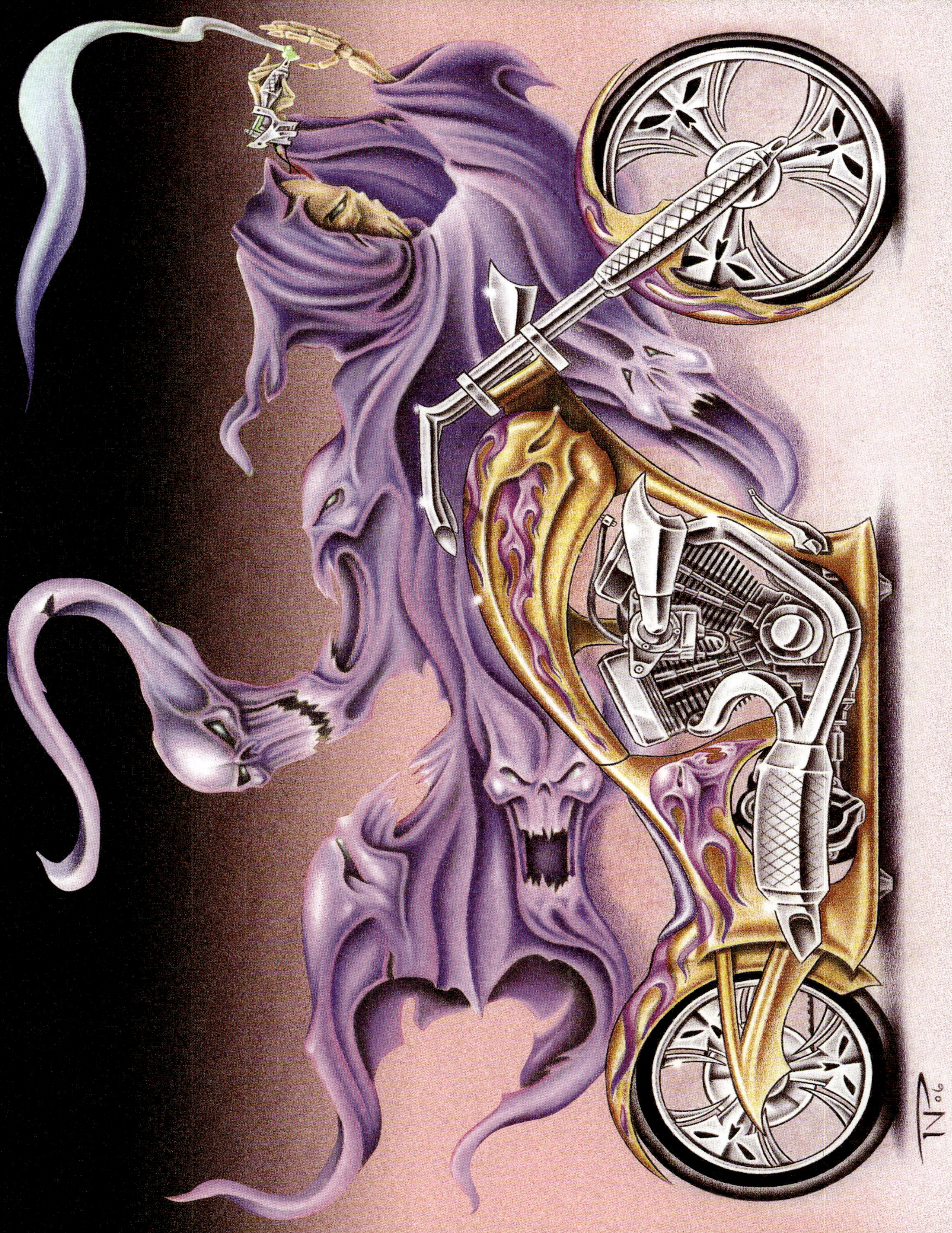

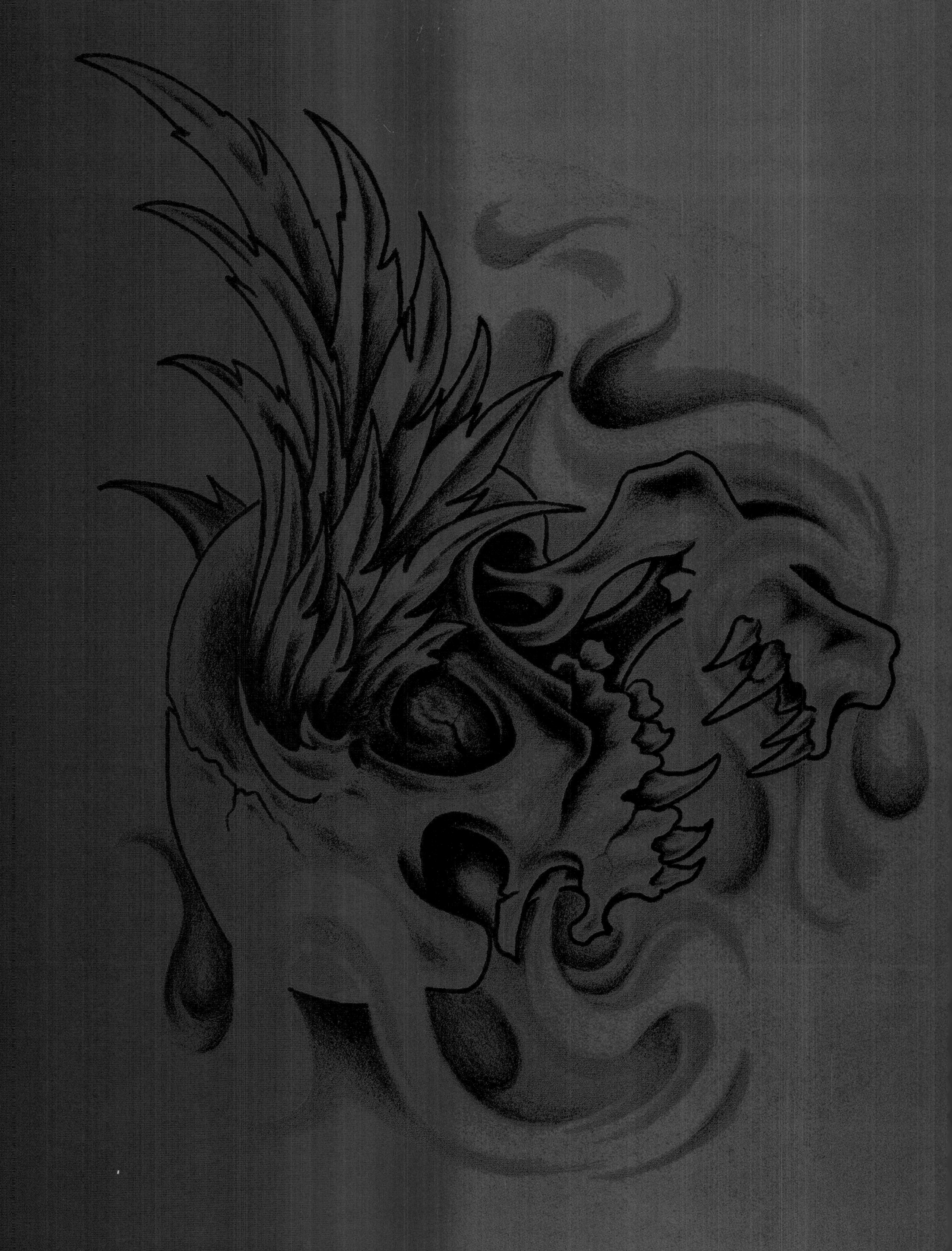

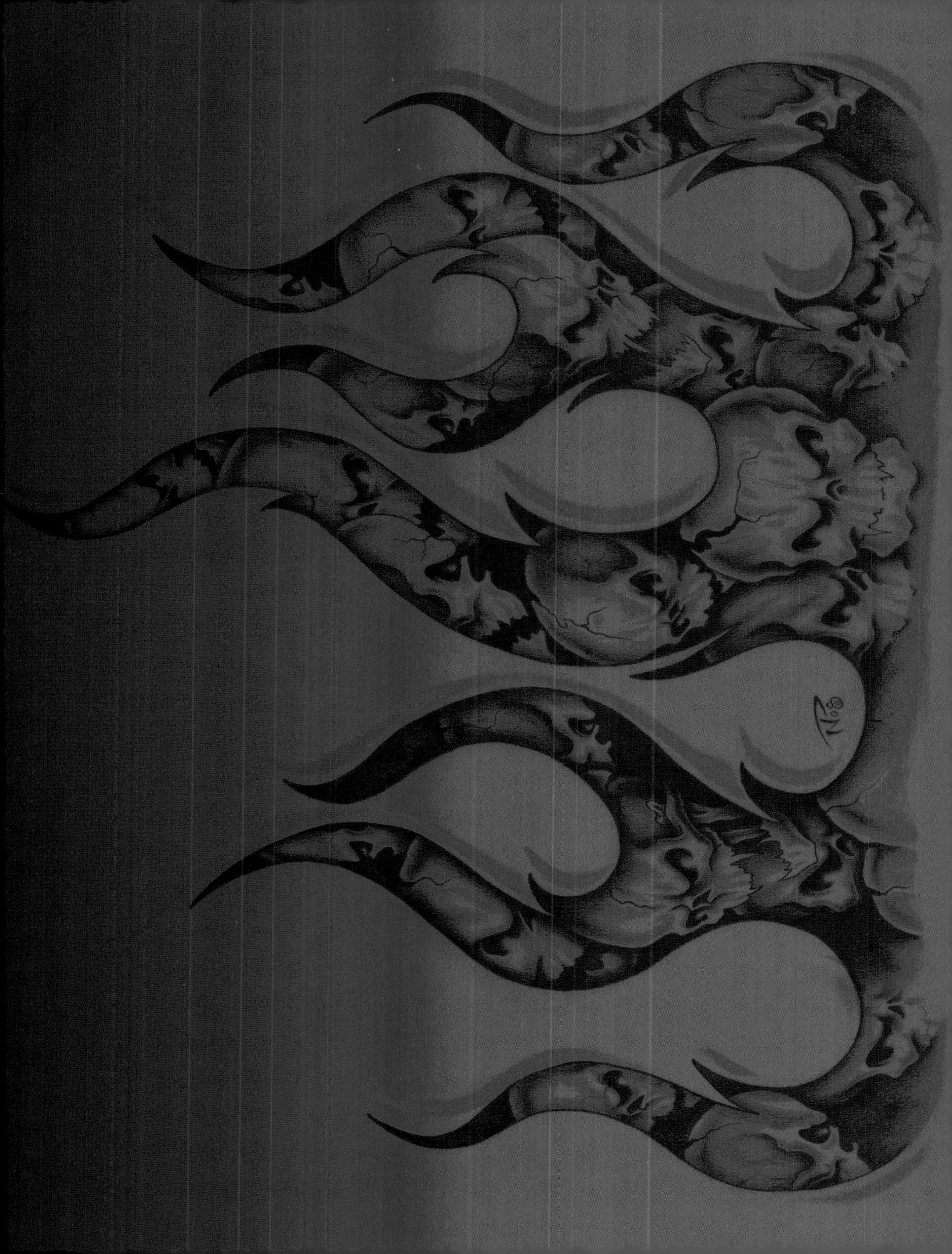

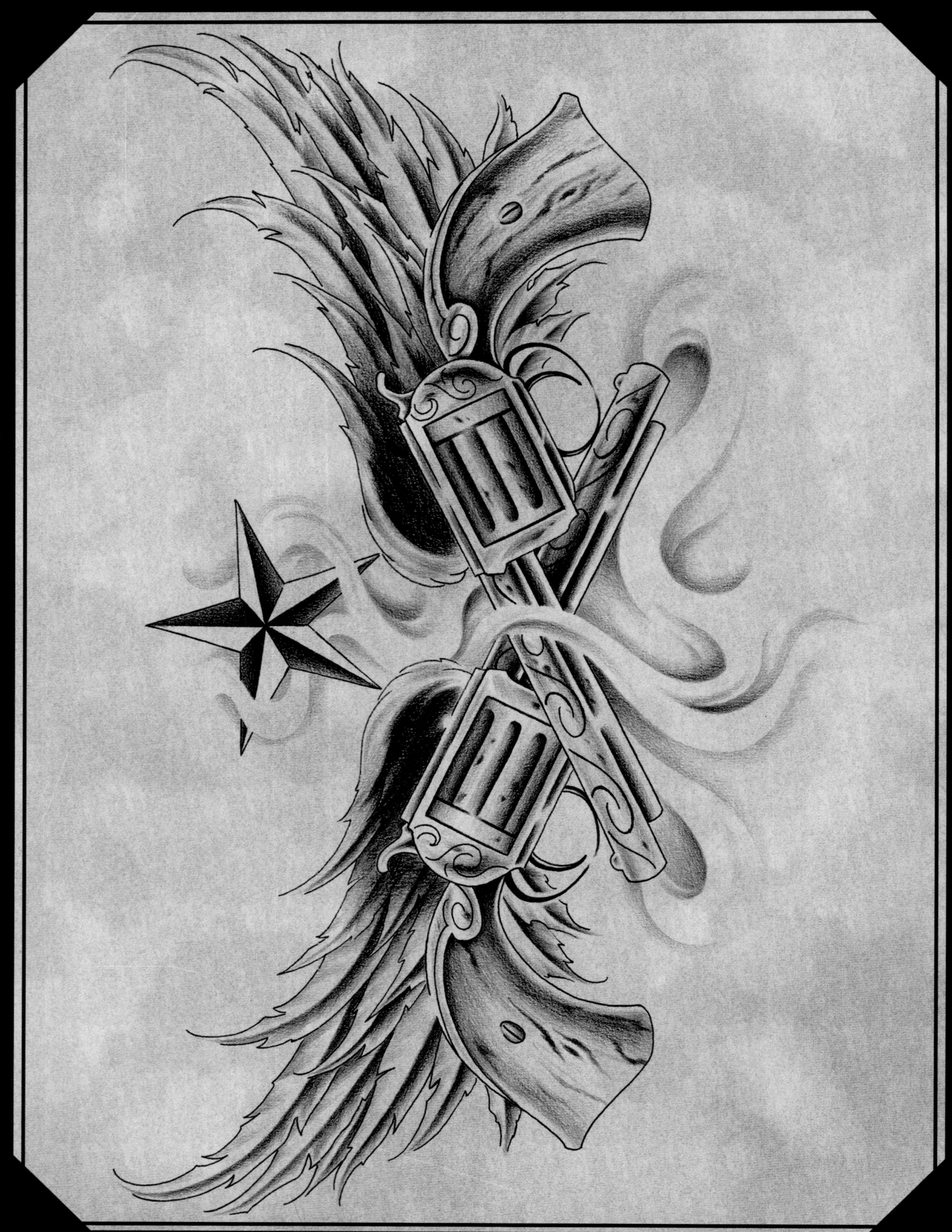

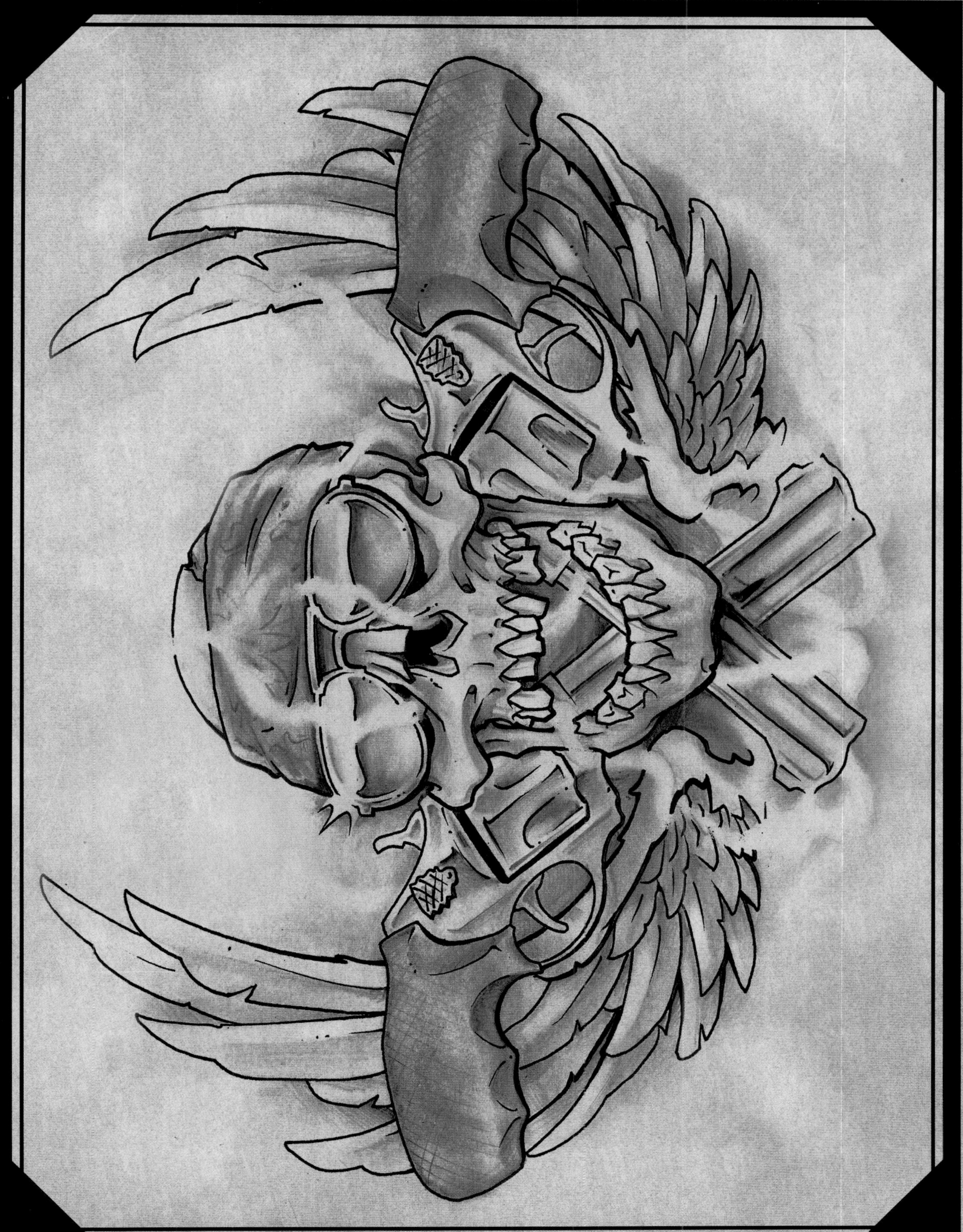

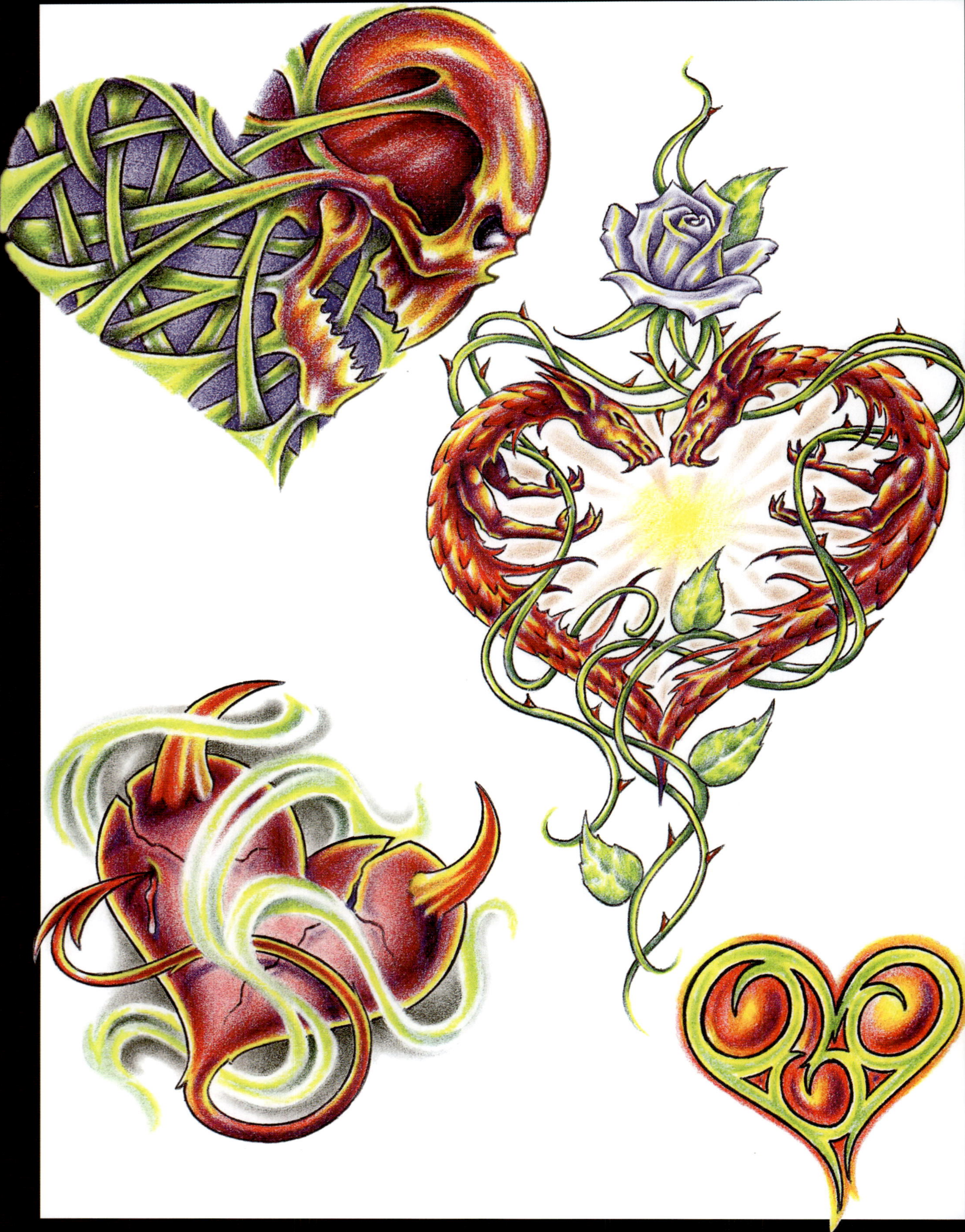

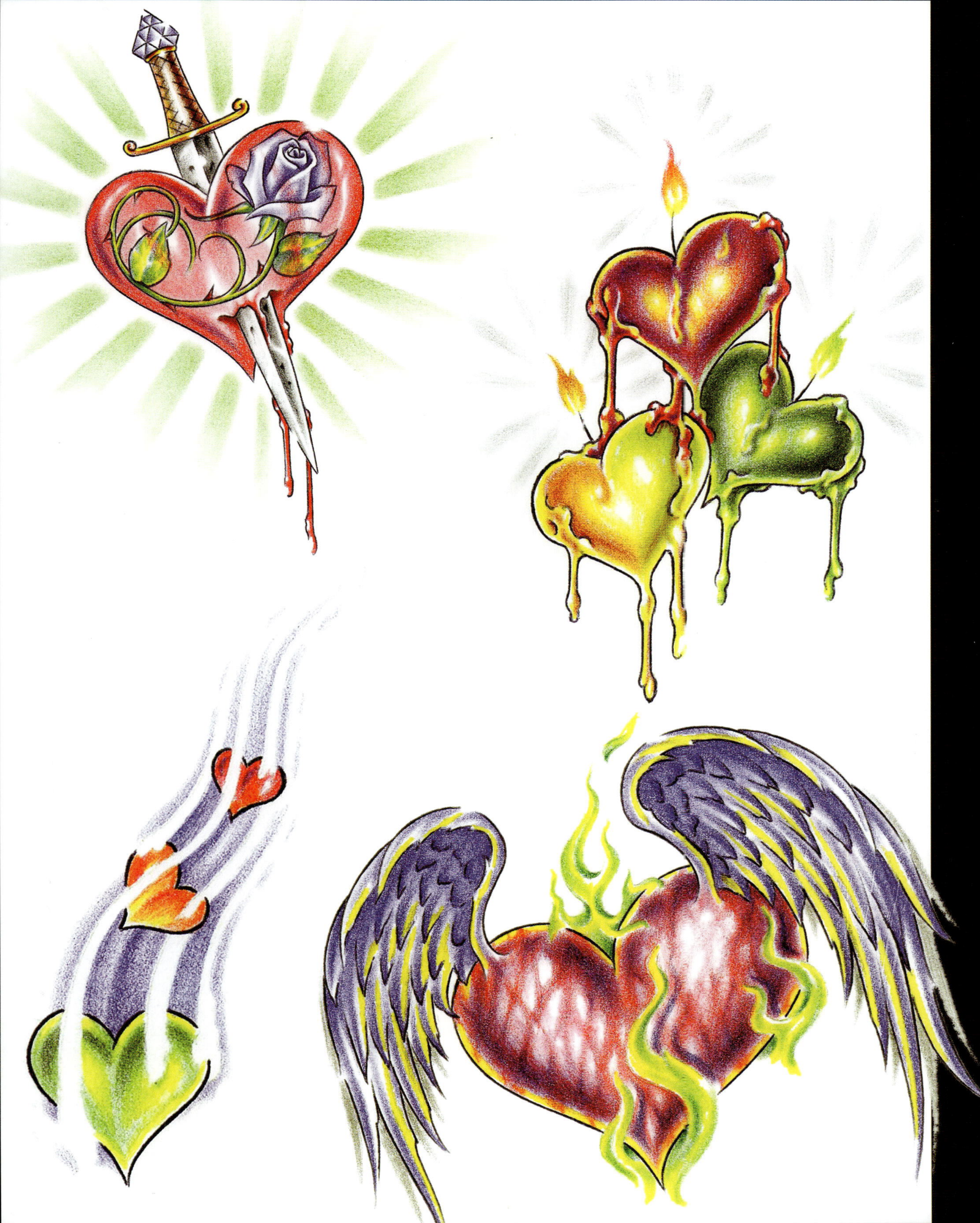

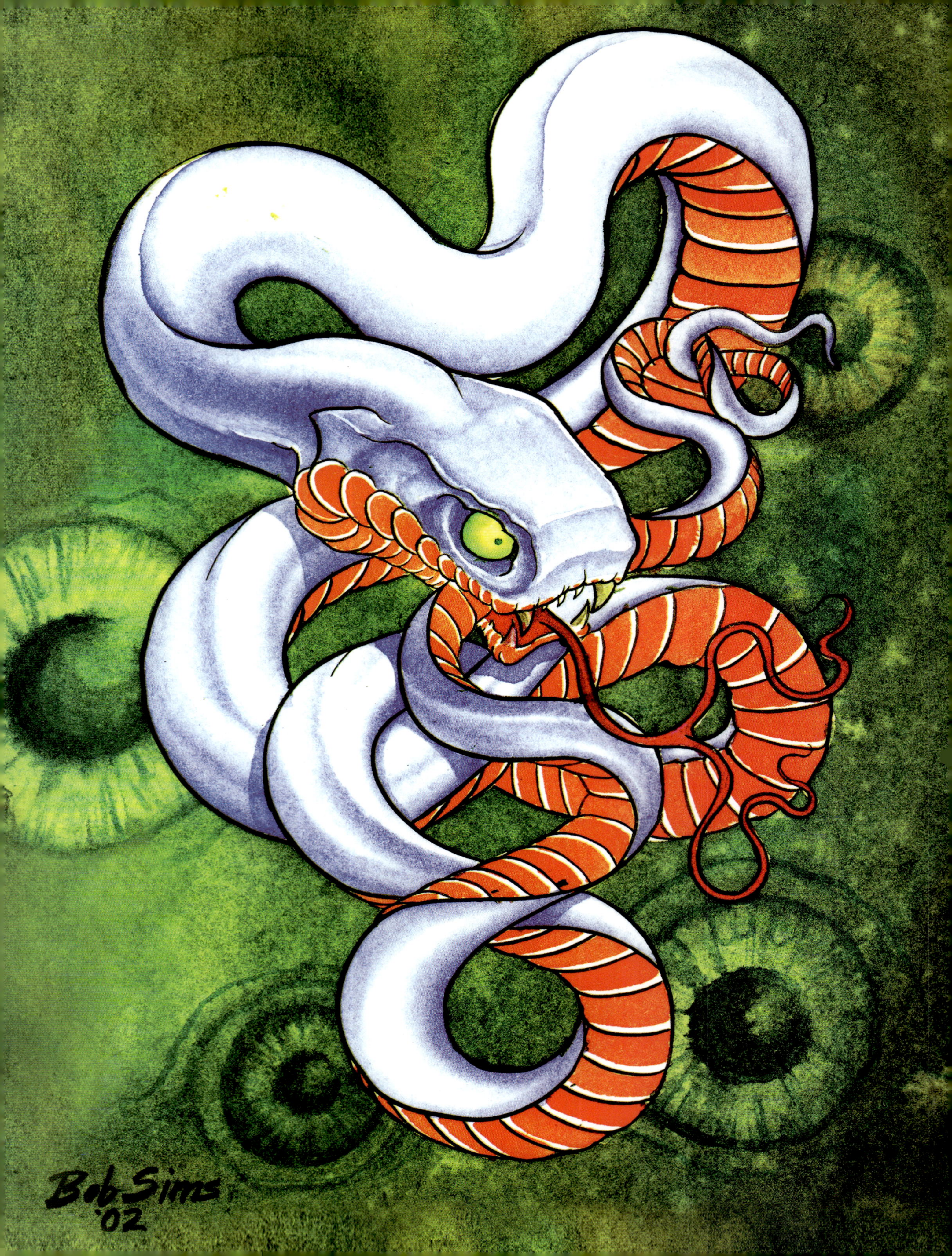
Bob Sims
'02

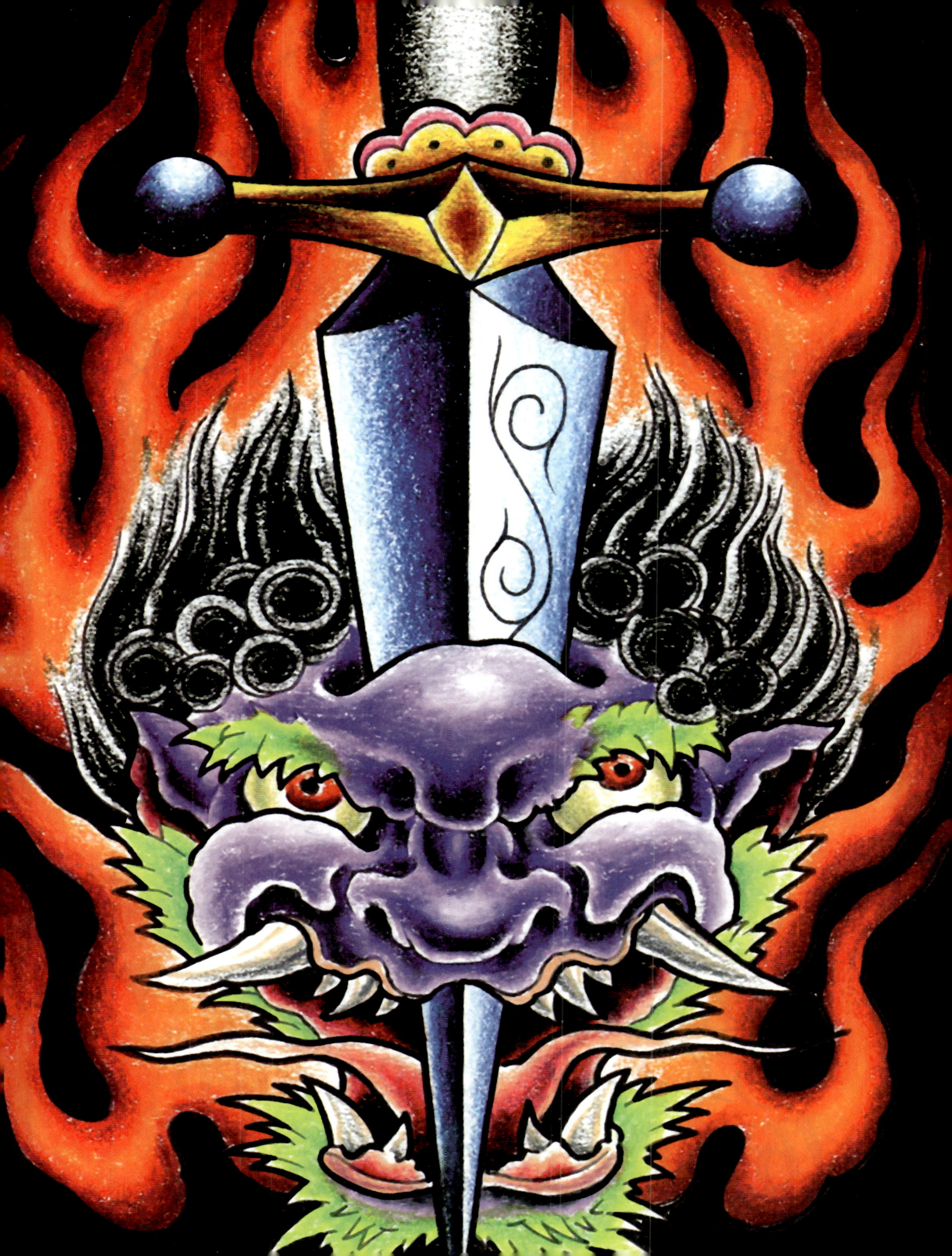

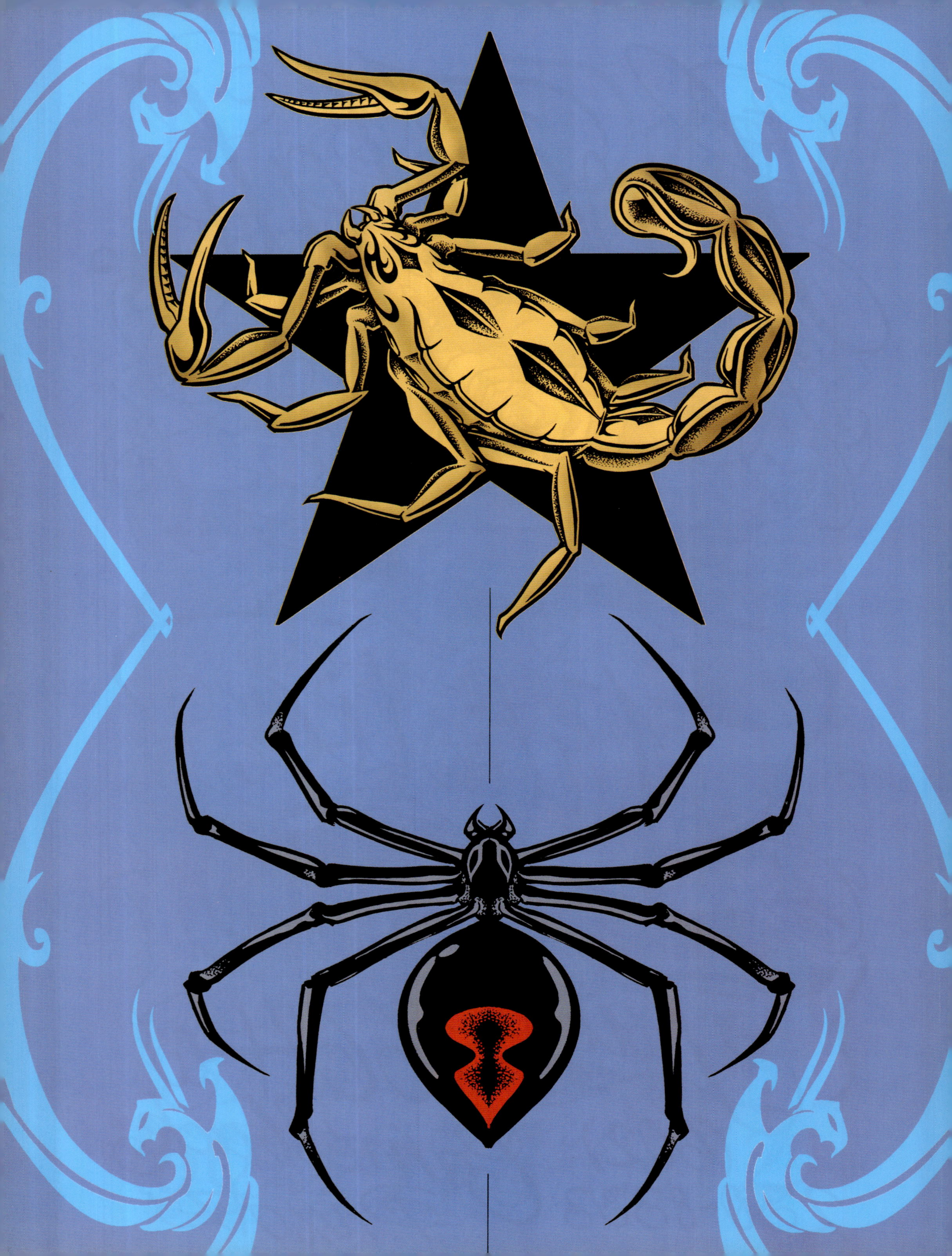

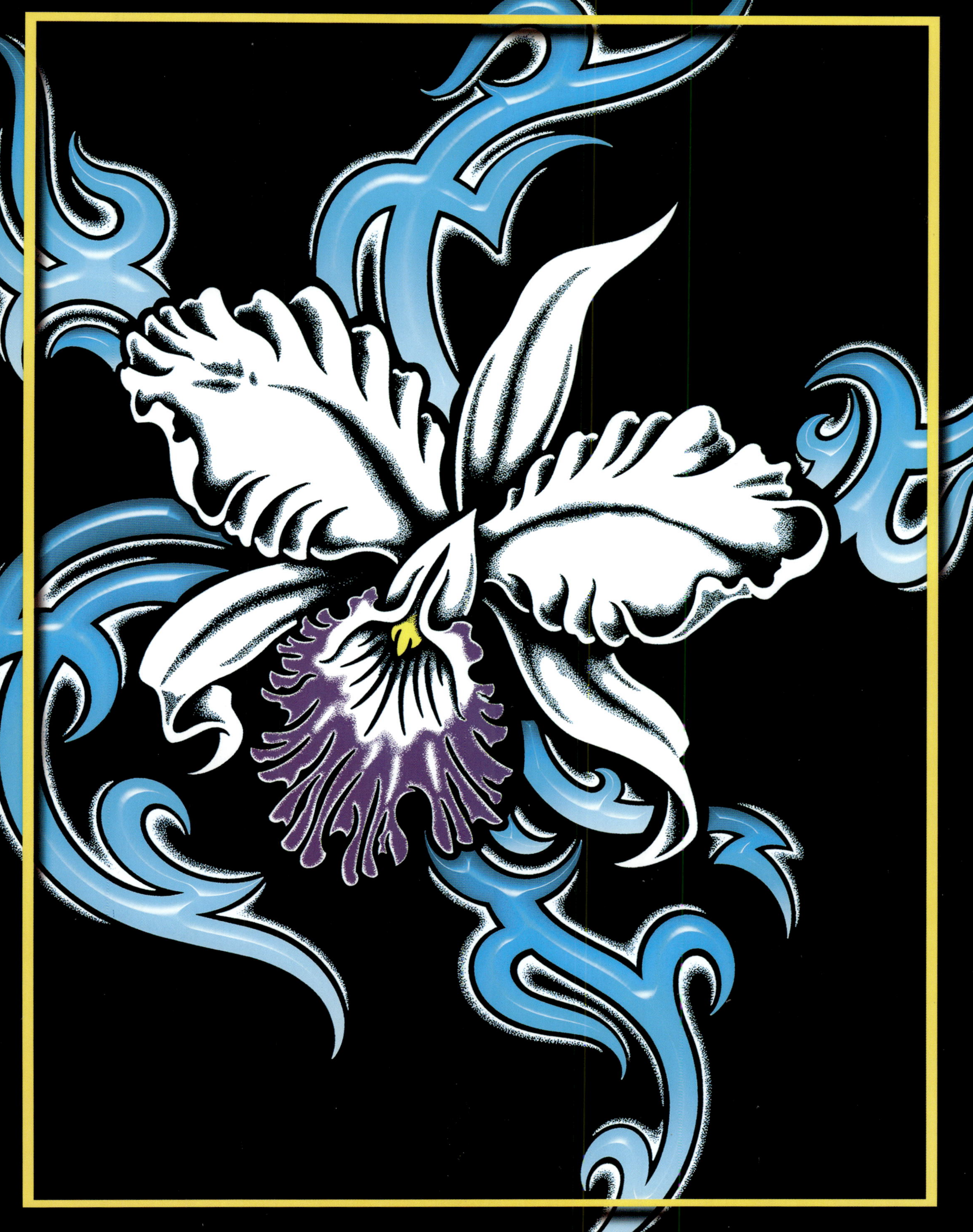

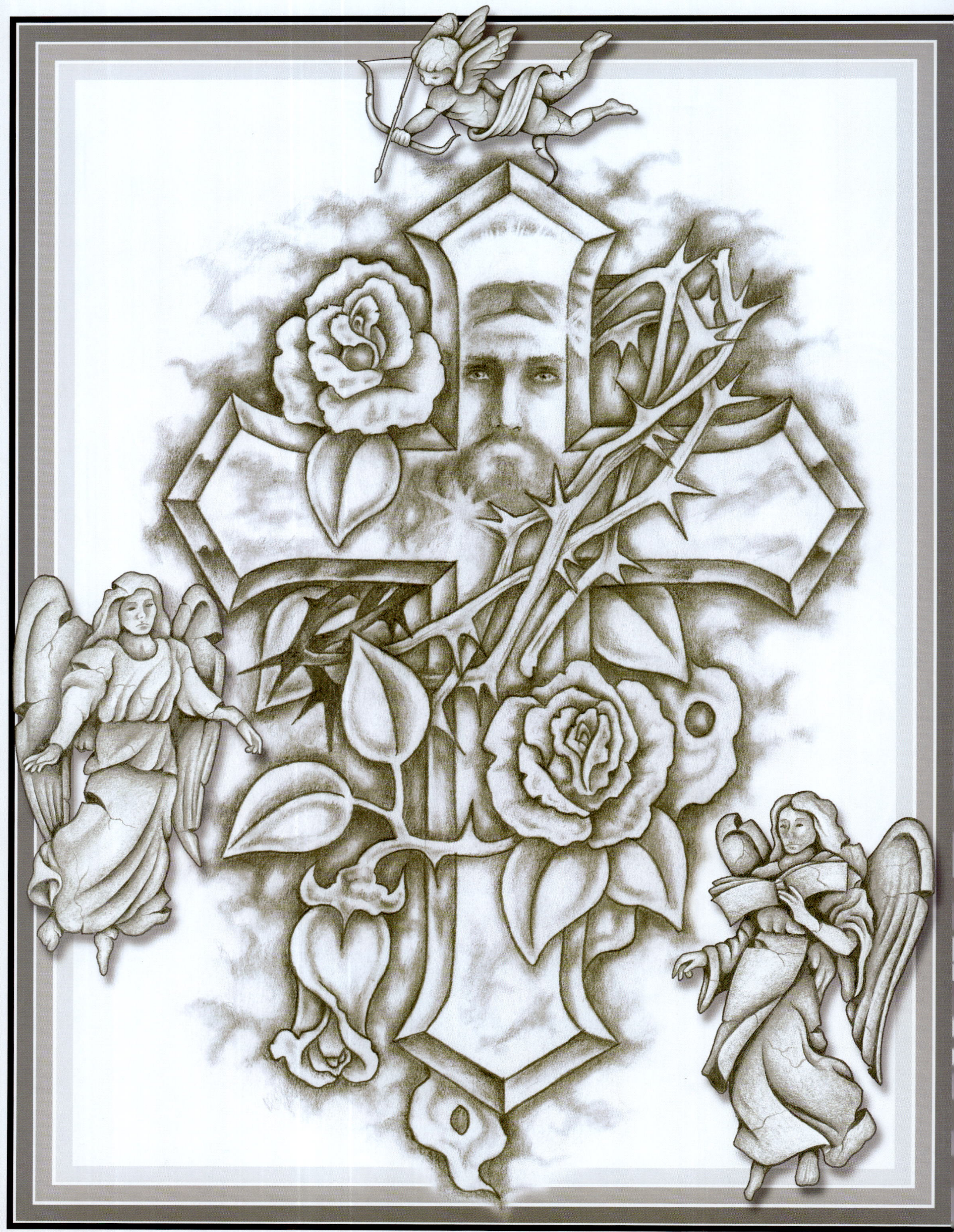

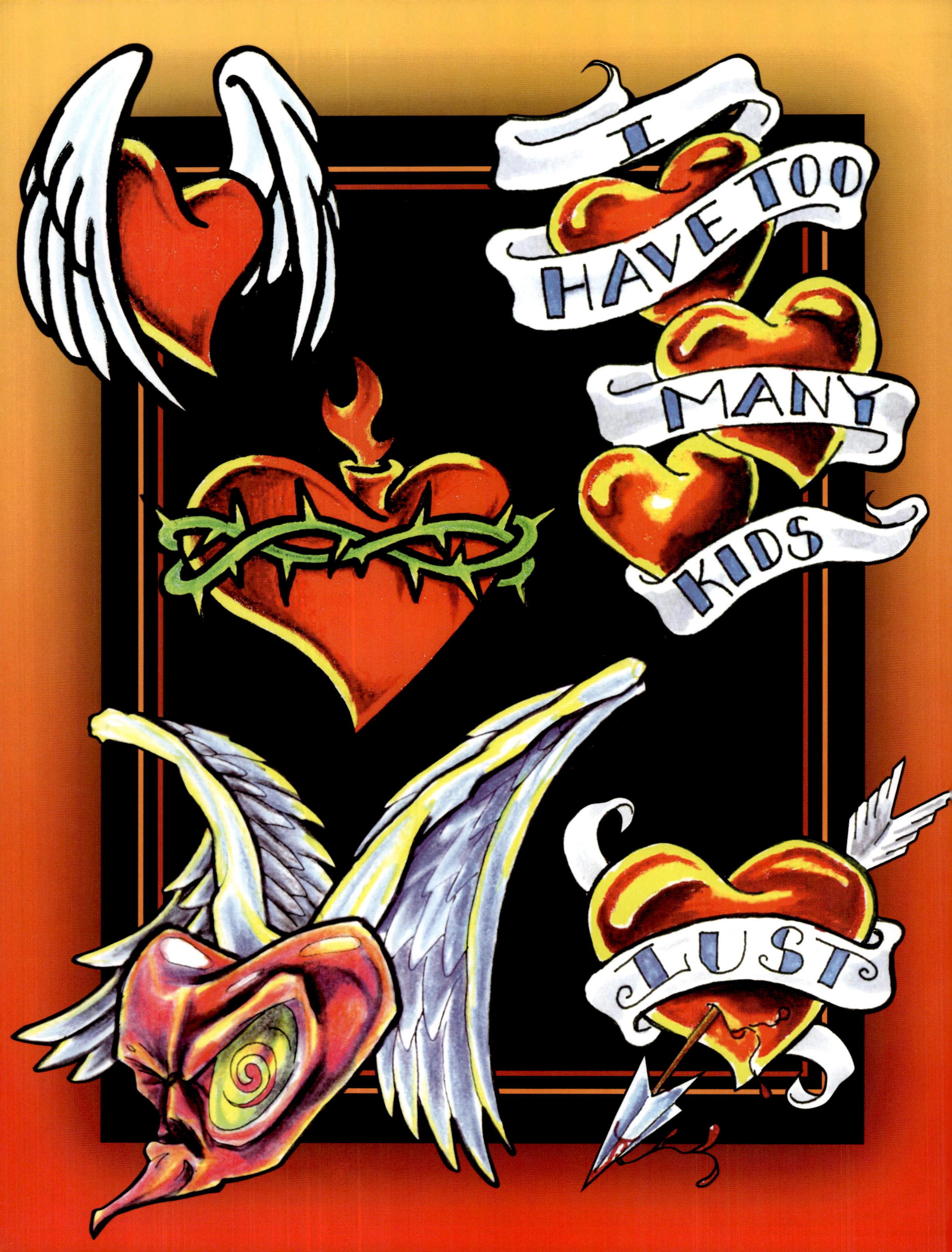
I
HAVE TOO
MANY
KIDS
LUST

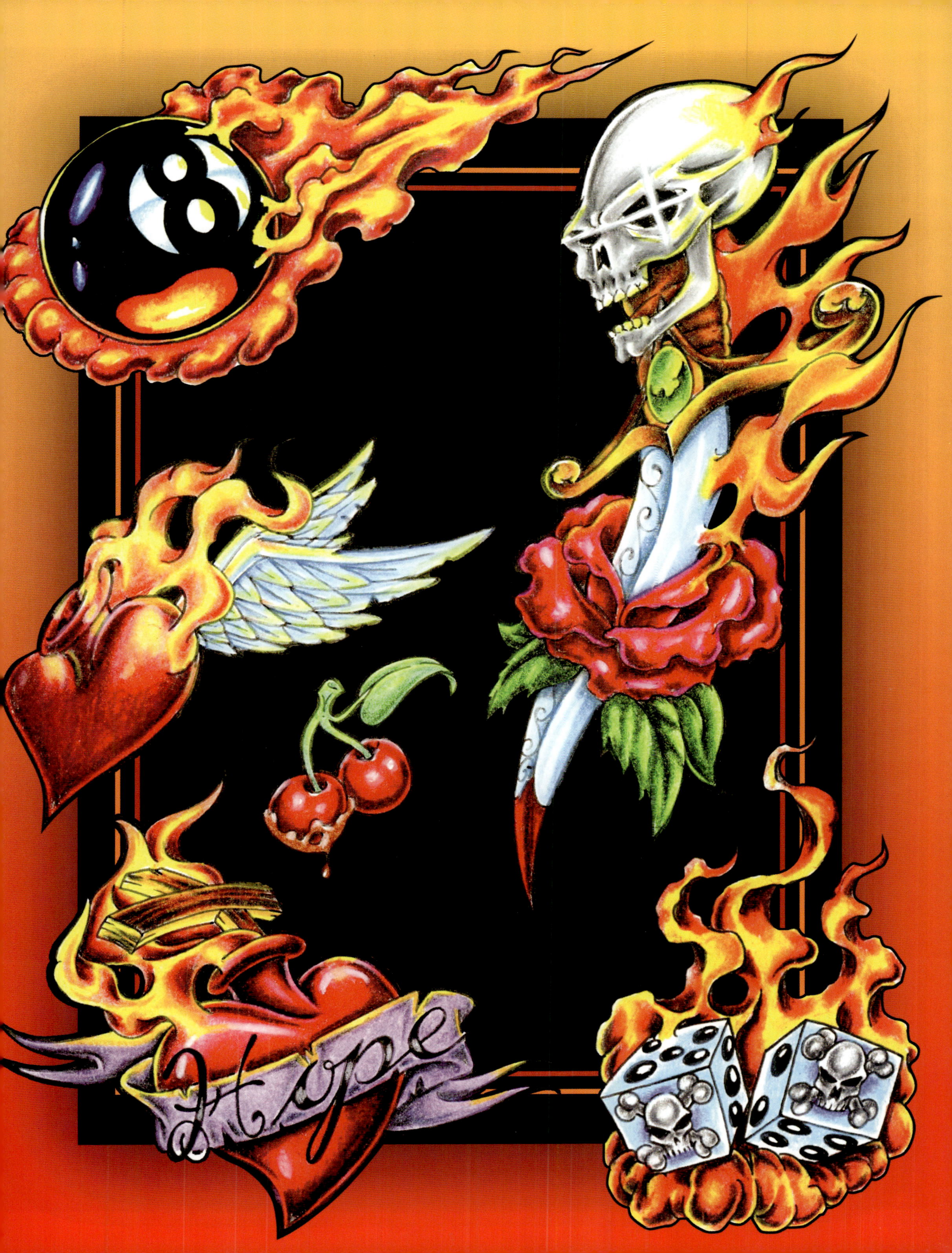
Hope

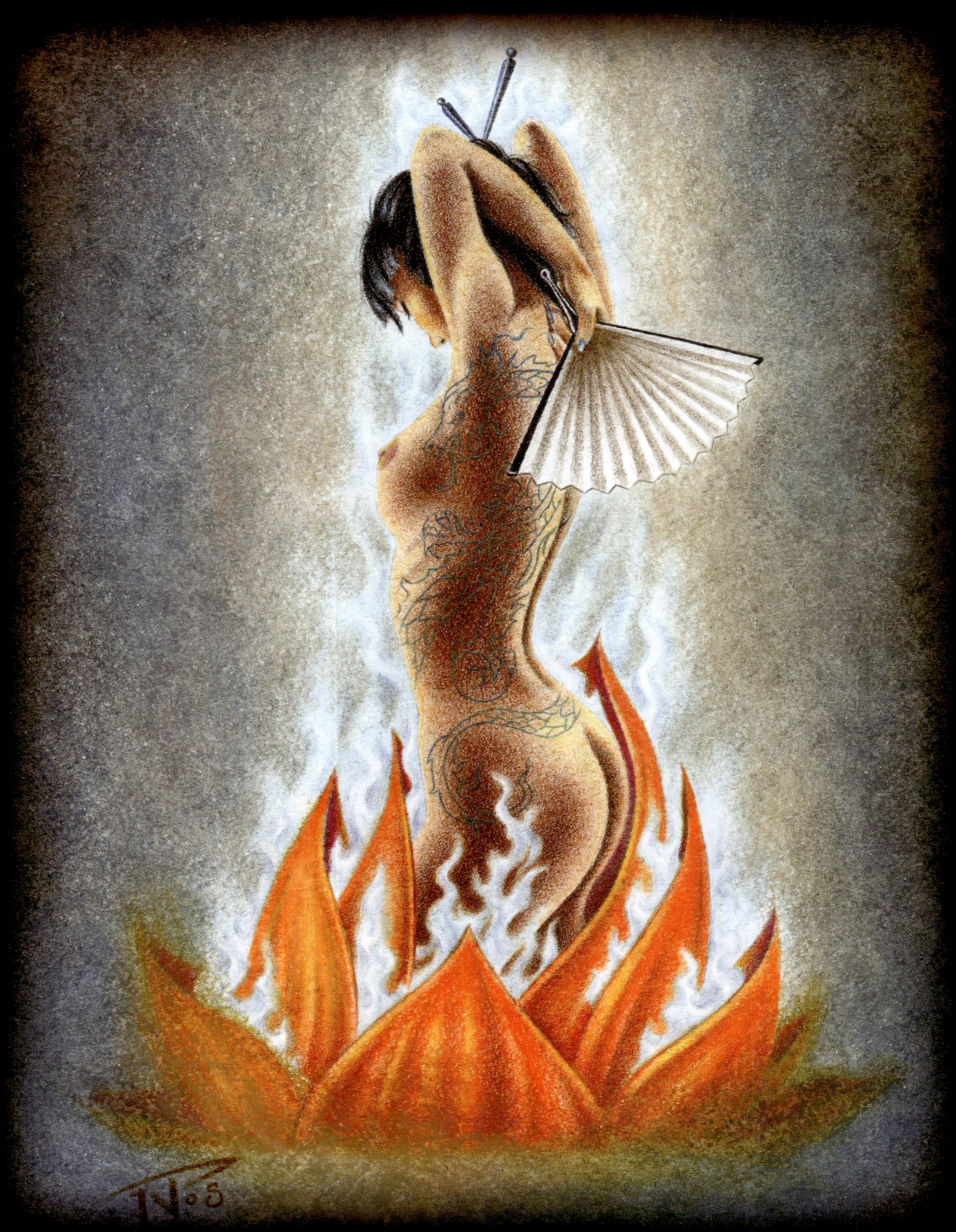

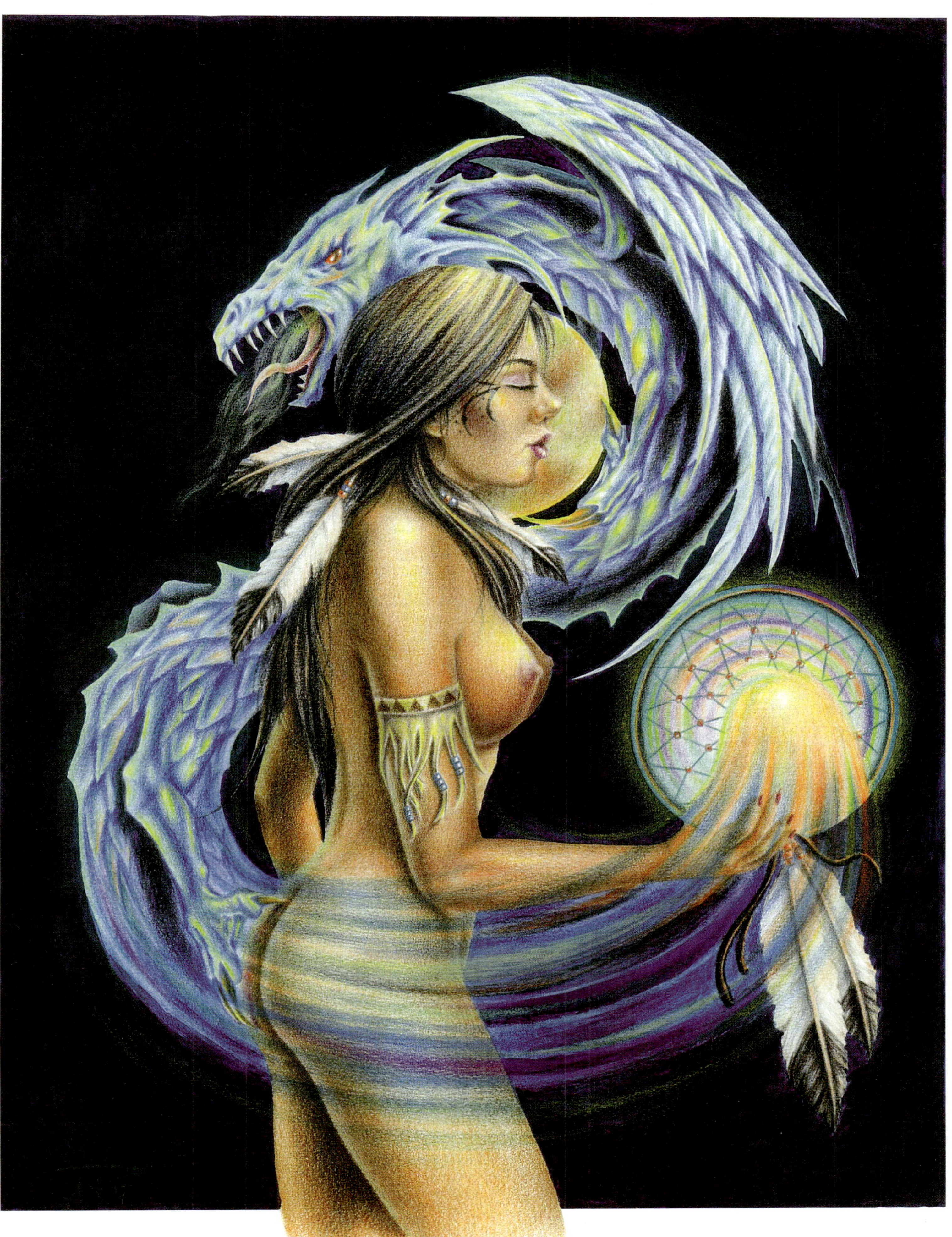

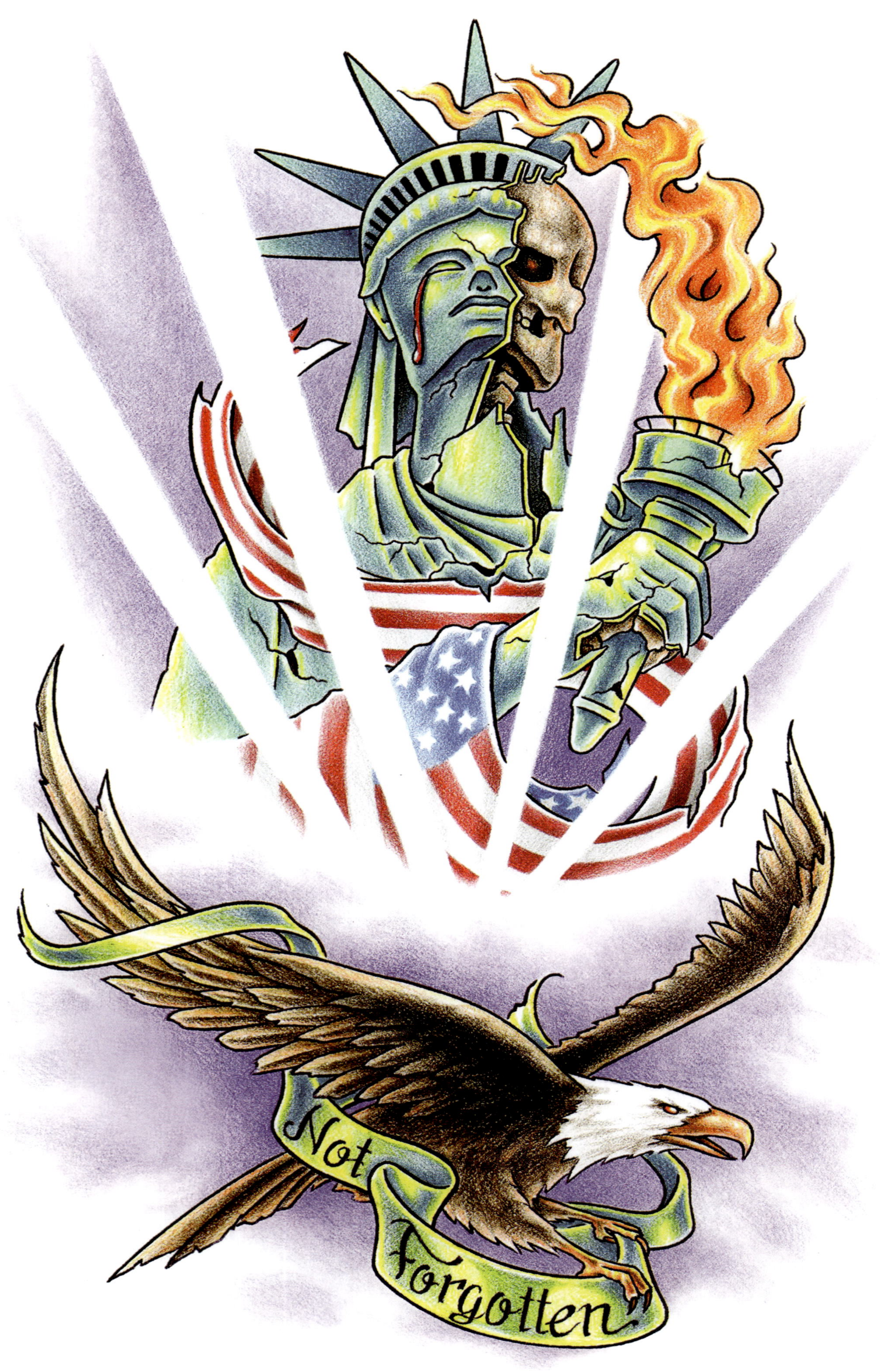
Not
forgotten

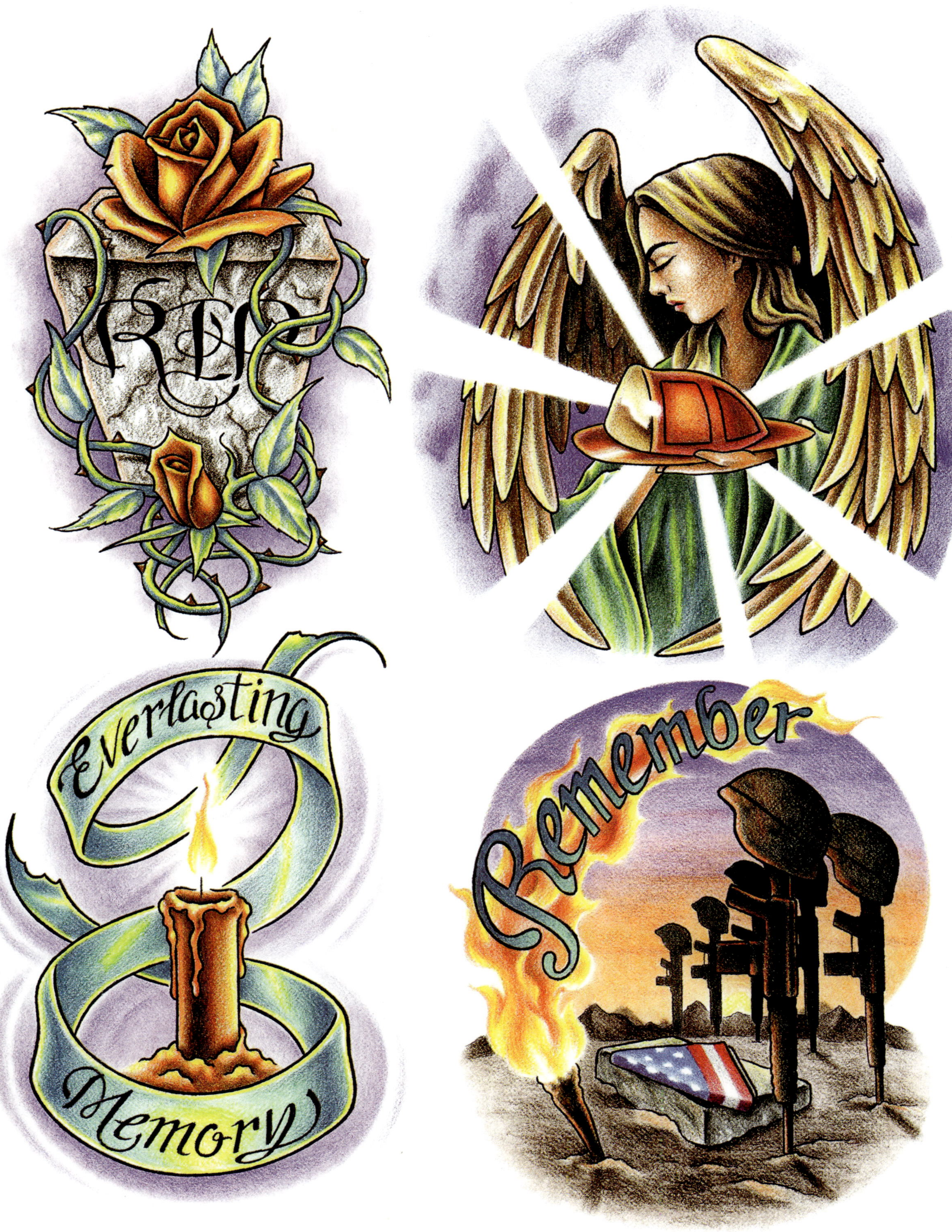
RIP
Everlasting
Memory
Remember

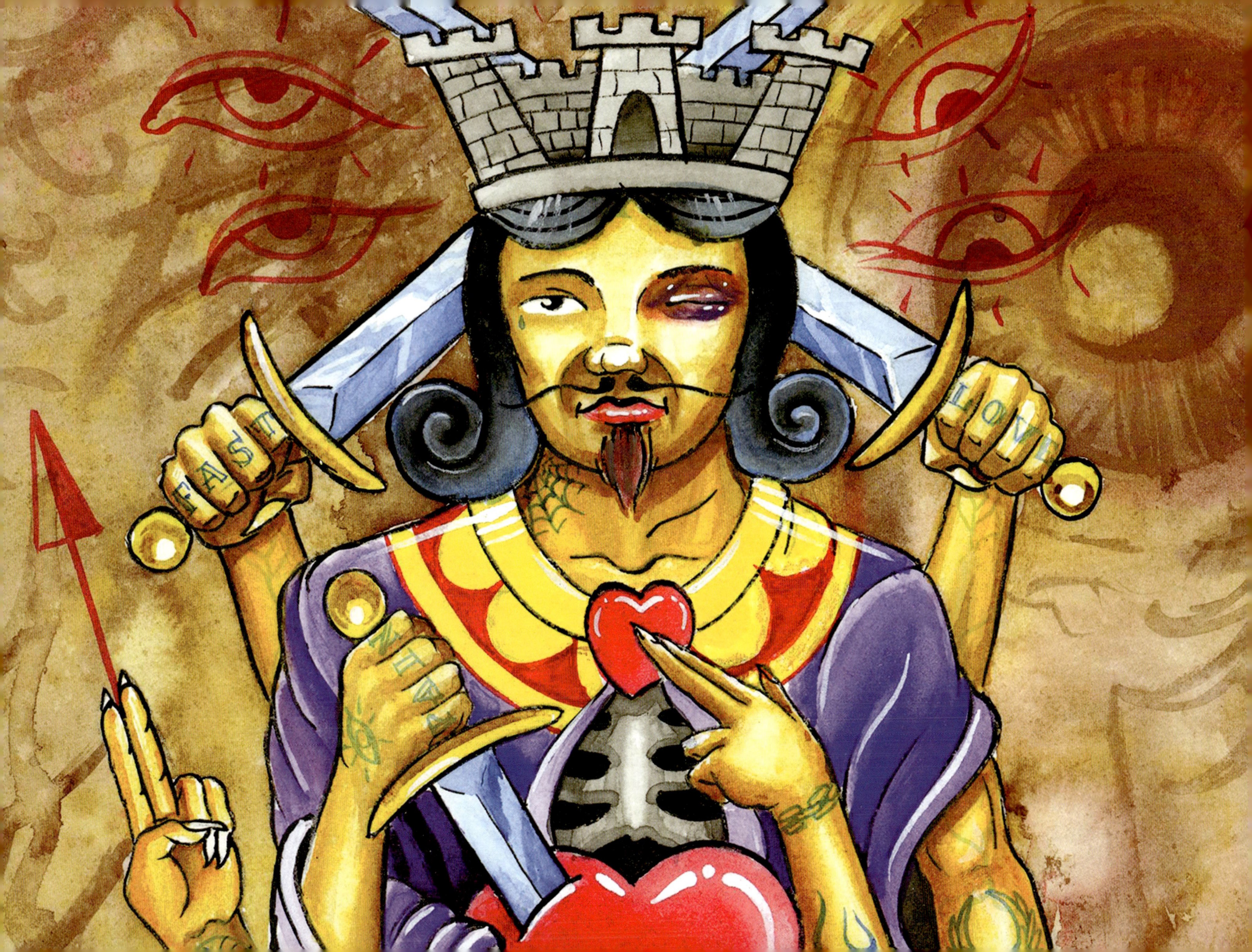
EAST
LOVE

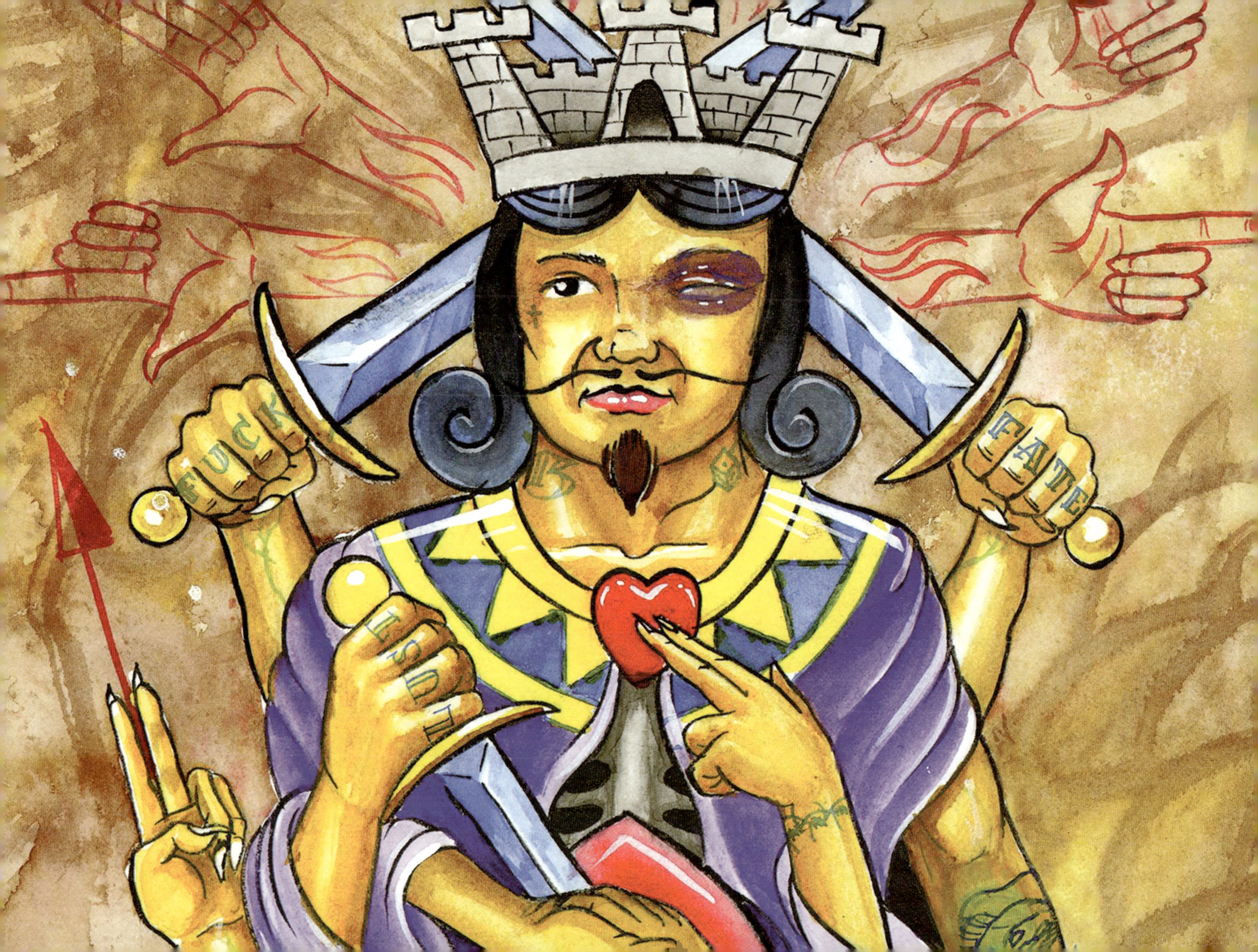
FUCK
FATE
LUST

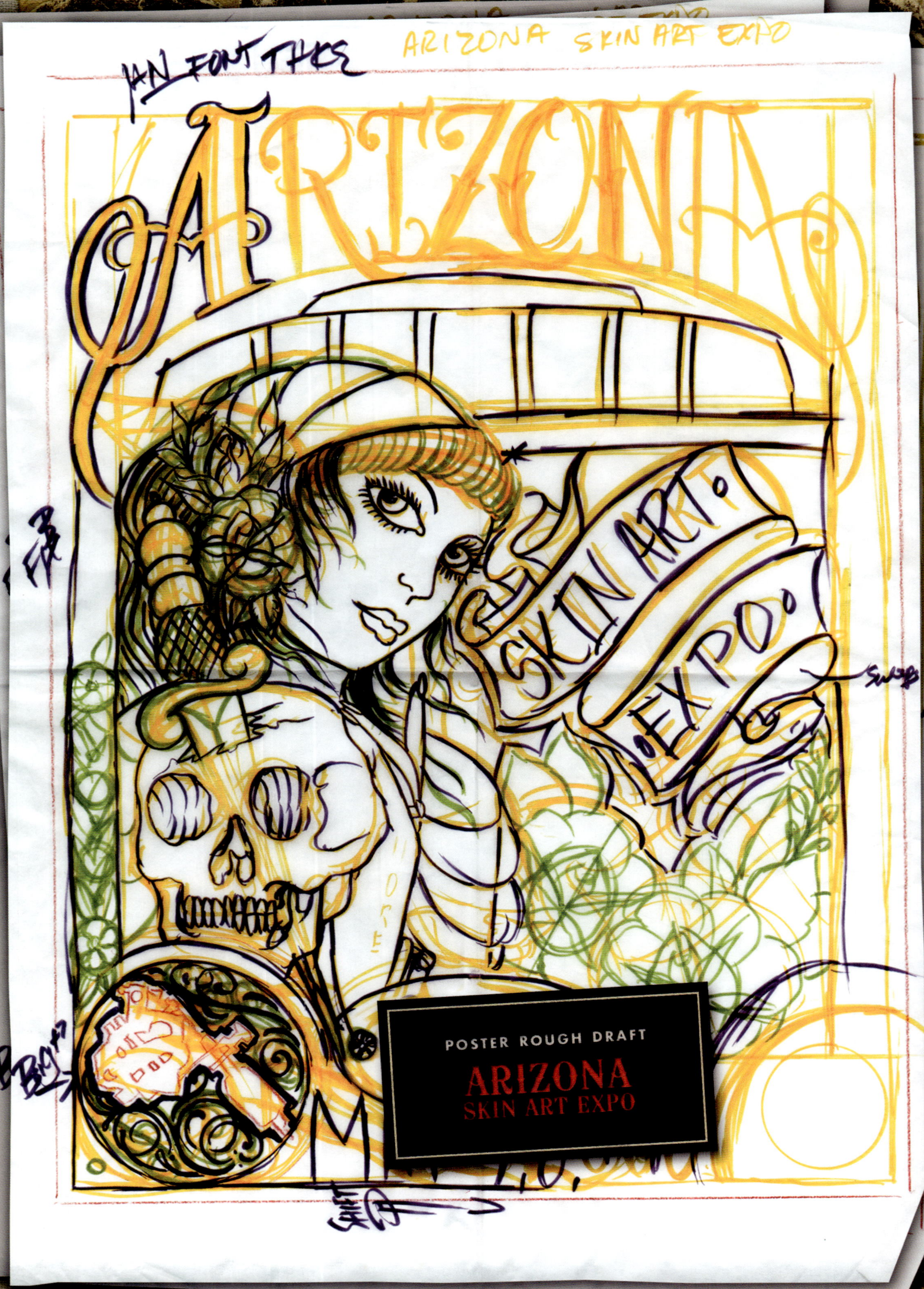

POSTER ROUGH DRAFT

ARIZONA

SKIN ART EXPO

ARIZONA

SKIN·ART EXPO

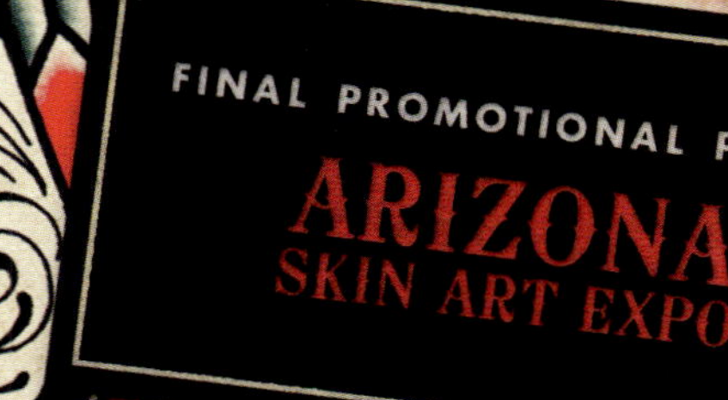

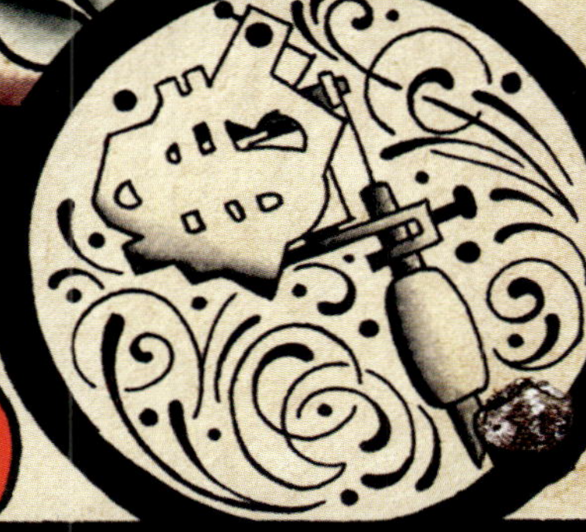

FINAL PROMOTIONAL POSTER

ARIZONA SKIN ART EXPO

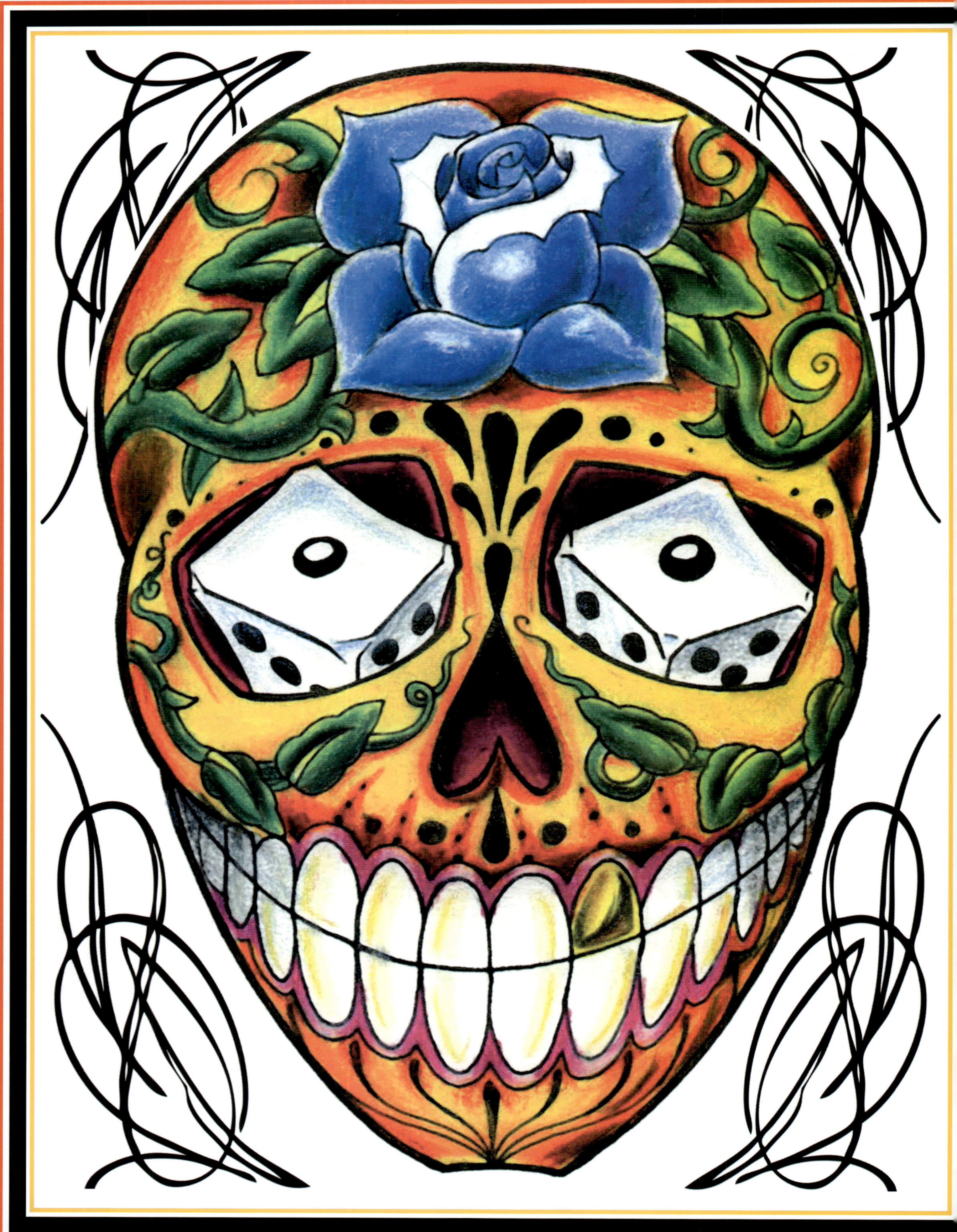

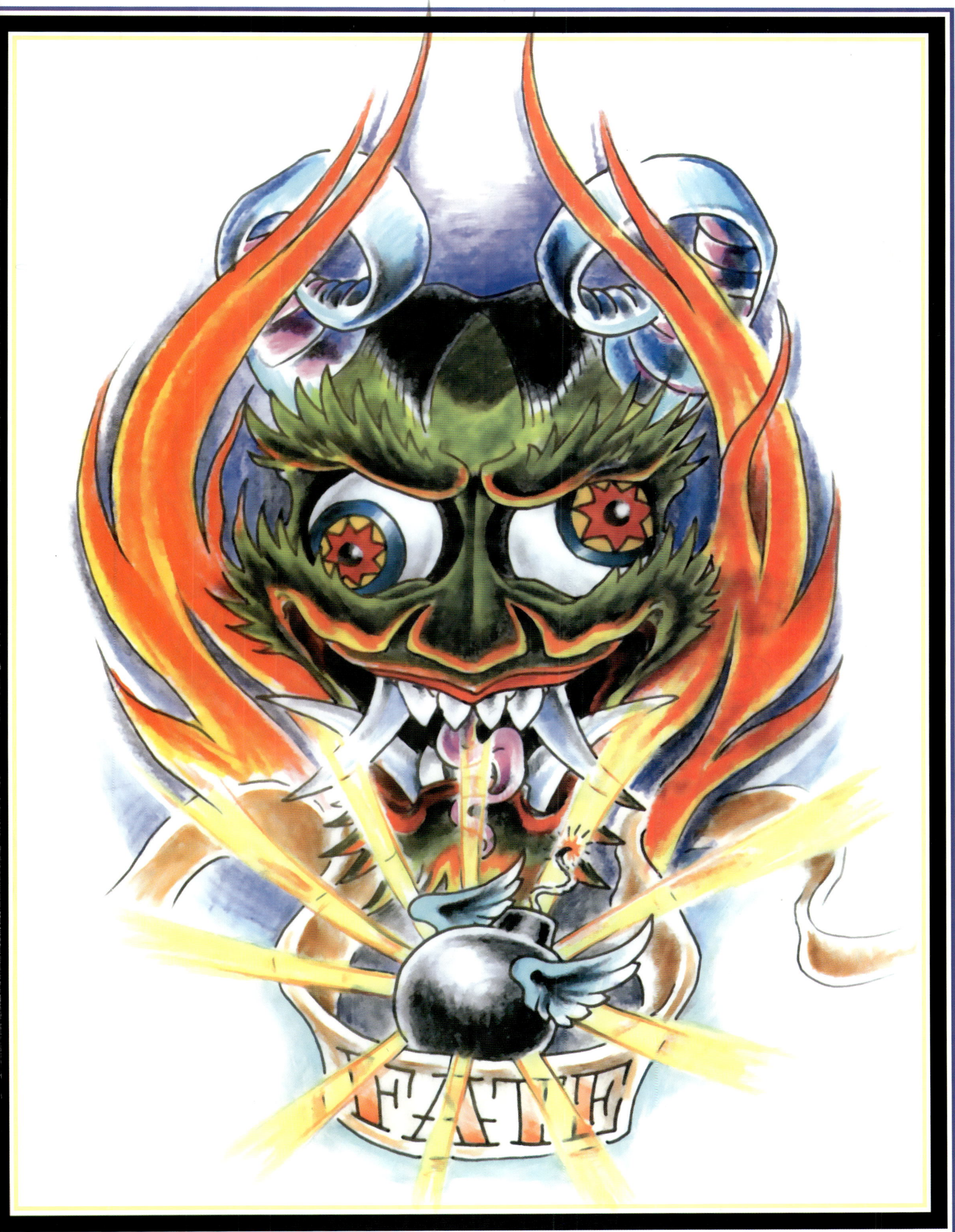

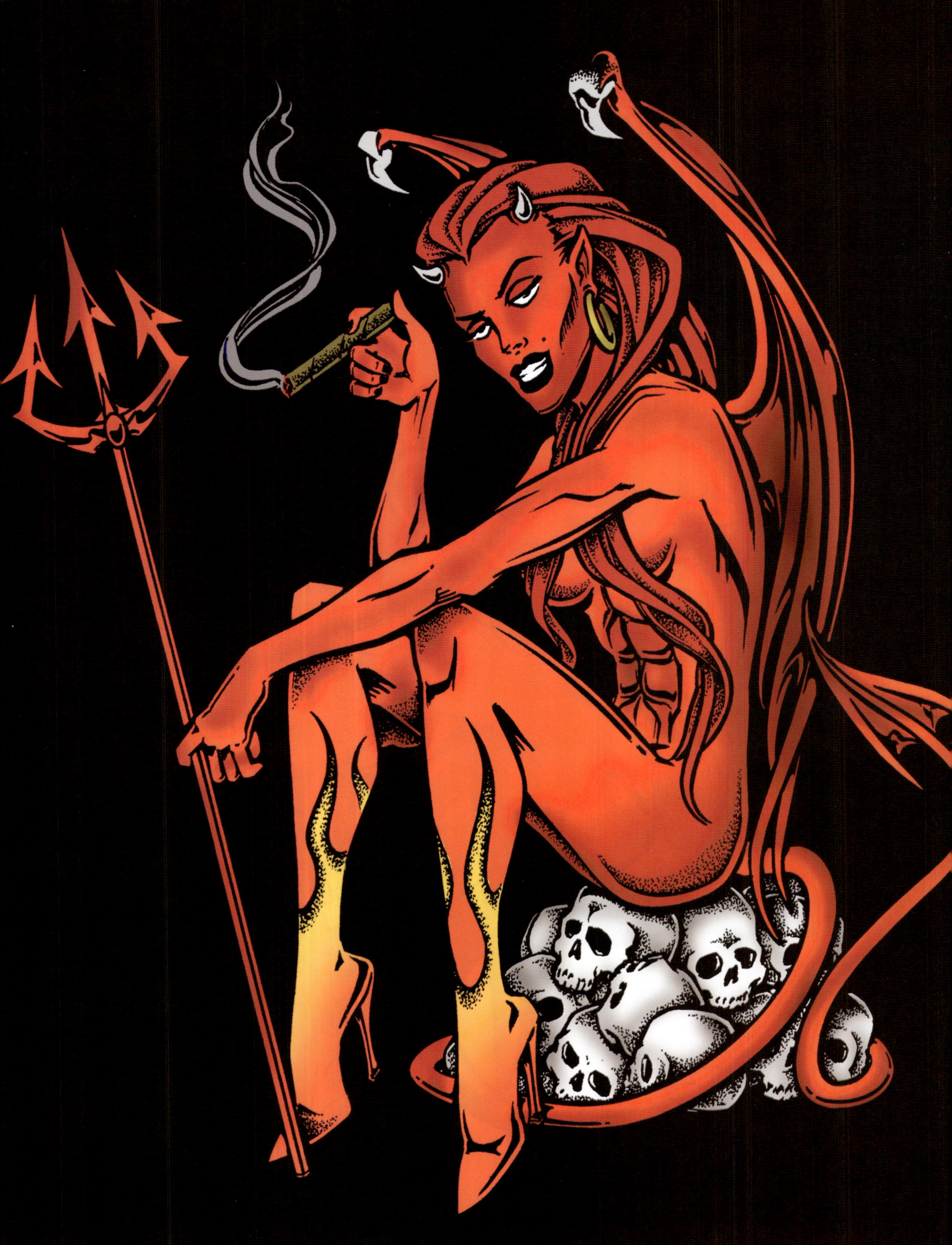

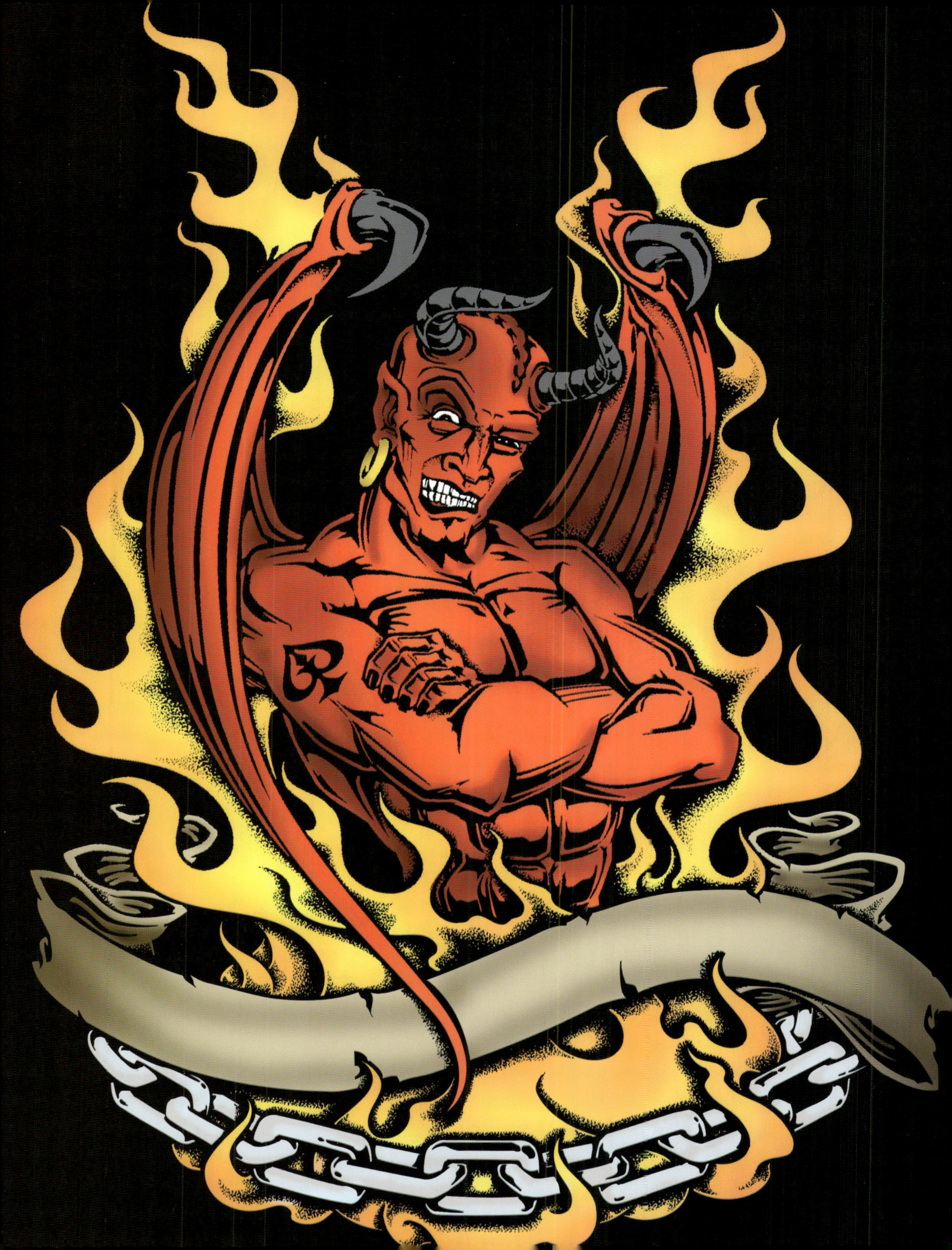

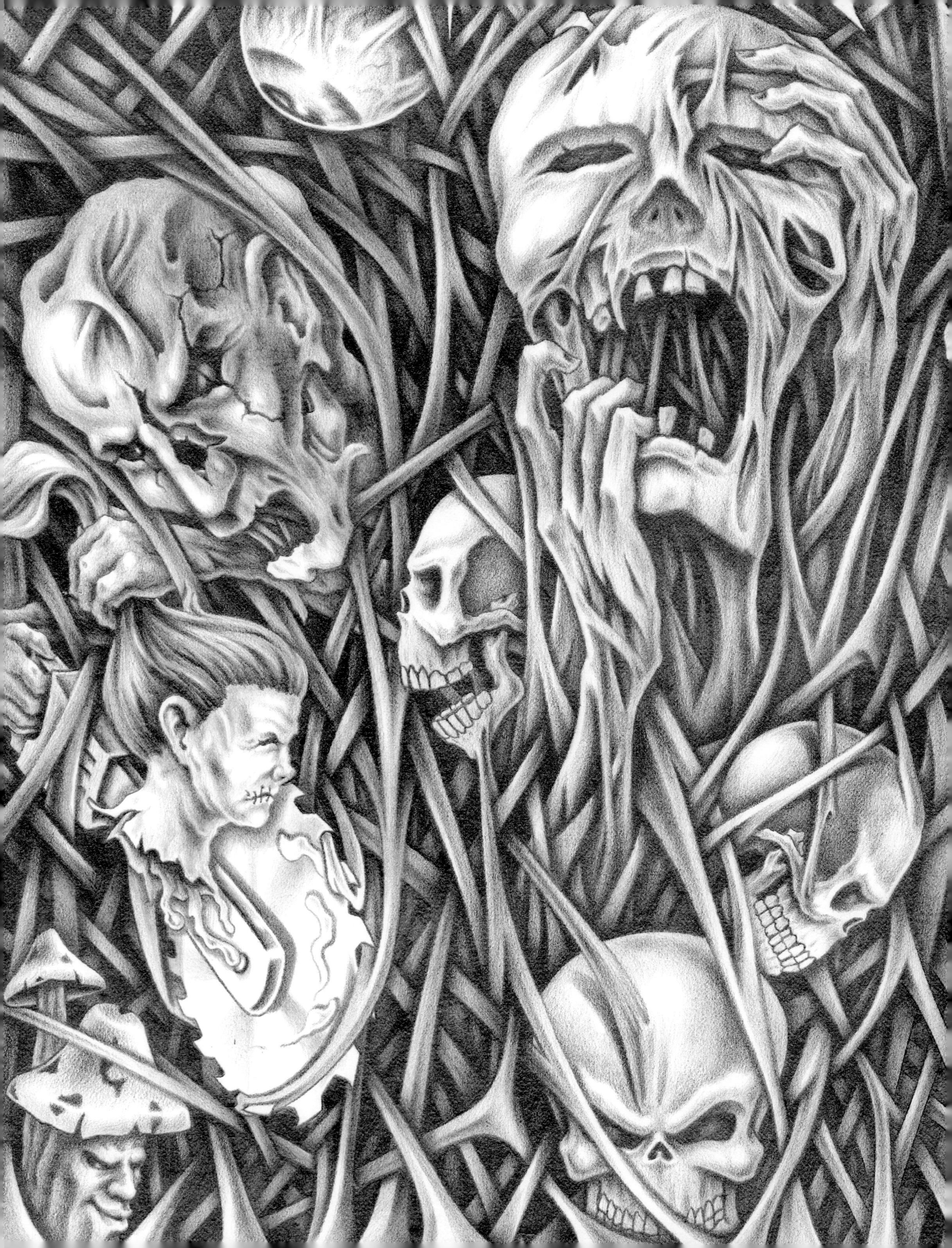

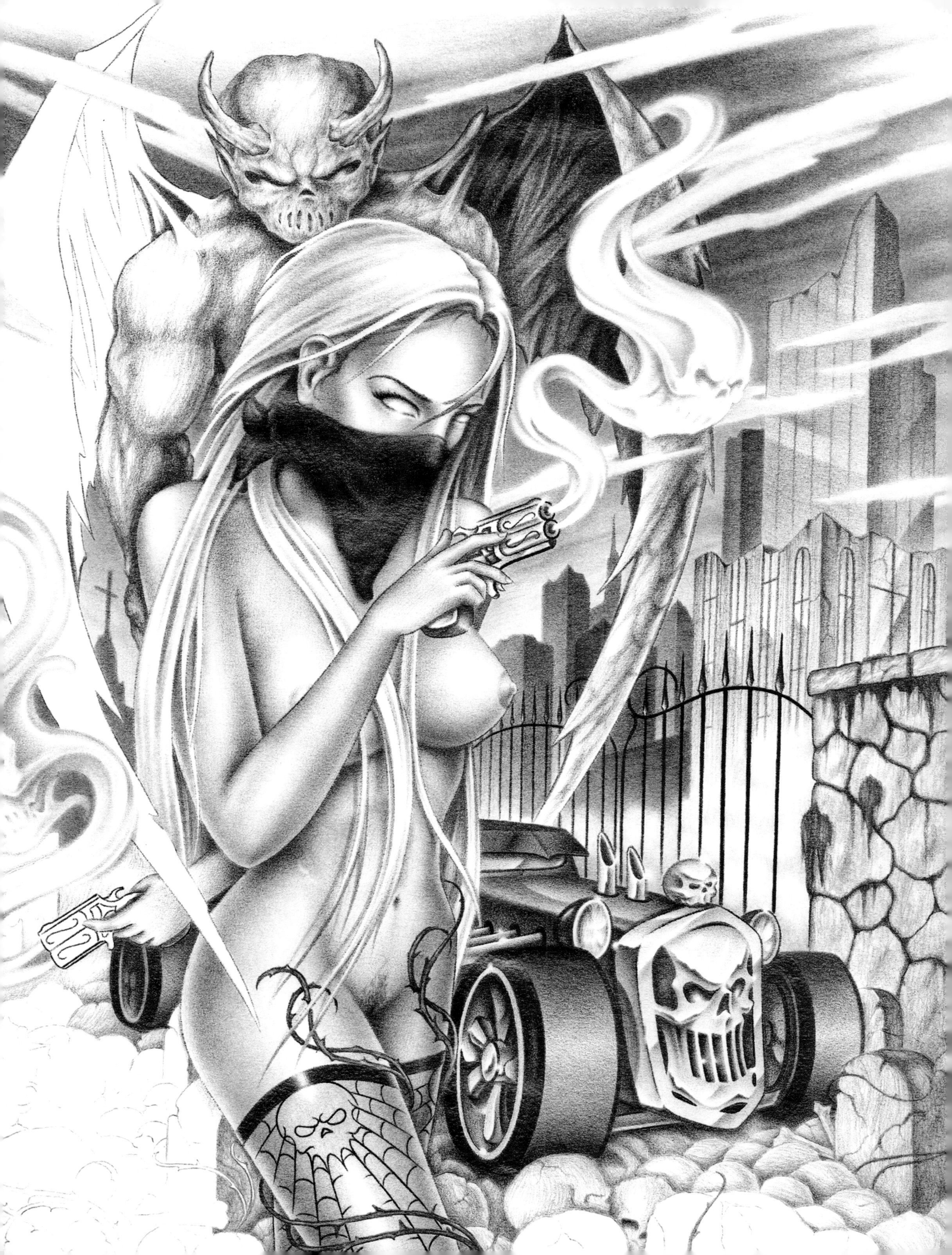

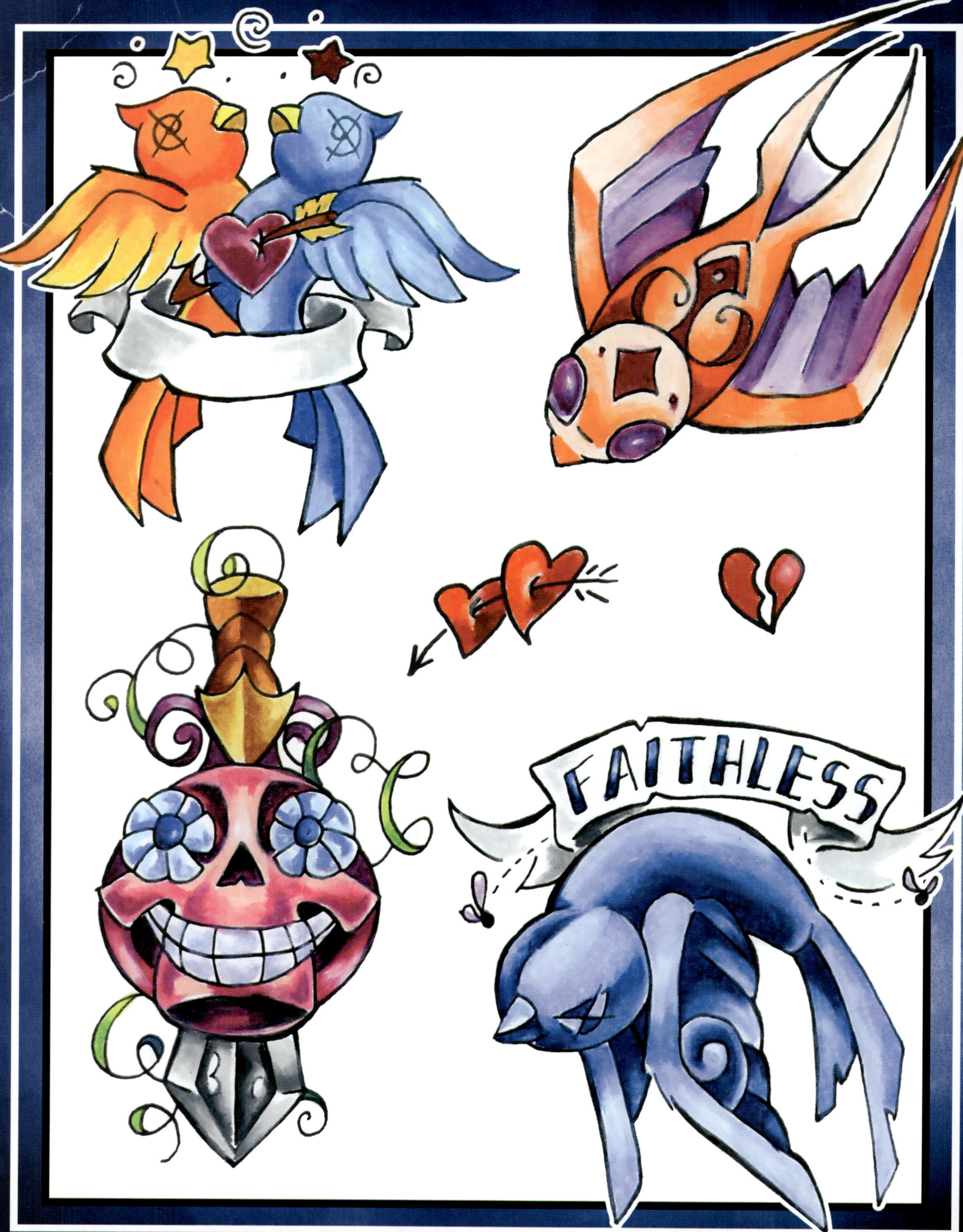
FAITHLESS

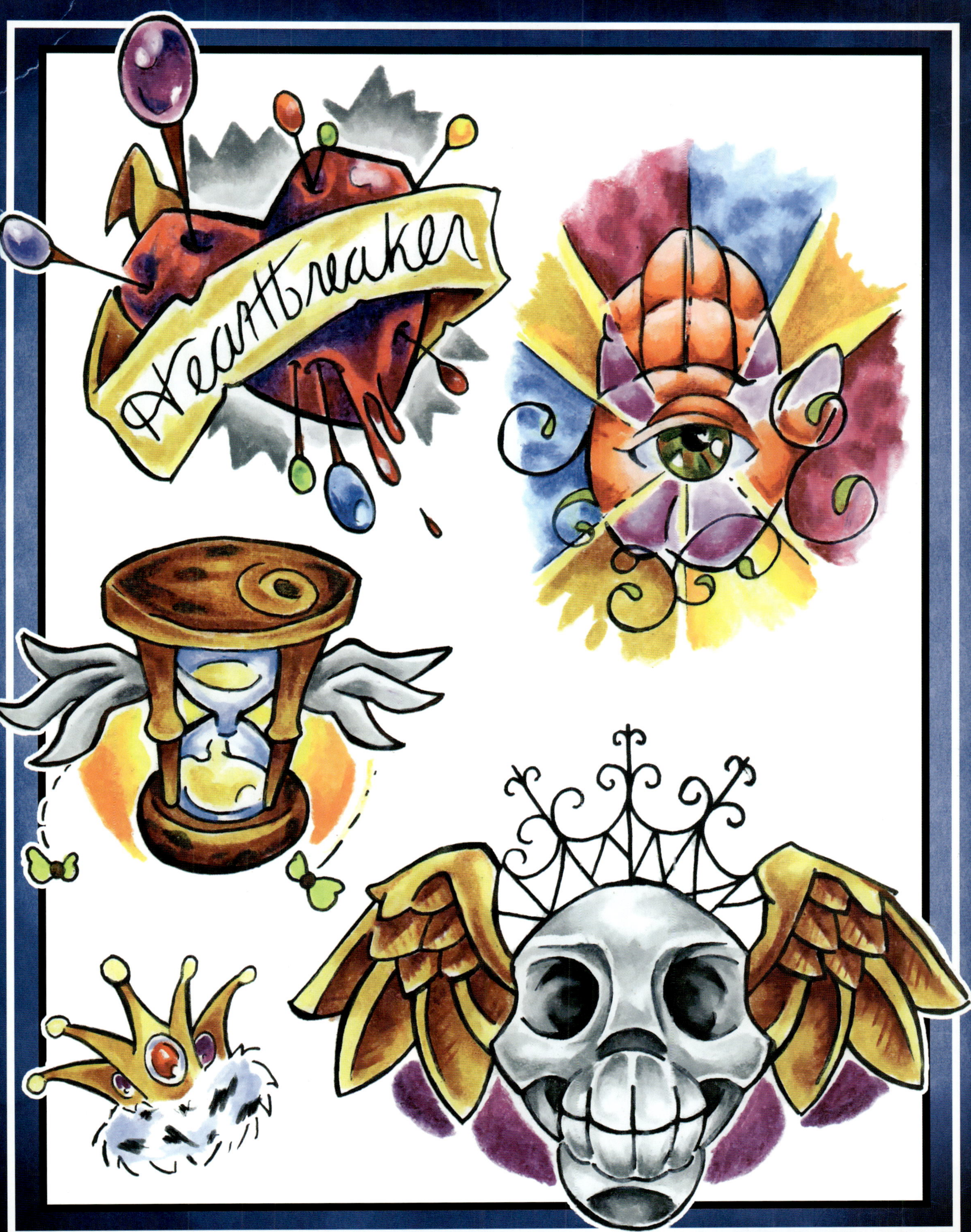
Heartbreaker

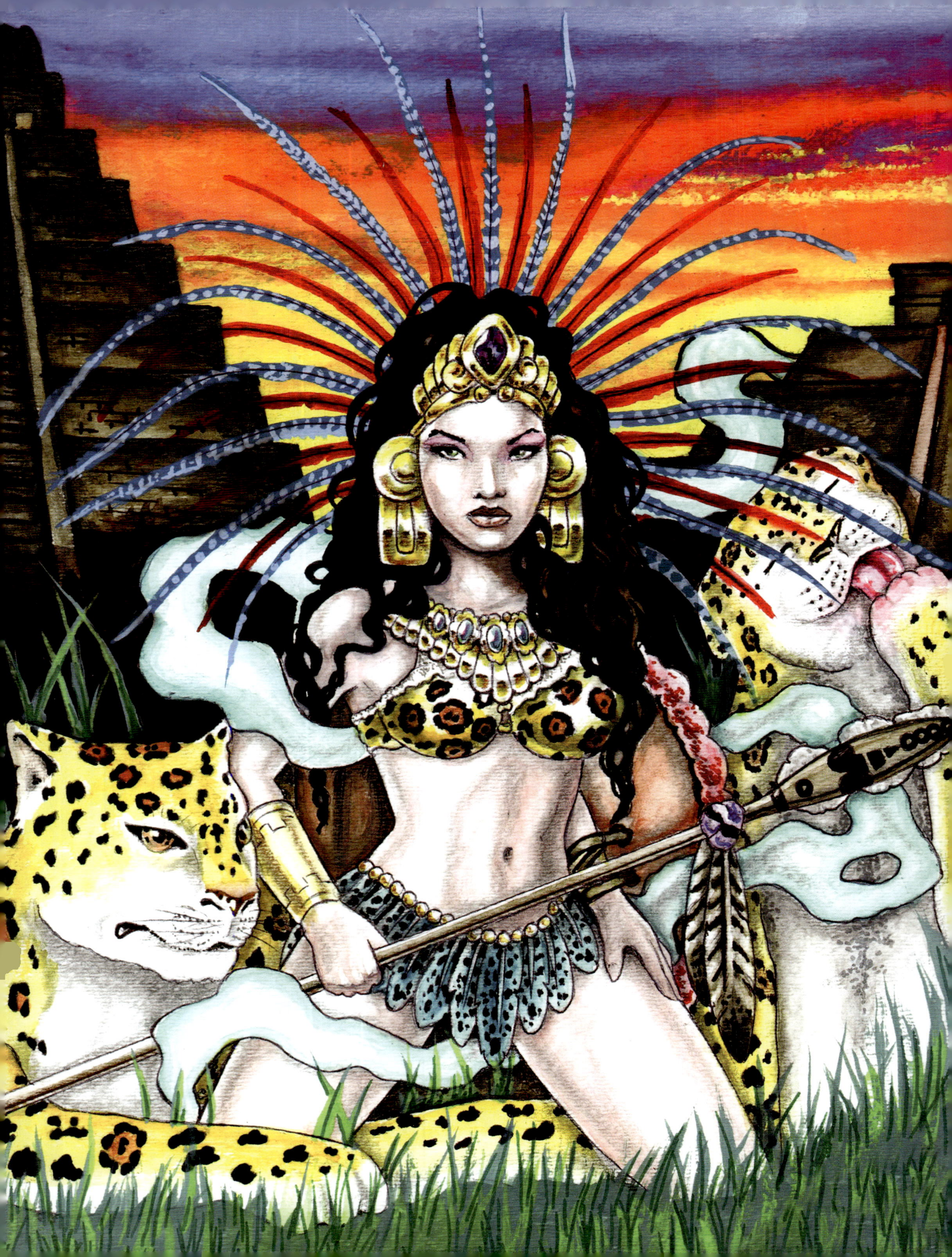

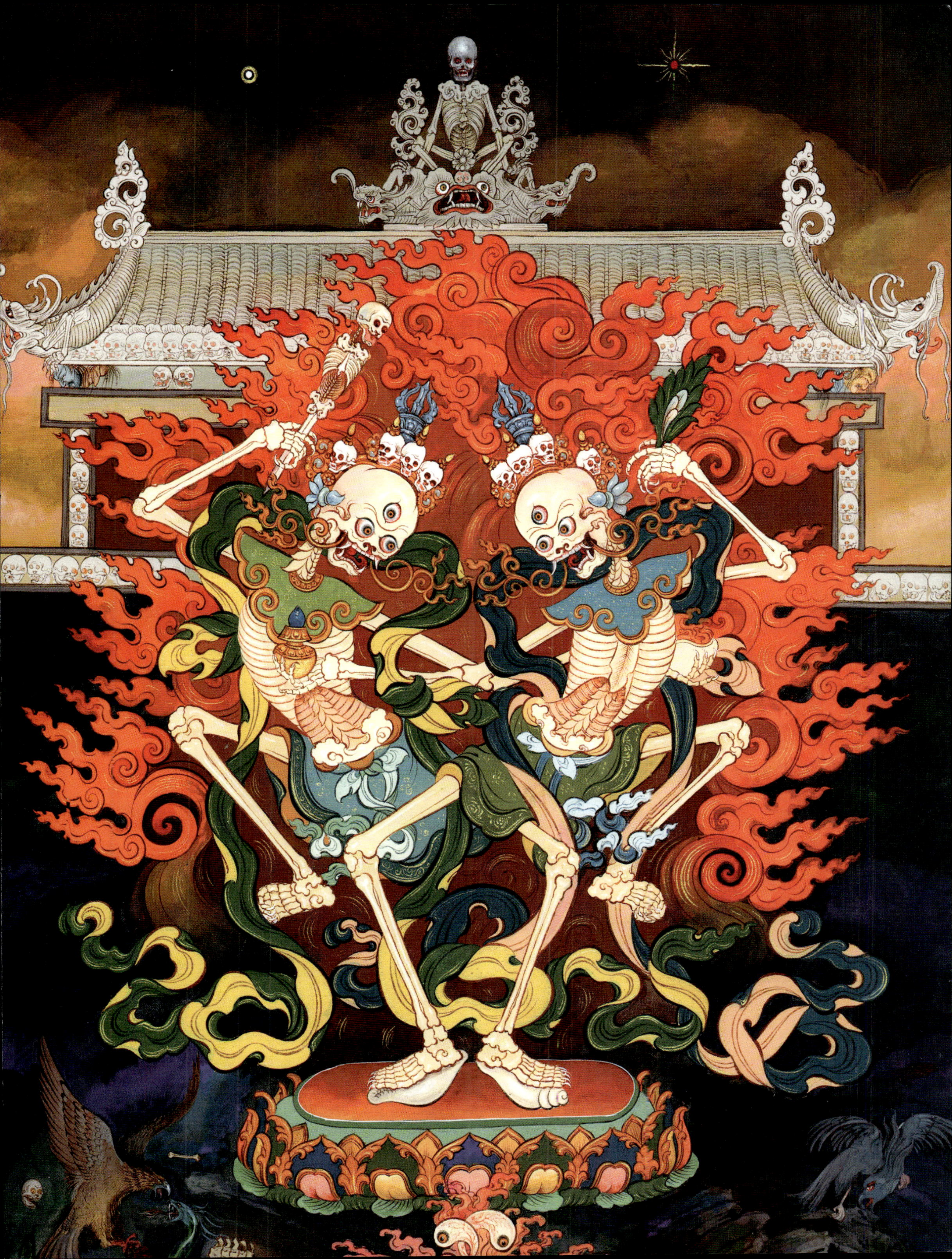

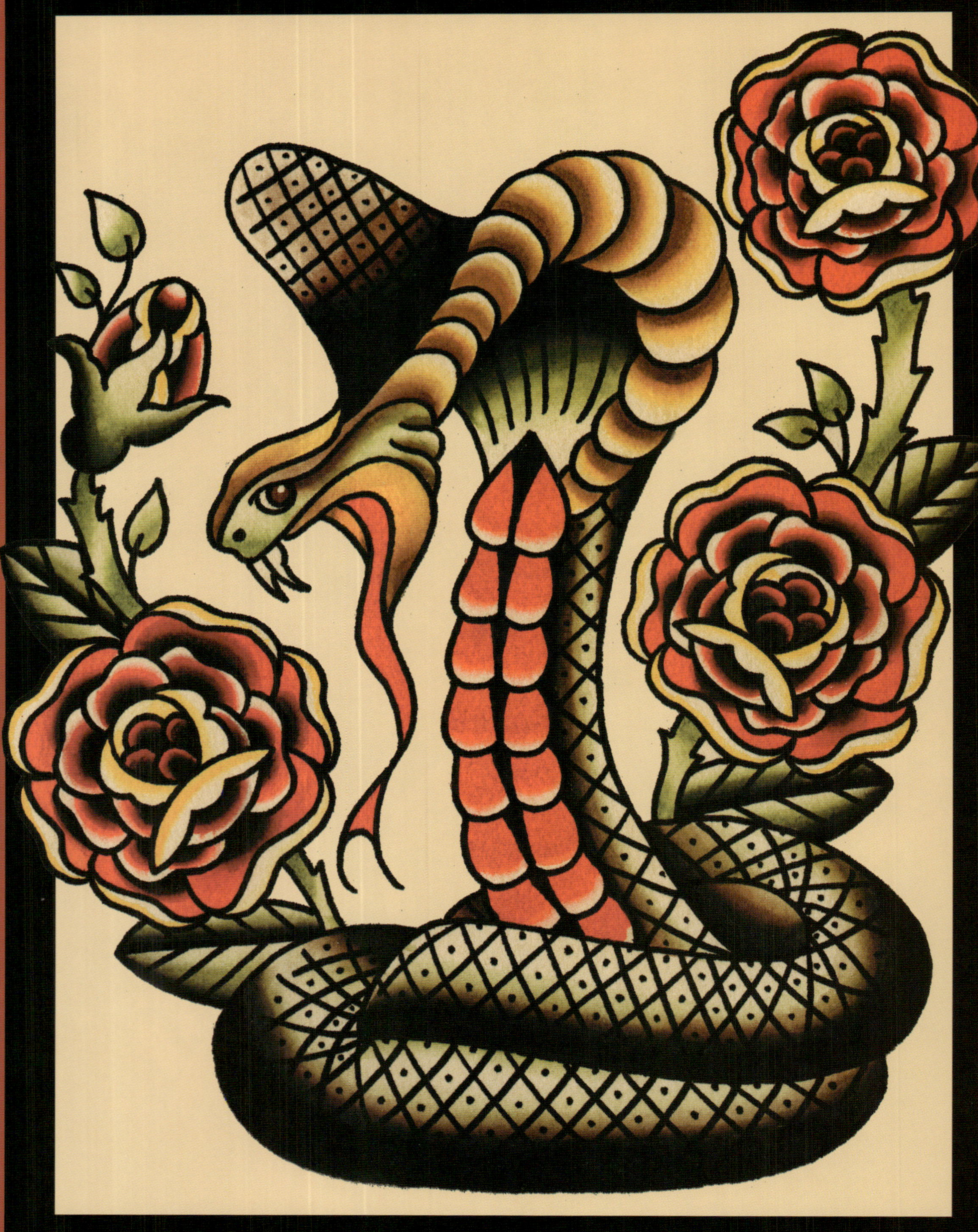

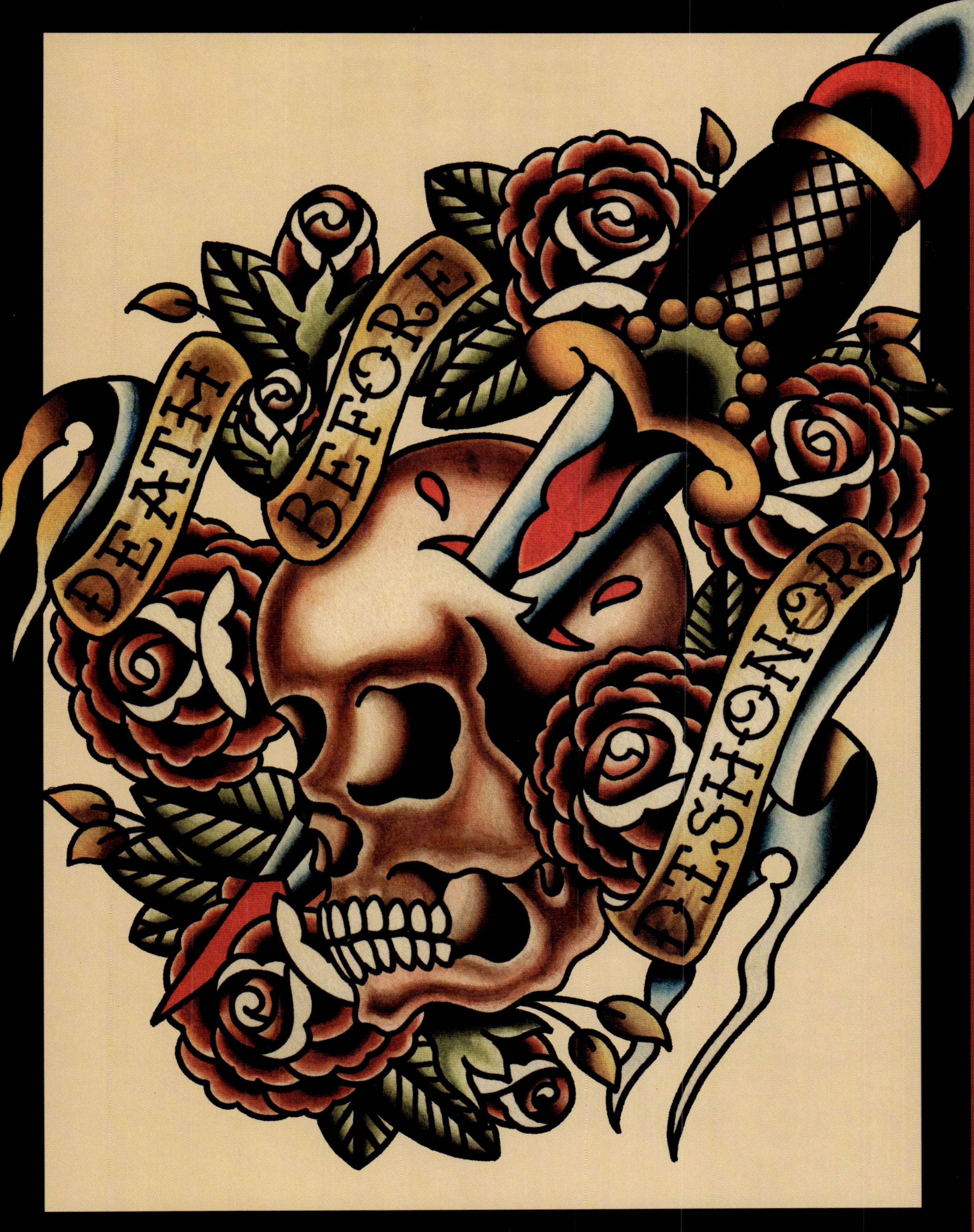
DEATH
BEFORE
DISHONOR

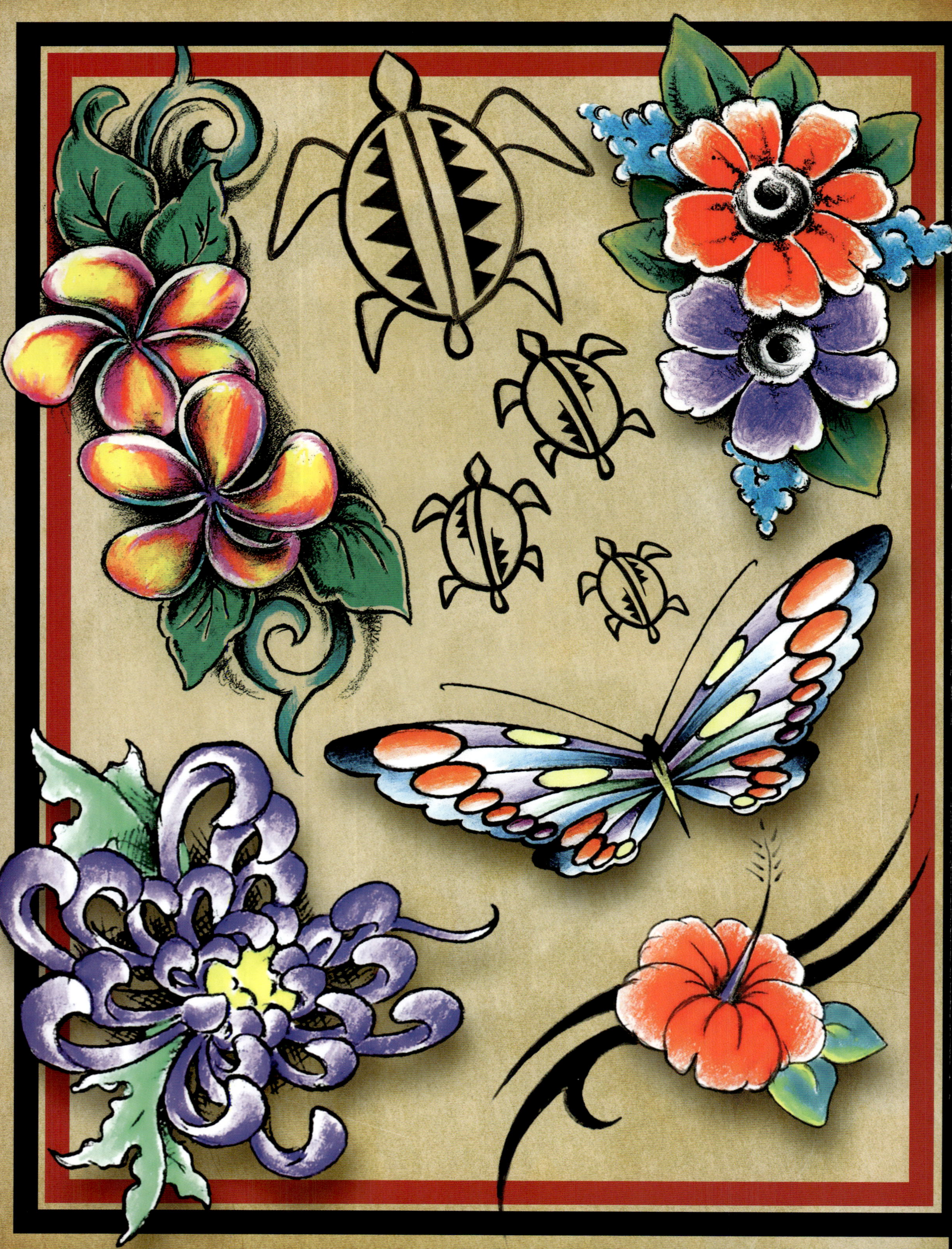

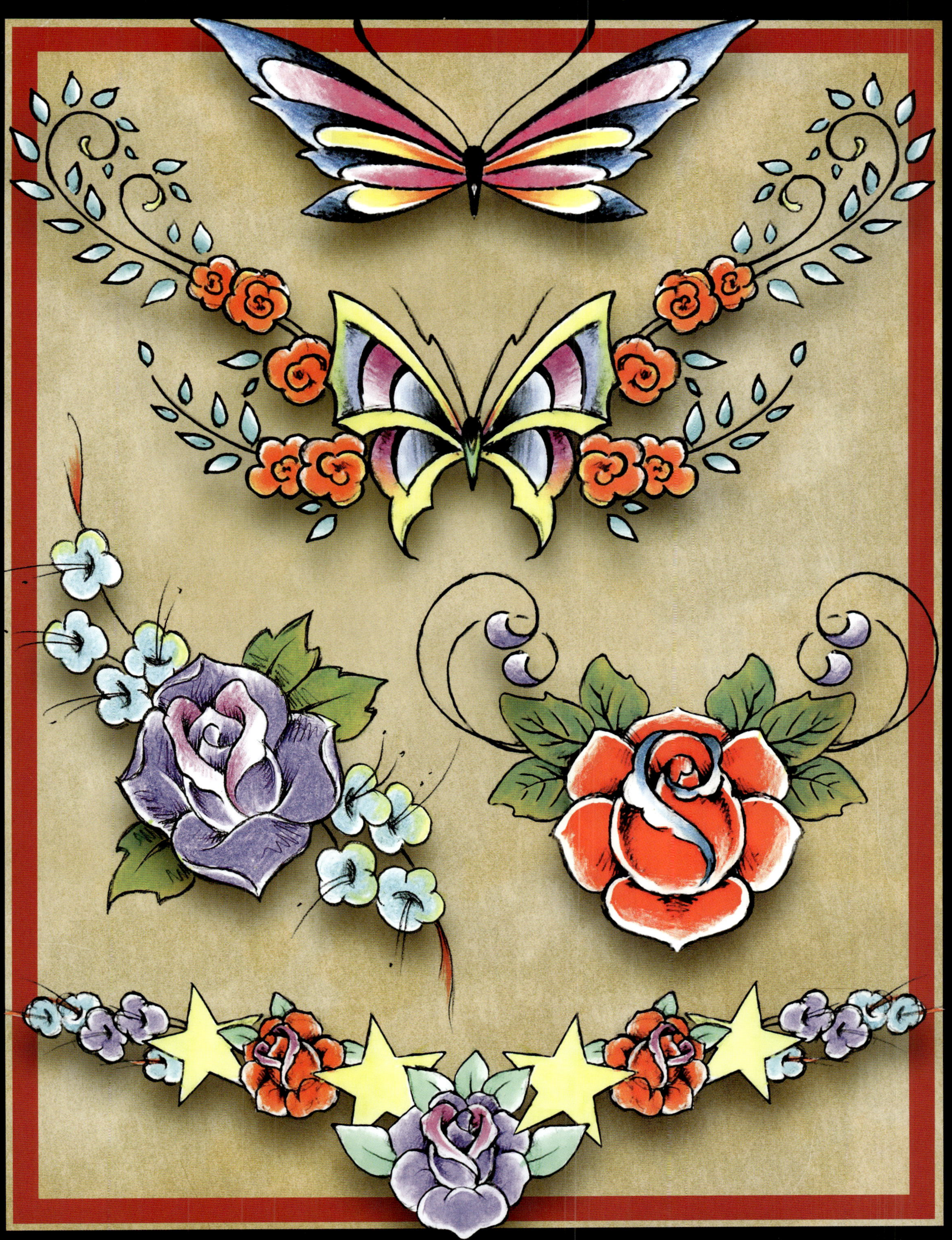

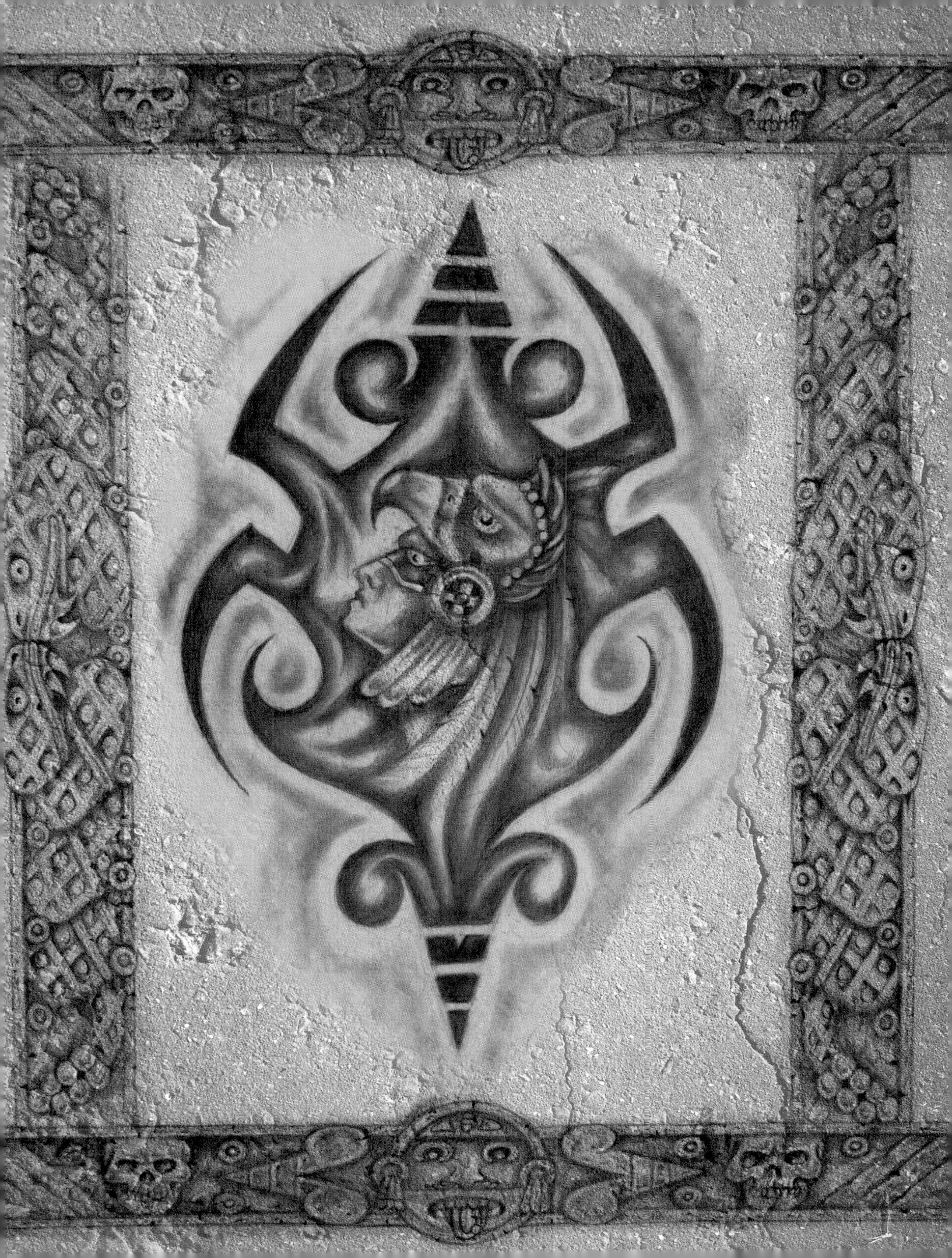

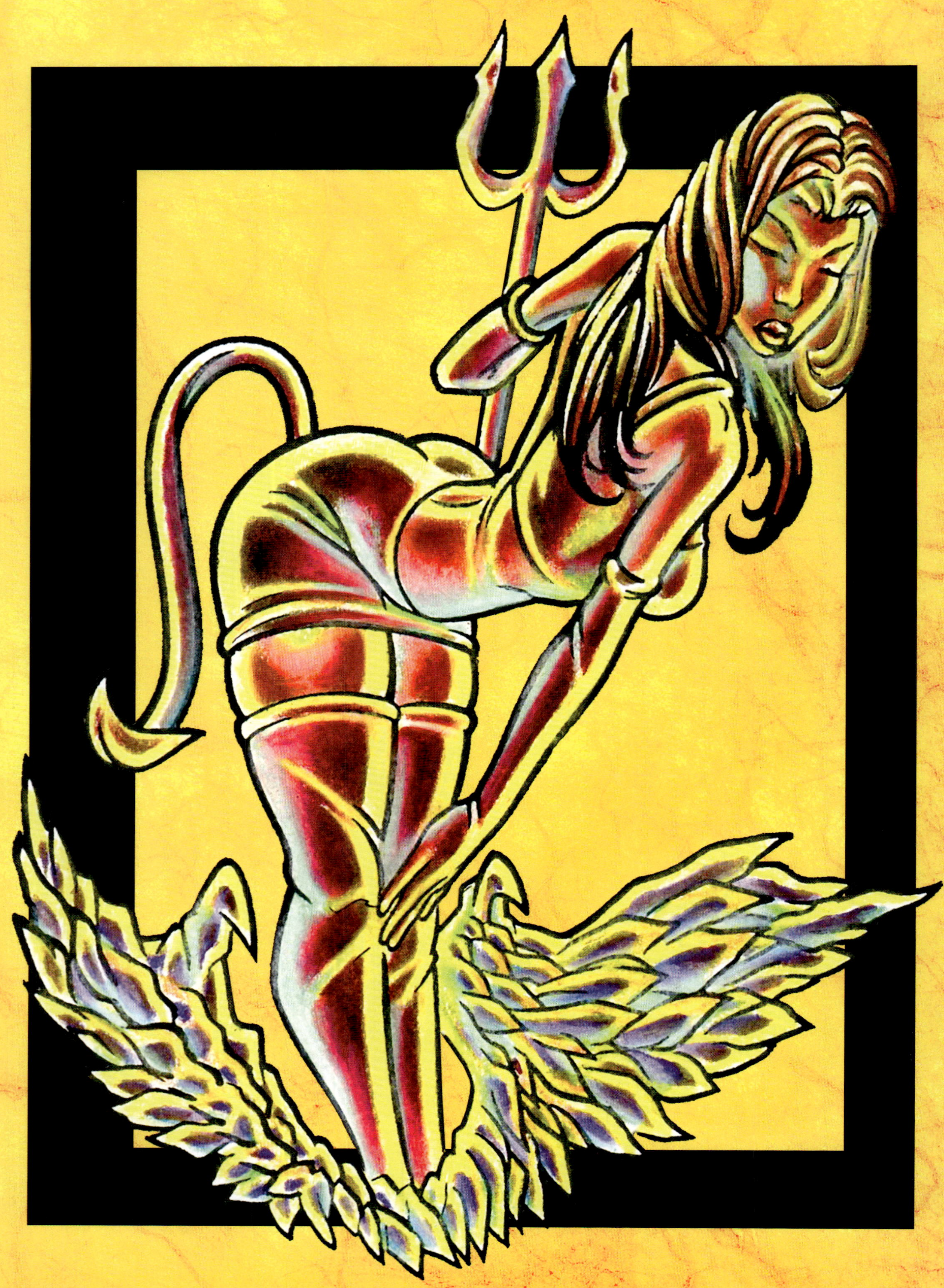

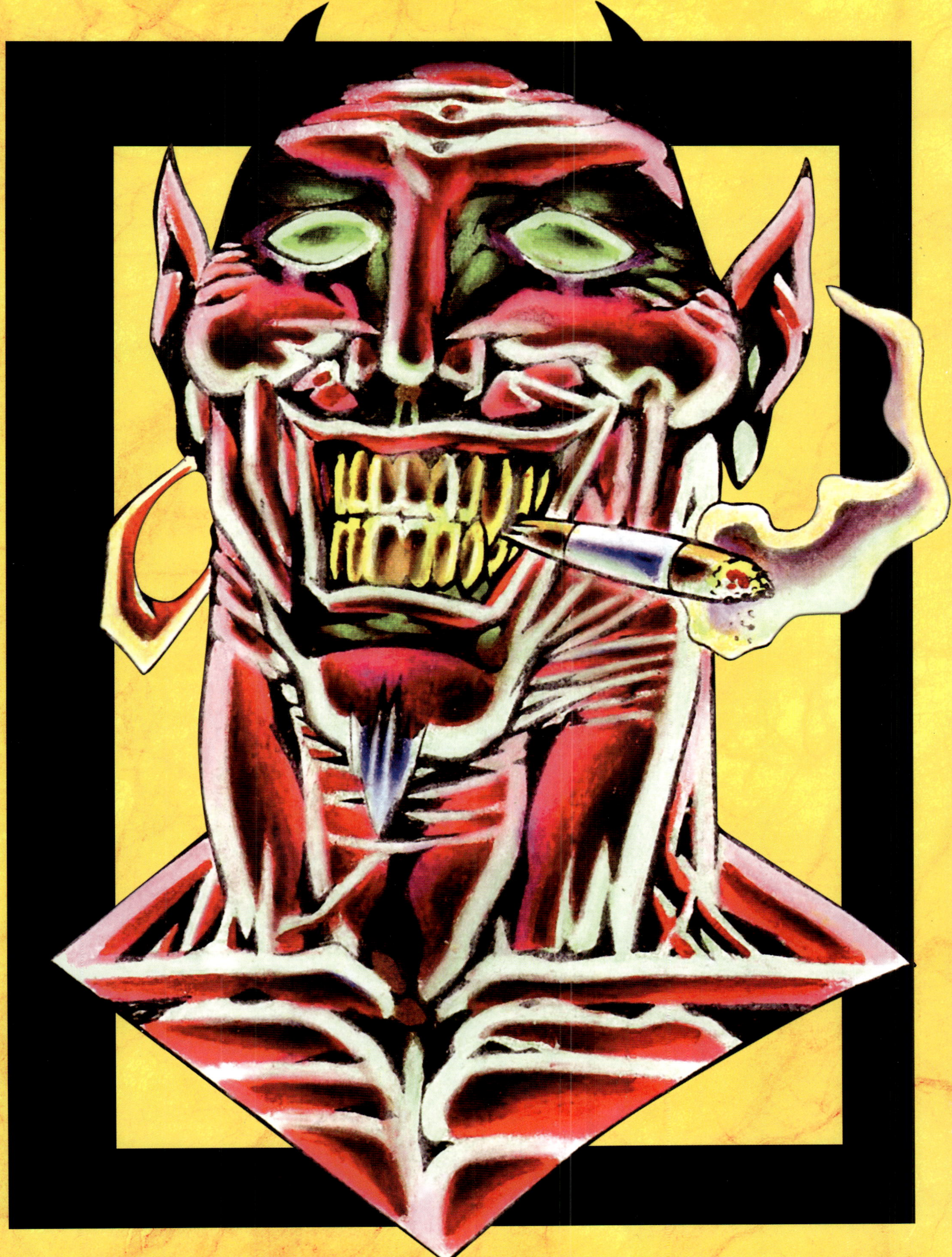

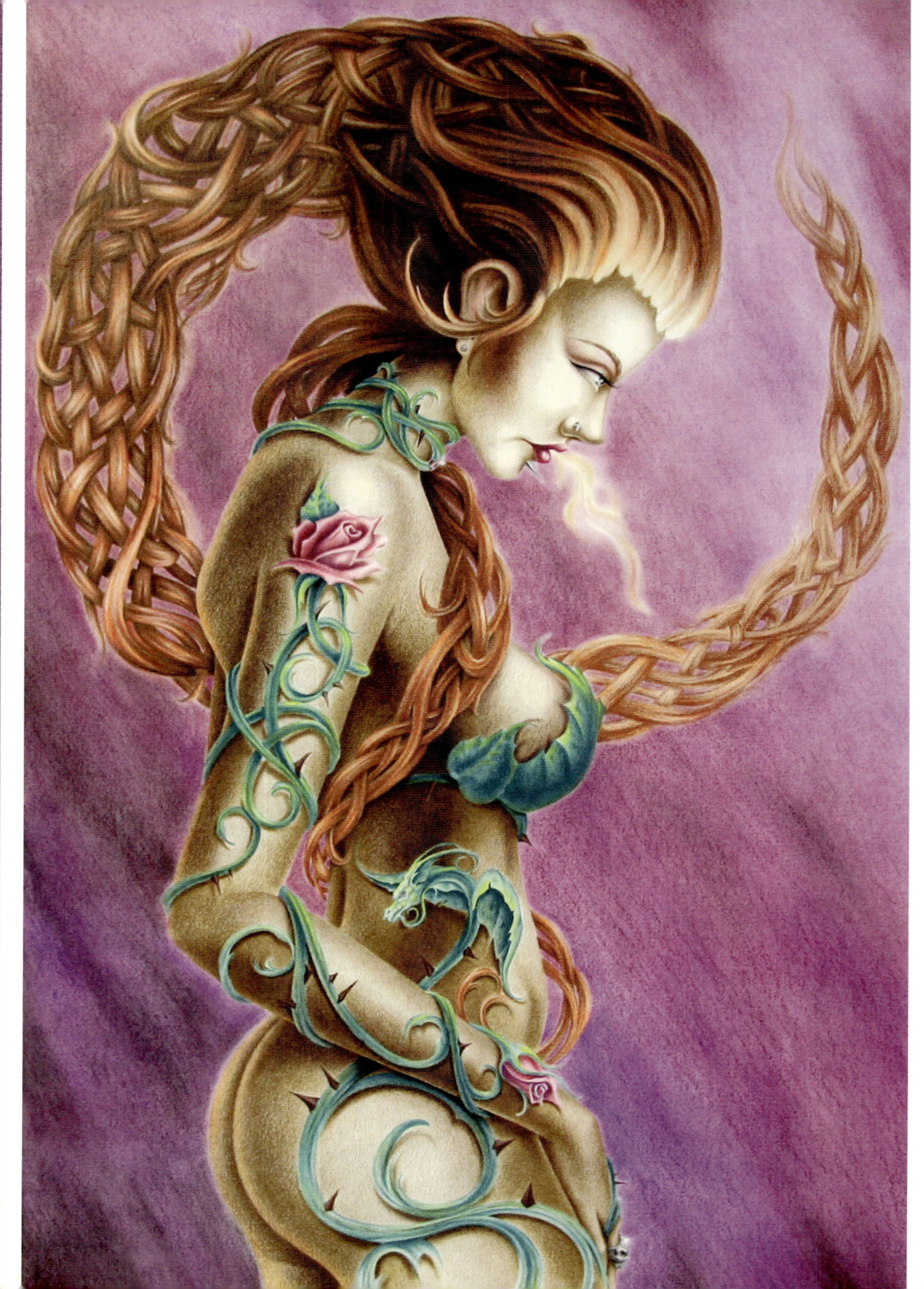

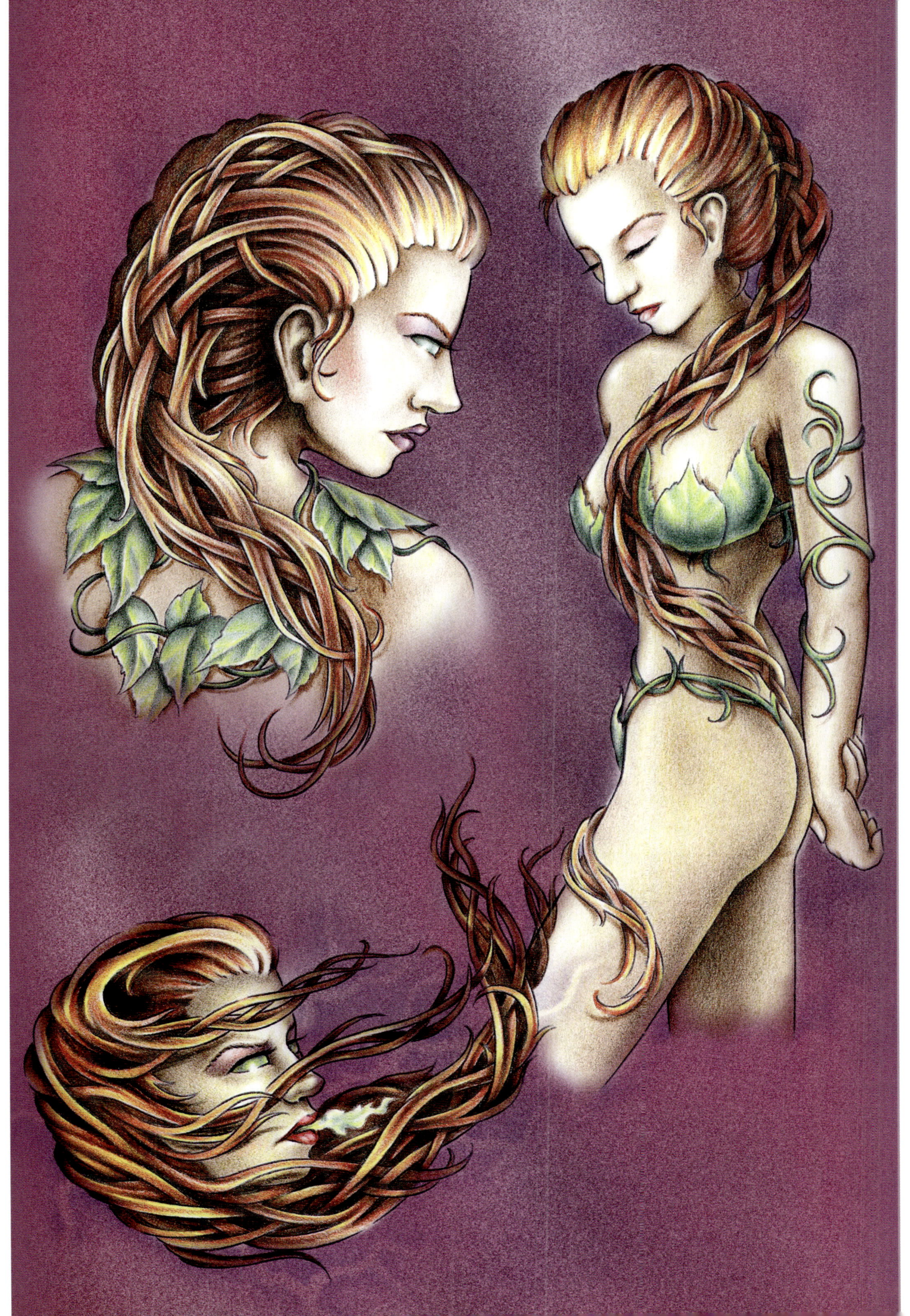

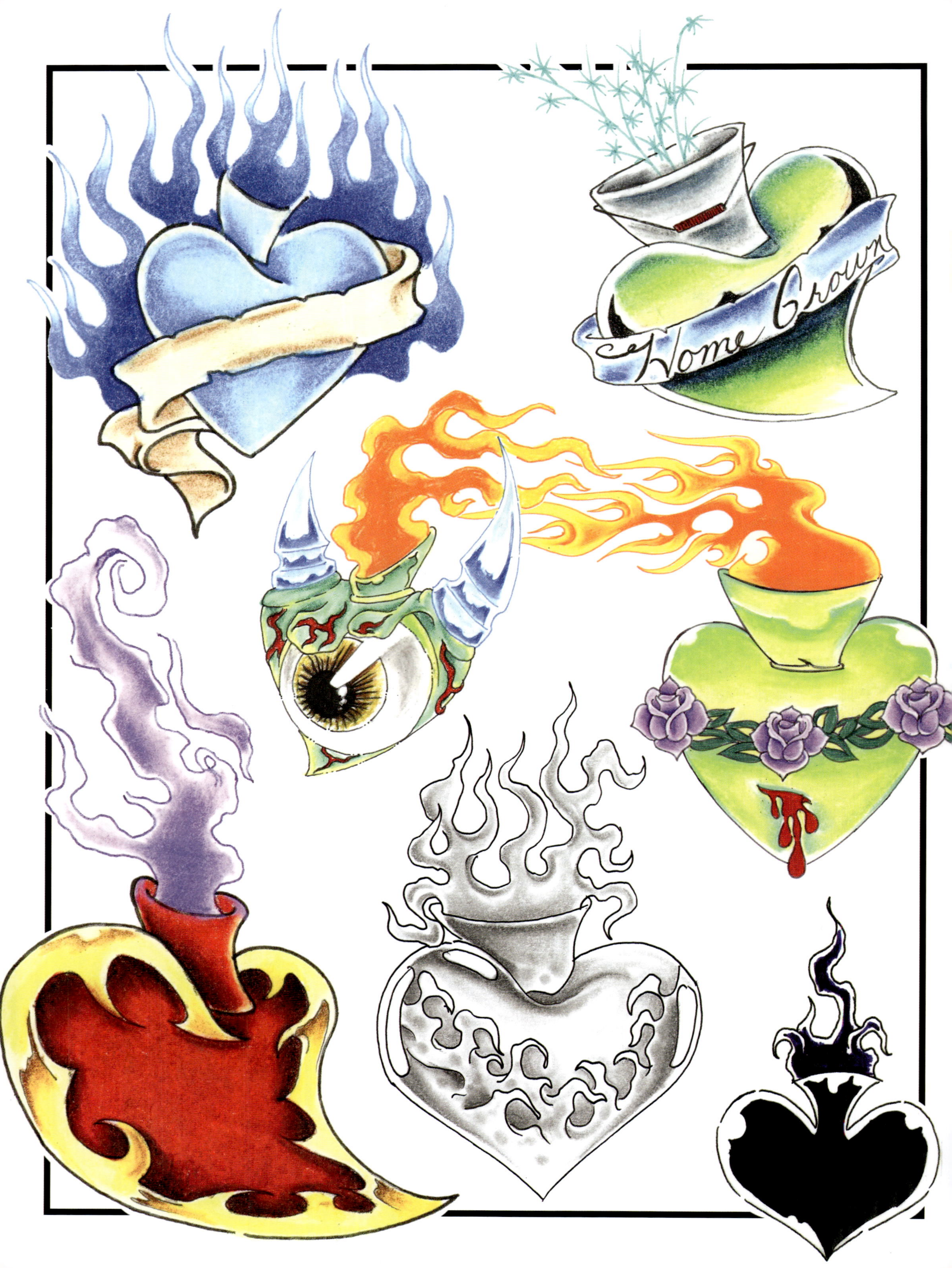
Home Grown

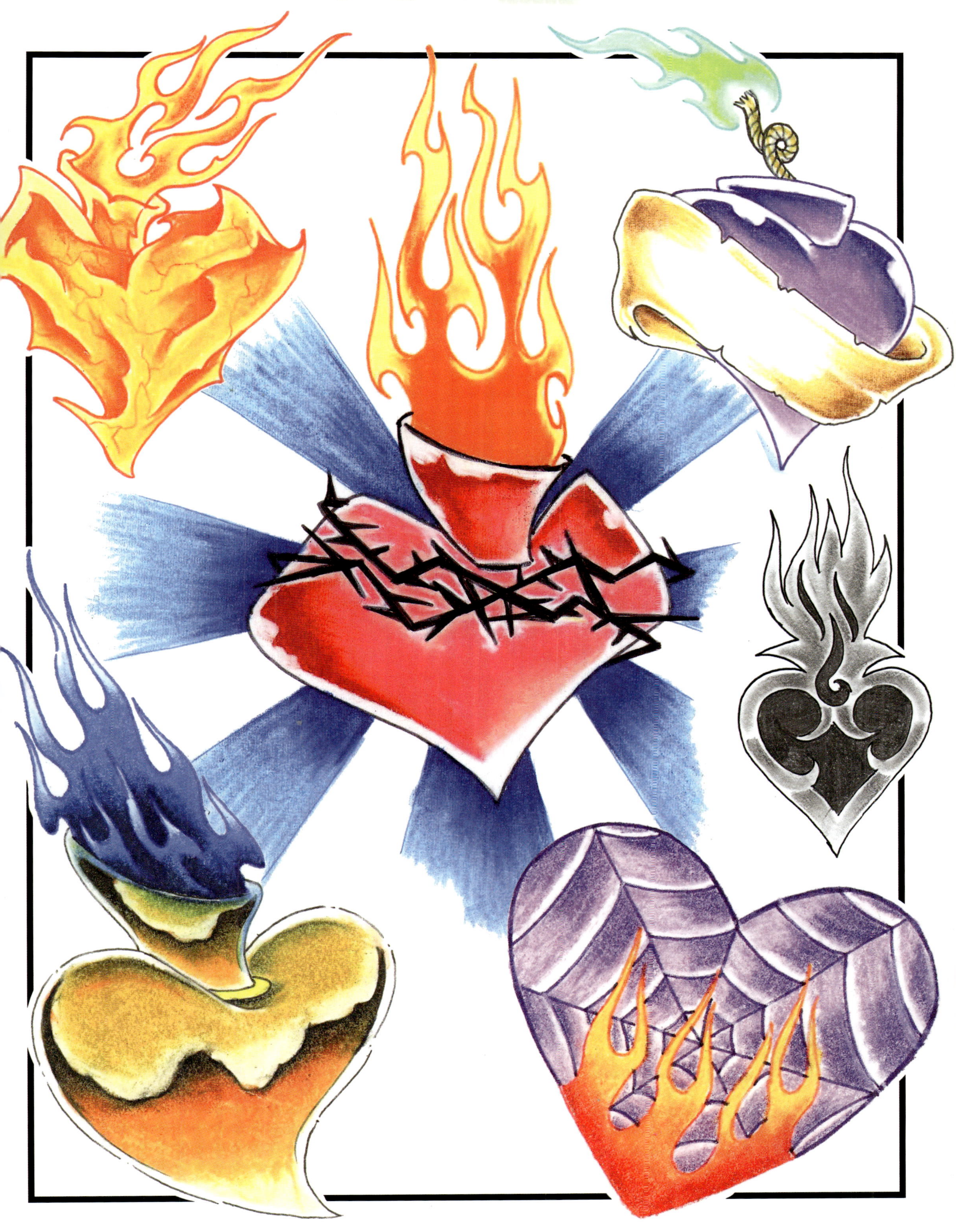

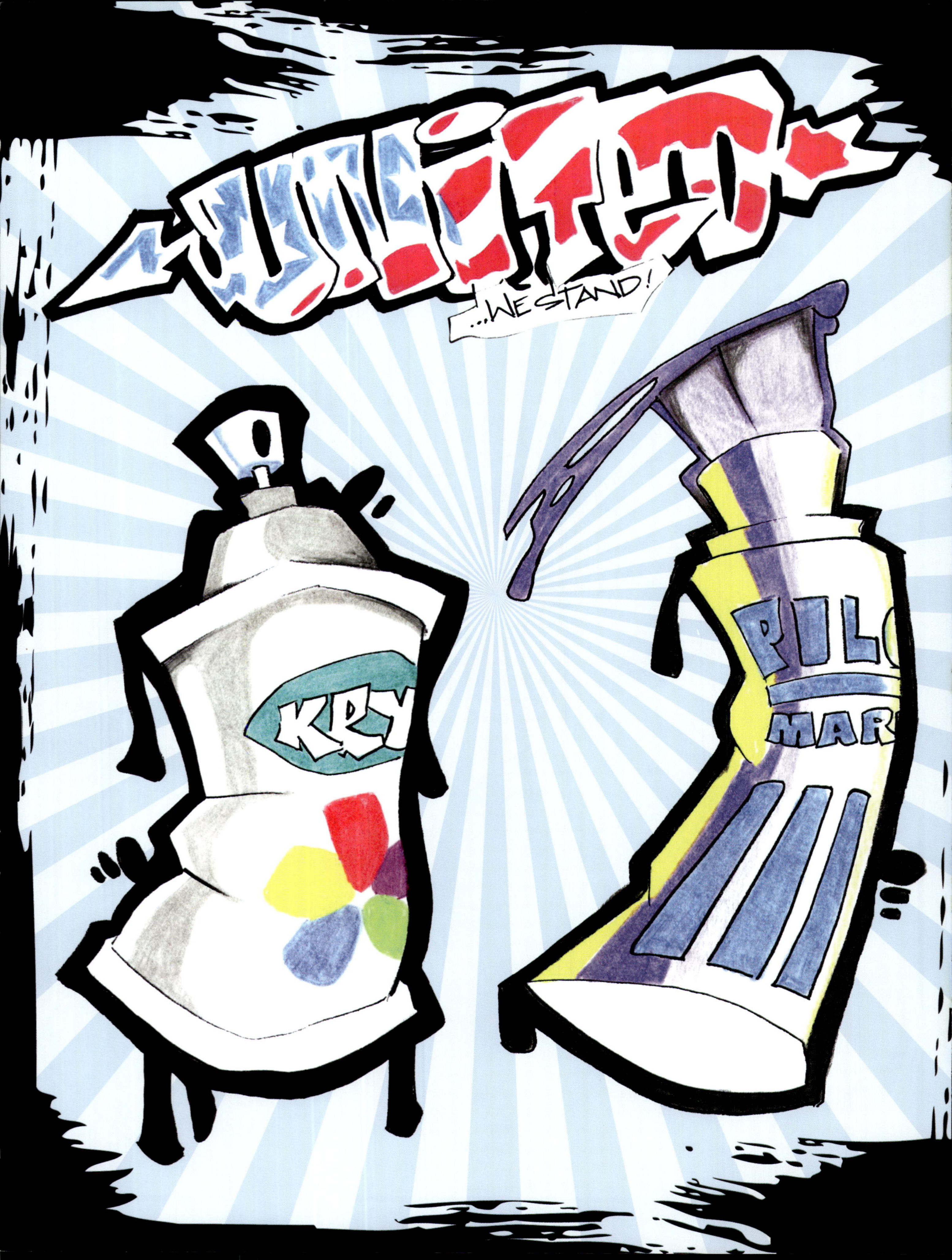
...WE STAND!

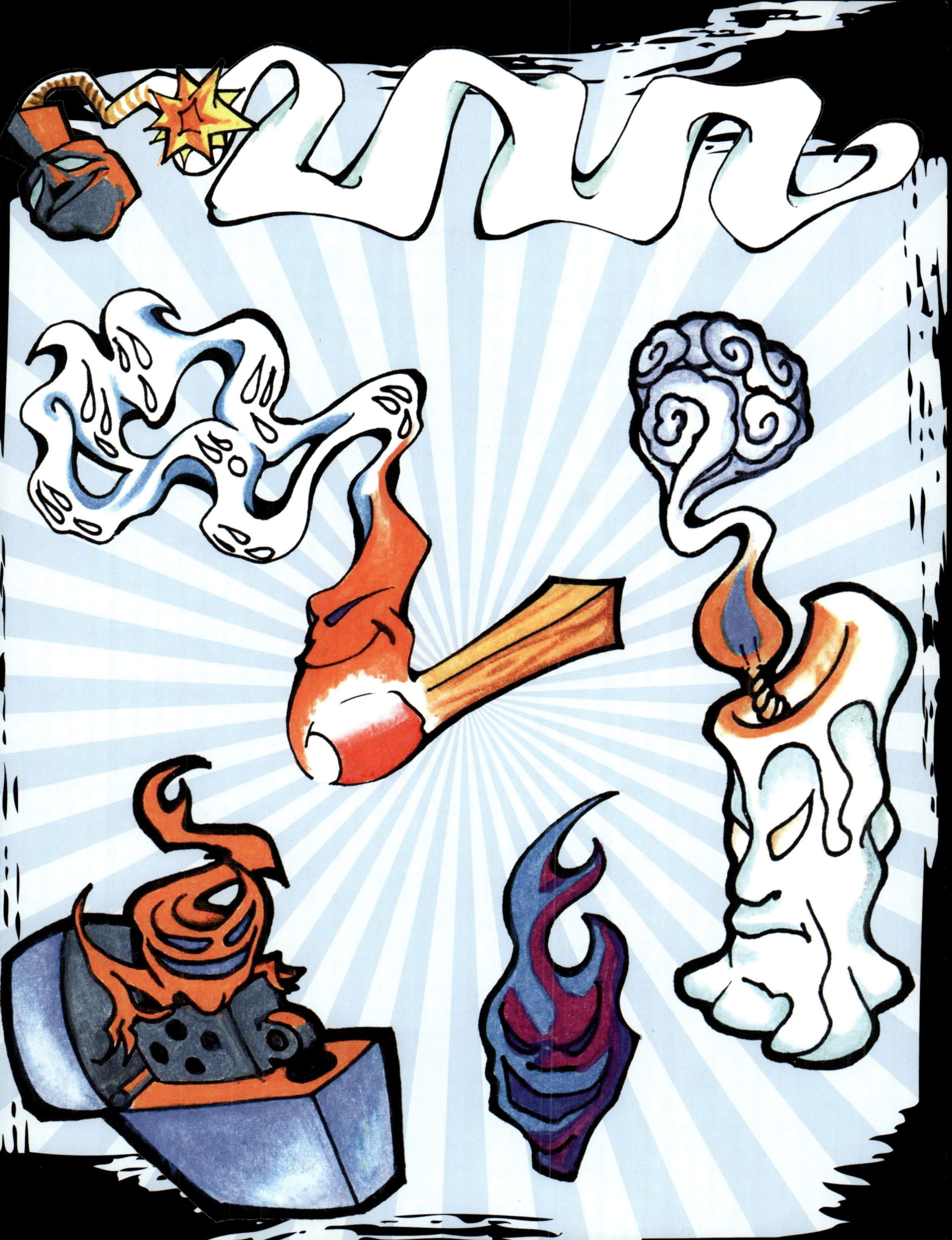

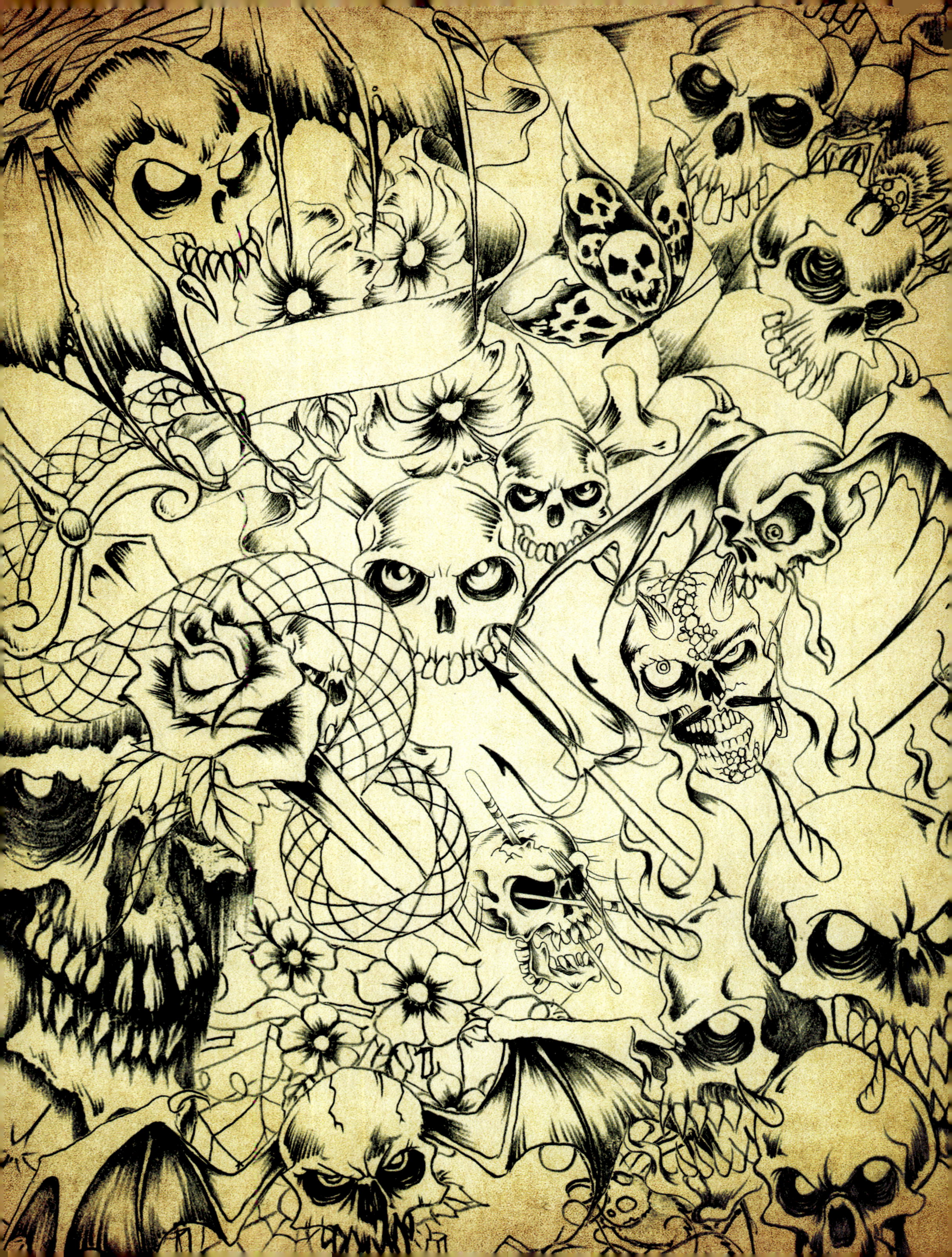

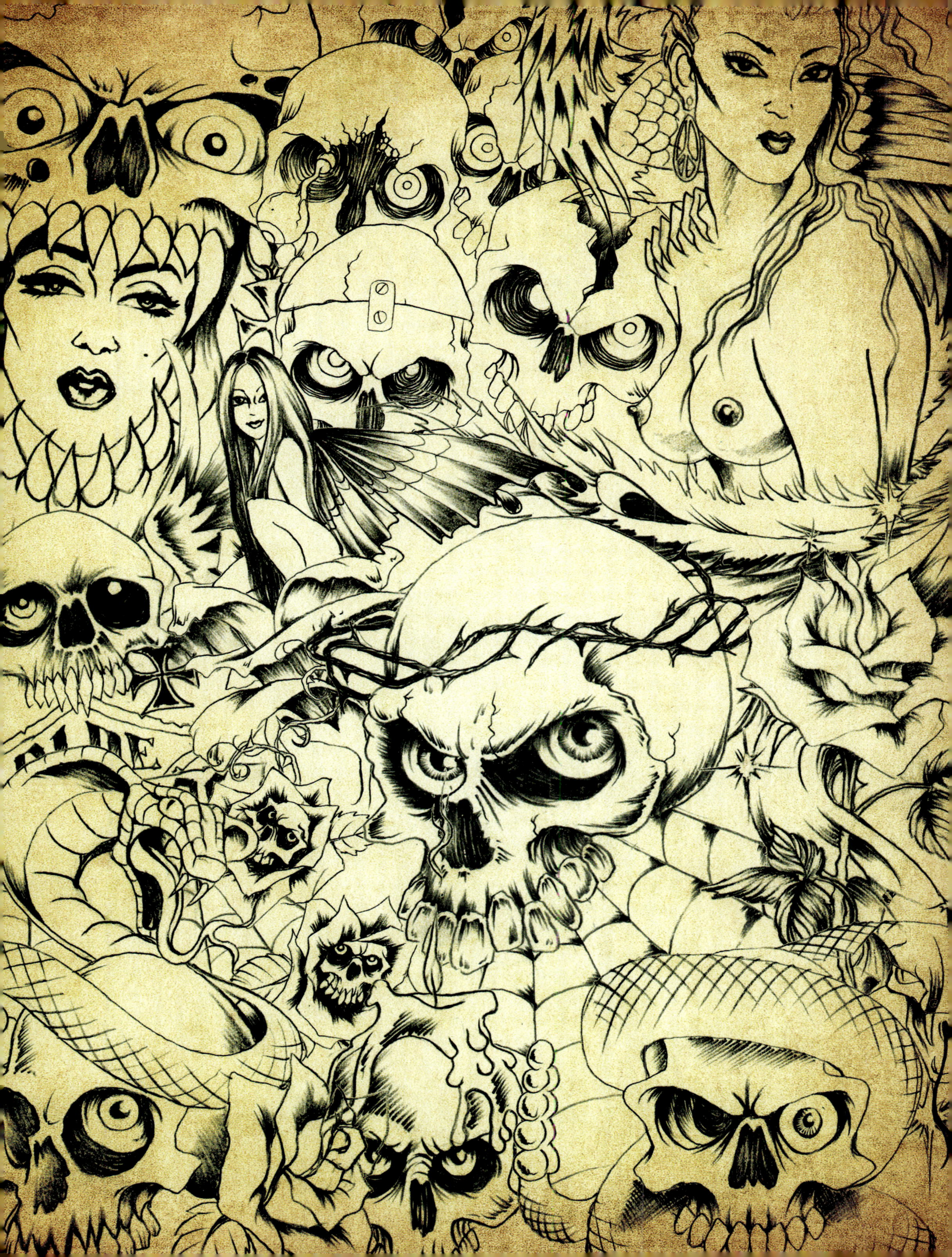

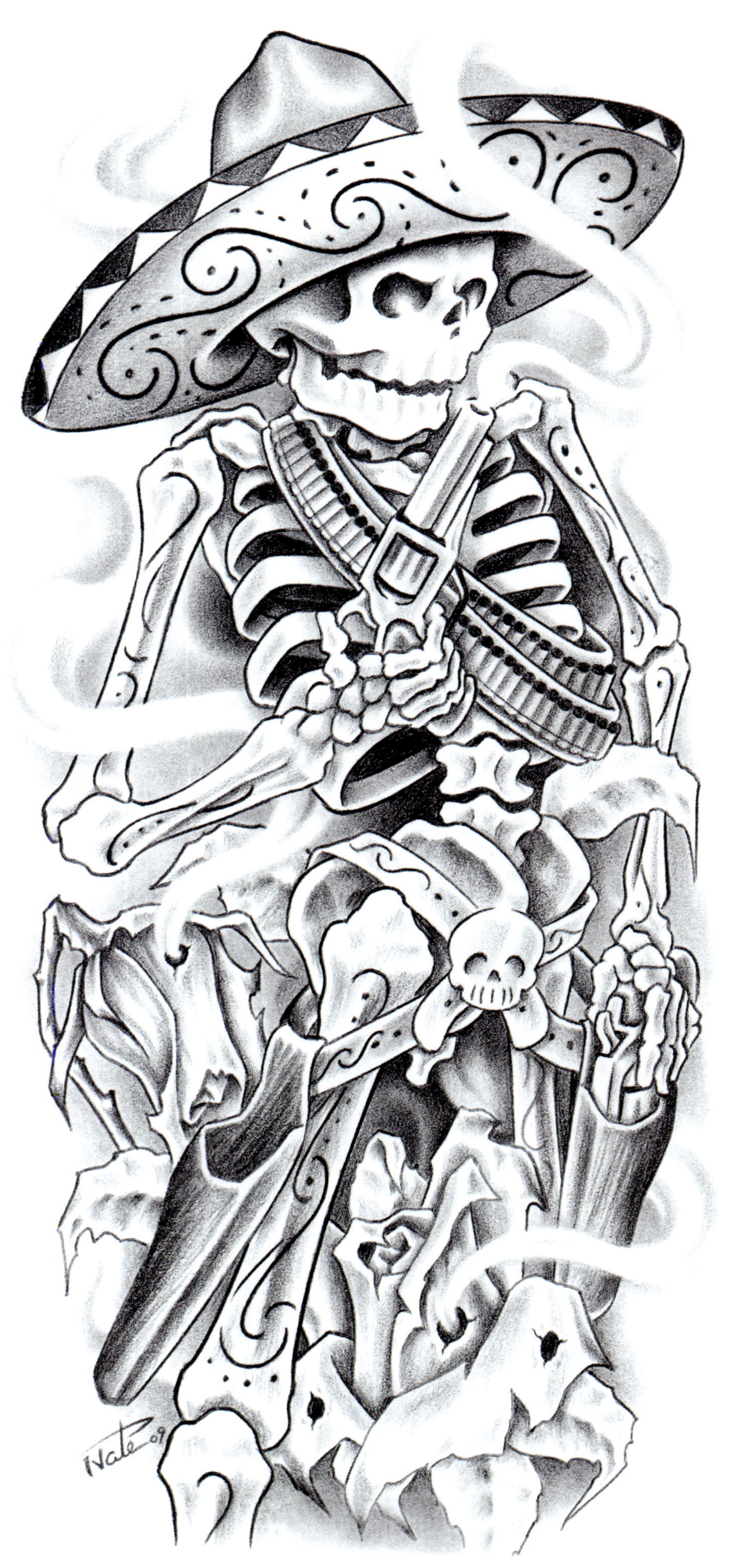
Nate 09

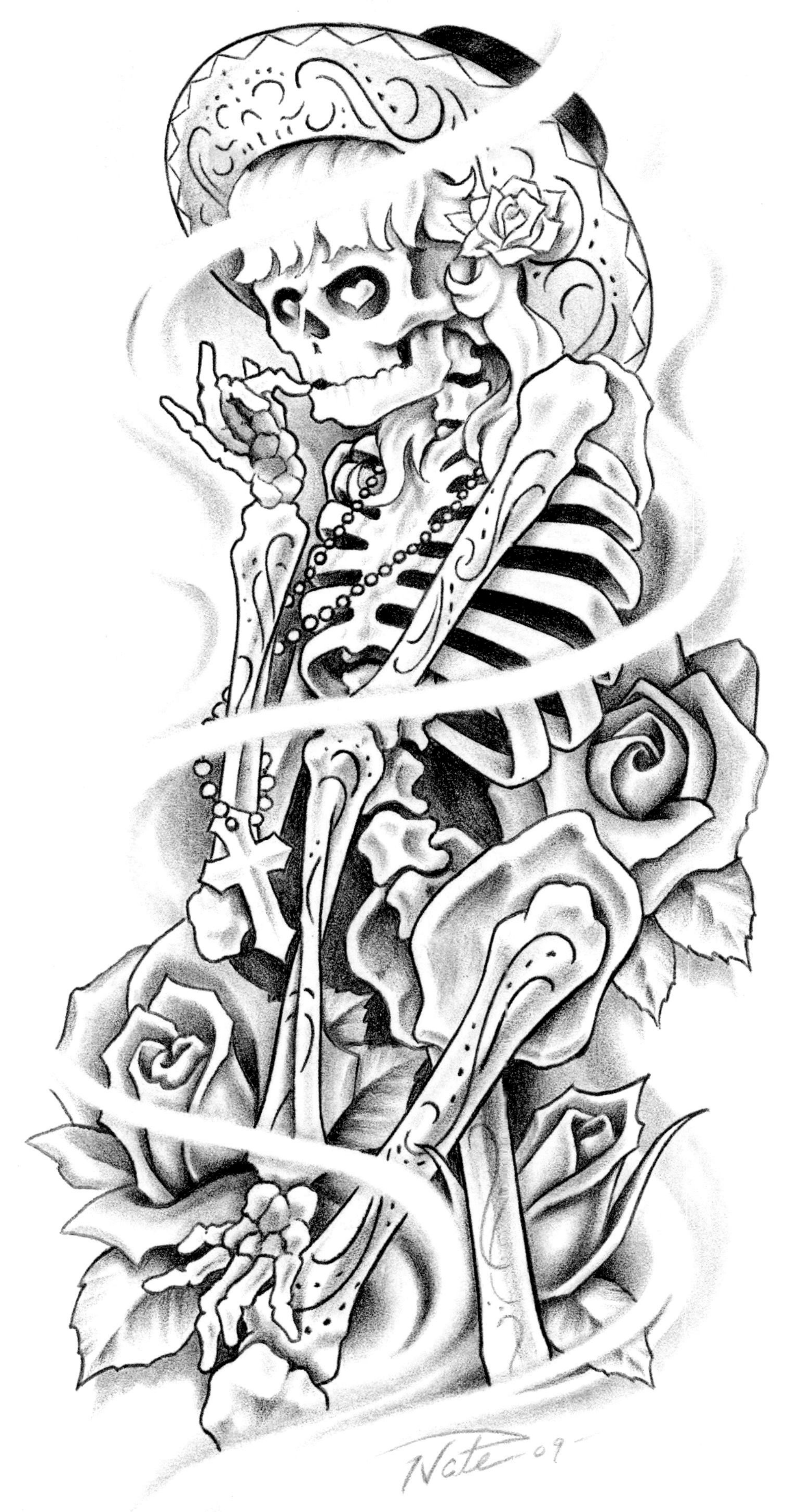
Nate 09

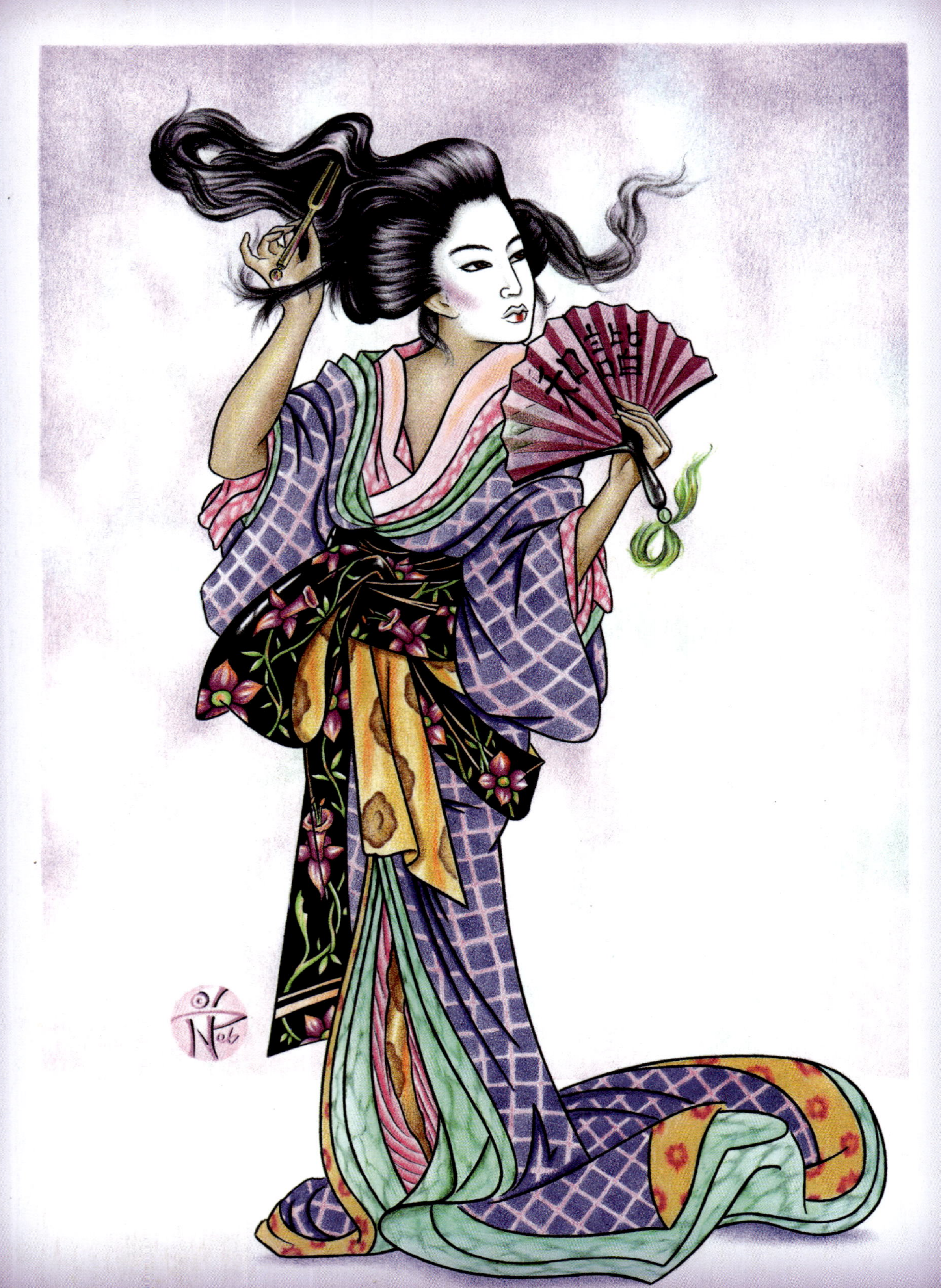
和諧

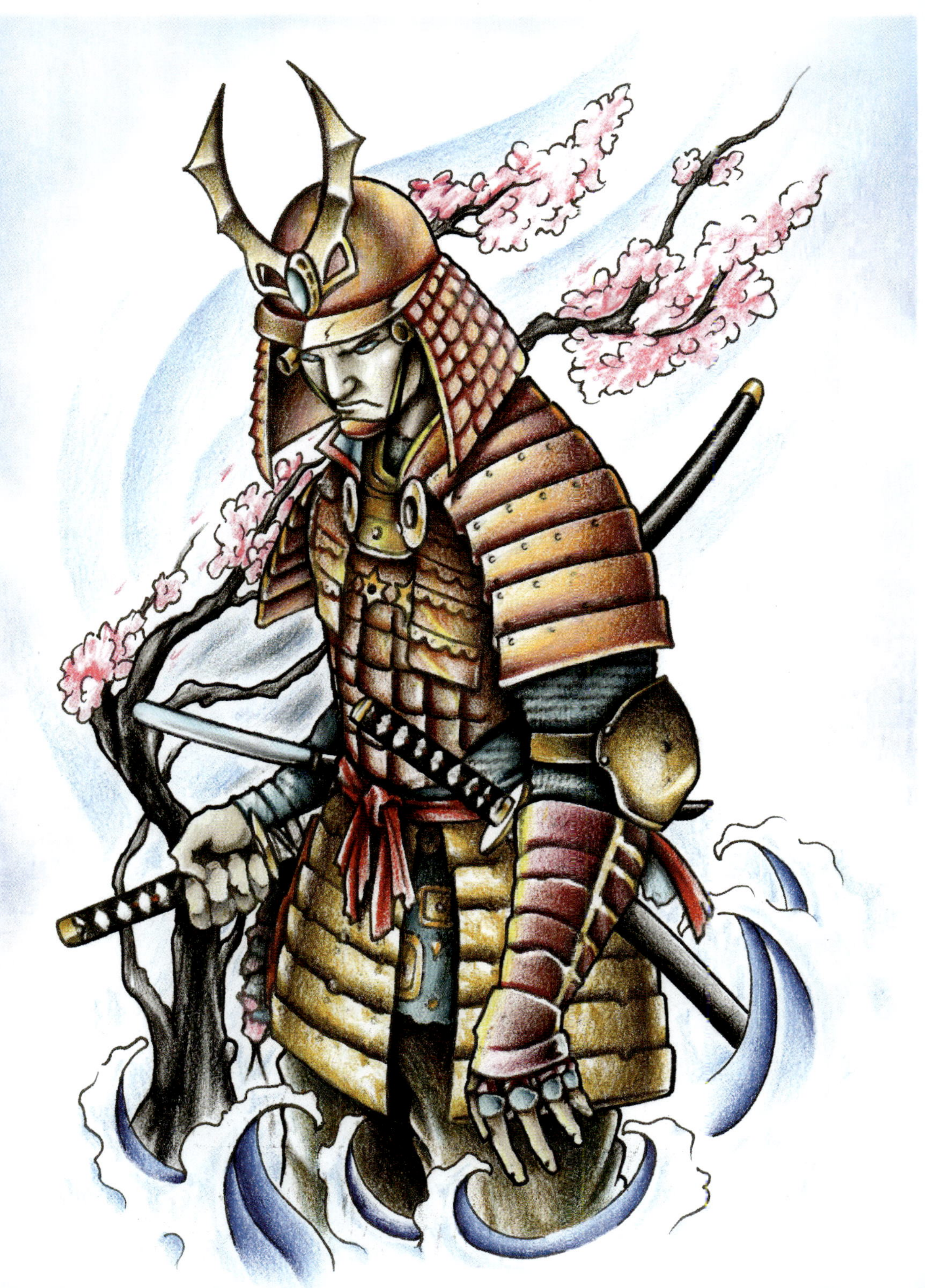

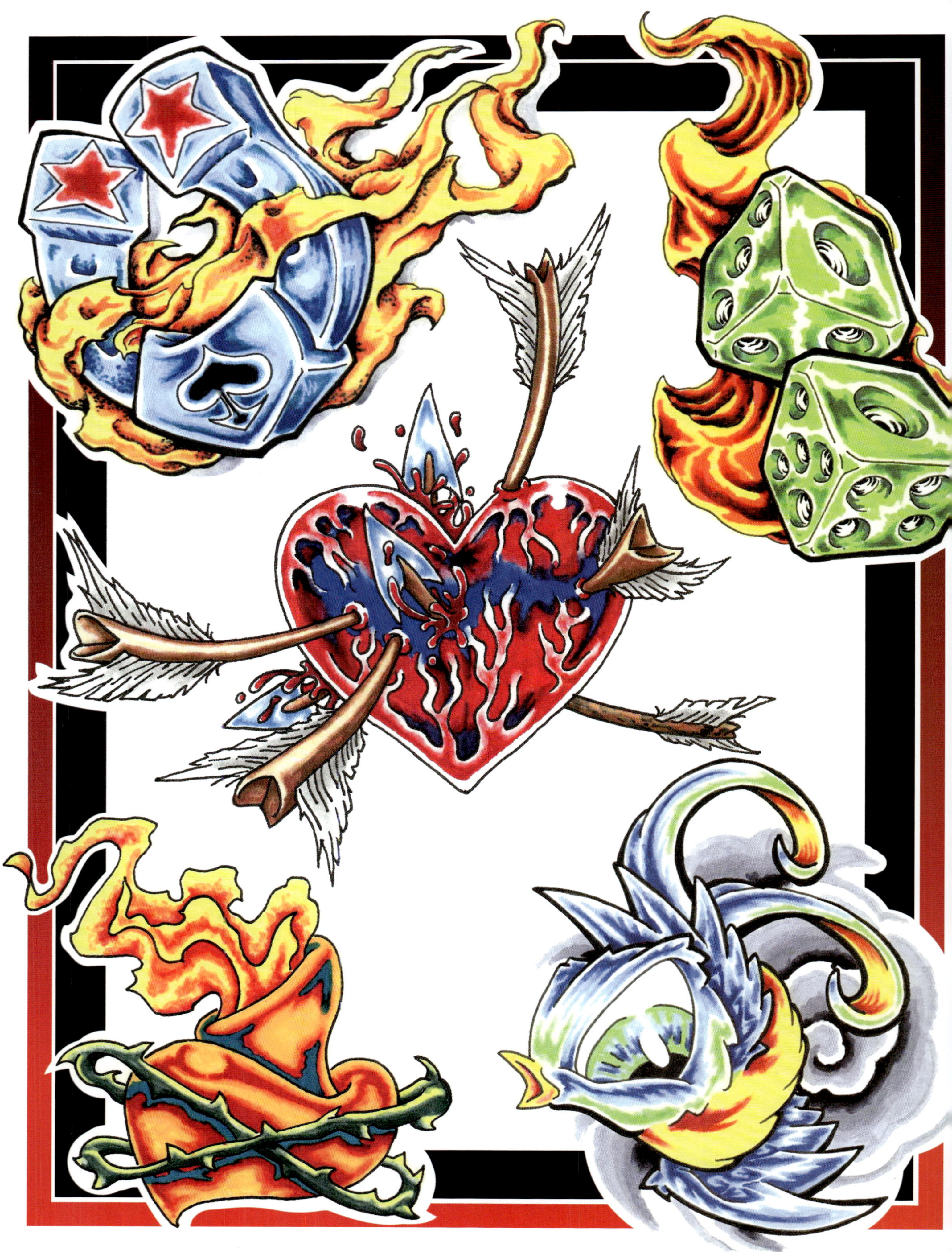

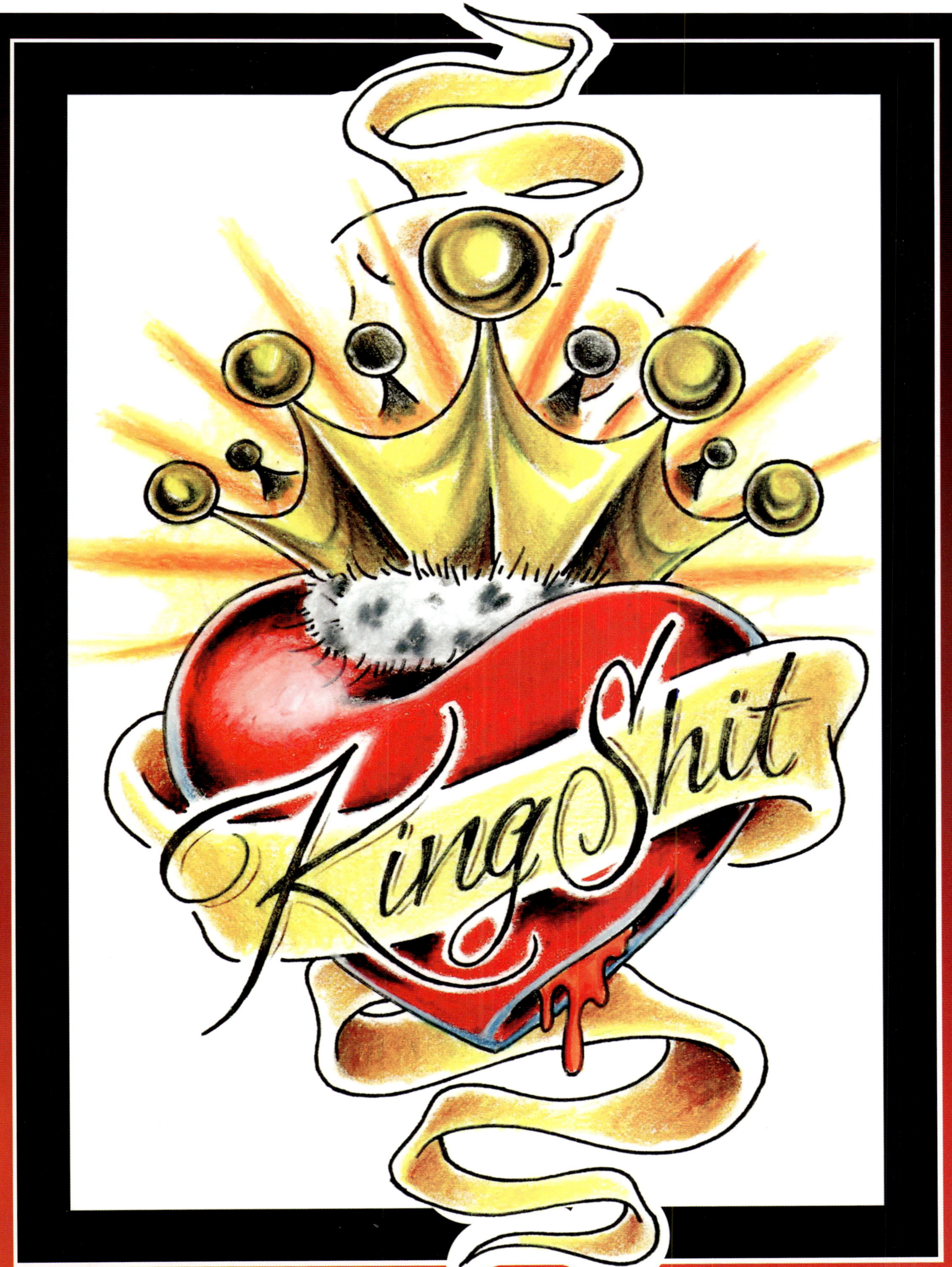
King Shit

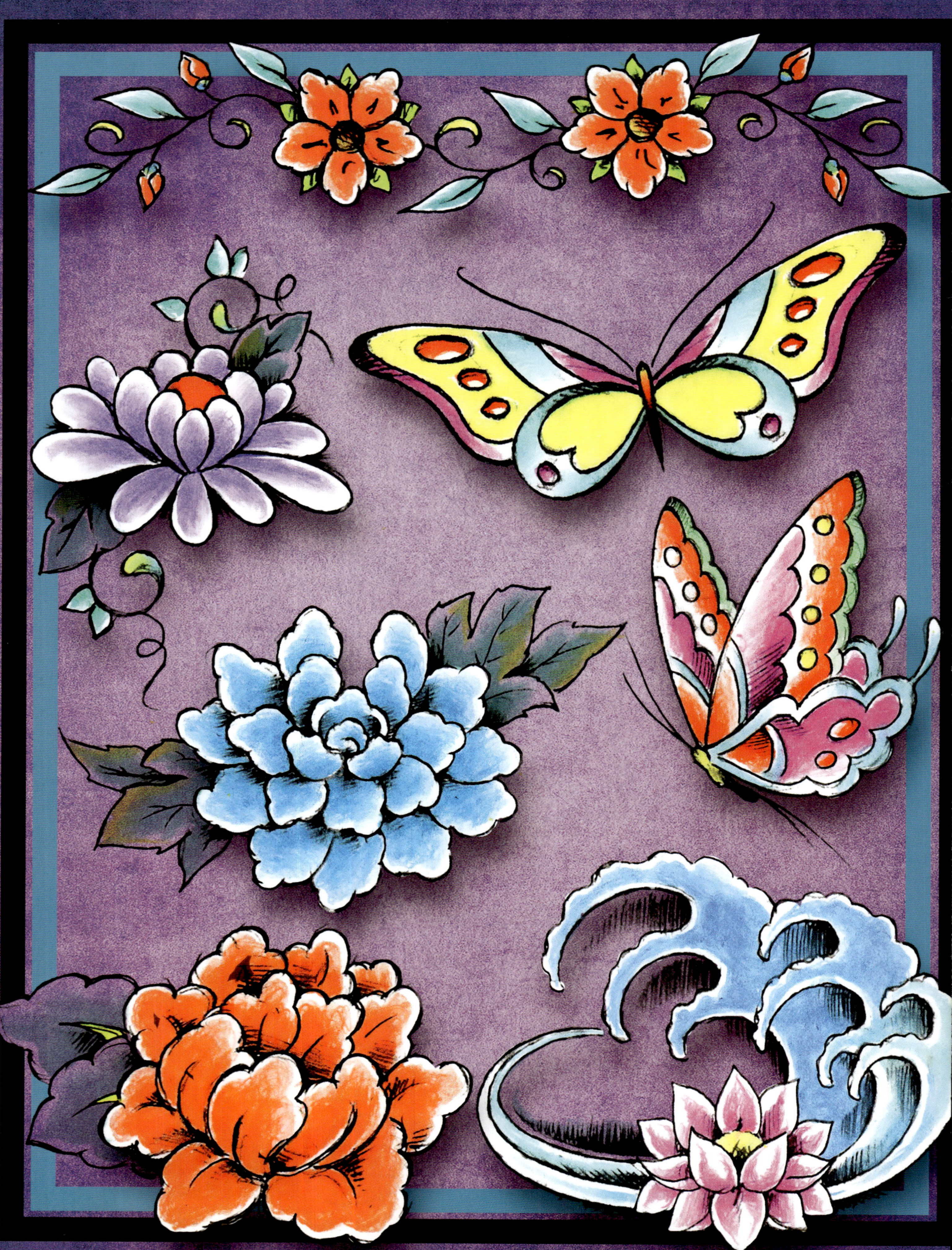

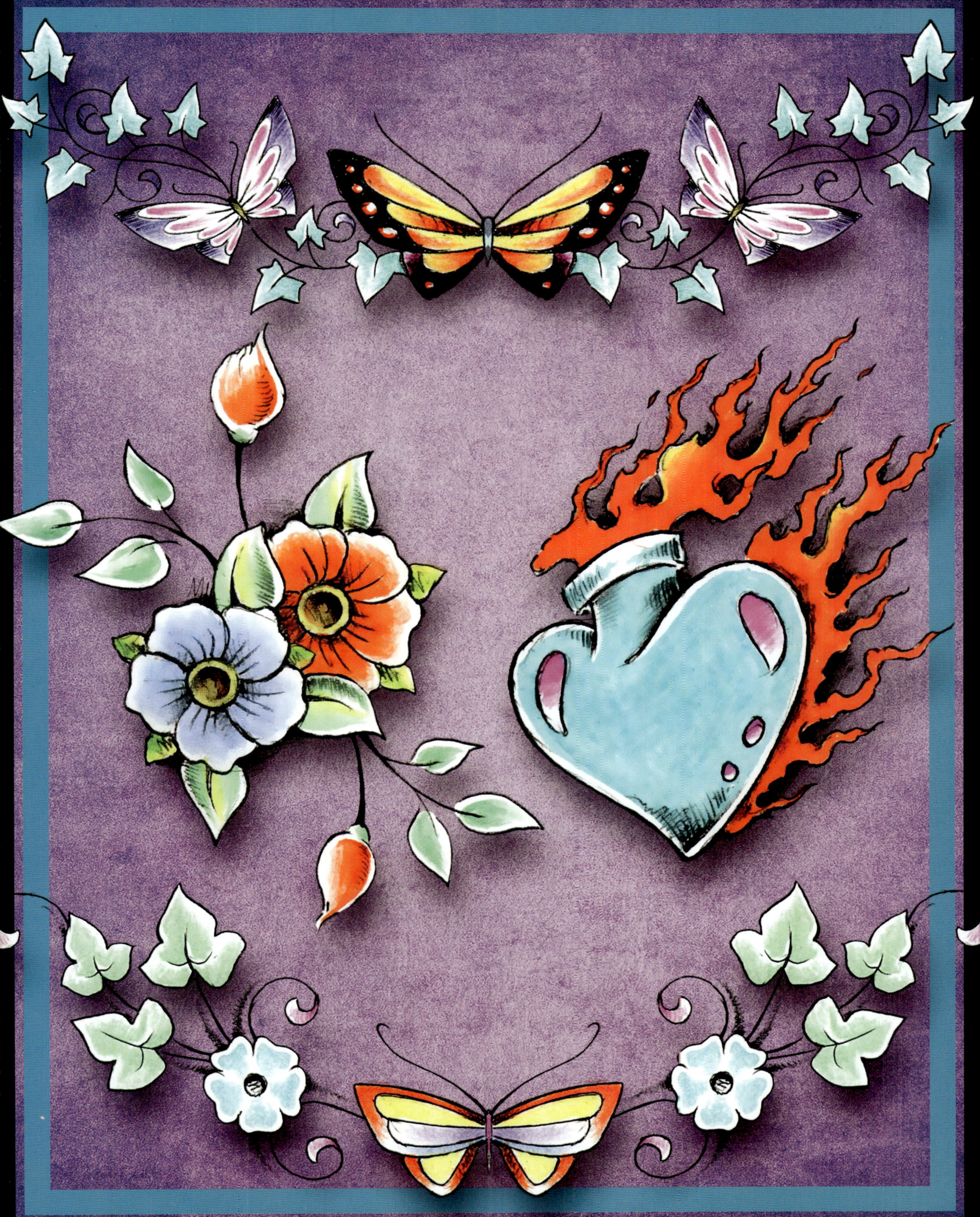

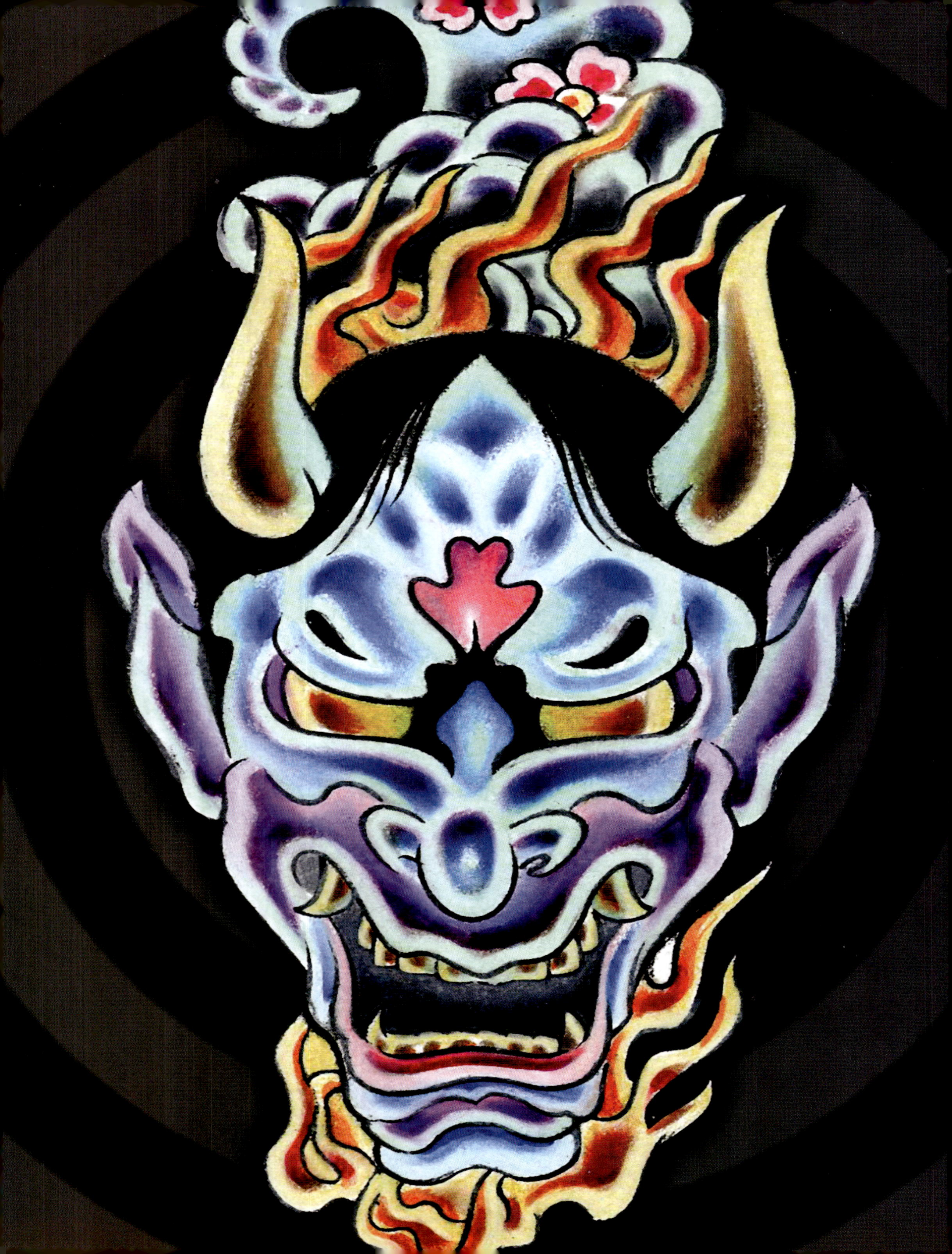

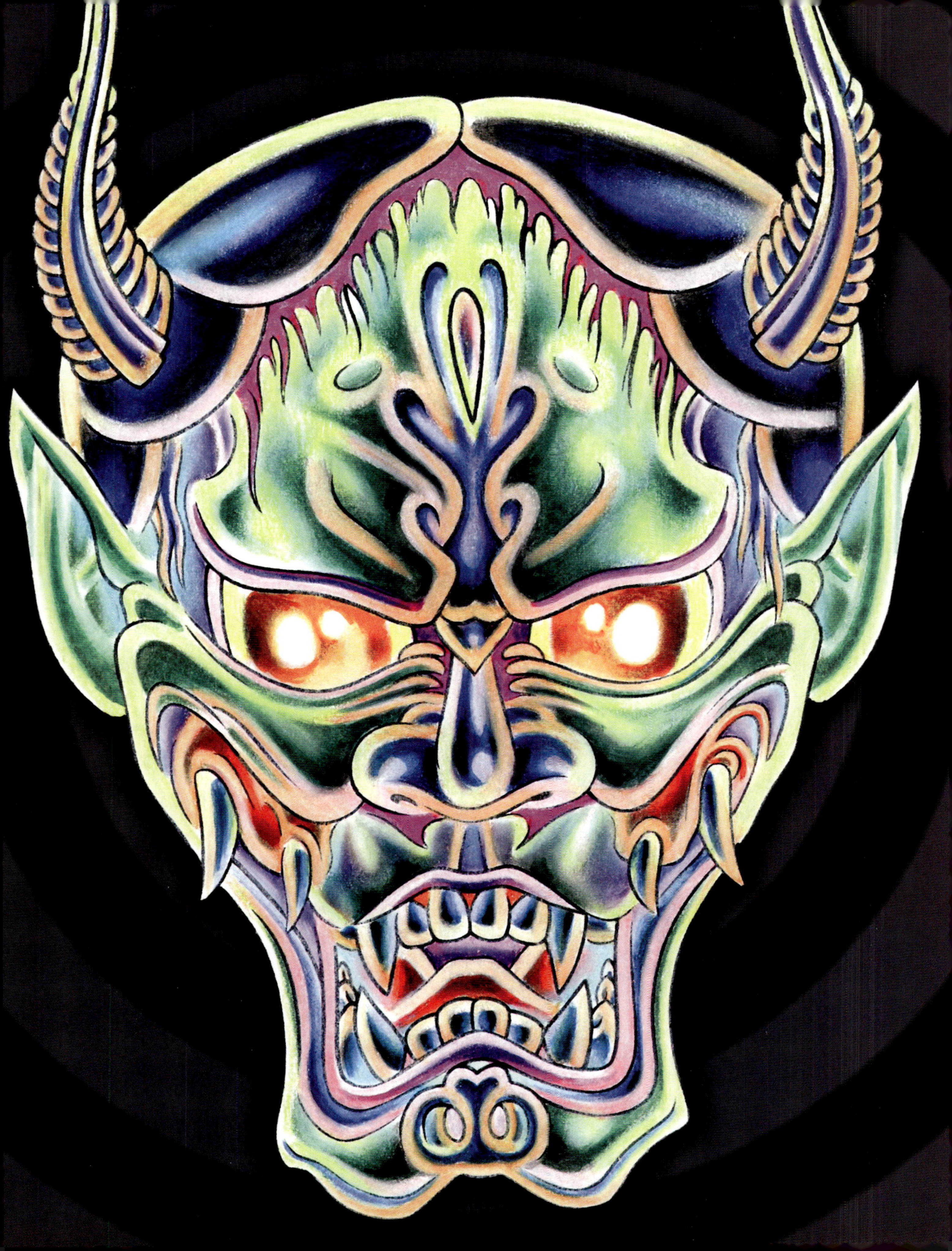

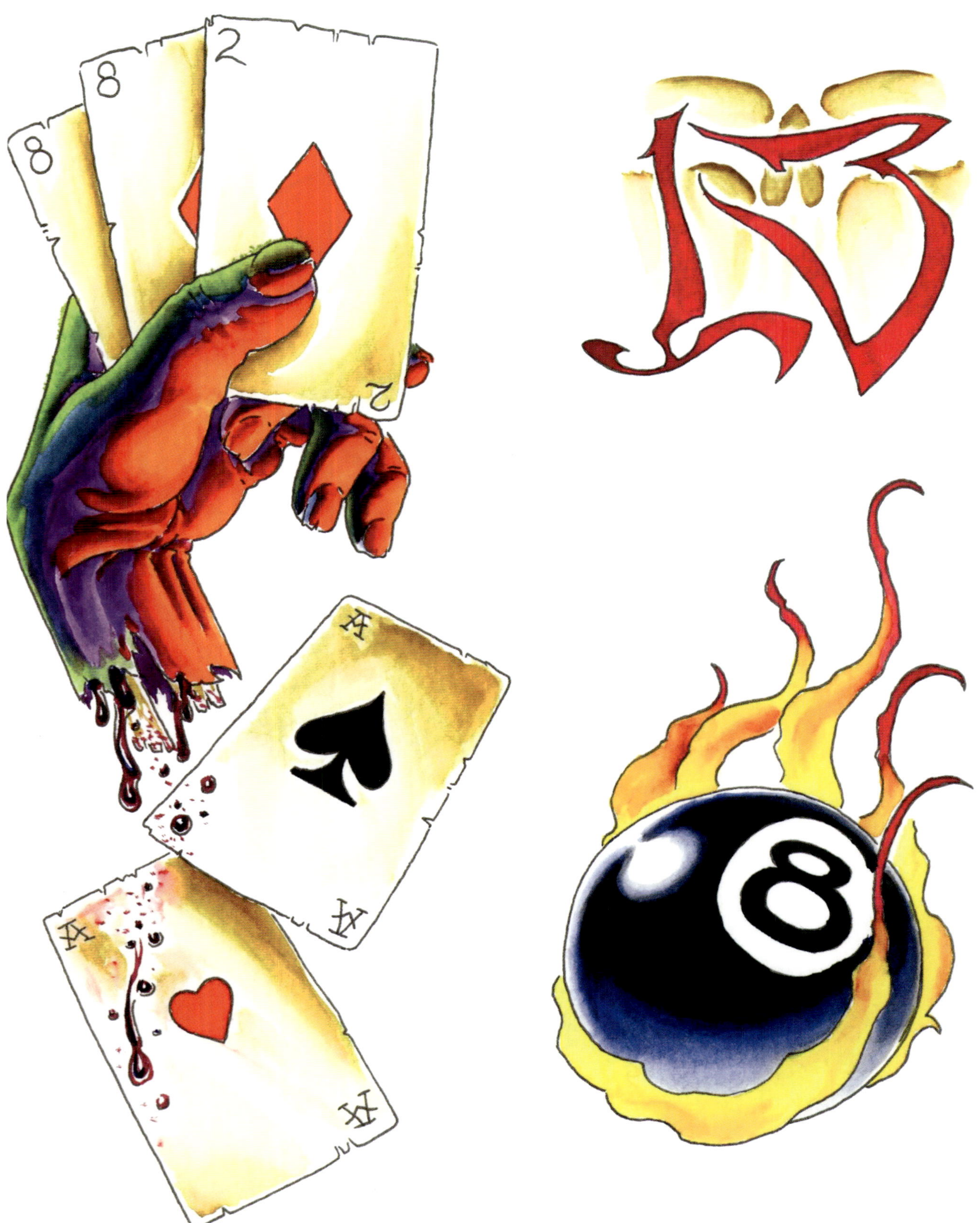

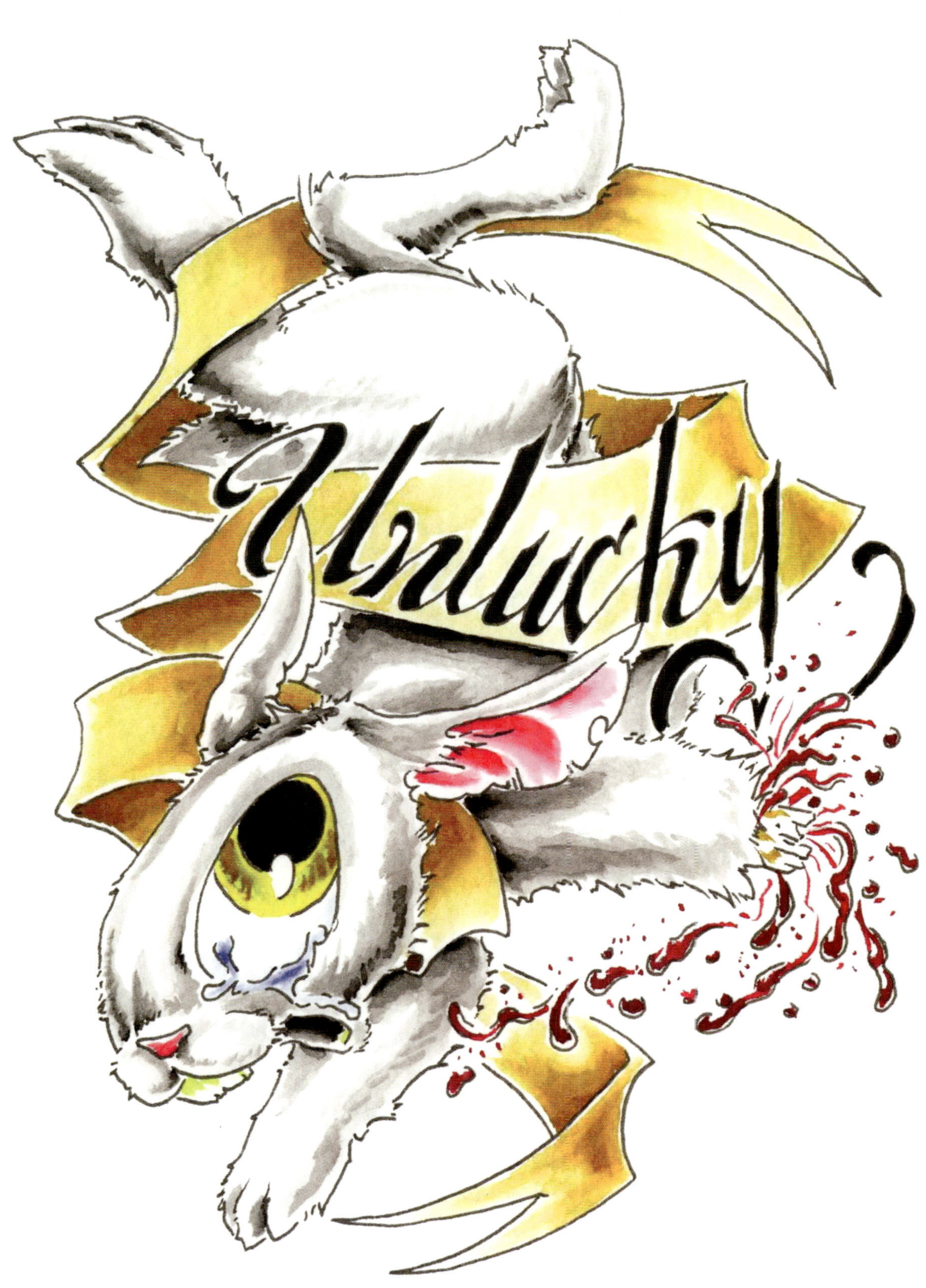
Unlucky

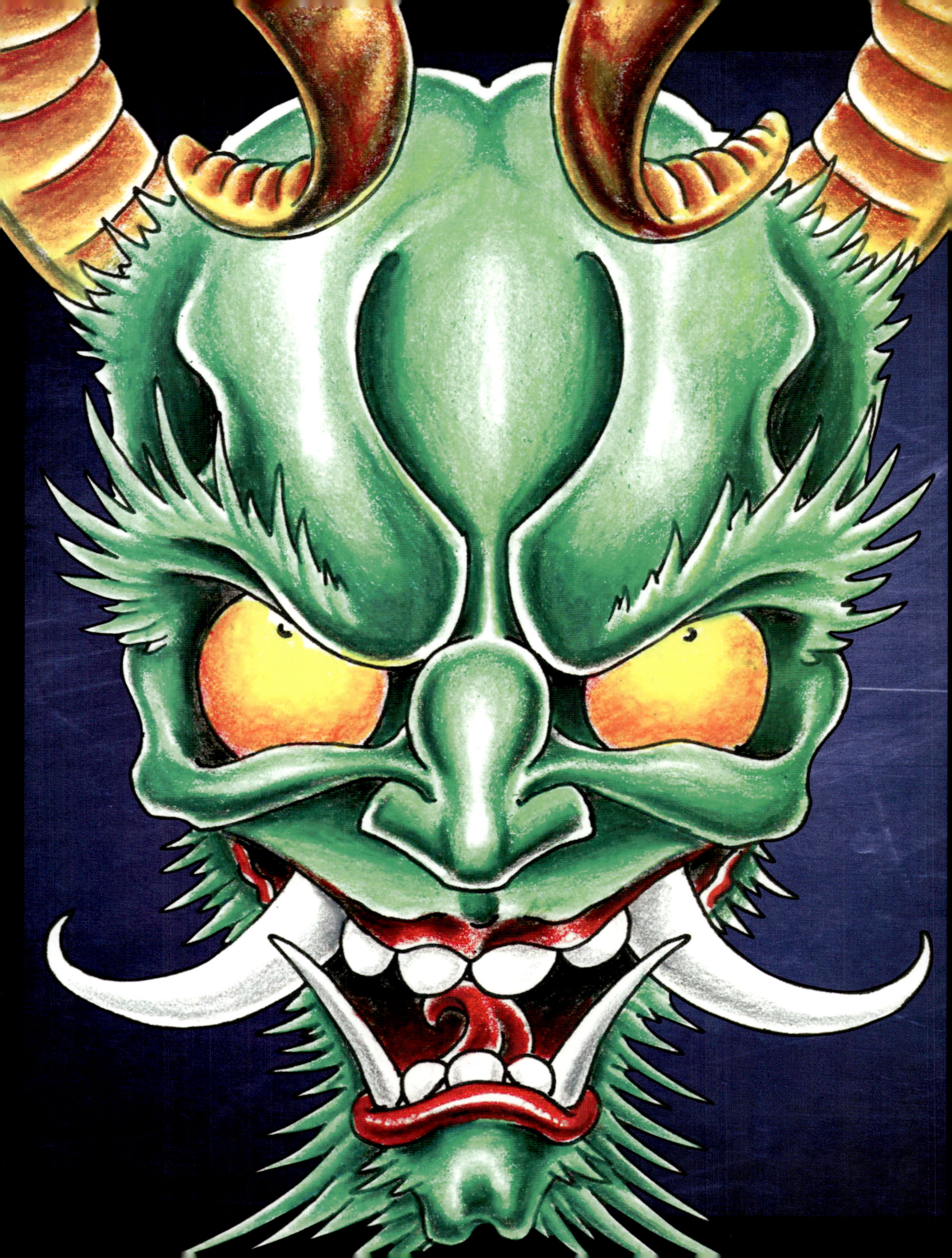

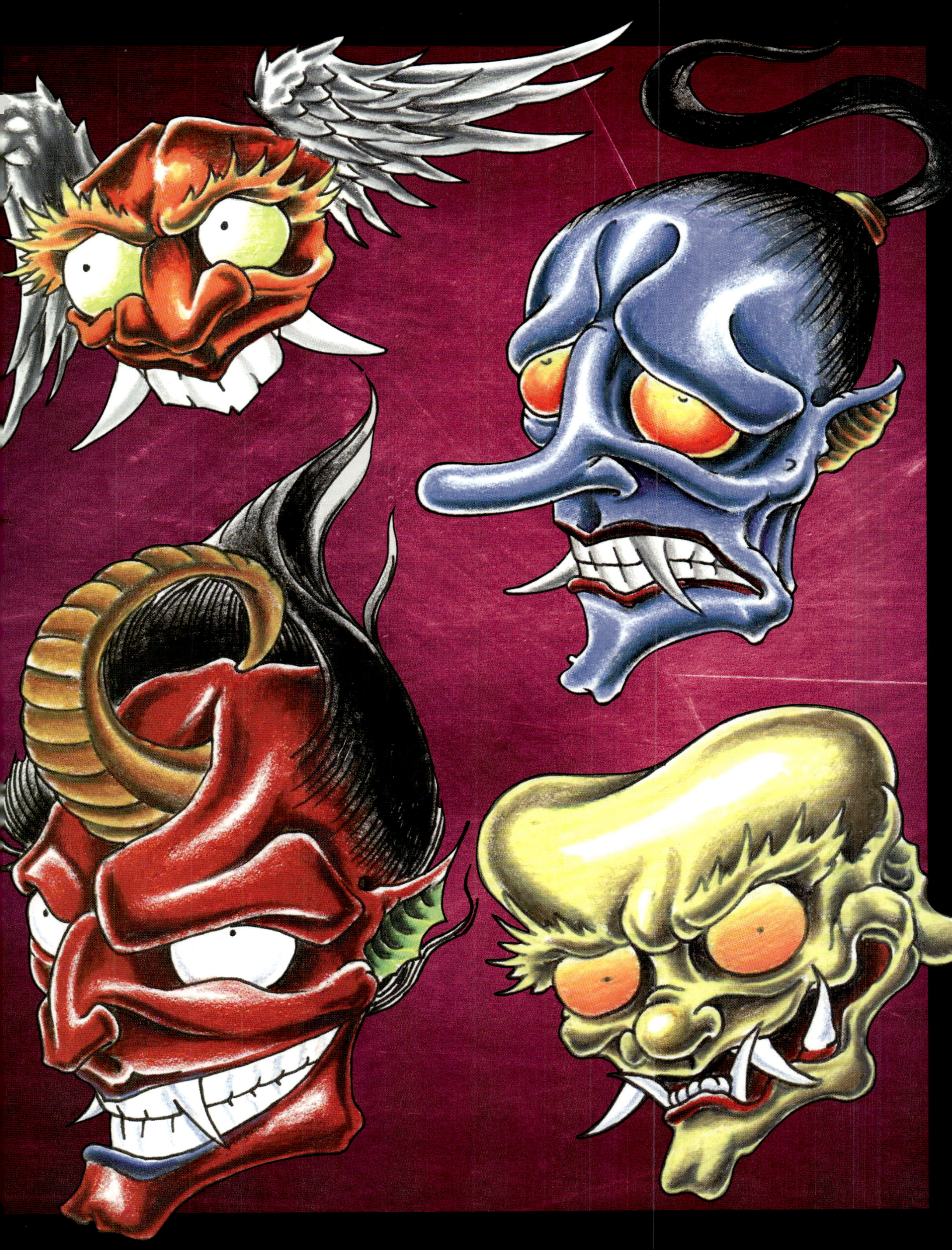

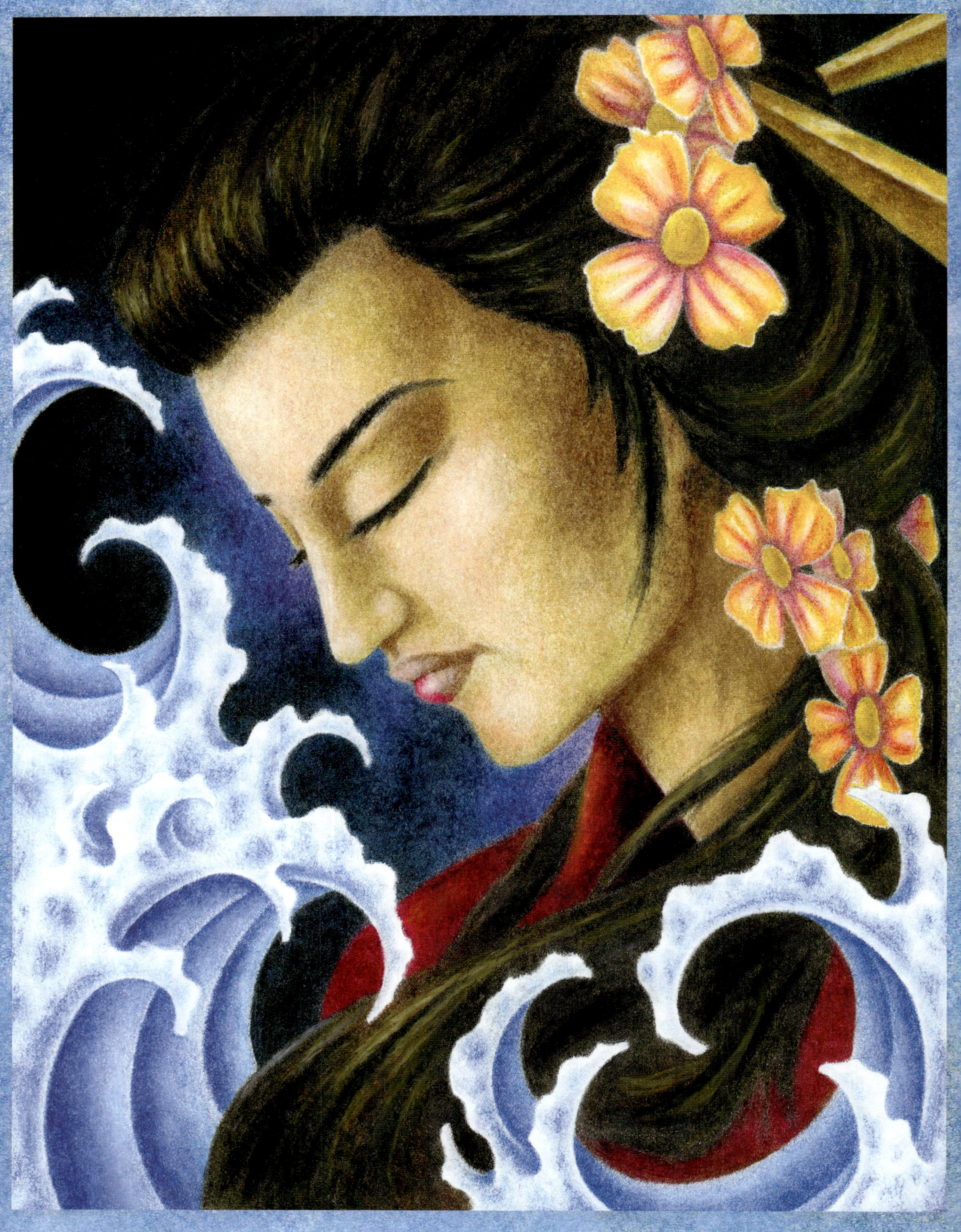

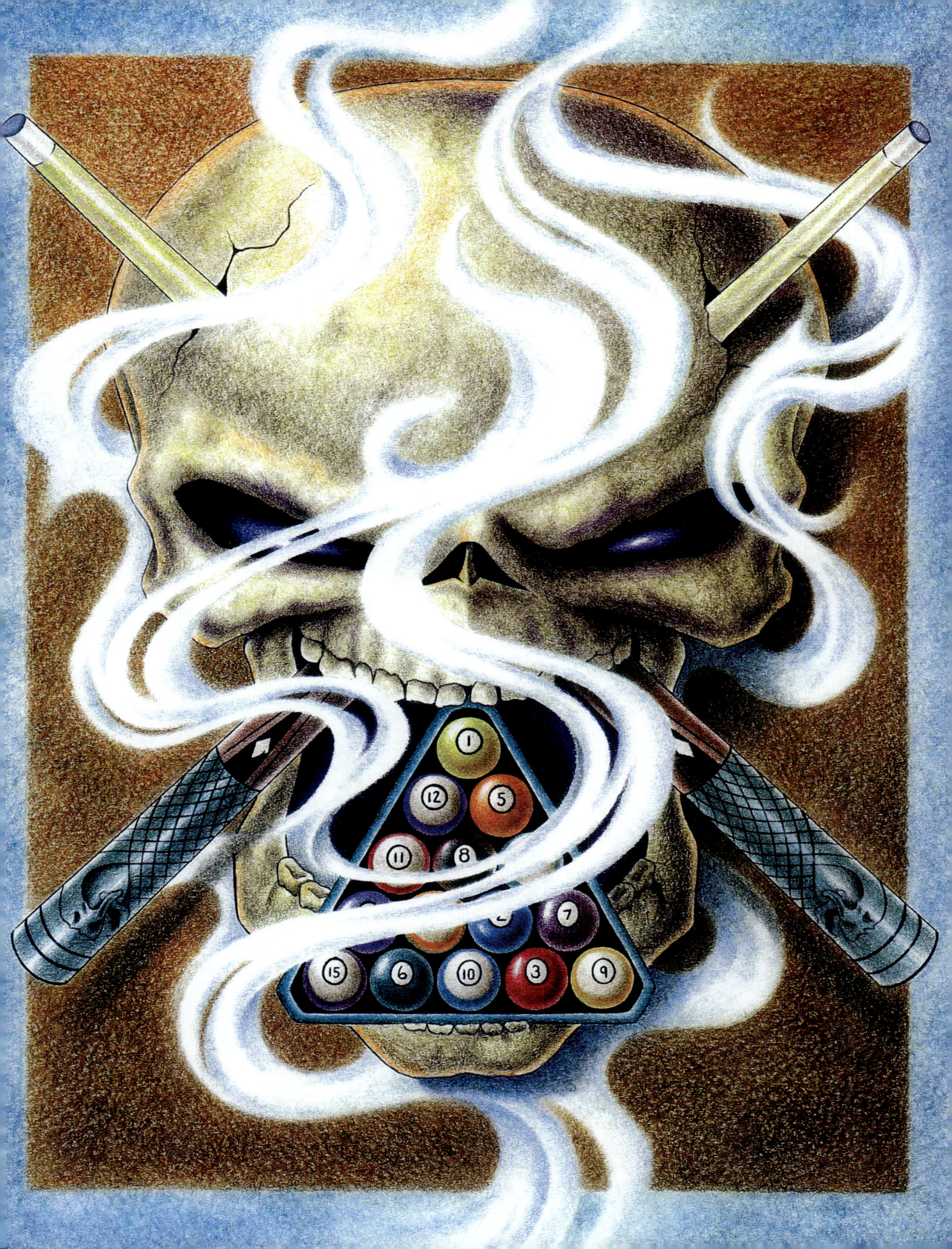
1
12
5
11
8
7
15
6
10
3
9

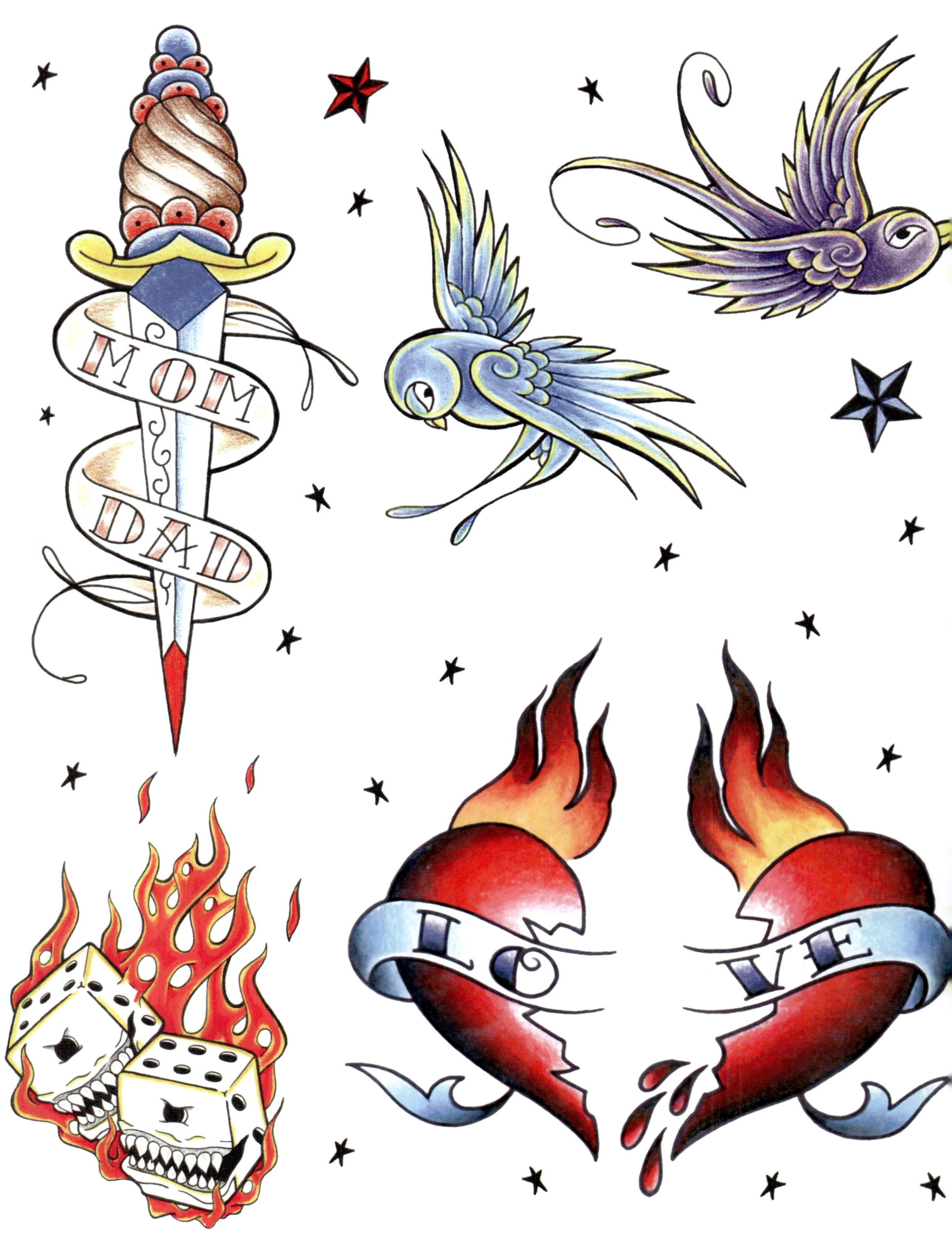
MOM
DAD
LO
VE

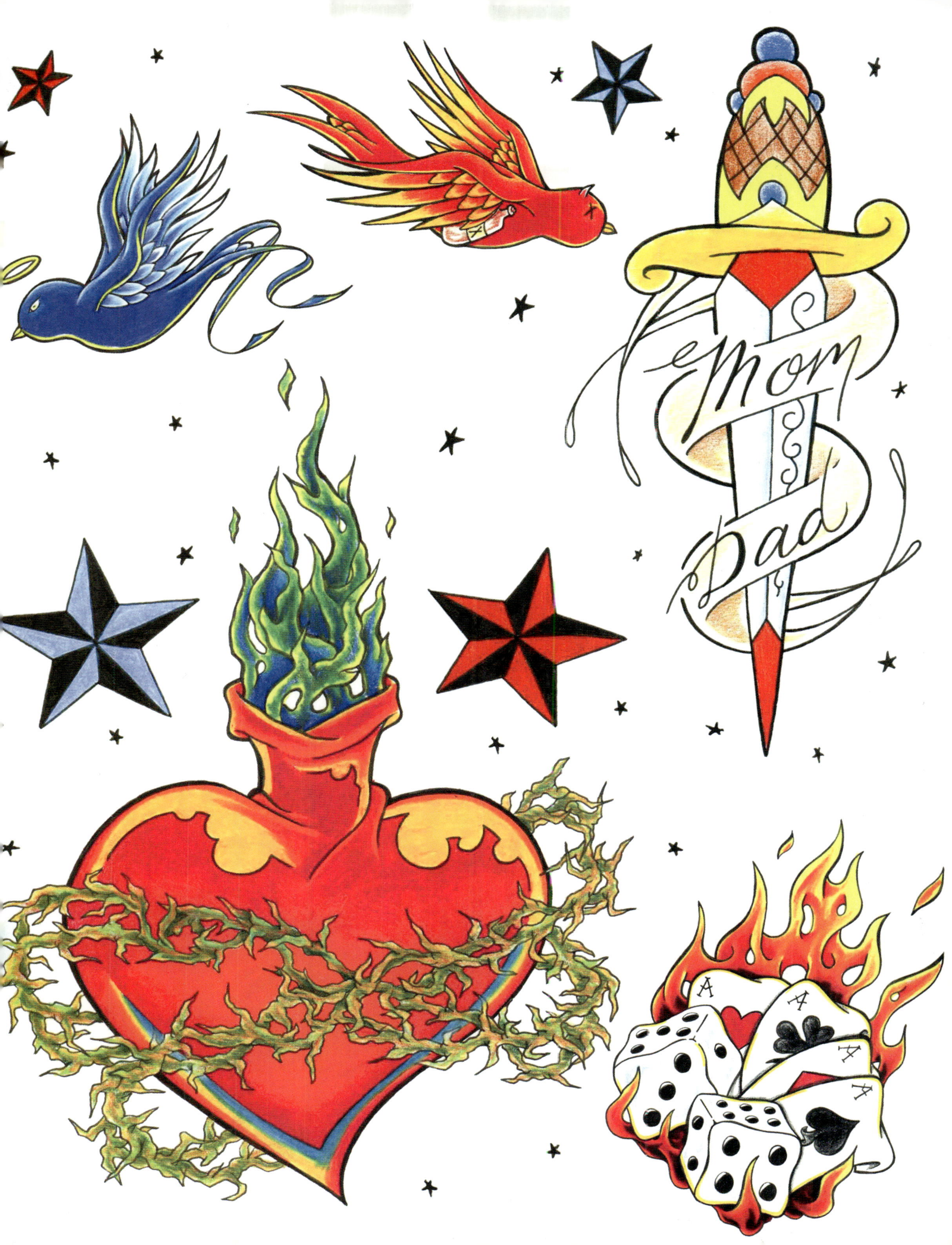
Mom
Dad

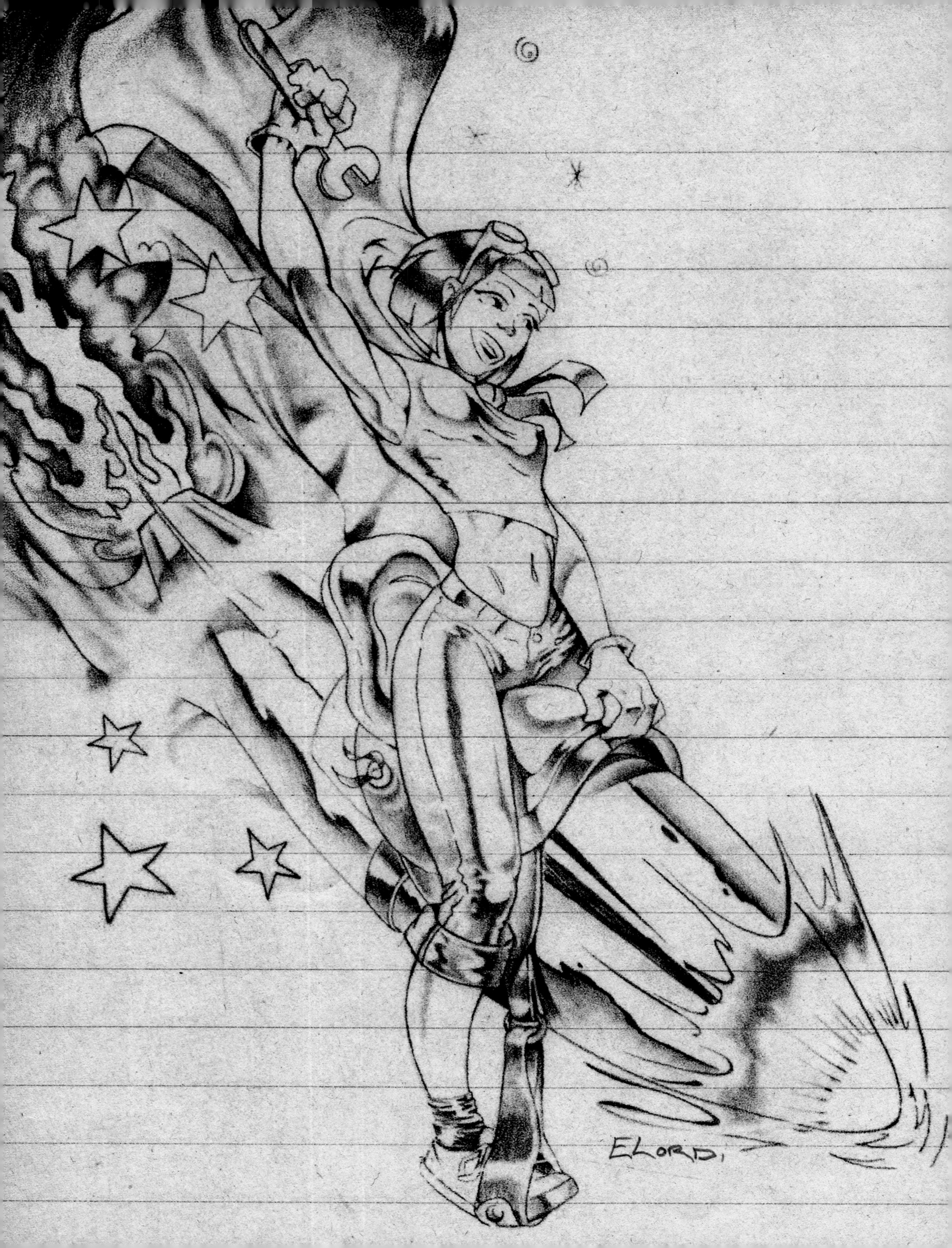
ELORDI

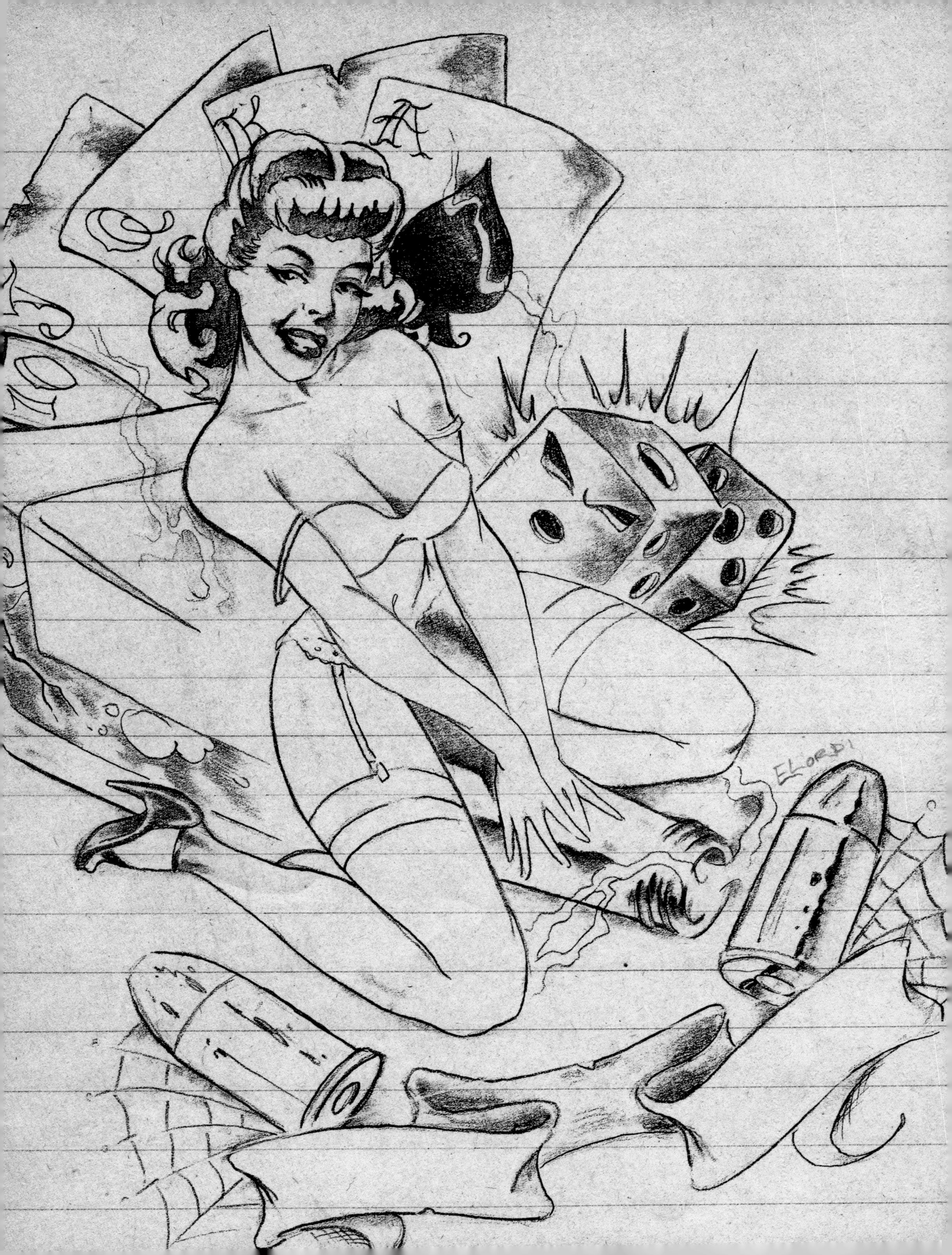
ELORDI

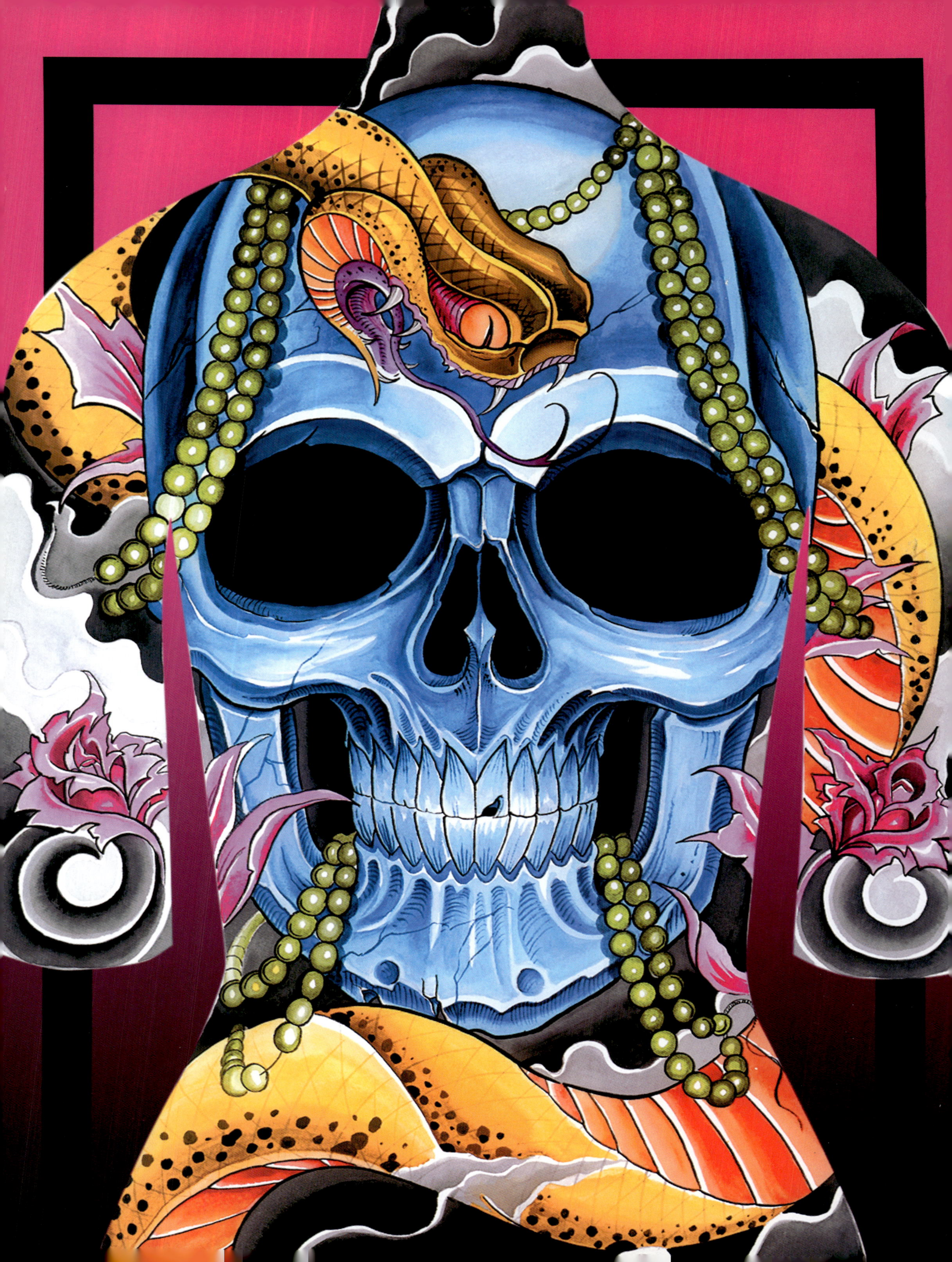

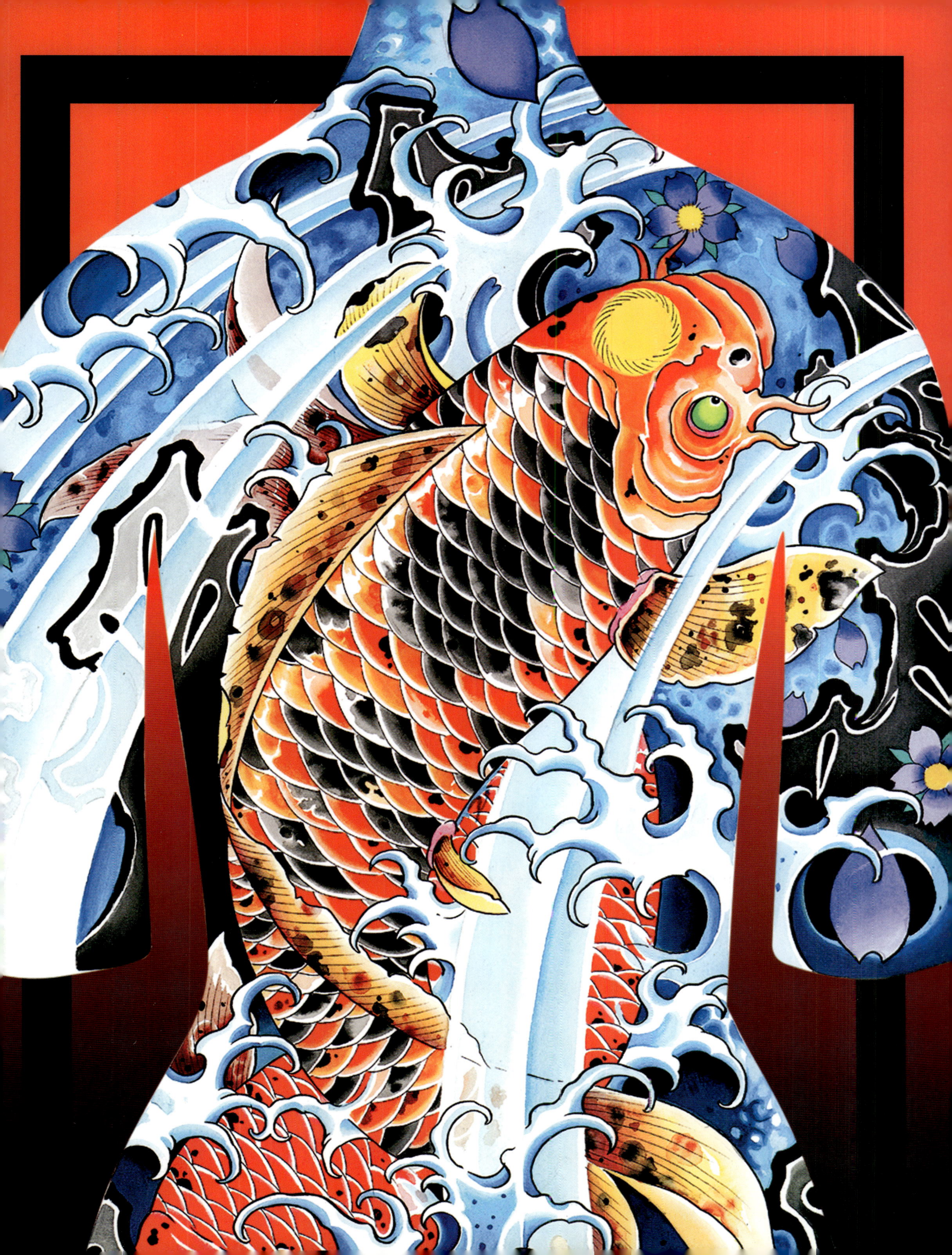

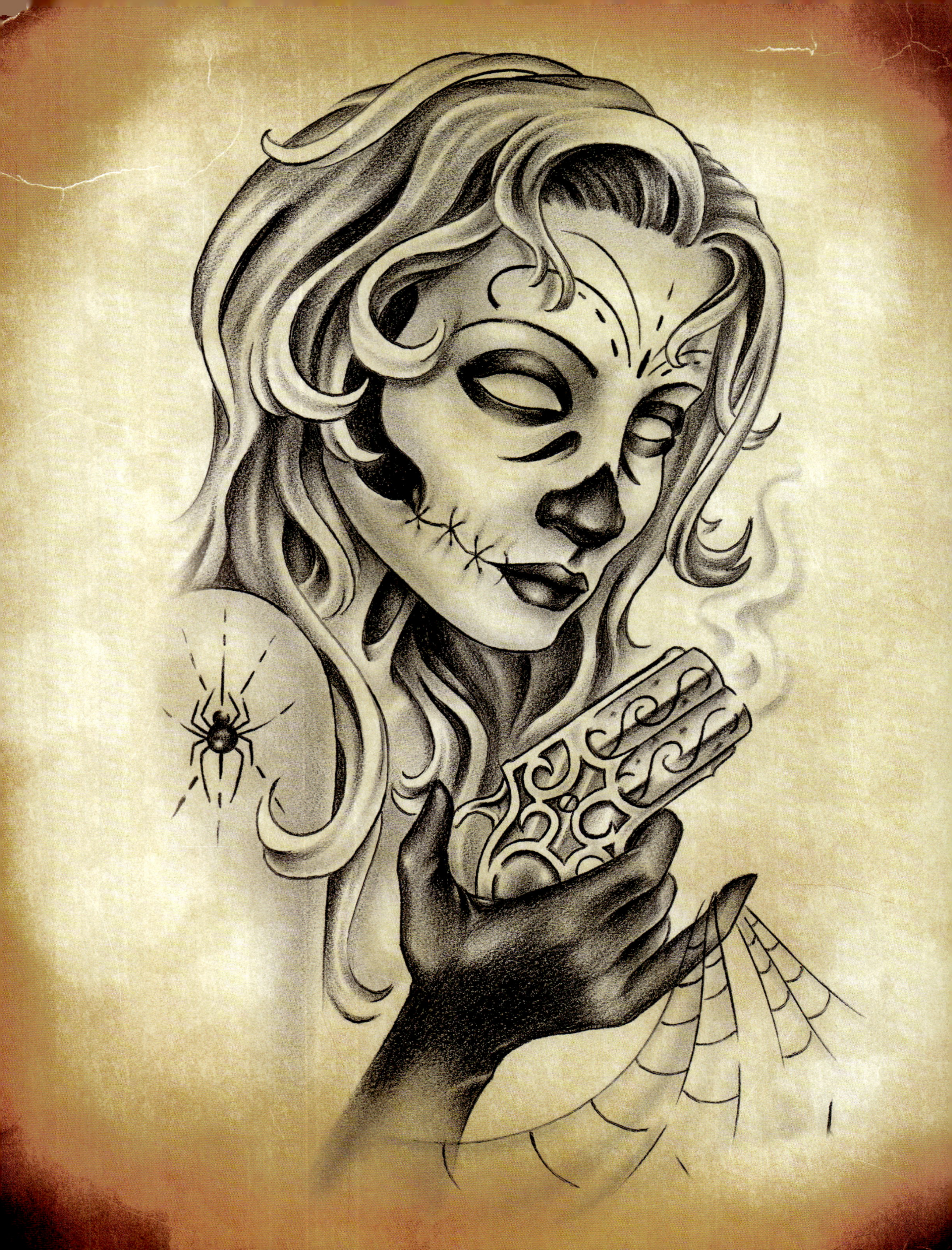

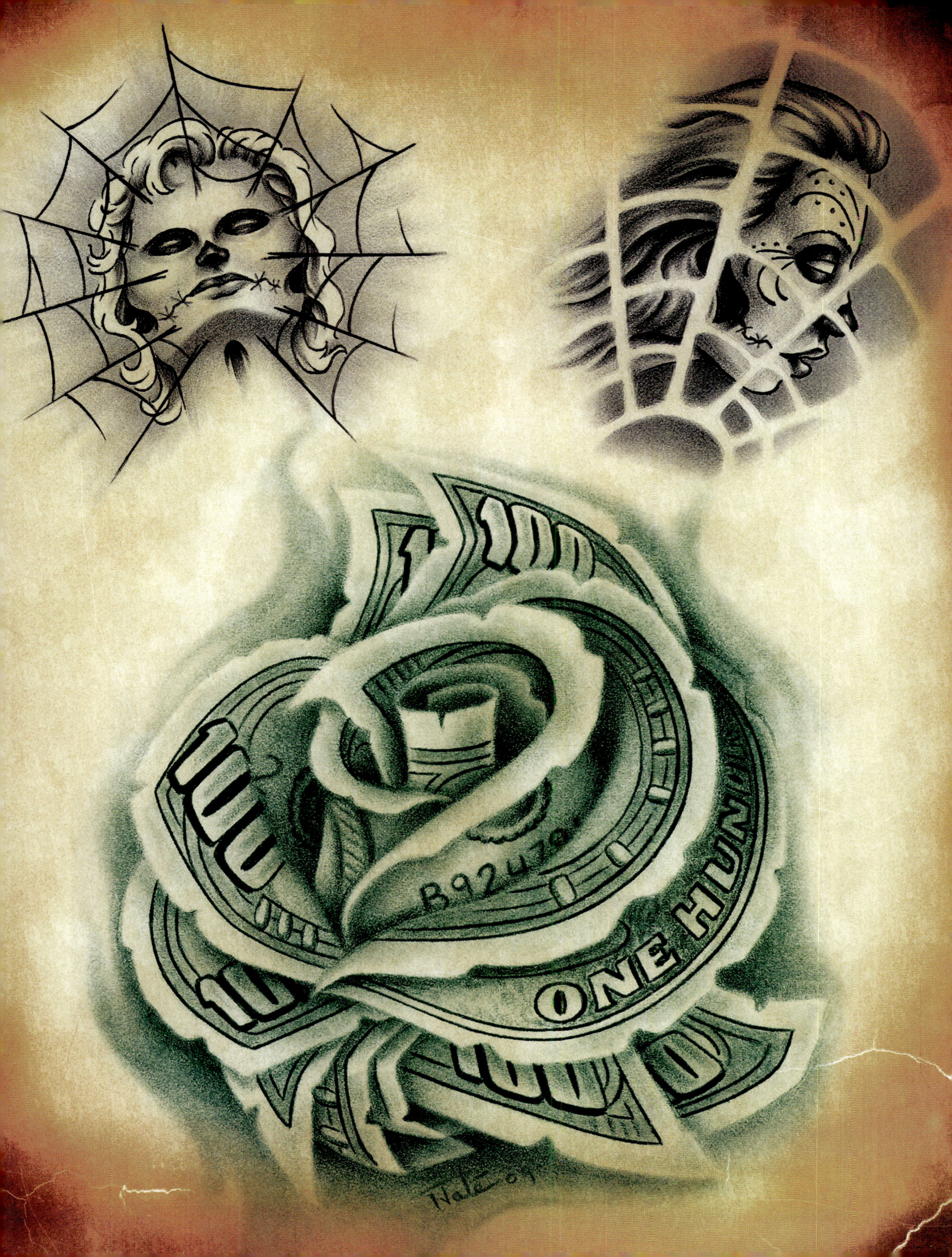
100
ONE HUN
B92479

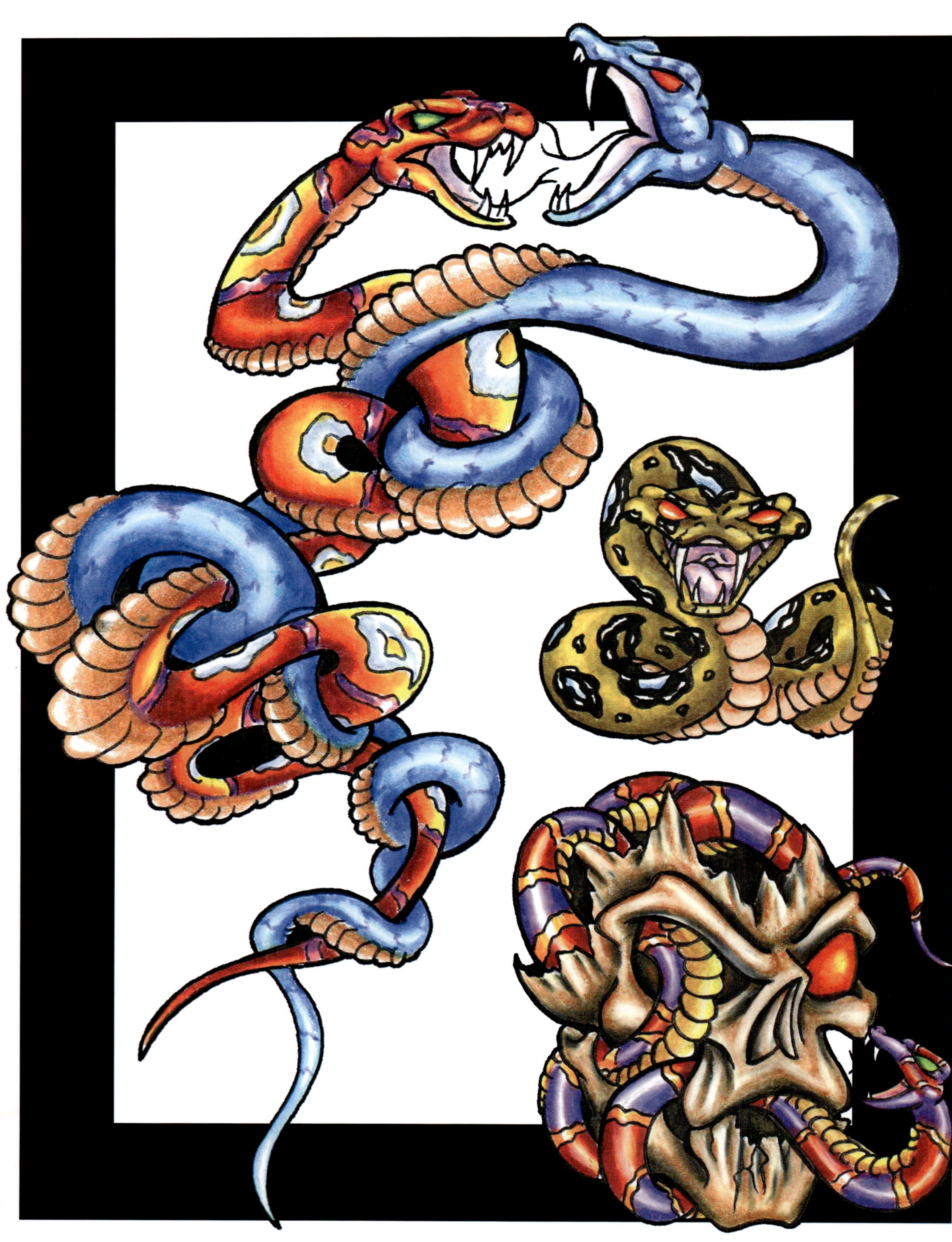

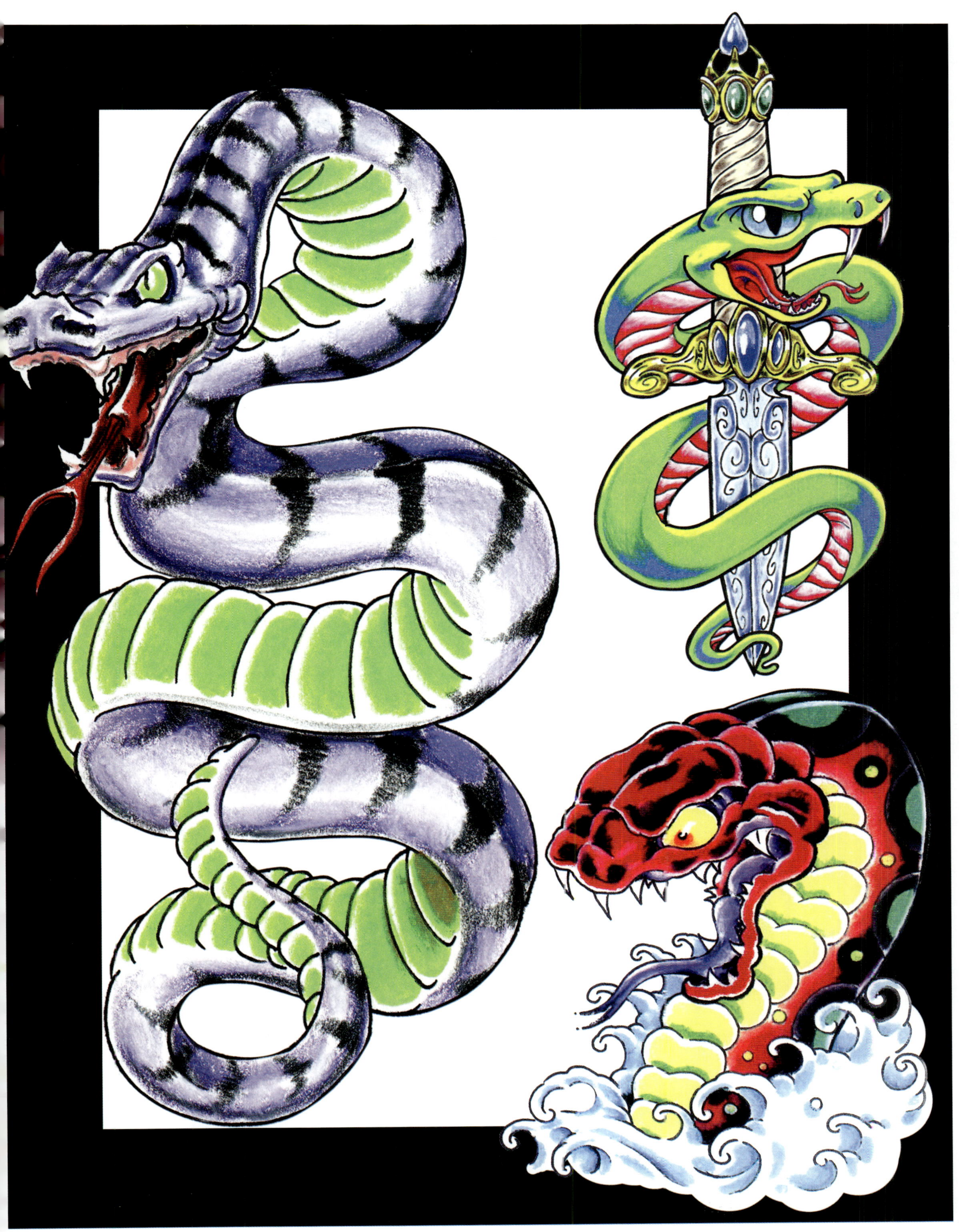

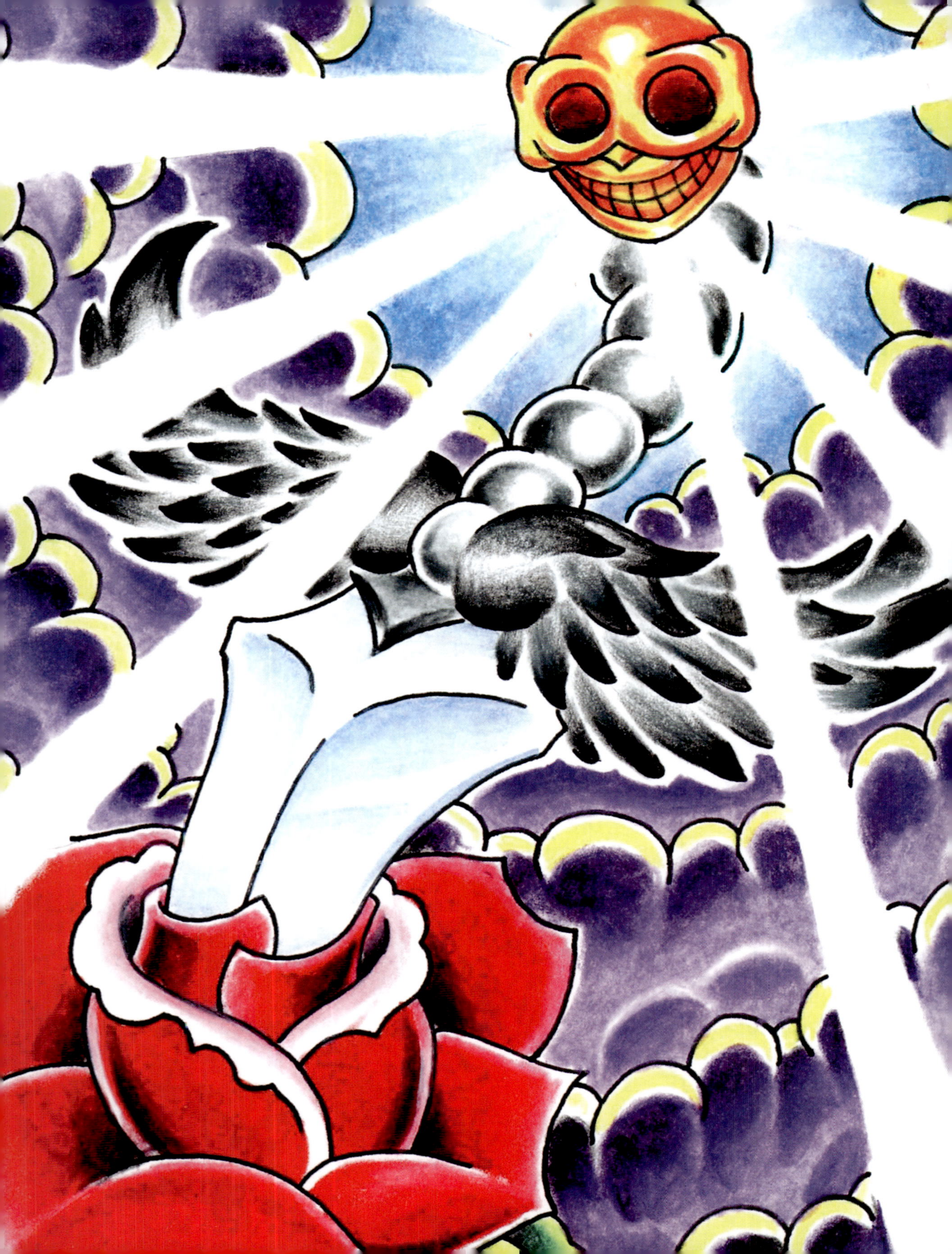

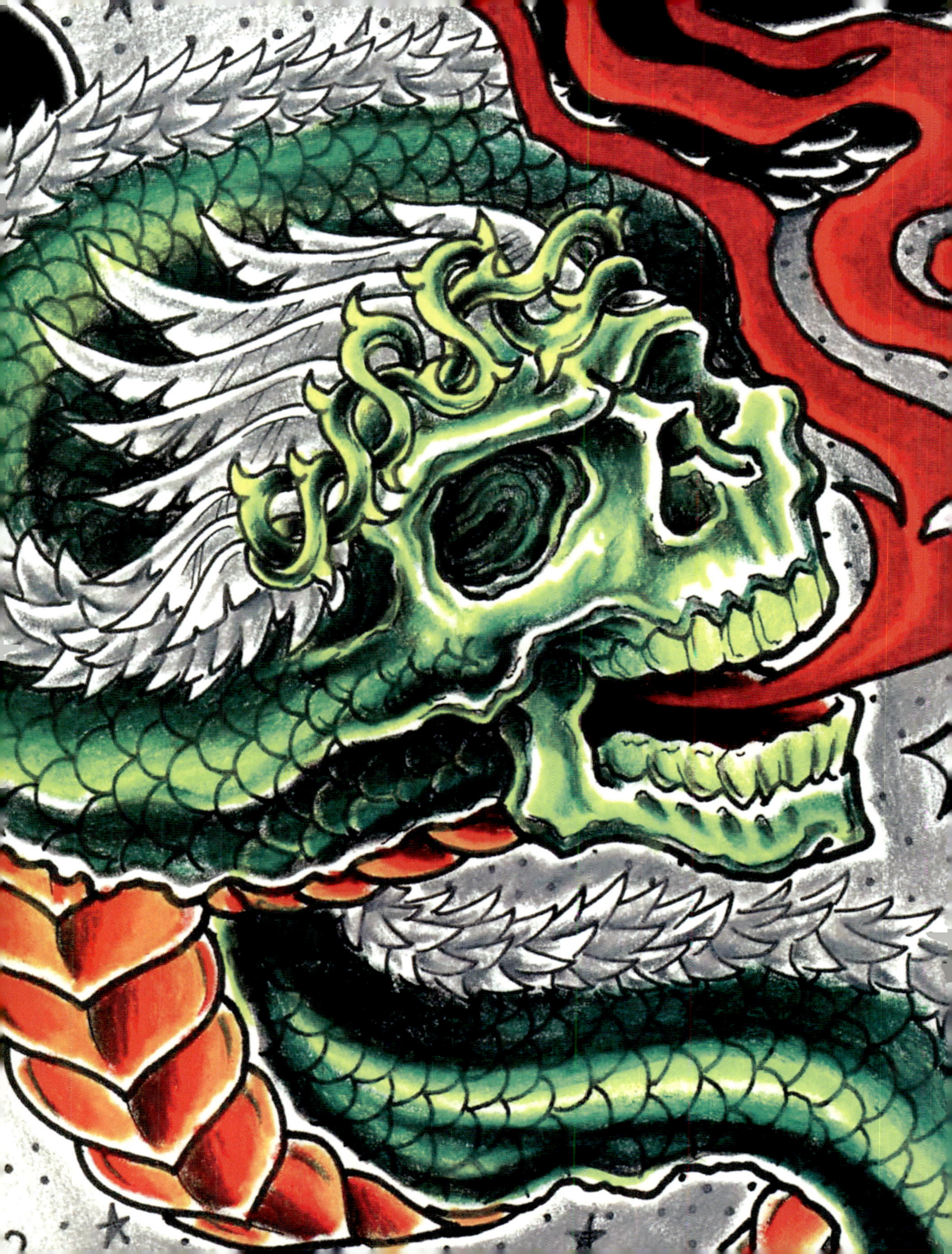

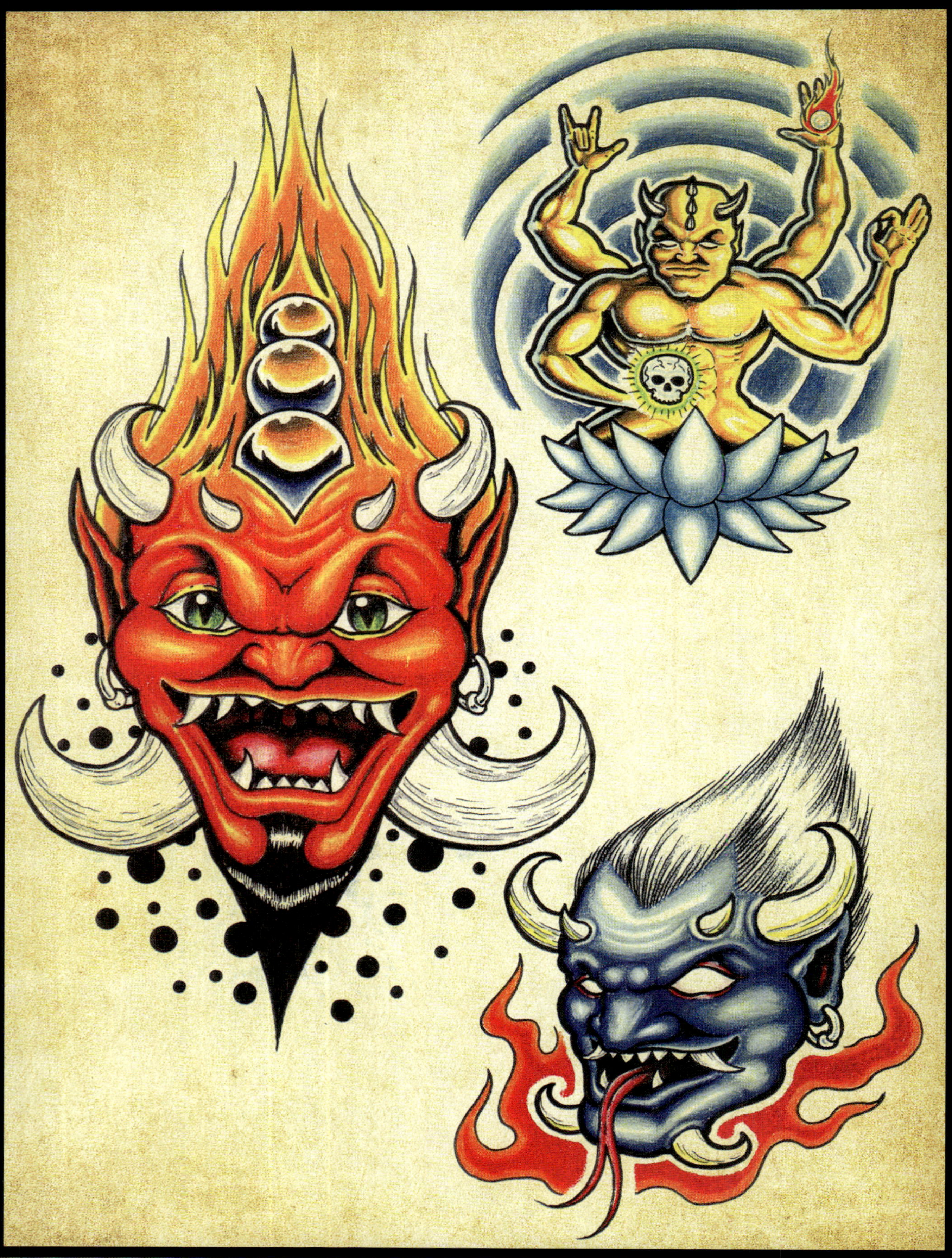

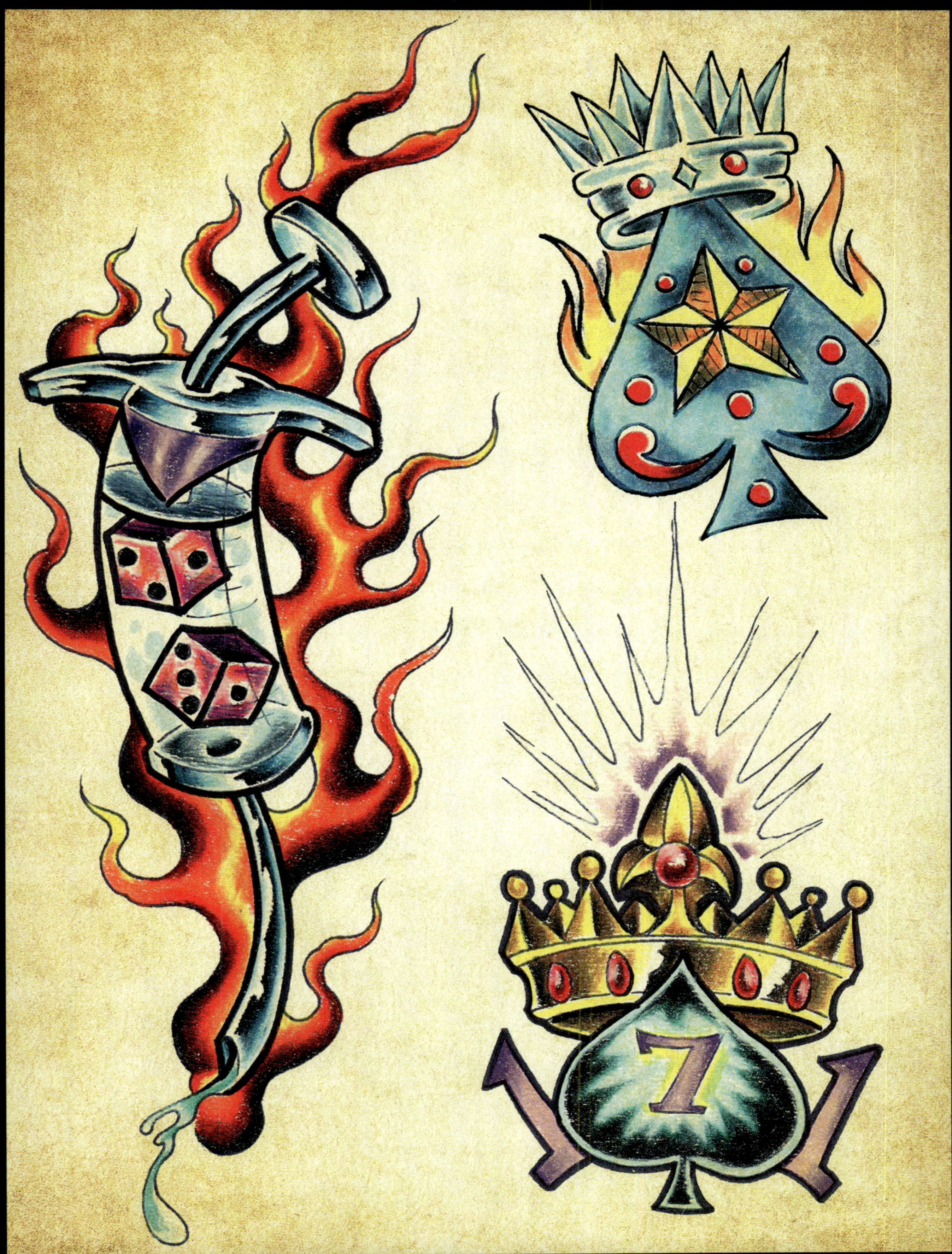
7

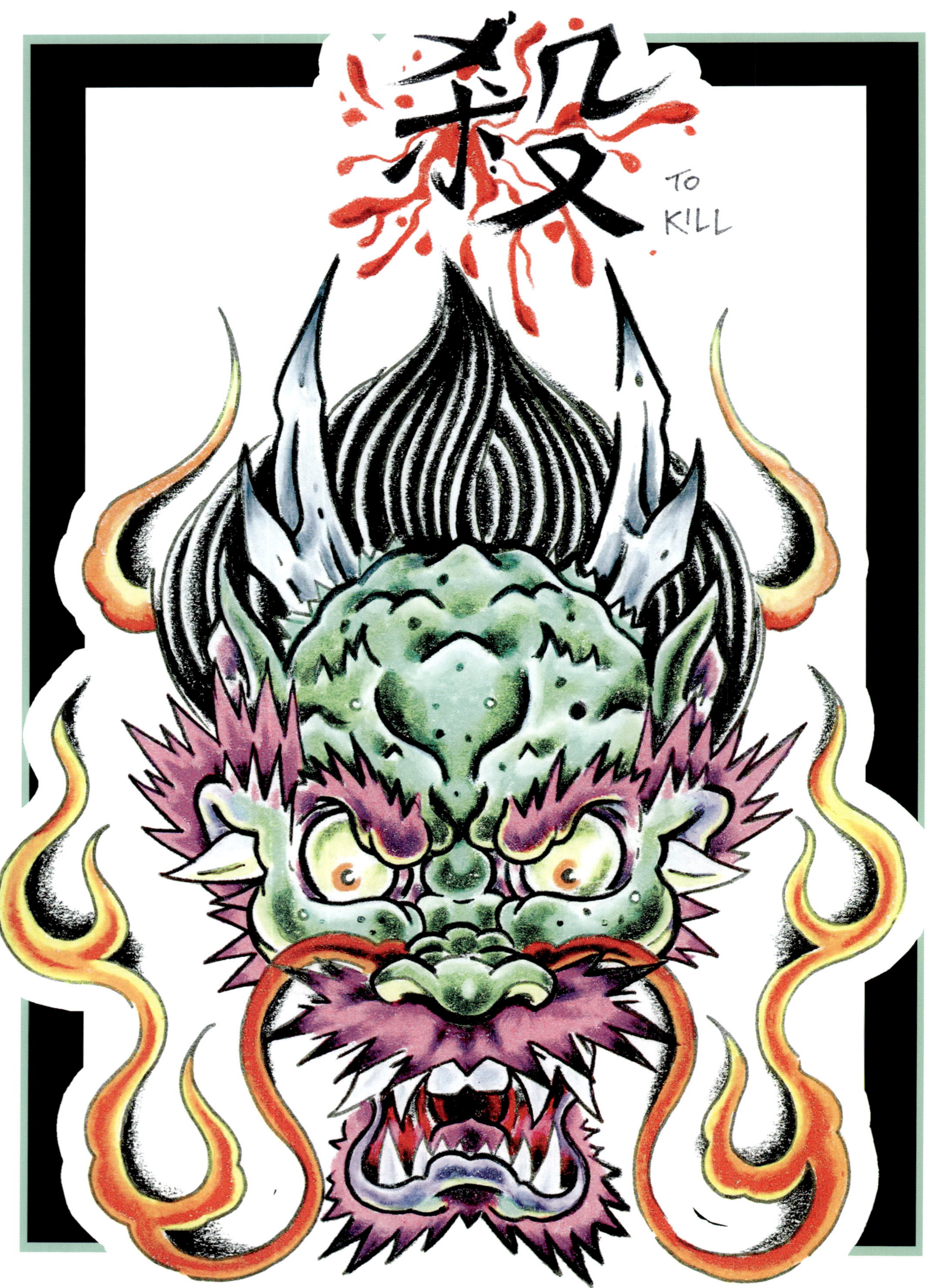
殺
TO
KILL

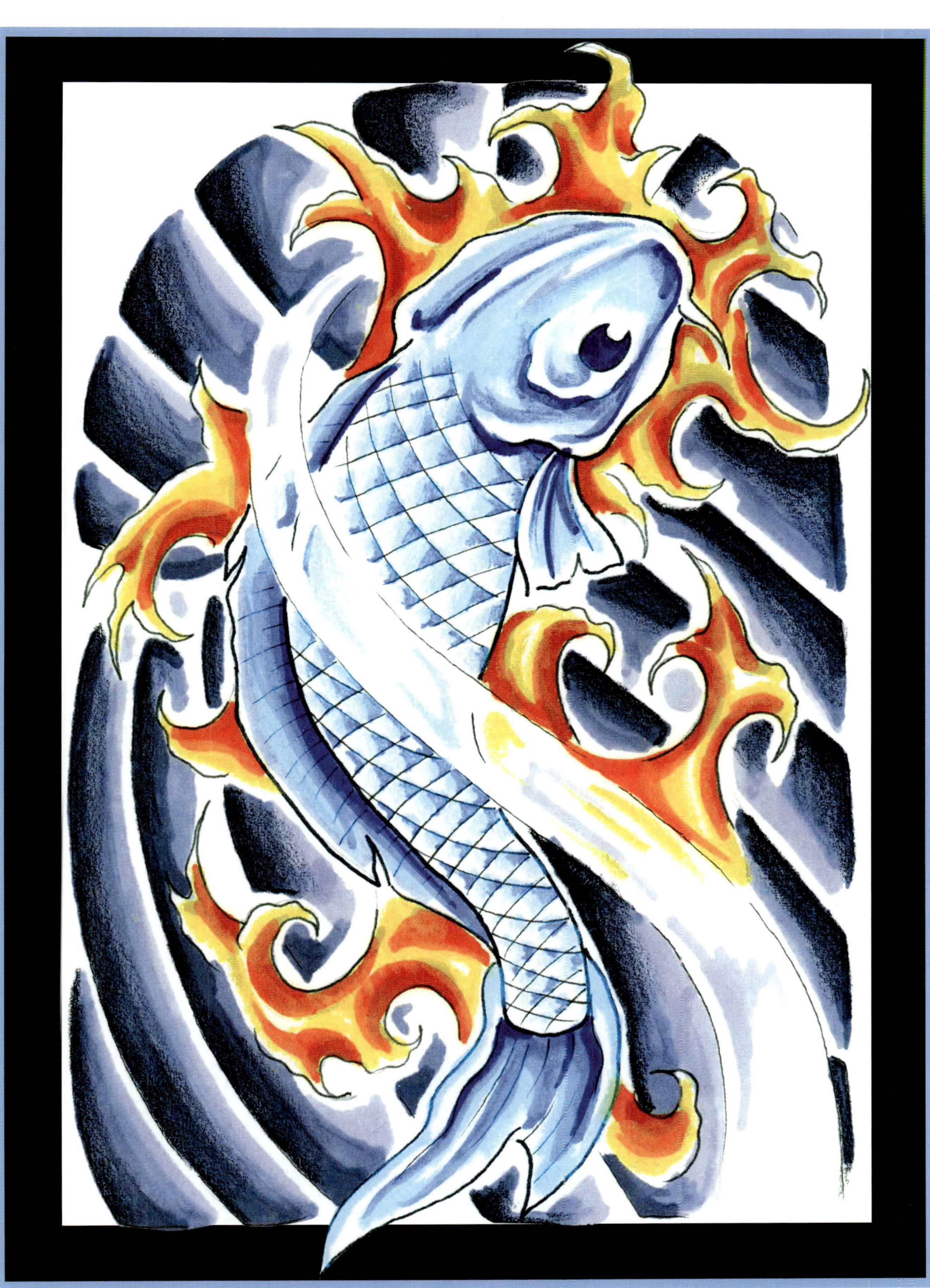

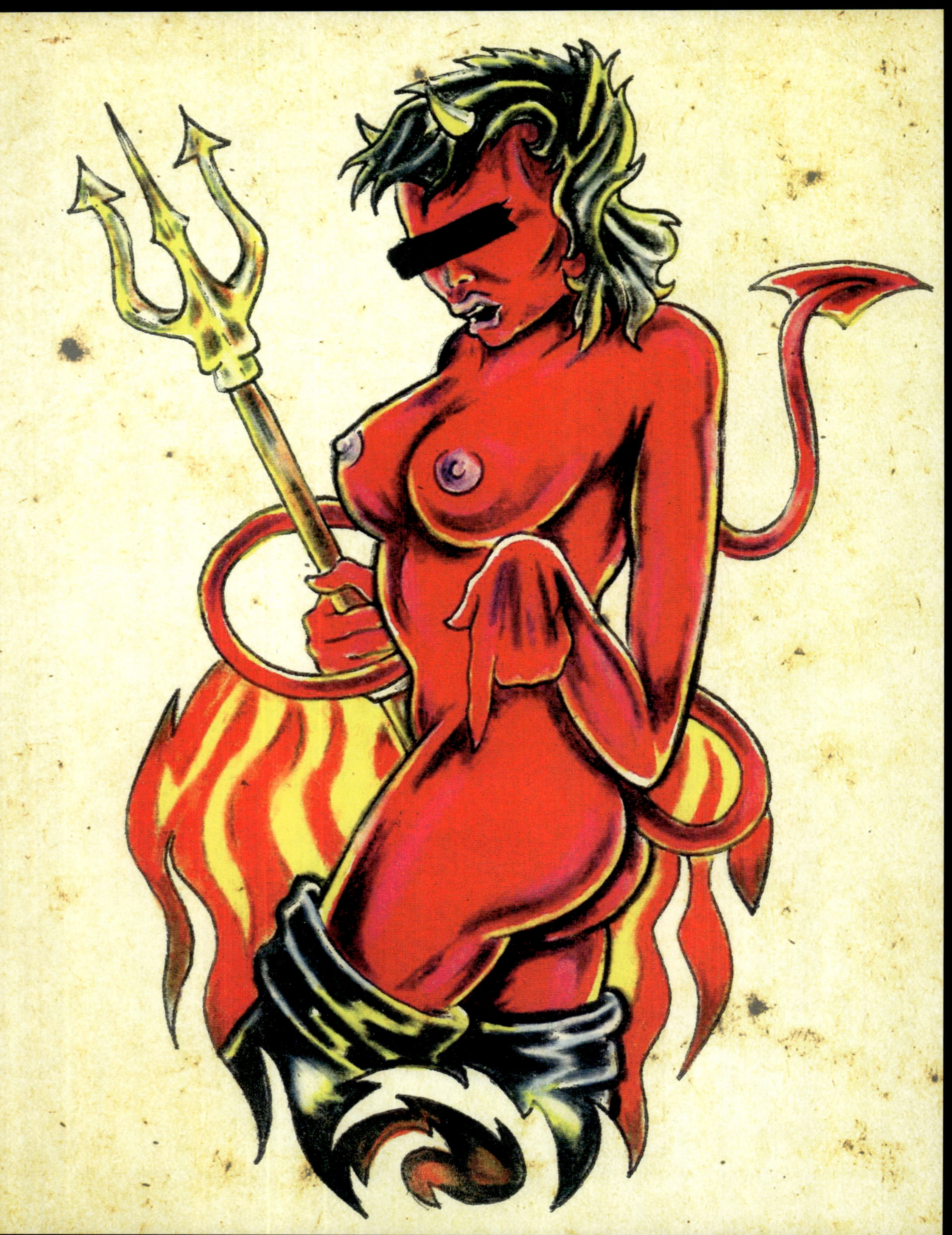

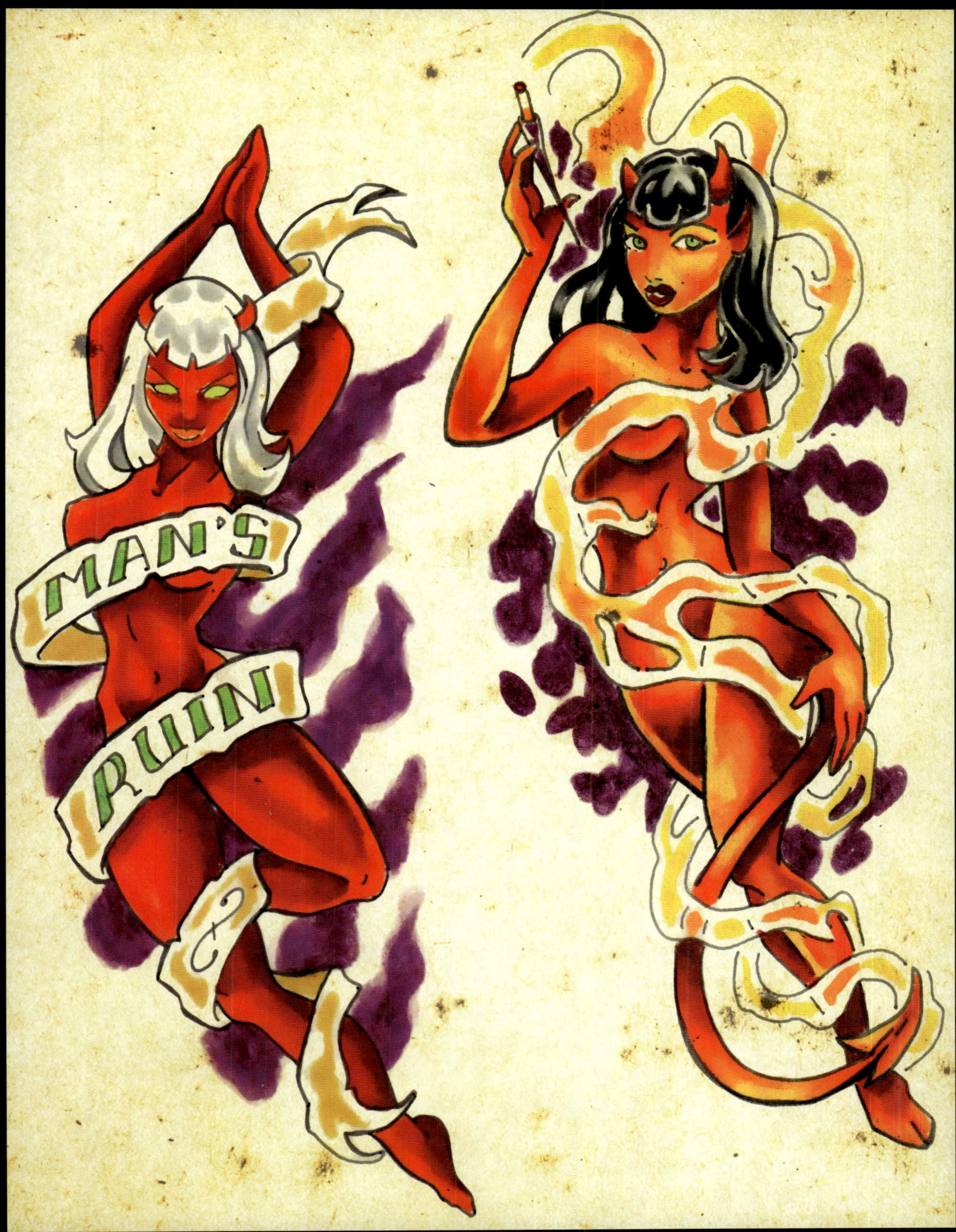
MAN'S
RUIN

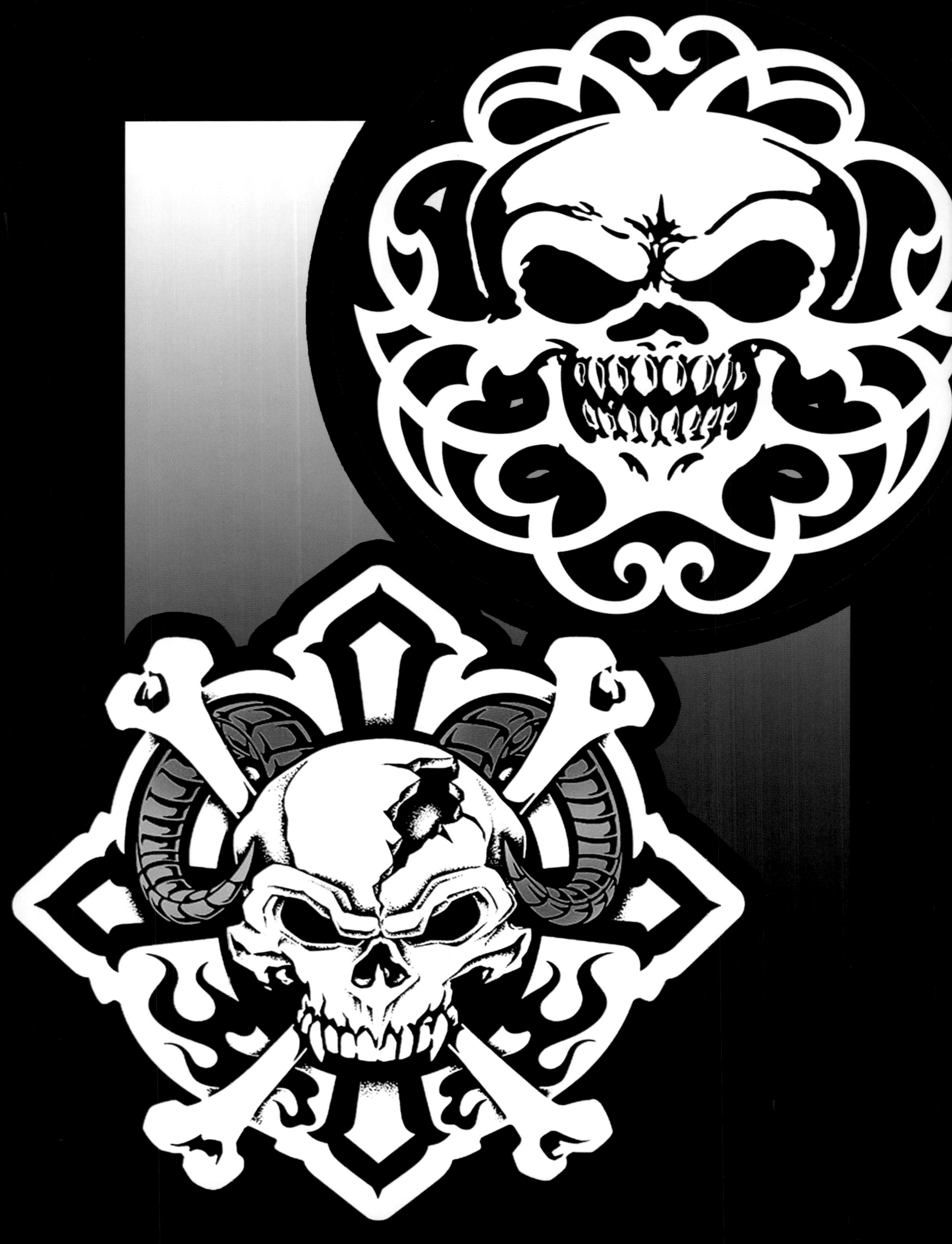

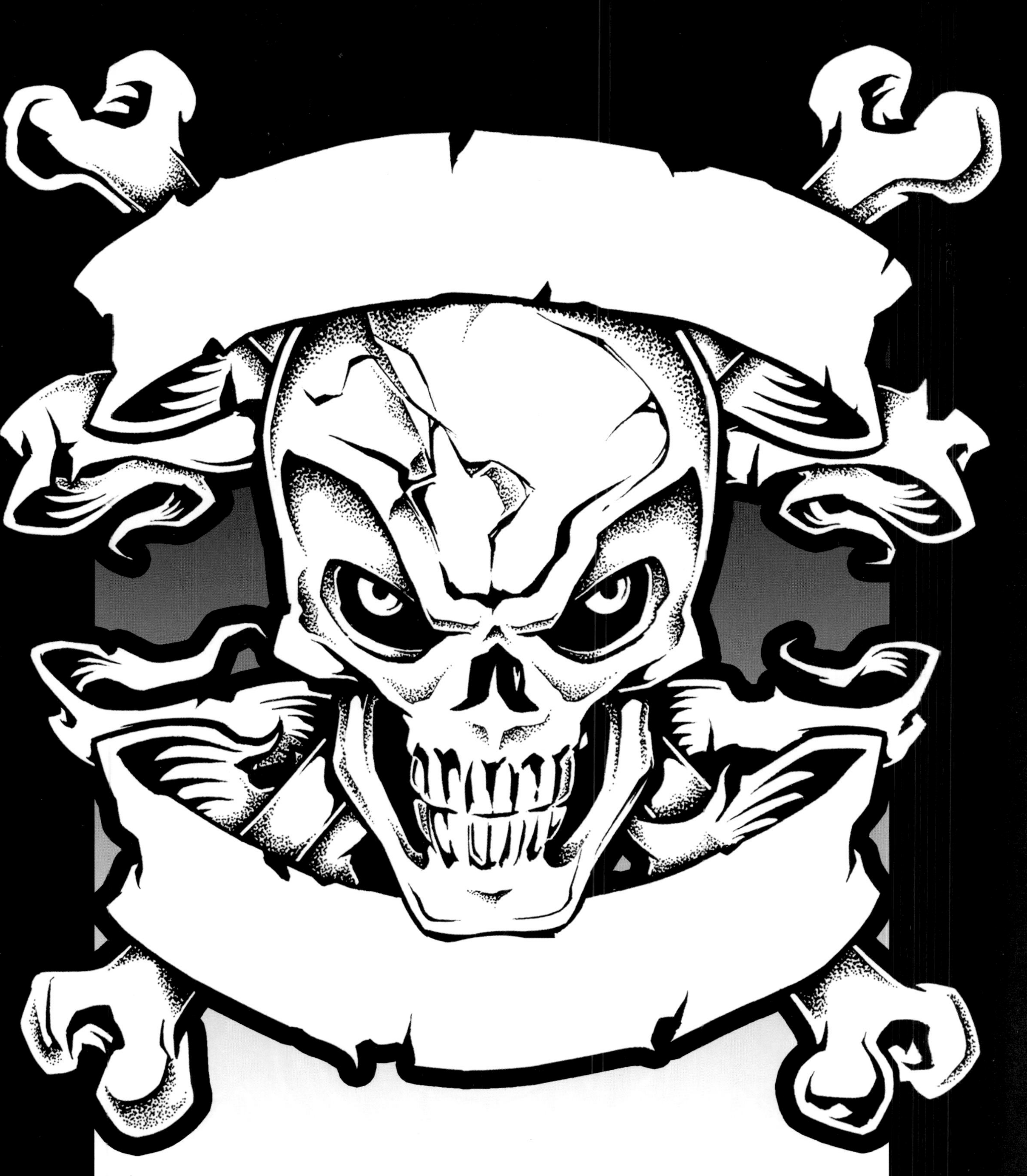

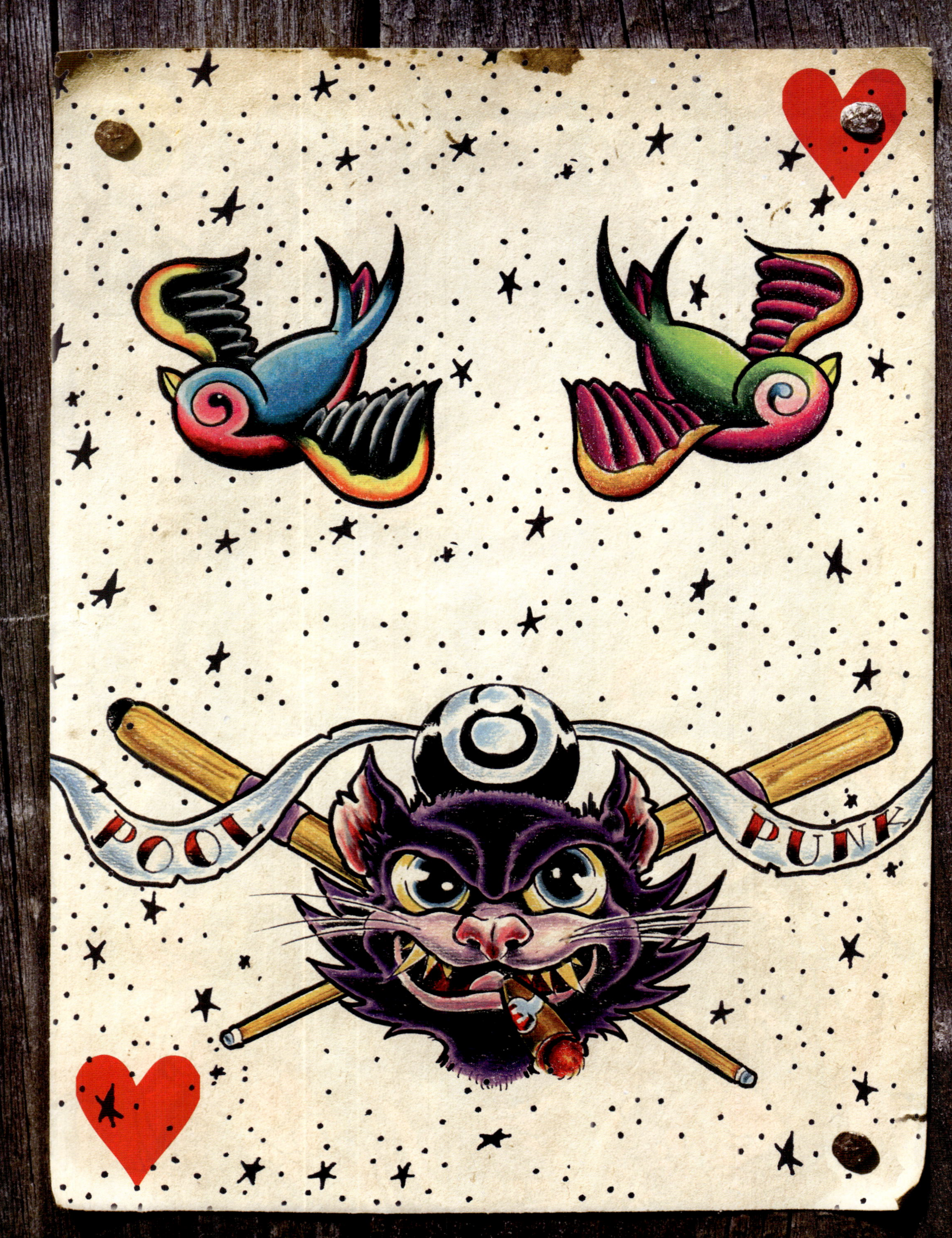
POOL
PUNK

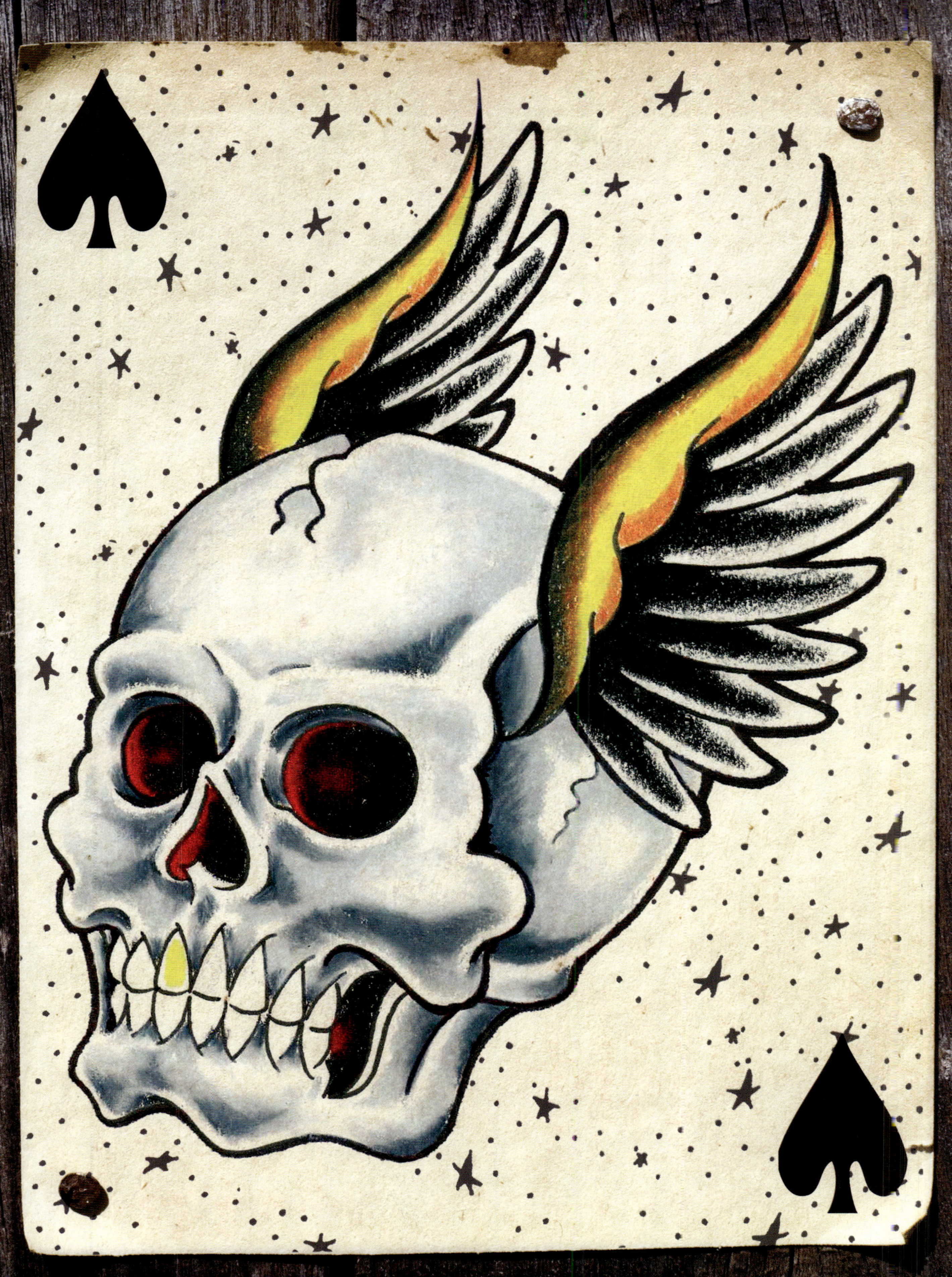

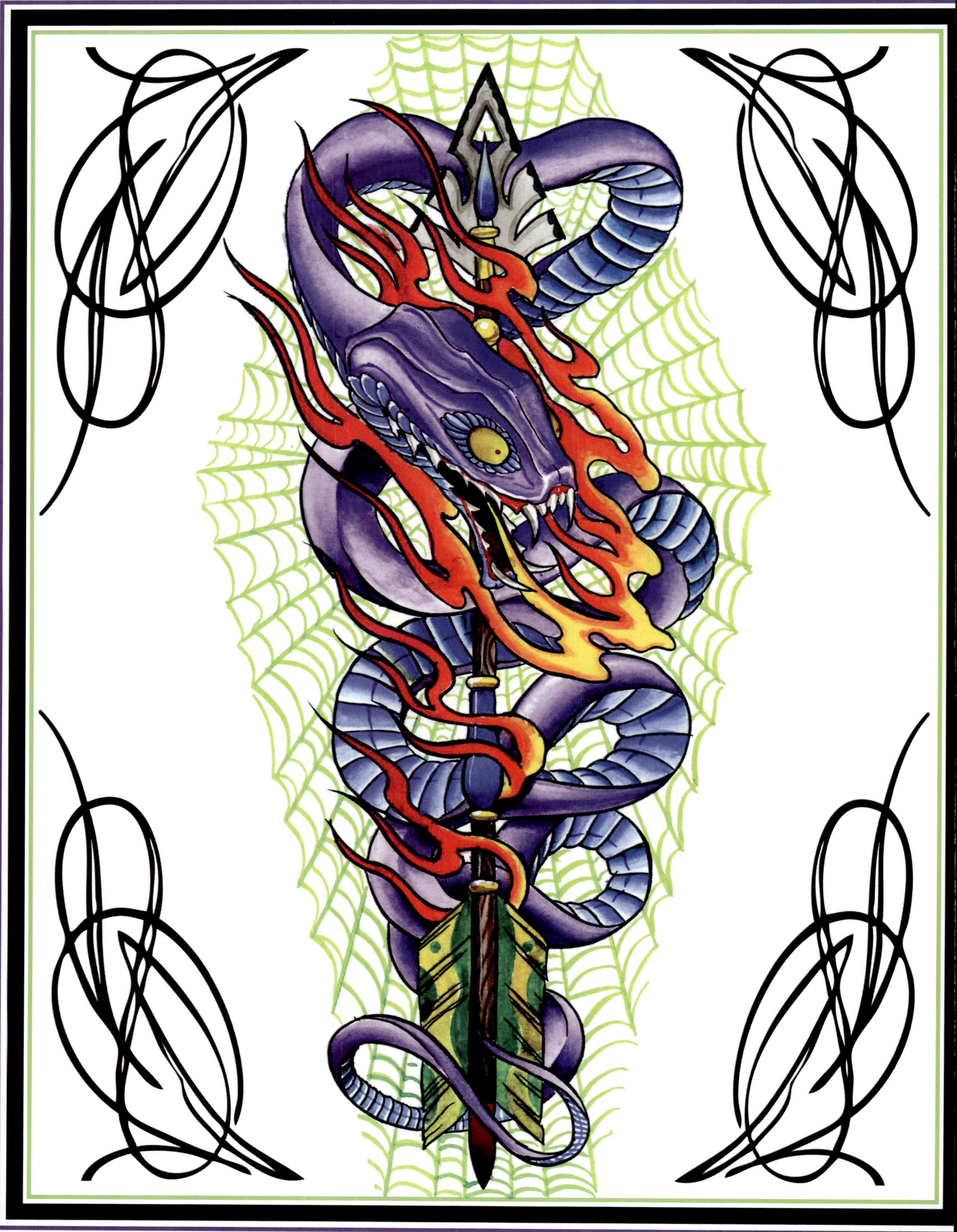

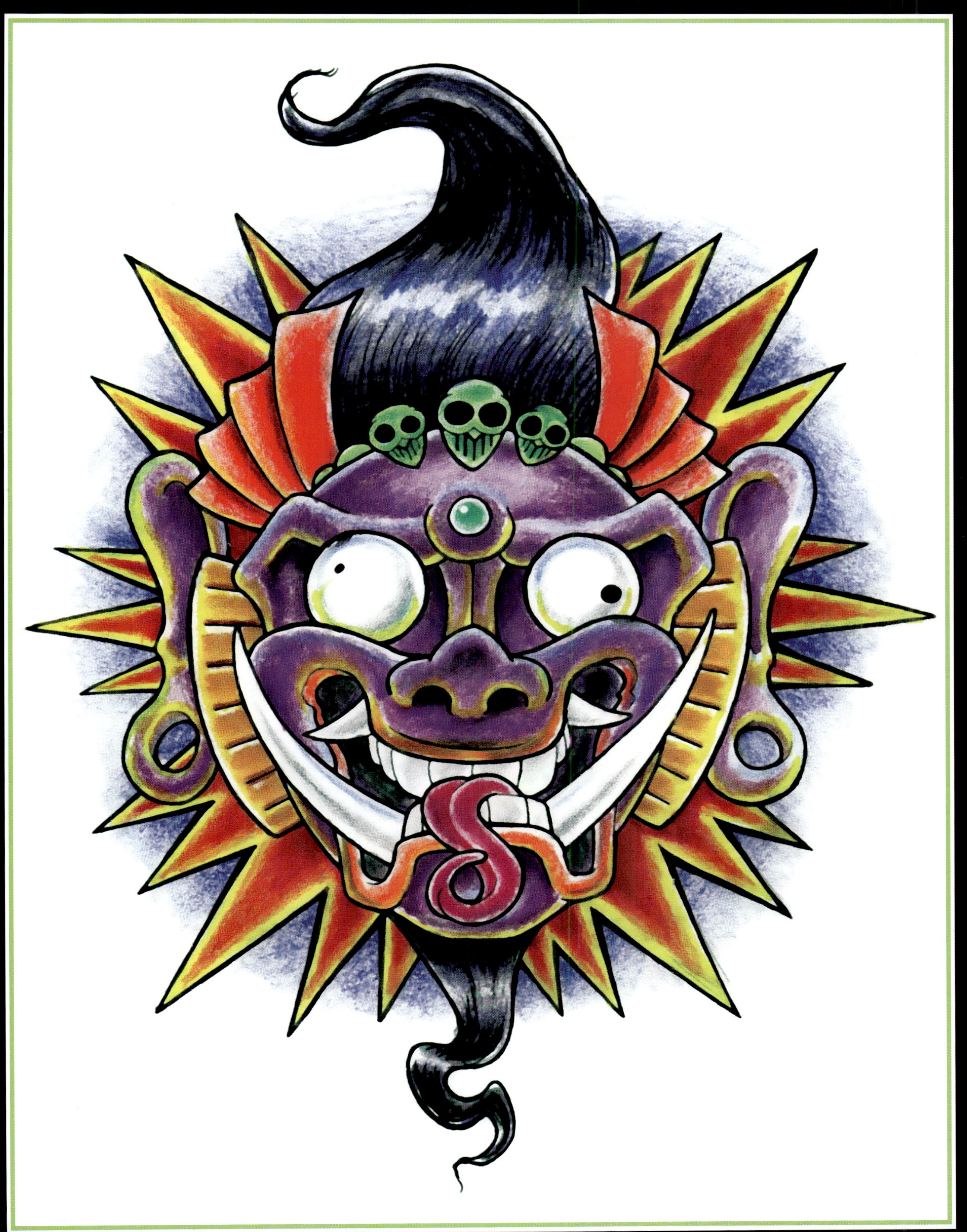

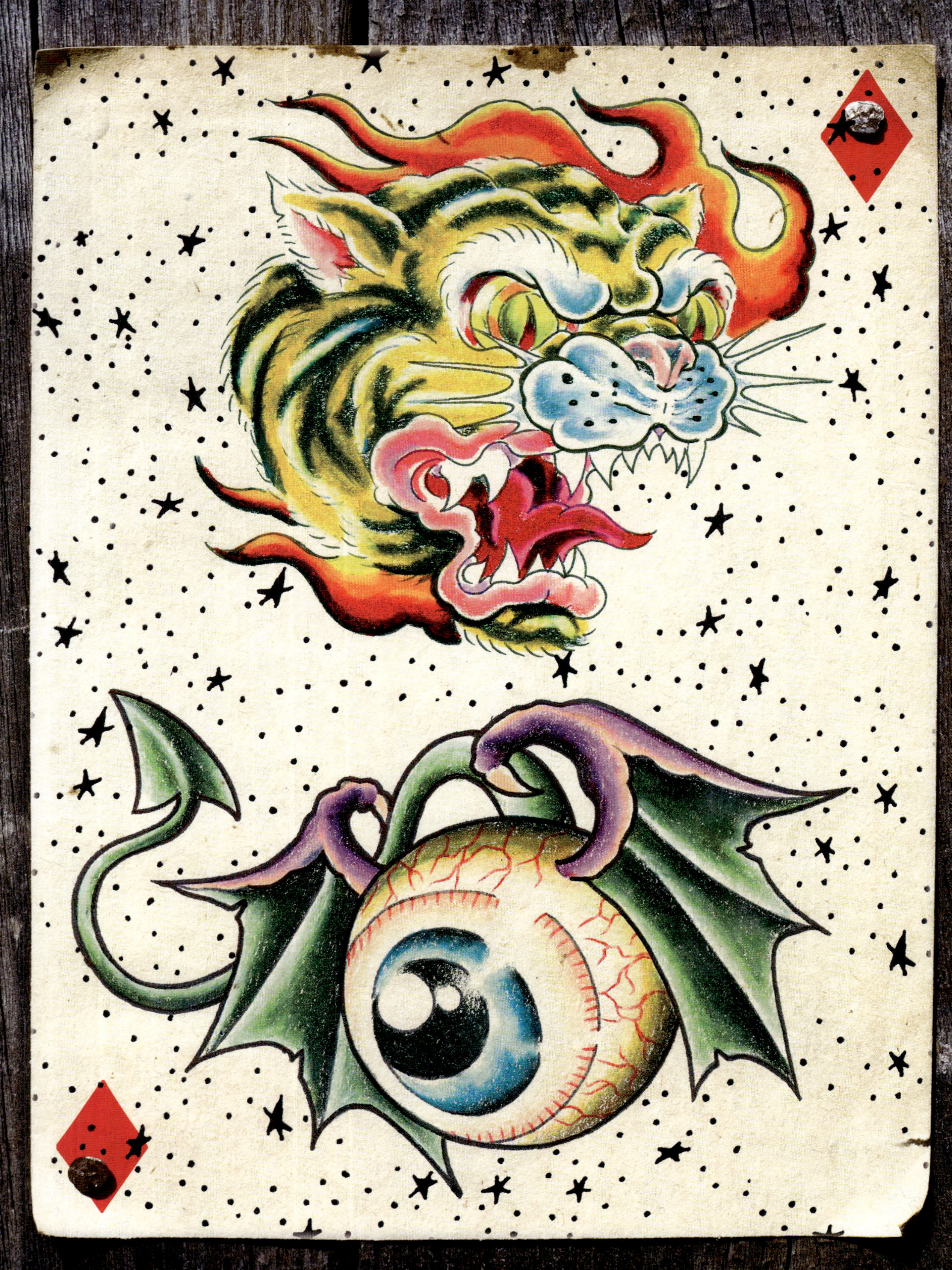

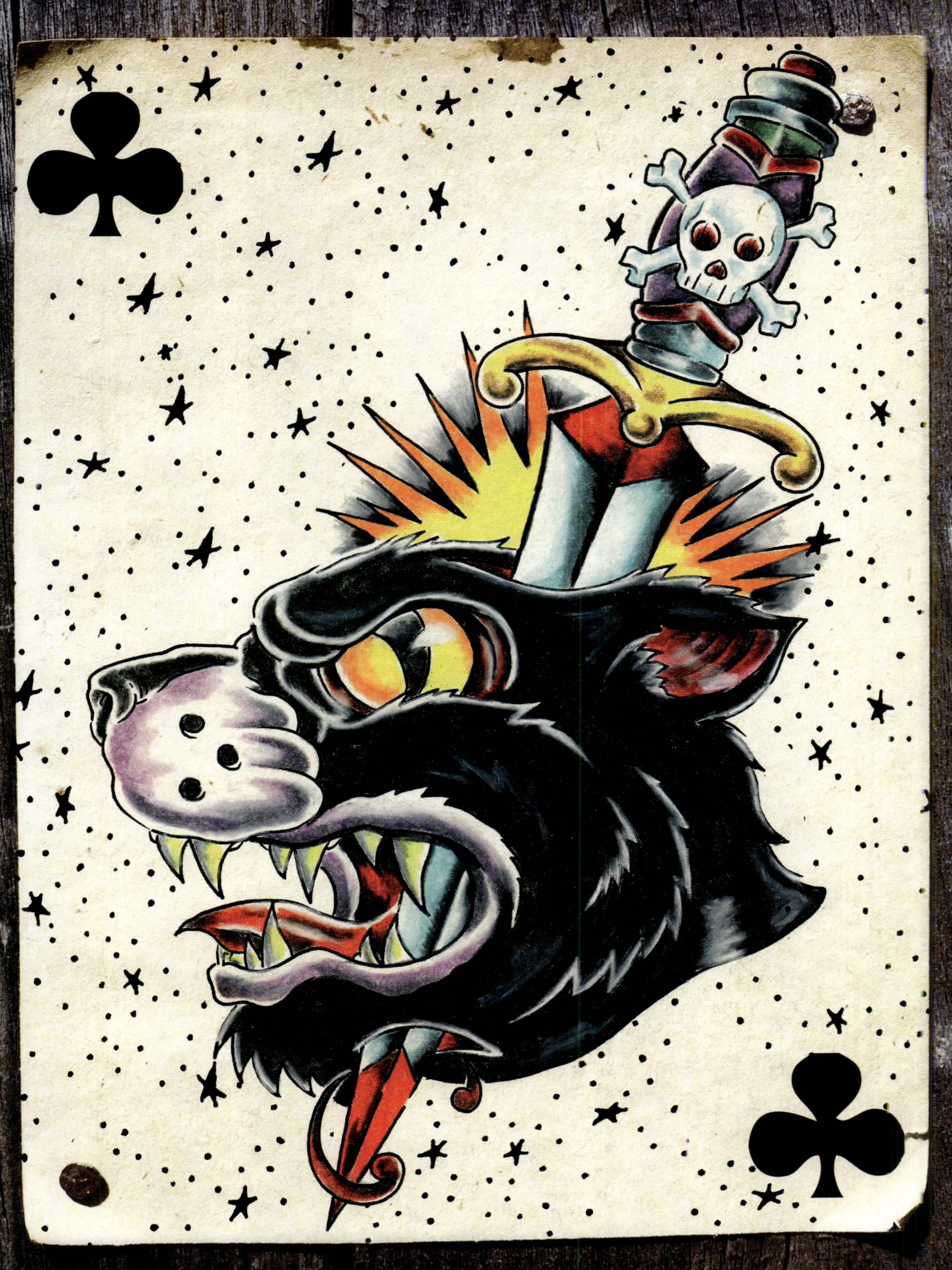

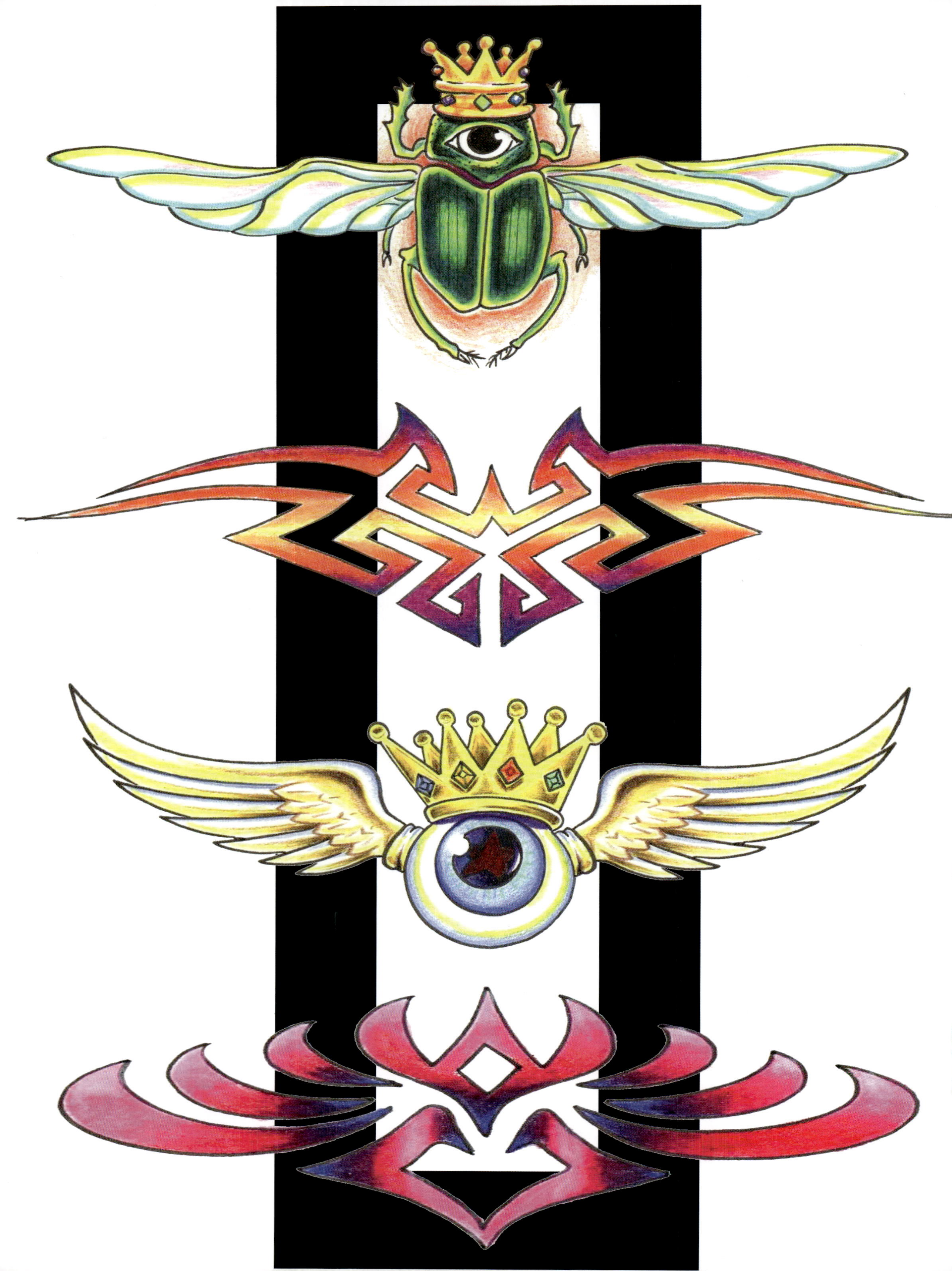

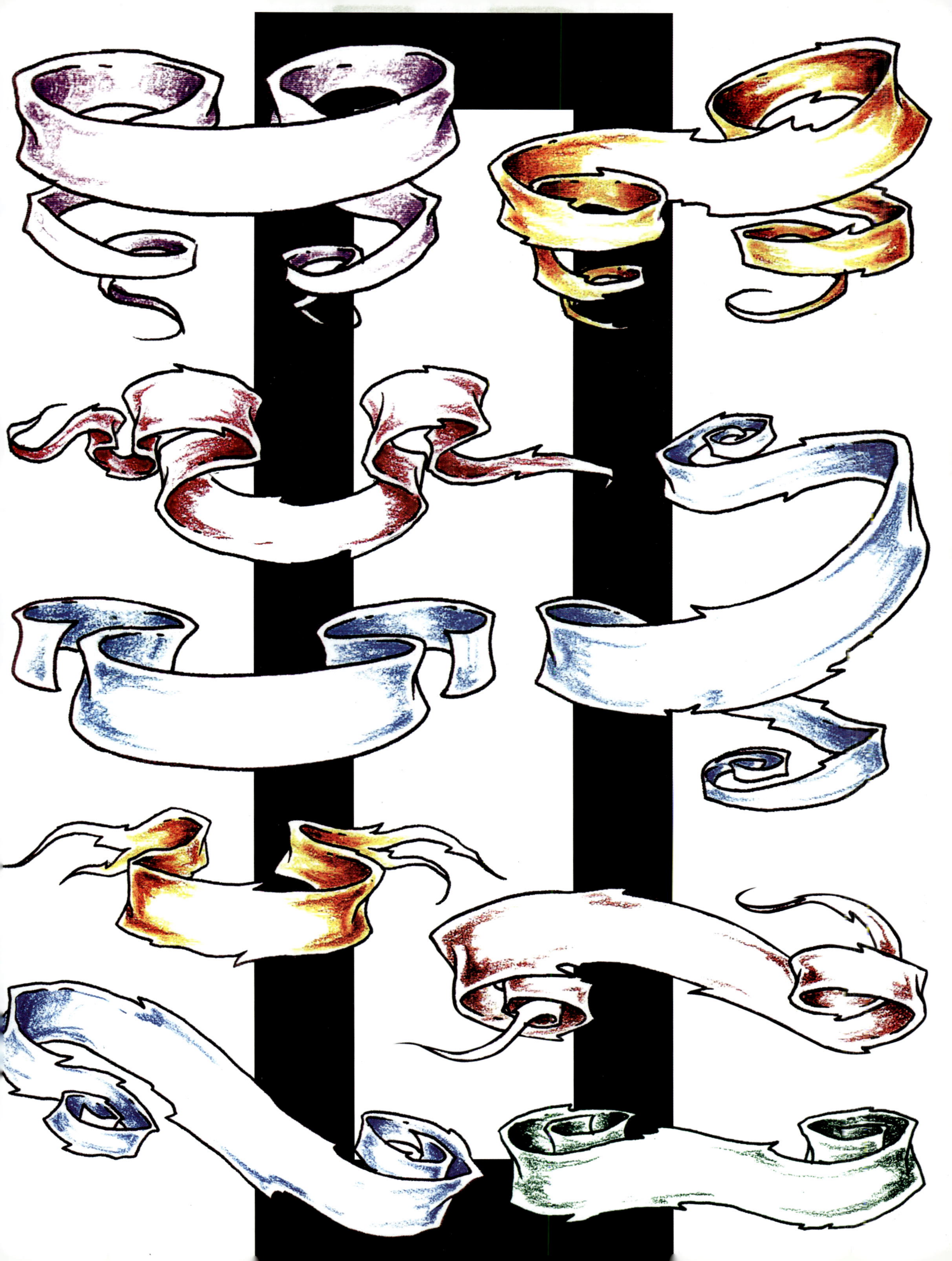

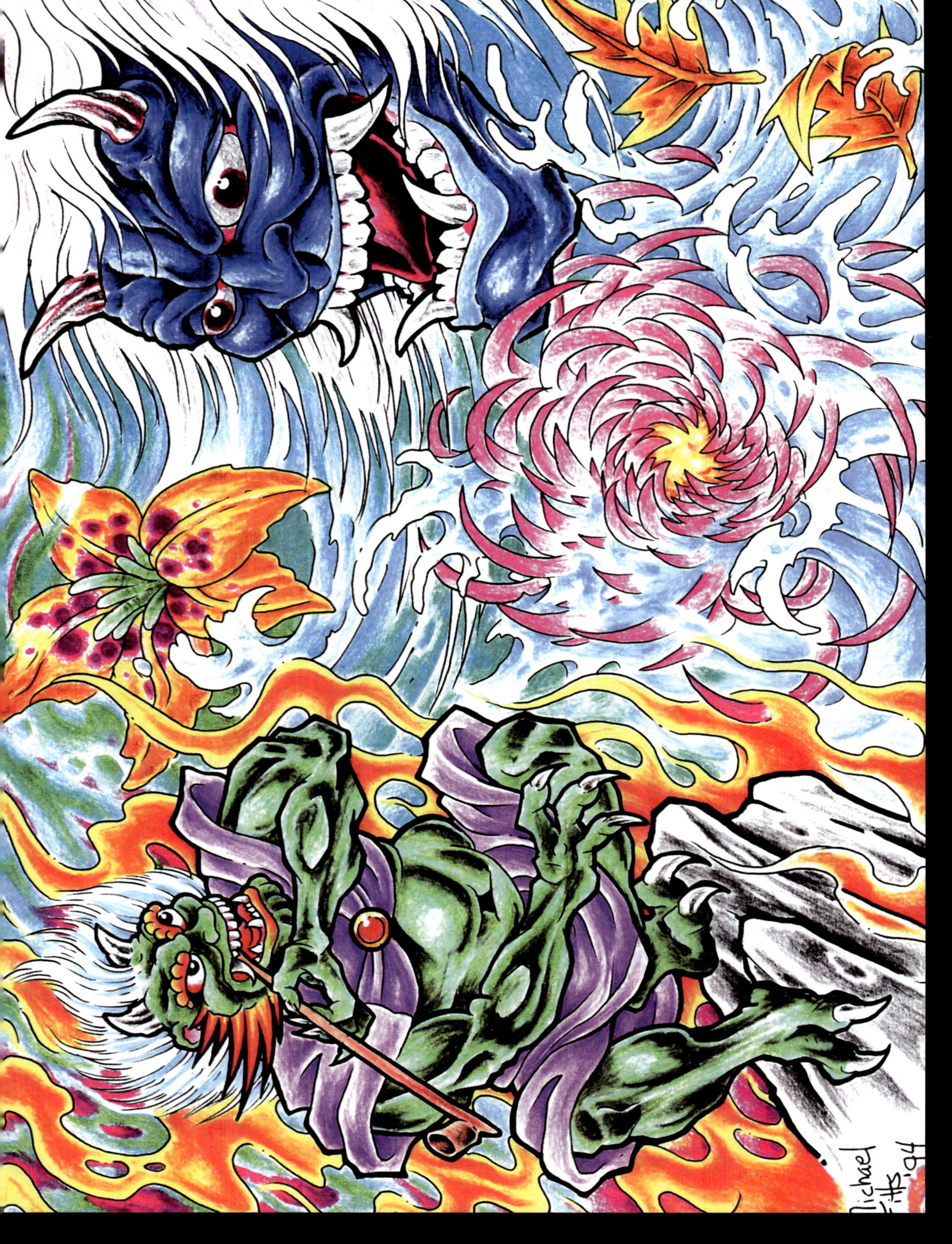

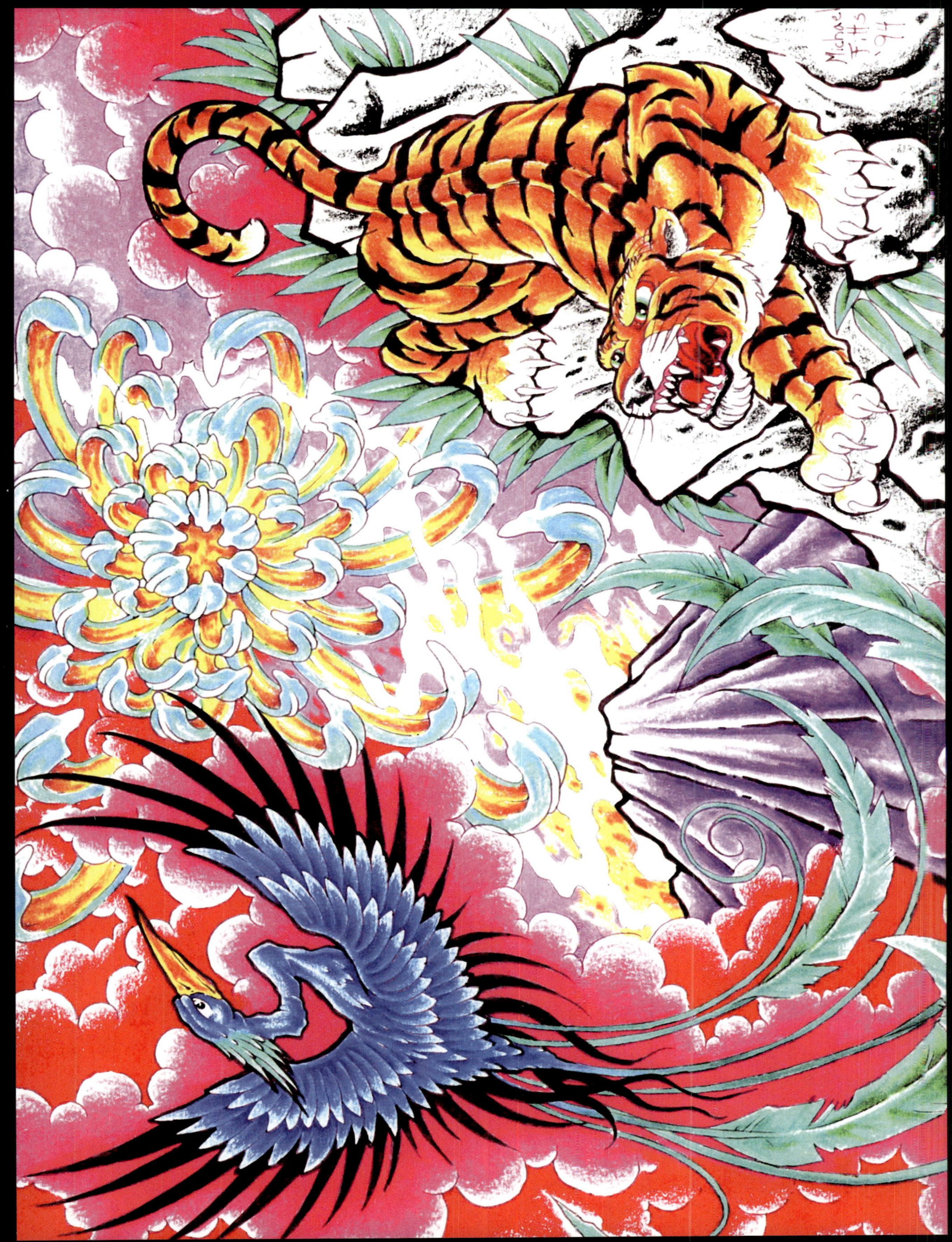
Michael
Fitts
'94

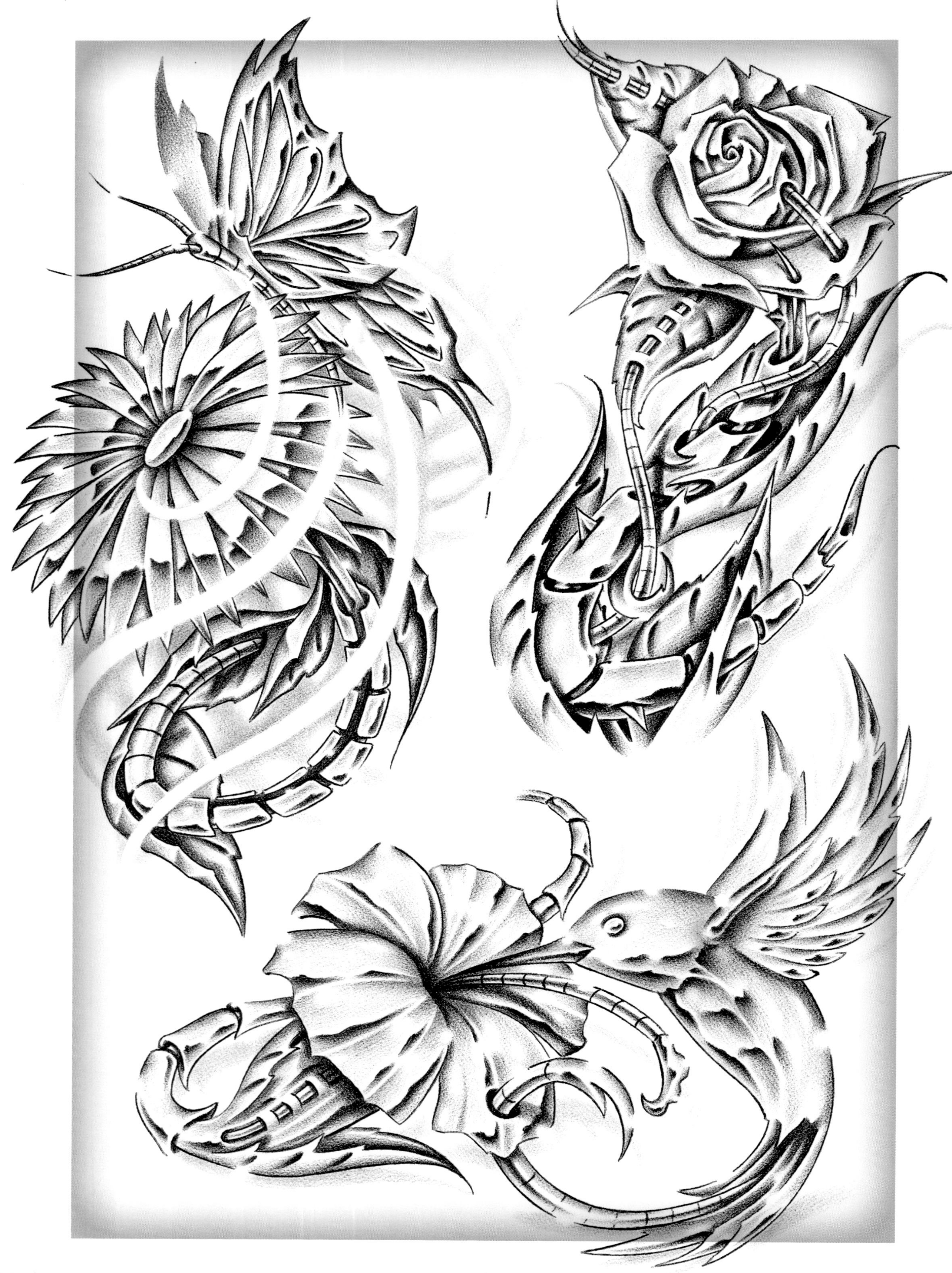

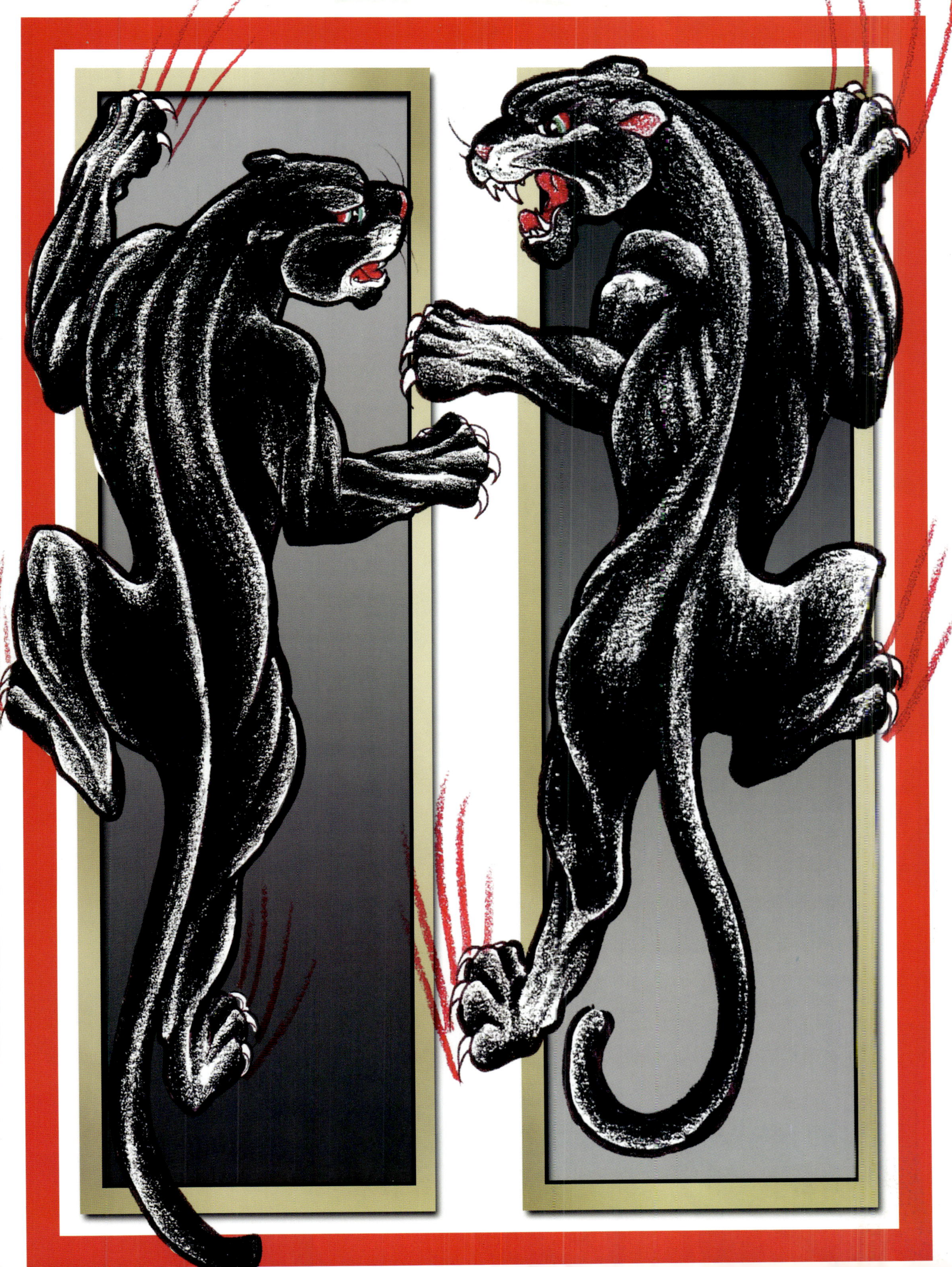

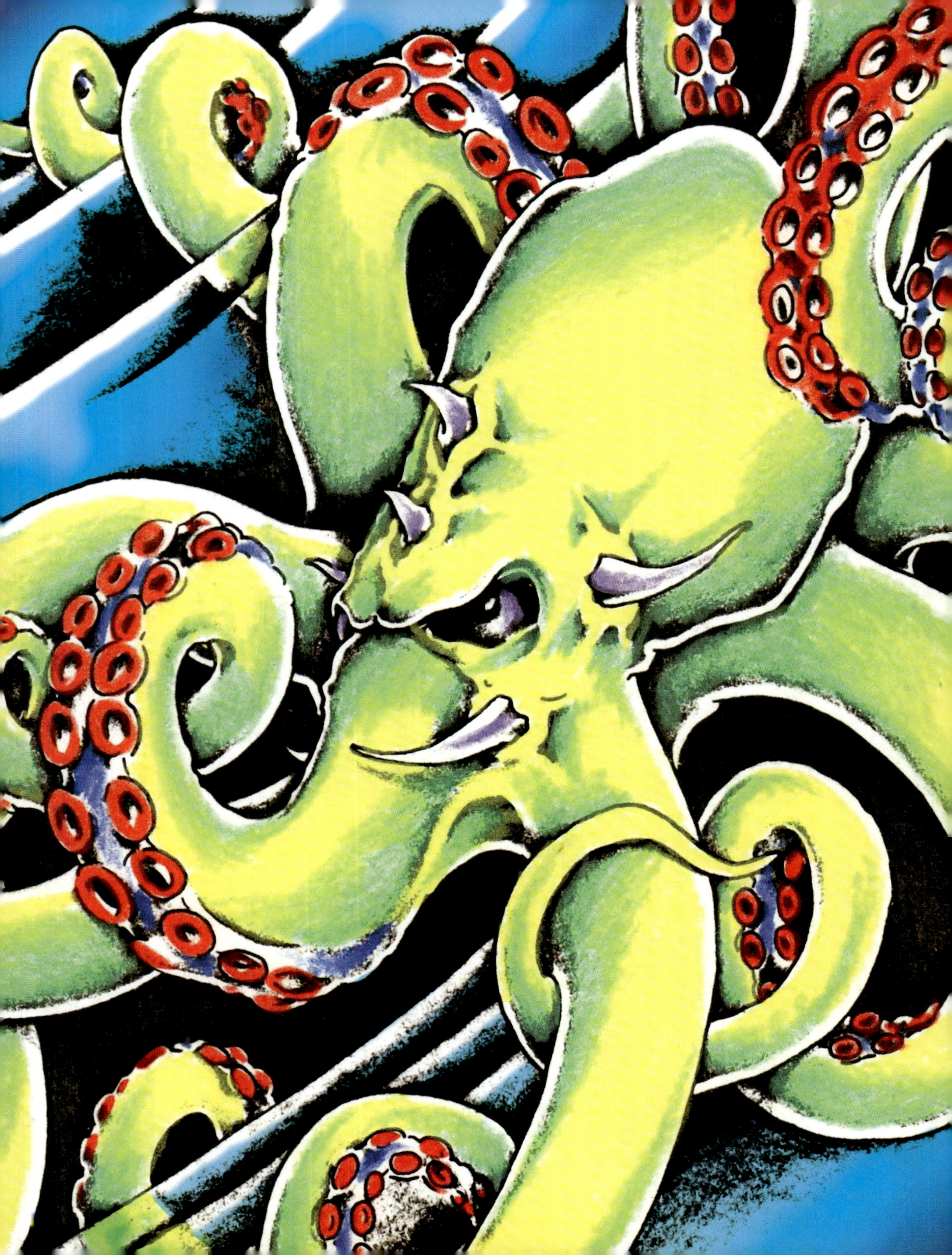

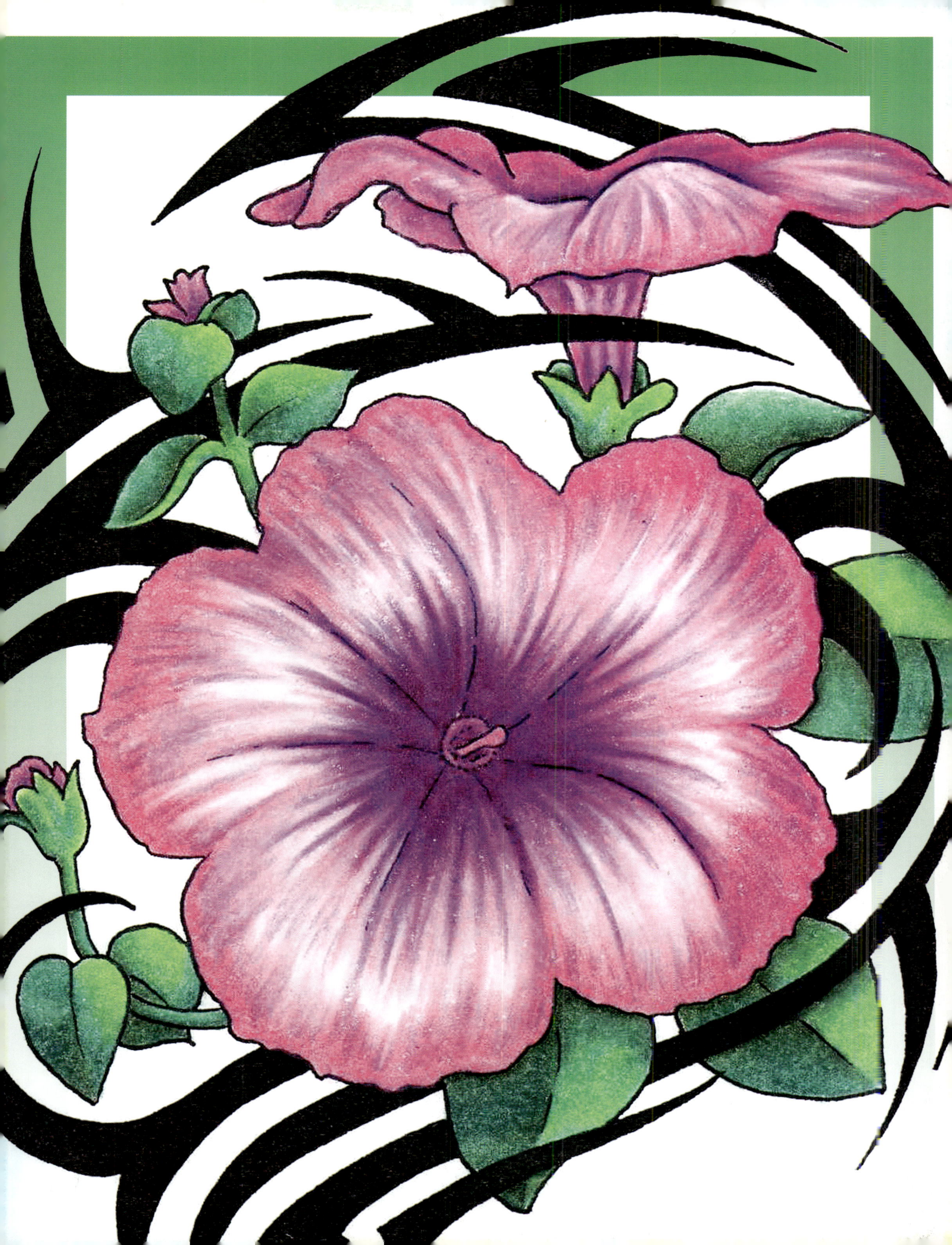

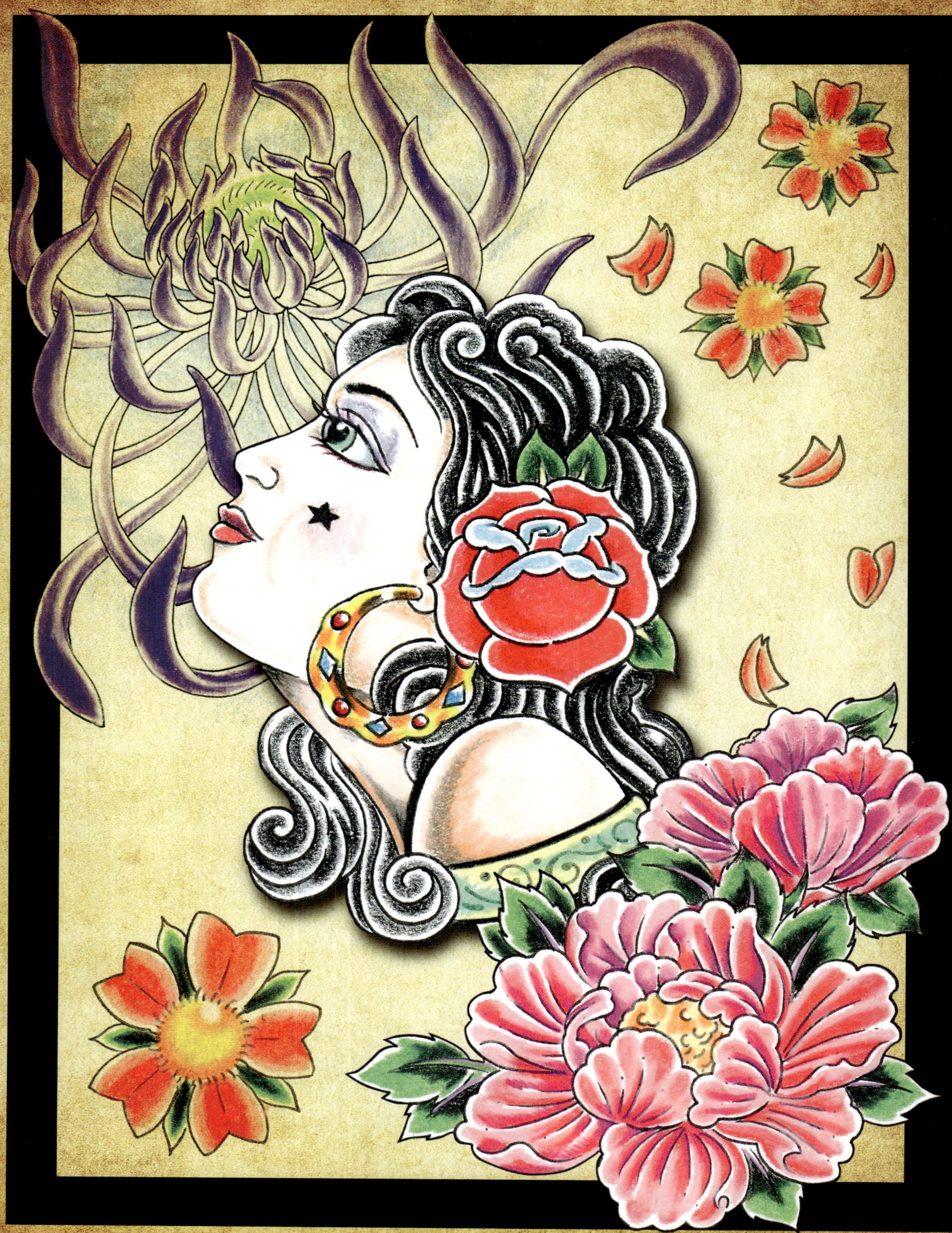

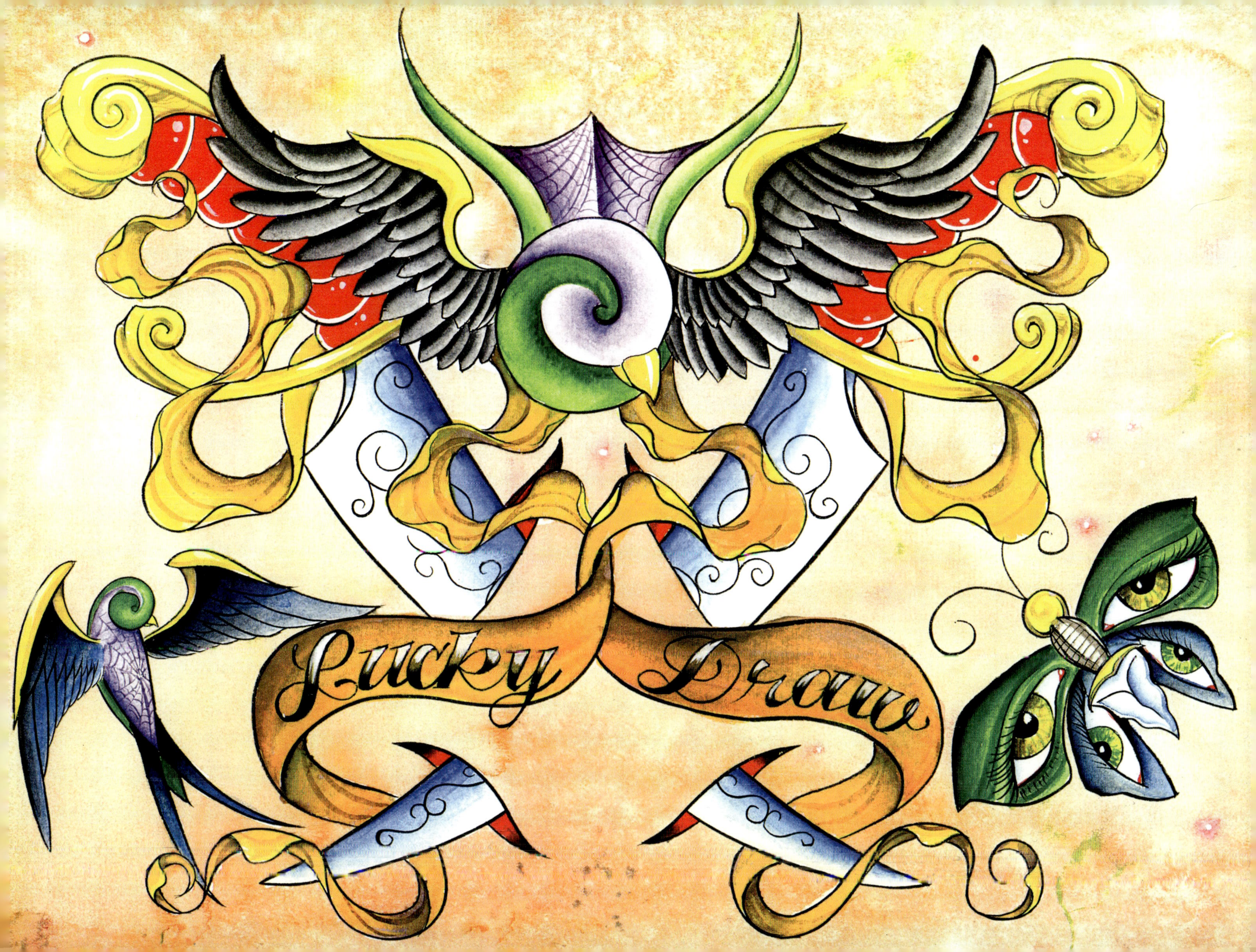
Lucky Draw

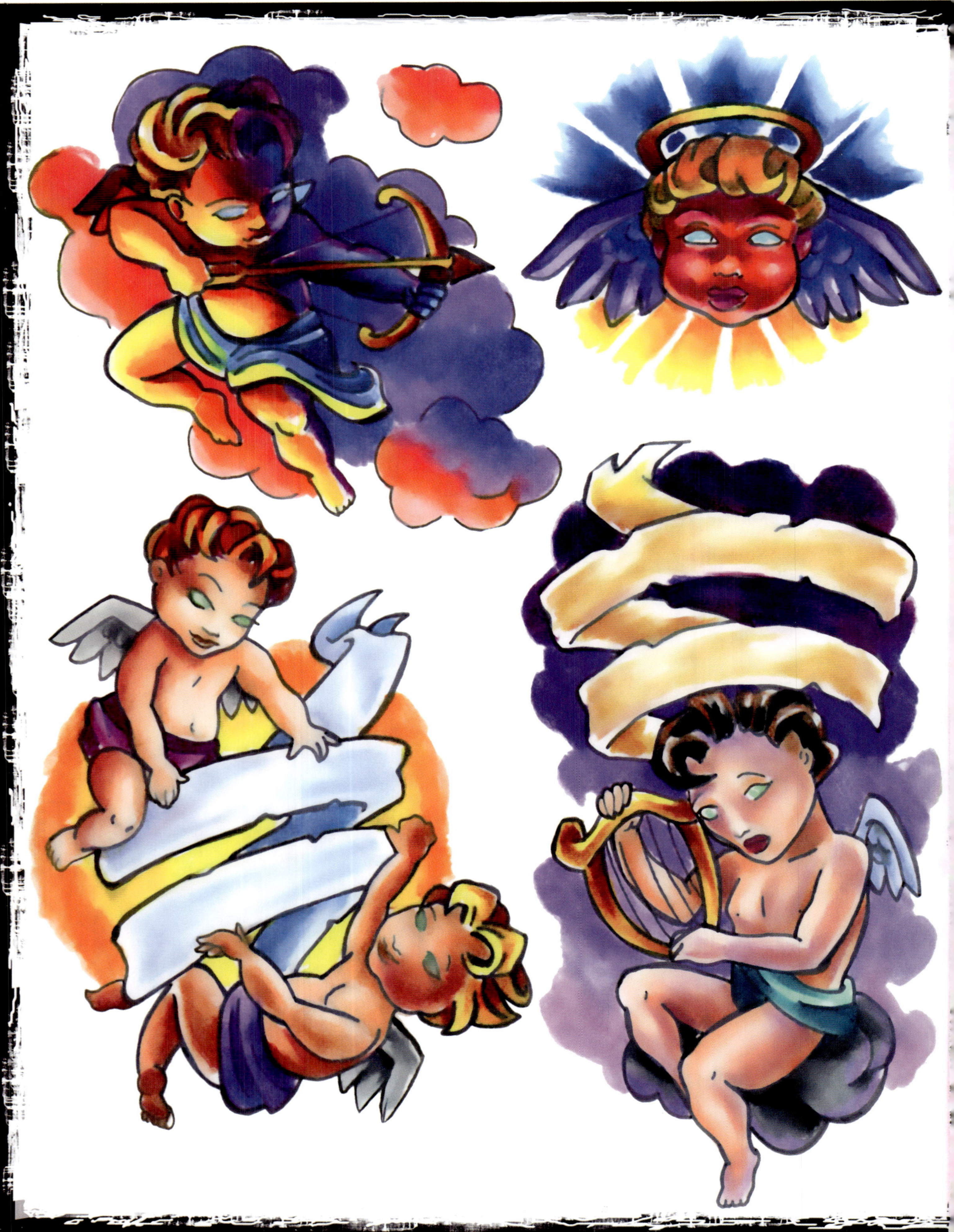

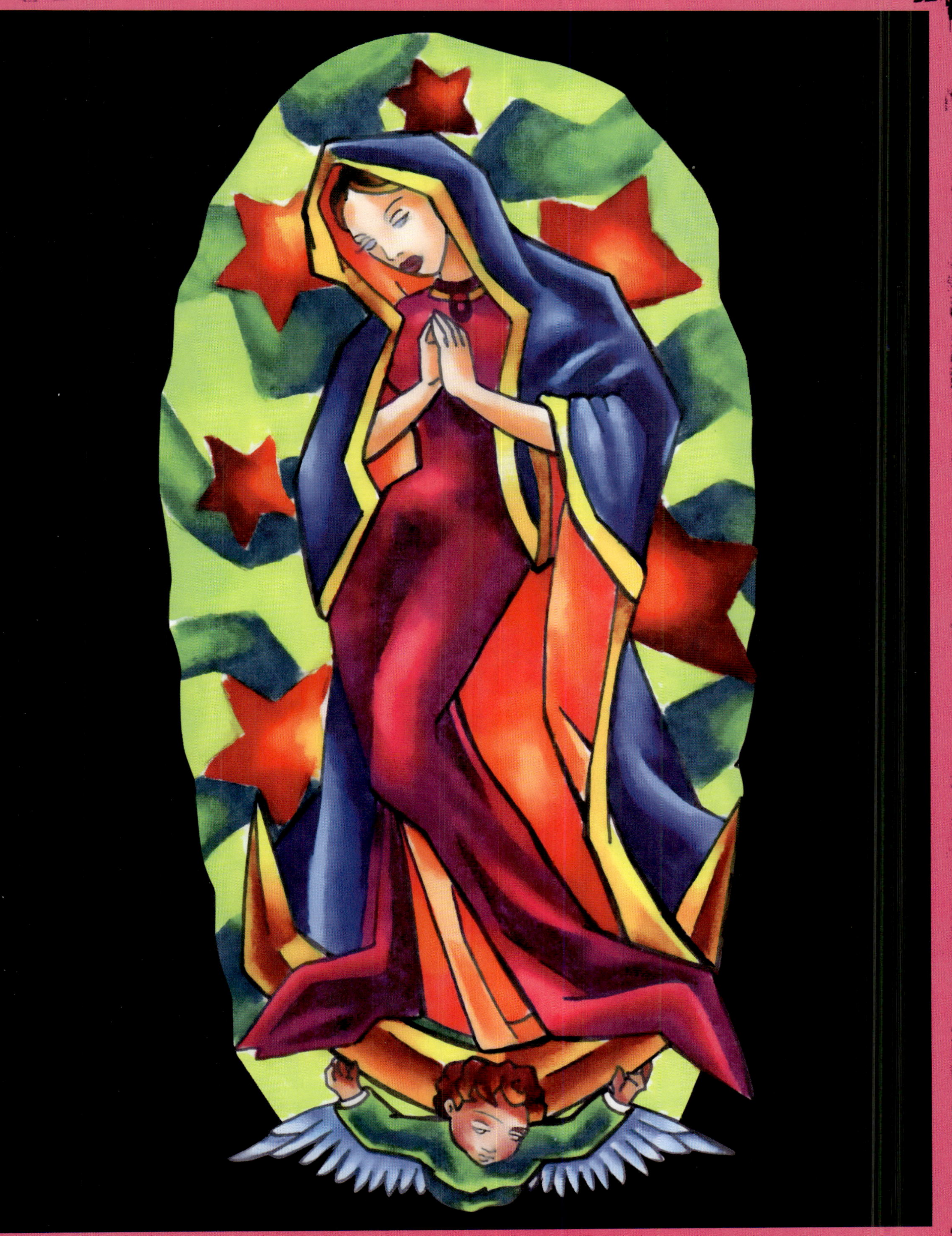

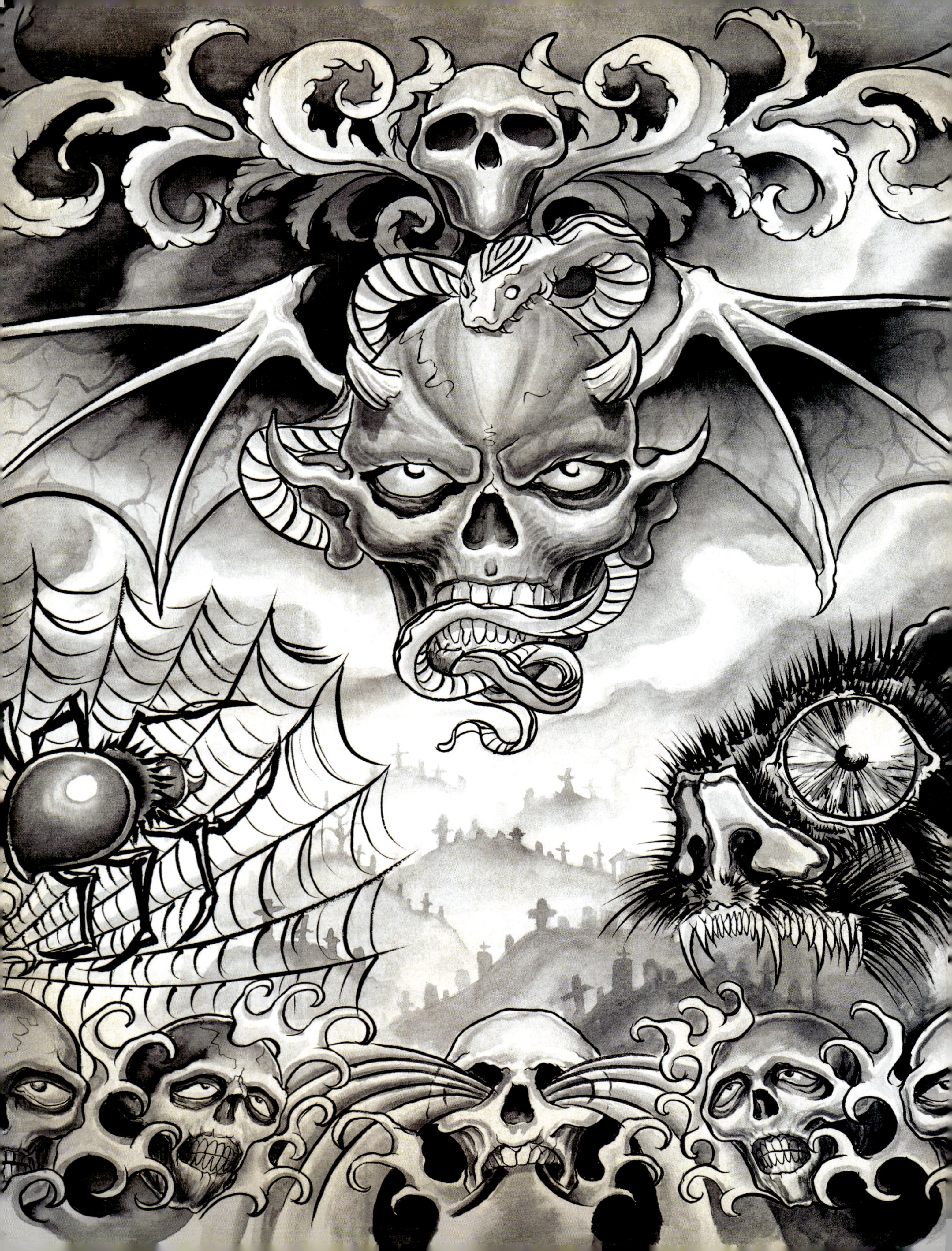

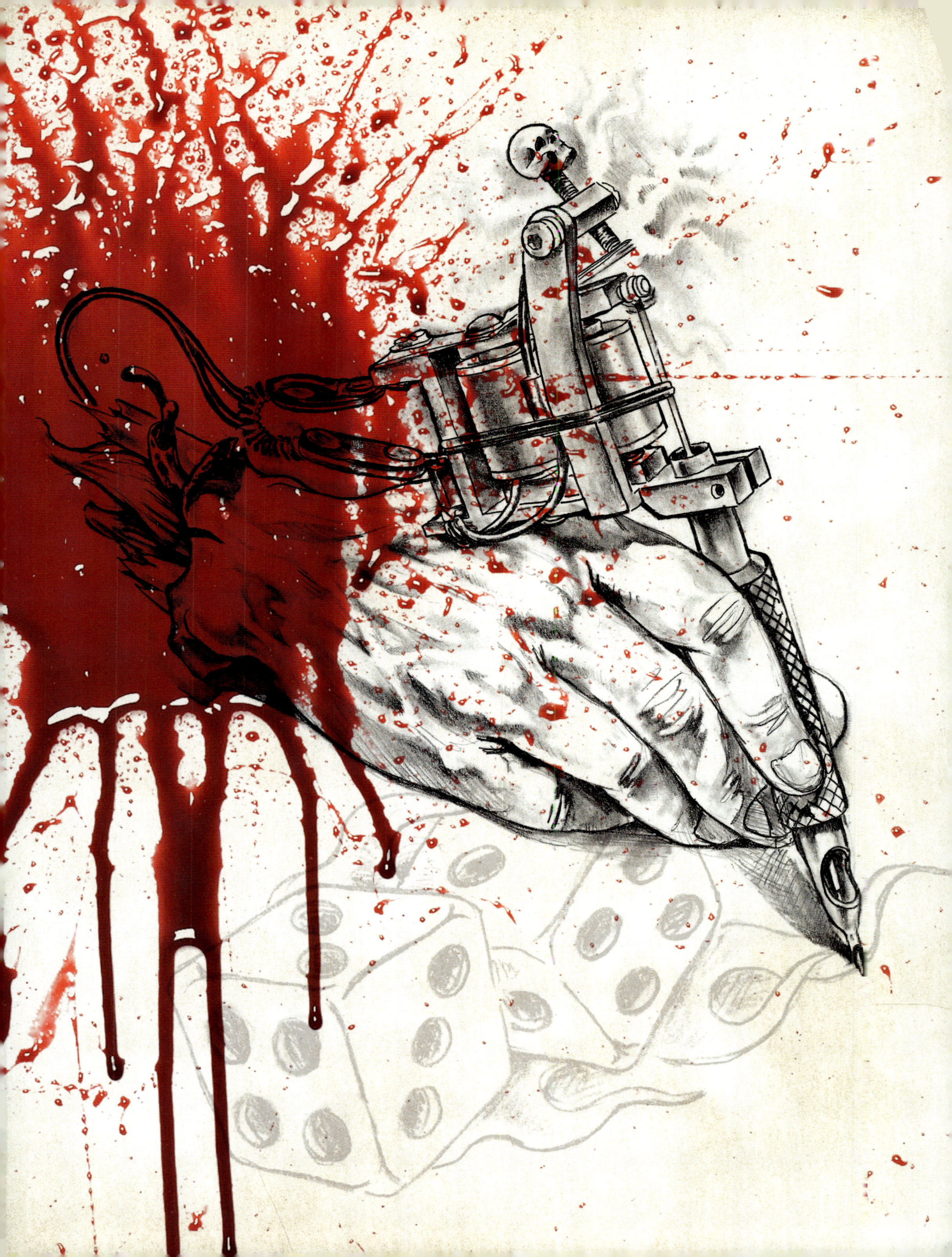

Wolfgang Books On The Web

http://www.wolfpub.com

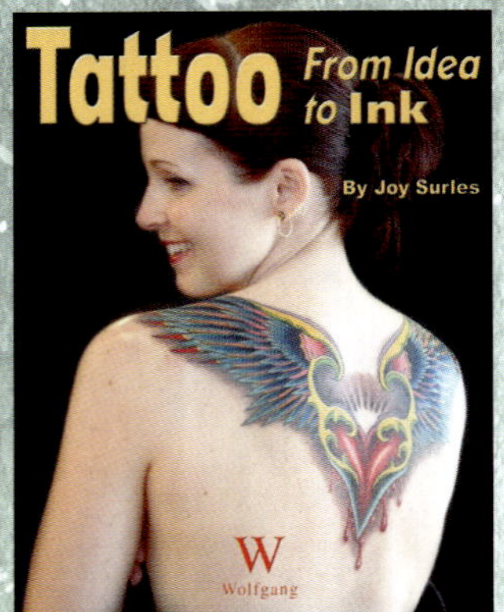

TATTOO - FROM IDEA TO INK

Tattoo: From Idea To Ink traces the origin of a tattoo from its initial inception through the process of design and finally implementation in the hands of talented artists like Amanda Wachob of Blue Moon Tattoo in Buffalo, New York. With an abundance of colorful images and insightful text, this book provides a first-hand look at the stages a custom client experiences in getting the tattoo of his or her dreams. From understanding this process and reviewing the different styles of art available, Tattoo: From Idea to Ink, offers artwork, artists, and suggestions for anyone looking for that perfect piece of art. In addition to a full section filled with original artwork from master tattooists, the book features work by industry legends like Brandon Bond, Sarah Peacock, Zsolt Sarkozi, Shannon Schober, Mario Desa, Corey Rogers, Josh Woods, Nate Beavers, and many more.

Eleven Chapters | 144 Pages | $27.95 | Over 400 photos, 100% color

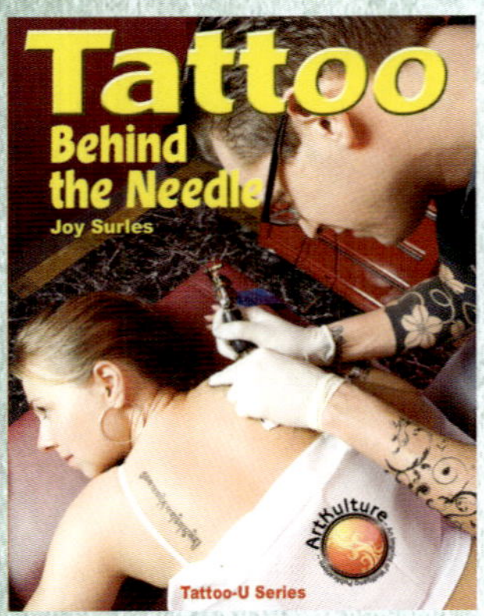

TATTOO BEHIND THE NEEDLE

Tattoo – Behind the Needle, takes the reader into the shop of 11 talented young tattoo artists. This is an opportunity to learn how and where each artist learned his or her skills, who they turn to for inspiration, and exactly how they create bright, colorful, living tattoos.

Behind the Needle includes interviews with well-known artists like Brandon Bond, Amanda Wachob and Shannon Schober. Each has a distinctive style, a unique philosophy, and a very personal approach to tattoo art.

Author Joy Surles gives each artist one chapter to explain who they are and what they do. A series of photographs illustrate and compliment what words cannot.

Eleven Chapters | 144 Pages | $27.95 | Over 500 photos, 100% color

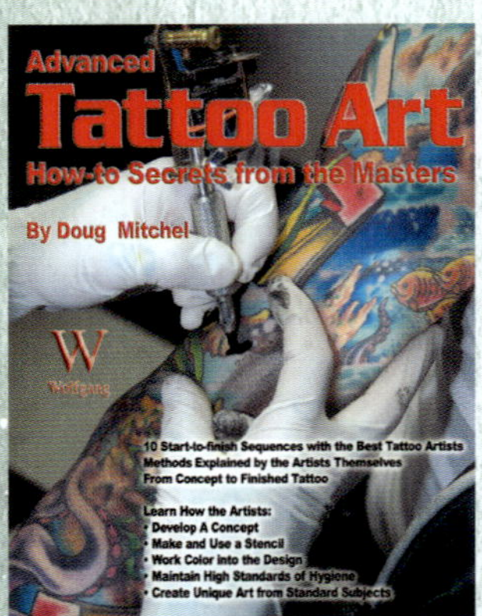

ADVANCED TATTOO ART

The art of the tattoo has emerged from the garage to the parlor, from the local bar to the boardroom. With interest in tattoos at a high point, the time is right for a detailed look at the art, and the artists, who create the elaborate designs.

Doug Mitchel take the reader inside the shops of ten well-known and very experienced artists spread across the country. Both a how-to book and a photo-intense look the world or tattoos; Tattoo Art includes interviews with the artists that explain not only how they do what they do, but also their personal preference for materials and methods.

Detailed photo sequences follow each artist through a tattoo project. From customer concept, to sketch, outline, and the finished colorful design. The chapters document not only the techniques, but also the inks and tools used during each step of the process

Ten Chapters | 144 Pages | $27.95 | Over 400 photos, 100% color

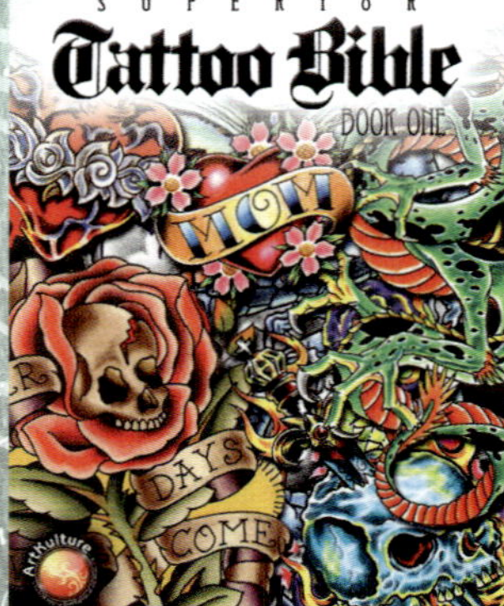

TATTOO BIBLE - BOOK ONE

Whether you are preparing for your first tattoo or your twenty-seventh, you need artwork and designs that are just-right. Tattoo Bible, authored by Superior Tattoo, provides well over 500 pieces of unique flash art - flash never before compiled into one single book.

While most tattoo books available today concentrate on one specific genre, this Tattoo Bible covers many different genres and the ideas are endless. This is not just a book to add to your collection - this is your collection. You can combine different pieces of art from within the book, or just take them as is. This book is for you and your imagination to do with as you wish.

Tattoo Bible is filled with images that are both striking and very useful to both the tattoo shop, and the tattoo aficionado.

Eleven Chapters | 144 Pages | $27.95 | Over 500 photos, 100% color

Wolfgang Publication Titles

For a current list visit our website at www.wolfpub.com

ILLUSTRATED HISTORY
Triumph Motorcycles $32.95

BIKER BASICS
Sheet Metal Fabrication $27.95
How to FIX American V-Twin MC $27.95

COMPOSITE GARAGE
Composite Materials $27.95

HOP-UP EXPERT
How to Hop & Customize Your Bagger $27.95
How to Hop & Customize Your Softail $27.95

OLD SKOOL SKILLS
Barris: Grilles,Scoops, Fins and Frenching (Vol. 2) $24.95
Barris: Flames Scallops, Paneling and Striping (Vol. 4) $24.95

HOT ROD BASICS
How to Air Condition Your Hot Rod $27.95
How to Chop Tops $24.95
How to Wire your Hot Rod $27.95

MOTORCYCLE RESTORATION SERIES
Triumph Restoration - Unit 650cc $29.95
Triumph MC Restoration Pre-Unit $29.95
Harley-Davidson Panhead Restoration $34.95

AIR SKOOL SKILLS
How Airbrushes Work $27.95
How to Airbrush Pin-Ups $27.95
Air Brushing 101 $27.95
Airbrush Bible $27.95

PAINT EXPERT
Adv. Custom Motorcycle Painting $27.95
Advanced Airbrush Art $27.95
Advanced Custom Painting Techniques $27.95
Advanced Pinstripe Art $27.95
Kustom Painting Secrets $19.95
Custom Paint & Graphics $27.95
Pro Airbrush Techniques $27.95

SHEET METAL
Advanced Sheet Metal Fabrication $27.95
Ultimate Sheet Metal Fabrication $24.95

CUSTOM BUILDER SERIES
Adv Custom Motorcycle Wiring $27.95
Adv Custom Motorcycle Assembly & Fabrication $27.95
Adv. Custom Motorcycle Chassis $27.95
How to Build a Cheap Chopper $27.95
How to Build a Chopper $27.95

TATTOO U Series
Body Painting $27.95
Tattoo- From Idea to Ink $27.95
Tattoos Behind the Needle $27.95
Advanced Tattoo Art $27.95
Tattoo Bible Book One $27.95
Tattoo Bible Book Two $27.95

HOME SHOP
How to Paint Tractors & Trucks $27.95

NOTEWORTHY
Guitar Building Basics
Acoustic Assembly at Home $27.95

Superior Tattoo Biography

We at Superior Tattoo Equipment, Inc. are proud to be the leading supplier of equipment and supplies in the industry. We strive to provide the best equipment, supplies, designs, and assistance to our customers. This means that our Research and Development department is creating and improving products all the time. Within the last year alone, we have introduced over 100 new products. Check our website often and look for the new products button; it's located on the home page.

By updating our website daily with new products and sales we set ourselves apart from our competitors. We brought the process in house to allow us to make changes in real time. We have streamlined our order process and our company to react quickly. There is no other company that can take an order and ship faster. What this means is that, in many cases, if an order is placed at 4:45pm we can still ship it out the same day. In fact, we guarantee if it is placed by 4:00pm it will go out the same day. In Arizona, six months of the year 4:00pm is 7:00pm EST, and 6:00pm EST the remainder of the year. We take orders 24 hours a day, 365 days a year.

We have contracted with several professional companies like Sullen Clothing, and with new companies like M.O.B. Irons to provide you with the best products that are out there. Stencil Magic is a good example, the reviews on this product are amazing. Stencil Magic is second to none when it comes to keeping the stencil on during the entire tattooing process. There is no need to re-apply or extend your outline with a marker. You can try it in a one ounce size to prove it to yourself.

Although many of our competitors have increased prices over the last several months we have been maintaining, or even lowering, prices on many products. As we move forward we are developing new products that will help artists perform the best they can for their clients. Please visit superiortattoo.com for the latest in the materials you need.

PS: There are companies popping up all the time. They are even trying to use our good name. Please make sure you stay with the original Superior Tattoo Equipment, Inc.

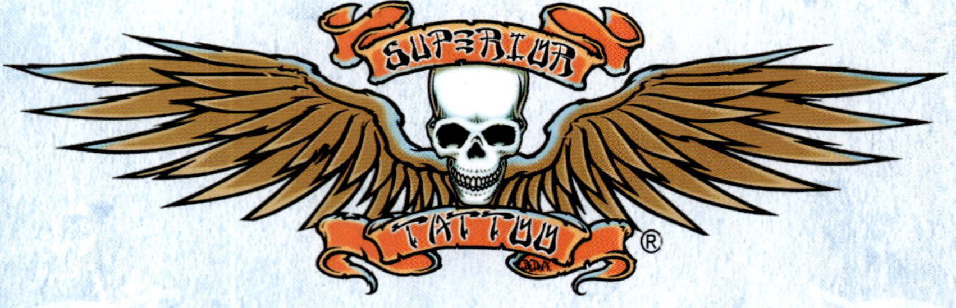

www.superiortattoo.com

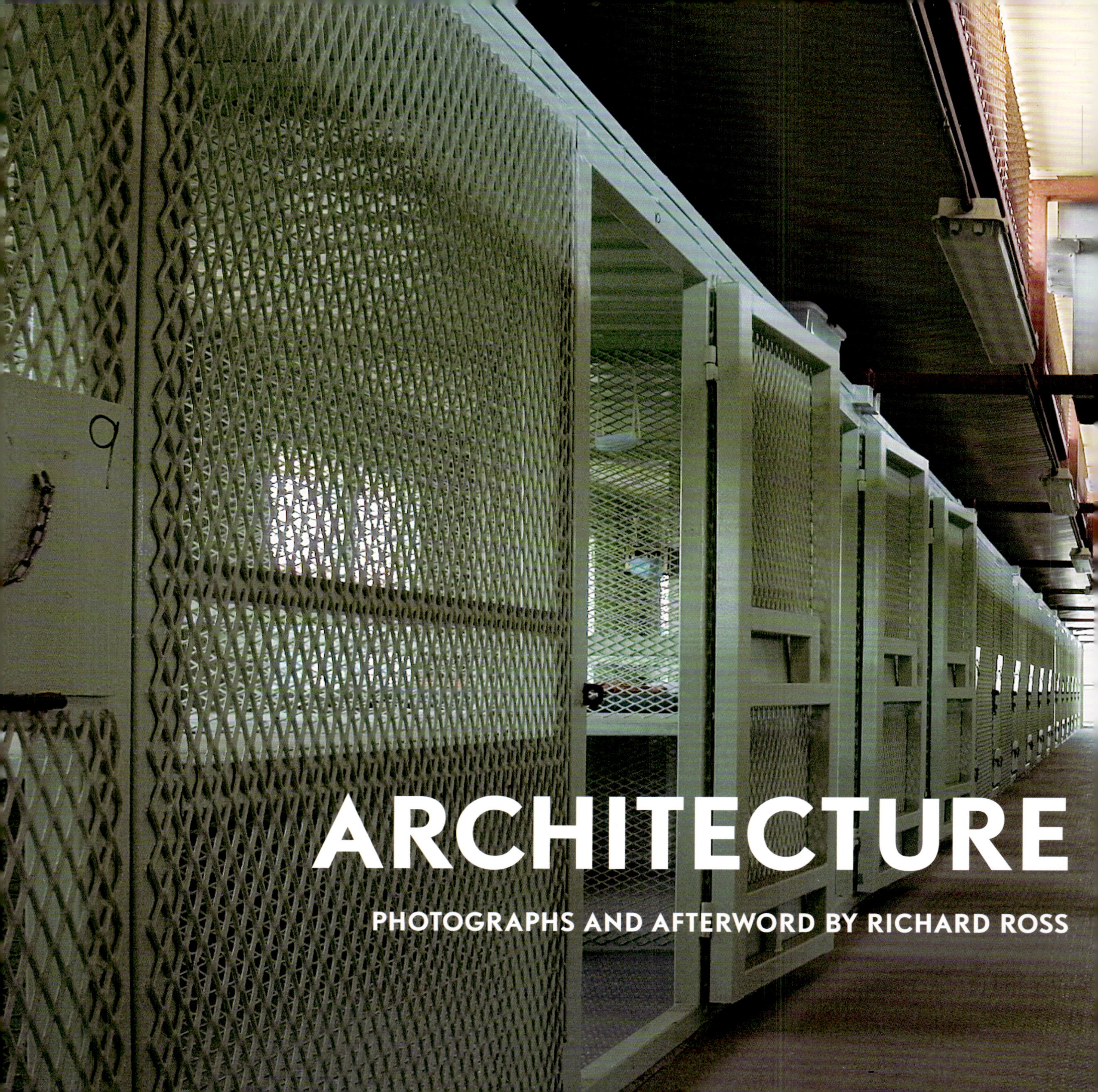

ARCHITECTURE

PHOTOGRAPHS AND AFTERWORD BY RICHARD ROSS

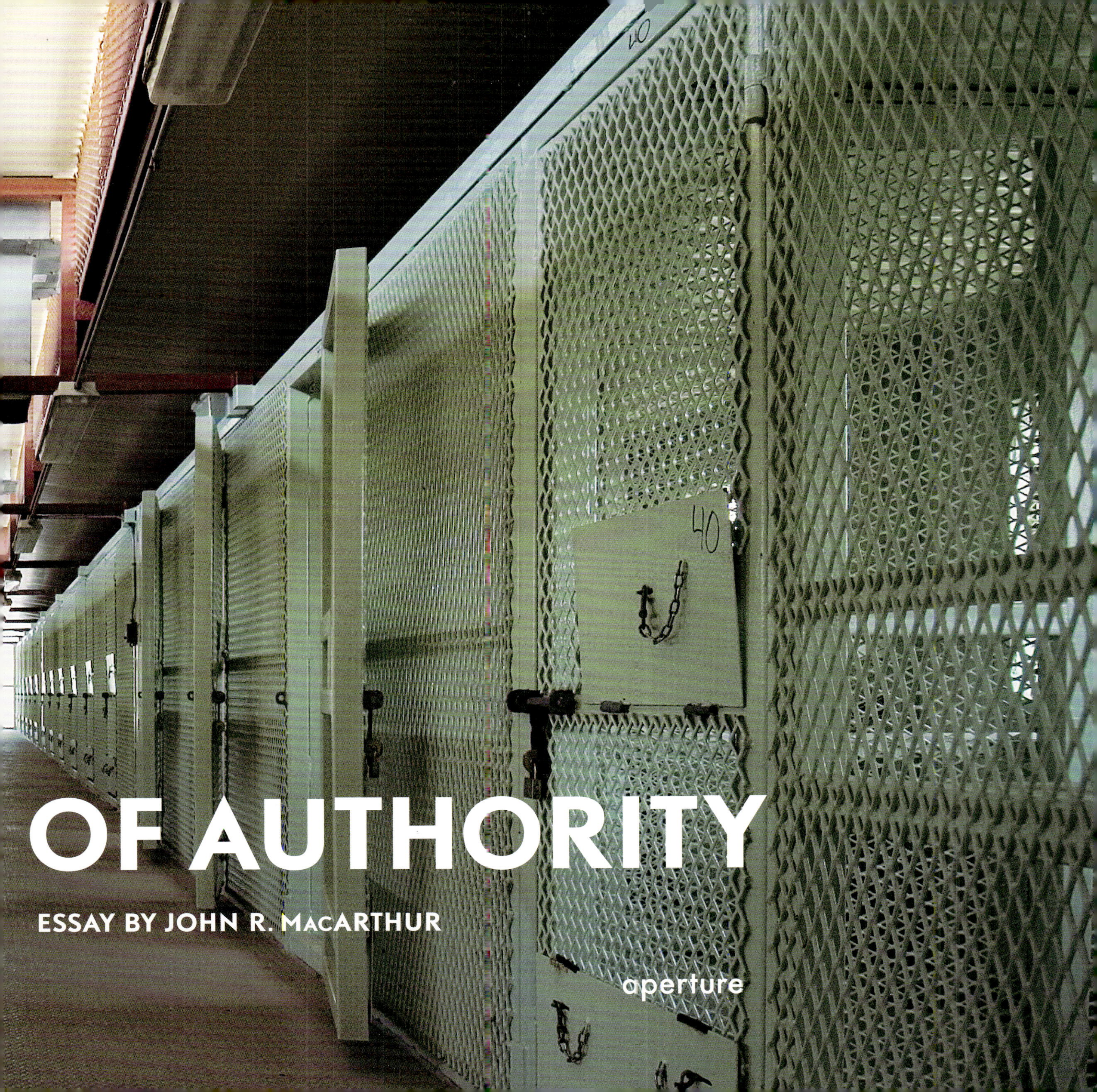

OF AUTHORITY

ESSAY BY JOHN R. MACARTHUR

aperture

To Josef K.

FRONT COVER: Isolation room ("rubber room"), U.S. Customs and Border Protection, San Ysidro, California
BACK COVER: Office of Assistant Principal for Attendance and Discipline, Santa Barbara High School, Santa Barbara, California
HALF-TITLE PAGE: Holding-cell slot, Metropolitan Police, Collingwood Road, Hillingdon, London
TITLE PAGE: Holding cells, Joint Task Force, Guantánamo, Cuba
OPPOSITE: Citadel, Aleppo, Syria

Editor: Nancy Grubb
Designer: Laura Lindgren
Production: Matthew Pimm

The staff for this book at Aperture Foundation includes:
Ellen S. Harris, *Chief Executive Officer*; Michael Culoso, *Director of Finance and Administration*;
Lesley A. Martin, *Executive Editor, Books*; Susan Ciccotti, *Production Editor*; Sarah Henry, *Production Manager*;
Andrea Smith, *Director of Communications*; Kristian Orozco, *Director of Sales and Foreign Rights*;
Diana Edkins, *Director of Exhibitions and Limited-Edition Photographs*;
Catherine Archias, Laura Cooke, and Julie Pilato, *Work Scholars*

This project was made possible, in part, with generous support from Lannan Foundation.

First edition
Printed in Hong Kong
10 9 8 7 6 5 4 3 2 1

Library of Congress Control Number: 2007900666
ISBN 978-1-59711-052-5

Aperture Foundation books are available
in North America through:
D.A.P./Distributed Art Publishers
155 Sixth Avenue, 2nd Floor
New York, N.Y. 10013
Phone: (212) 627-1999
Fax: (212) 627-9484

Aperture Foundation books are distributed
outside North America by:
Thames & Hudson
181A High Holborn
London WC1V 7QX
United Kingdom
Phone: + 44 20 7845 5000
Fax: + 44 20 7845 5055
Email: sales@thameshudson.co.uk

aperturefoundation
547 West 27th Street
New York, N.Y. 10001
www.aperture.org

The purpose of Aperture Foundation, a non-profit organization, is to advance photography
in all its forms and to foster the exchange of ideas among audiences worldwide.

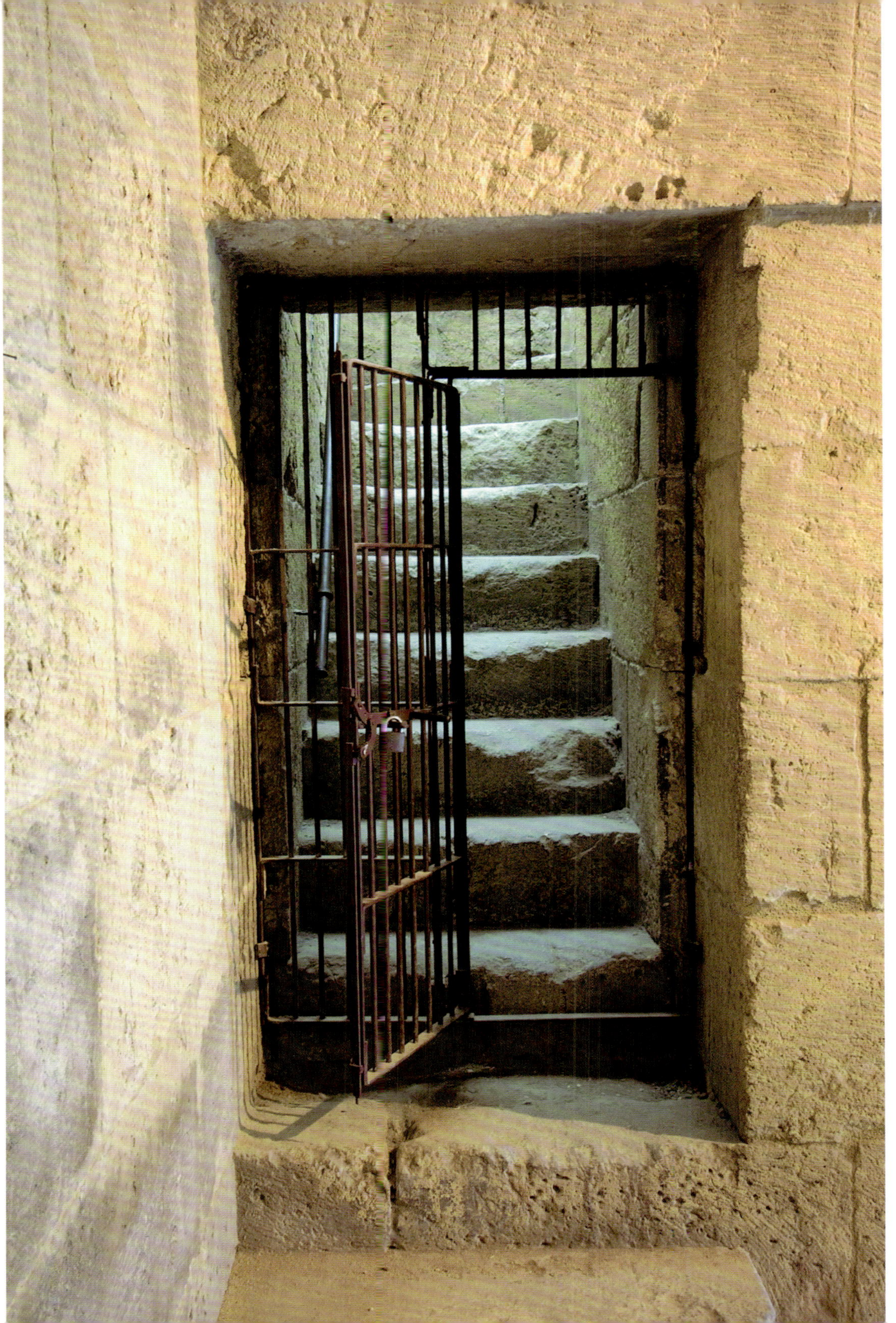

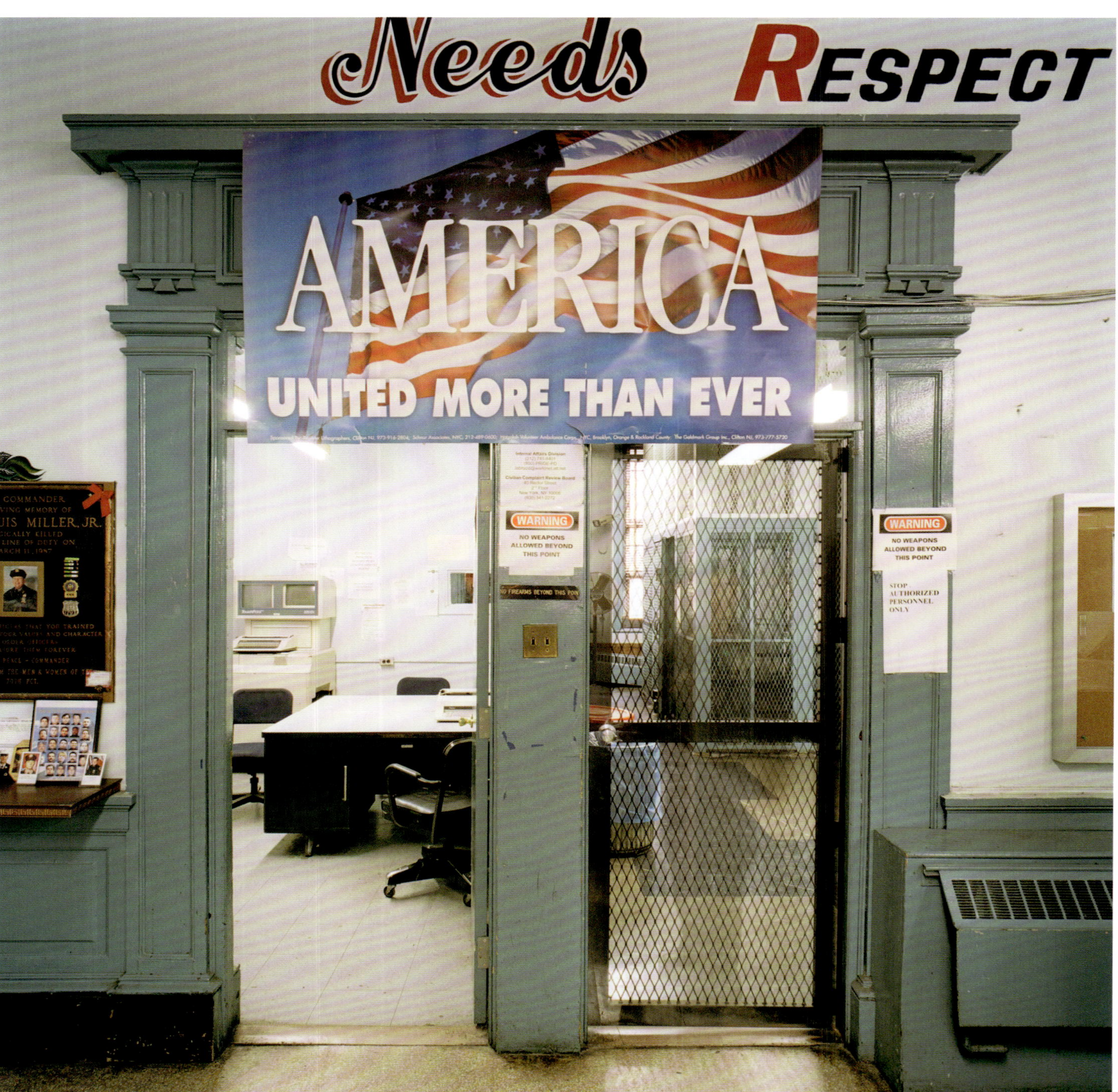
Needs RESPECT
AMERICA
UNITED MORE THAN EVER
WARNING
NO WEAPONS ALLOWED BEYOND THIS POINT
WARNING
NO WEAPONS ALLOWED BEYOND THIS POINT
STOP AUTHORIZED PERSONNEL ONLY
COMMANDER

BROOKLYN TO BAGHDAD

John R. MacArthur

Rigid political analysis tends to suffocate art. I once asked the eminent critic Alfred Kazin what he regarded as the greatest threat to literature. I thought he might single out something obvious, like television or consumerism, but he answered simply: "the ideologists." Which of course isn't to say that great art can't be mainly political. Picasso painted the iconically antifascist and antiwar *Guernica* and famously refused to return the painting or himself to Spain as long as Francisco Franco remained in power. He wanted, he said, to "express my abhorrence of the military caste which has sunk Spain in an ocean of pain and death." Indeed, *Guernica* remains so politically threatening to authority that even a tapestry reproduction of the painting hanging outside the United Nations Security Council Chamber was covered up in February 2003—evidently so that TV cameras wouldn't relay the abstracted images of pain and death to millions of people around the world while Colin Powell promoted the fraudulent case for war against Iraq.

Nevertheless, I wouldn't call Picasso a political artist or *Guernica* an entirely political statement. As Arthur Danto writes, *Guernica* is "a Cubist work that can serve a purely decorative function if one is unaware of its meaning." And, in any event, we should be cautious about taking an artist's words at face value when we consider his politics or his oeuvre. The self-exiled Spaniard may well have declined to revisit his authoritarian homeland on principle, but he seems to have had little difficulty returning to Nazi-occupied Paris.

So when I study the photographs that make up Richard Ross's *Architecture of Authority*, I find myself struggling to evaluate the harsh political meaning versus the gentler artistic content, just as I do with *Guernica*. I don't mean to be ironic. However menacing Ross's images may be, there is an appreciation of beauty and a clear personal aesthetic running through them, whether they are drop-dead frightening, chicly sinister (like the postmodern pat-down room at LAX), or even occasionally elegant and inspiring. On this softer side, I happen to love the Scandinavian interior design of the United Nations, the "Workshop for Peace" that has so often been subverted by the realpolitik of the great powers. Ross's elegiac depiction of the empty Security Council Chamber, designed by the Norwegian Arnstein Arneberg, restores faith in a stunning, if tarnished, emblem of universal moral authority. The very opposite of sinister, this image evokes a forceful optimism that might yet sweep the world if only the member nations truly believed in the ideals of the UN (not to mention the message of the *Guernica* tapestry).

Seventieth Precinct house, New York Police Department, Brooklyn

Likewise, the lovely Spanish Colonial–accented Santa Barbara Superior Court (in Ross's adopted hometown) and its carpeted jury box fill me with hope that equal justice under law is more than just a slogan. And I feel raised up by the scales of justice, not weighed down, when I contemplate the cheerful design of the law courts in Göteborg, Sweden—a parquet-floored enclosure that could double as the reception area of a comfortable country inn. Like the Security Council Chamber, this courtroom murmurs fairness and equity for all. If I ever commit a crime, I hope it's in Santa Barbara or Göteborg.

More surprising, perhaps, is Ross's picture of the spacious, light-filled Blue Mosque in Istanbul, built before the European Enlightenment. Such an image raises the happy possibility of Western rapprochement with militant Islam, because you can't look at Ross's rendering of this soaring seventeenth-century interior and believe that the Taliban and al-Qaeda are the only forces to be reckoned with in the Muslim world. It's no wonder Pope Benedict XVI chose the Blue Mosque for his grand gesture of reconciliation, in November 2006, with Turkish Muslims outraged by his remarks linking Islam and violence. Not that Ross gives official Islam a free pass. His image of the female prayer area in a Syrian mosque astutely represents the vast veil of orthodoxy that covers so much of Middle Eastern womankind. Already hidden (to a large degree) in plain sight on the street, the devout daughters of Homs find themselves hidden altogether in their local house of worship, whether they consent to it in principle or not.

These mostly edifying pictures are about what might be viewed as softer, more legitimate authority. But what provoked Ross to do this book was his horror at the sudden rise of hard, illegitimate authority in America, the abrupt lane change in our political culture that took place after 9/11. This self-righteous, vindictive, and reckless divergence by the Bush administration was aimed at justifying actions at once unconstitutional and shameful: torture, the suspension of habeas corpus, "preemptive" invasions, and bald-faced lying to Congress, the American people, and the world. I'm a skeptic by nature, but talking with Richard Ross for any length of time makes it impossible to doubt his political sincerity and his outrage over the transformation of America into a country that practices waterboarding in the name of liberty. "The United States," says Ross, "is not America anymore."

Thus, his photographs of the "new" Abu Ghraib prison in Iraq (near the old Abu Ghraib) are devastating, and unique: these are the first publicly available pictures of the outdoor "segregation boxes" reserved for inmates who misbehave. Ross had to do some fast talking with the U.S. military to shoot these "bear cages," as he calls them. ("I don't get why they allowed me to take those pictures—because to me it seems like such an indictment.") I suspect that readers will be horrified by the crude structures with their fabric coverings held down by sandbags, as well as by their cruelly small dimensions. According to Lt. Kristy Miller, infractions punishable by segregation in these boxes include "talking between compounds, throwing 'rock notes' between compounds, failure to obey guard orders, failing to appear for head count, failing to obey curfew, and fighting." Not to worry, says Lt. Miller—nobody has to stay in the box for more than twelve hours, and they're "kept out of direct sunlight and provided with plenty of food and water."

Even more disturbing, to my mind, are the two photos—exterior and interior—of Cell 101 at Camp 5, the high-security wing of the U.S. prison at Guantánamo, Cuba. Antiseptically denuded of almost anything human save the trademark orange jumpsuit, a copy of the Koran, and a pair of thongs, Cell 101 looks like a fate worse than Abu Ghraib, where at least a prisoner might plausibly dream of a jail break or manage to bribe a guard for some contraband. According to Joseph Margulies, a lawyer representing Guantánamo detainees, congressional delegations and the media never see Camp 5, "where prisoners spend more than twenty-three hours a day in solitary confinement."

But there's much more underlying this panorama of authoritarian imagery than simple anger about constitutional America gone awry. I suppose if Ross had enrolled in law school the way he planned (the way his parents expected), he might be representing Guantánamo inmates today in federal court. But whatever good he might have done as a lawyer, we're fortunate that the artist in Ross got the upper hand. In the late summer of 1967, while he was cruising from New York to Washington at the wheel of his green Triumph TR-4A on the way to his first year at Georgetown, it suddenly became clear to Ross that law school wasn't going to work. So he made a U-turn on the New Jersey Turnpike and set out on a path of inquiry that eventually led to a camera instead of a courtroom.

Intuition drives a good photographer. Having grown up during the Cold War and Vietnam, the son of a none-too-law-abiding Brooklyn policeman, Ross intuitively understands that the aftermath of 9/11 marked not the end of American "innocence," but rather capitulation to a deep craving, common to all nationalities, for submission and control. That awareness, one of the disturbing currents running through Ross's work, is what sets it apart from more objective efforts to document the latest trends in worldwide authoritarianism. A conventional study of government torture produced by, say, Amnesty International records only the surface of authority, no matter how gruesome the descriptions, no matter how ugly the facts.

Beginning with the Montessori circle at his children's school, Ross reminds us that coercion starts young and wears many disguises. A less subtle photographer might have opened with grim images of public school architecture—for who can avoid making the association between the layout typical of a postwar American high school and that of a prison? But that would be too obvious for Richard Ross. The legendary open-classroom approach of the Montessori method is curiously contradicted by the big white circle on the floor. Here, as one Montessori Web site puts it, children will learn the "interdependence of freedom and discipline." Most people who have had preschool kids know about circle time, which often takes place at the end of the day. Circle time can function not only as a summing-up of the day's activities but also as a kind of formal consent by the kids to being in school at all. Ross seems to ask, not without irony: Does the circle have to be literally drawn to make the point about fitting into a system?

No doubt all kinds of potential dissent are smoldering in the blankly severe corridor of Santa Barbara High School (here's Ross making the explicit school/prison analogy), but it's hard to see where students could find a dark corner in which to rebel. And God help the troublemaker. Except for the bulletin board and the absence of handcuffs, the dean of discipline's anteroom is alarmingly reminiscent of the various "interview" rooms depicted by Ross: the Secret Service headquarters in Los Angeles, an interrogation room at Guantánamo, and the grungier robbery and homicide rooms in LA and Oakland, California. No distractions, no ornamentation to relieve the eye while you're thinking about whether to confess or resist. No place to hide.

Contemporary authority is icy cold, say these pictures, as frigid in sunny California as it is outside foggy Scotland Yard, as grim inside the lobby of the Secret Service headquarters in LA as it is approaching the border between Syria and Lebanon. In cool LA we're welcomed by framed photographs of smiling George Bush and Dick Cheney; in Syria, we're confronted by the unsmiling duo of the father and son tyrants, Hafez and Bashar al-Assad. Such national political distinctions tend to blur in the age of "rendition"—just ask Maher Arar, the Syrian-born Canadian who in 2002 was detained at John F. Kennedy Airport in New York, accused of belonging to al-Qaeda, and whisked by U.S. authorities to Syria, where he was tortured on and off for a year before being released without charge. Arar's experience is one reason you don't want to start an argument when you're being led into the military tribunal building at Guantánamo or the interview room at the old Abu Ghraib prison.

What's visually absent from Ross's hard-authority images is likely to be reflexively filled in by the viewer: the possibility of torture—in the interrogation room, in the prison cell, in the corridor in between. As an artist, Ross is principally interested in the style of authority—the way it's presented to both the innocent and the guilty. One hardly ever sees a human figure in his photographs. The empty spaces require you to fill in the blanks, and these blanks make it impossible for an American to avoid thoughts about Lynndie England, Charles Graner, and Sabrina Harmon surveying their *tableaux vivants* of suffering at Abu Ghraib. The amateur cell-phone snapshots of American authority humiliating Arabs in leering triumph cannot be topped, at least not by conventional photojournalism.

And no photojournalist would ever be permitted to capture Abu Ghraib the way it was, or Guantánamo the way it may still be. The government claims that it has halted "stress and duress" and the near-drowning of detainees, and that it has closed the CIA-run "black site" prisons. Abu Ghraib today is allegedly run by Iraqis, not Americans. Whether you believe this or not, you can understand why Ross makes no pretense about presenting his pictures as photojournalism. The really awful stuff has to be left to your imagination.

By taking us on a journey from the LAPD to Abu Ghraib, Ross reminds us that Lynndie and Charles and Sabrina are homegrown products of the USA. Ross's shot of the grimy LAPD interrogation room immediately reminded me of a notorious Chicago police detective named Jon Burge, who in the 1970s and '80s tortured robbery and murder suspects on the city's South Side. He and his subordinates used homemade, hand-cranked electric shocks and, in a sinister prelude to Abu Ghraib, would sometimes place plastic bags over their victims' heads. Burge evidently learned these techniques as a military policeman in Vietnam.

If such behavior was unthinkable during Ross's Flatbush boyhood, it's not because horrible things didn't happen, in jails and elsewhere. After all, lynching remained common in the United States well into the 1940s, and still occurred sporadically during the 1950s. But in 1955—the year Ross's Brooklyn Dodgers (employing Jackie Robinson, Don Newcombe, Jim Gilliam, and Roy Campanella) finally won the World Series; the year Ross refers to, with only partial irony, as the pinnacle of American civilization—you could still believe in progress, you could still believe in the advance of liberalism.

Dad, it's true, was a bagman for the big-time bookmaker Harry Gross. Sidney Rosenstock ("Rosie from the seven-oh") escaped prosecution, but he eventually had to leave the NYPD when the ring was busted and Gross went to jail. But Sidney (he changed the family's last name to Ross in 1955) was no thug—he was a working-class sophisticate of the old-time, public-schooled New York variety. He took Richard to museums all over the city, but most often he dropped him off at the Brooklyn Museum for Saturday-morning art classes before heading to his handball game at nearby Union Temple. These visits had a profound effect on Ross; indeed, his first book, *Museology*, was inspired by those "magical" self-guided tours of the Brooklyn Museum before the lights were even turned on. According to Ross, "a photograph is the illusion of space and time," so the illusory aspects of American-style torture (recall the goofy, play-acting expressions of the Abu Ghraib guards juxtaposed with the obvious suffering of their faceless victims) might well appeal to him.

As Ross told me over the din of a noisy restaurant in Chelsea (a Flatbush childhood trains you to be heard in a crowd), his approach to photography is "about showing you an idea and saying, What do you think? This is Abu Ghraib, these are four cells in the middle of the desert; what the fuck is this about?" Well, for starters, I think it's about Ross's upbringing. "My father was the authority figure and the hero." That Sidney the father was for some years a small-time criminal only serves to underscore the depth of insight provided by Richard the son. Richard slips in his nostalgic shot of Brooklyn's old-fashioned Seventieth Precinct house not only to show us where his father worked in the 1940s and '50s but also to make a larger point. On the door is a sign announcing "Crime Prevention," and on the blackboard is a crudely drawn Christmas tree with the handwritten observation, "4 paychecks left until Christmas." What's going on here? Given that Sidney helped support his large extended family with graft, this photo might be taken as ironic. But think a bit more, and you may recall something dreadful: the Seventieth Precinct house was also the place where, in August 1997, a Haitian immigrant named Abner Louima was sodomized with a broom handle by a police officer named Justin Volpe.

The point is clear. In the 1950s, America was not a state that officially practiced torture, either in the Seventieth Precinct or on the battlefields of Korea. Torture was something the bad guys did to Americans. By the 1960s, the covert CIA assassination program known as Phoenix was torturing and killing thousands of Vietcong guerrillas. But American soldiers arriving in Vietnam were still instructed in the rules of the Geneva Conventions and handed a card titled "The Enemy in Your Hands." It said, in part: "YOU CANNOT AND MUST NOT MISTREAT YOUR PRISONER HUMILIATE OR DEGRADE HIM TAKE ANY OF HIS PERSONAL EFFECTS WHICH DO NOT HAVE SIGNIFICANT MILITARY VALUE.... ALWAYS TREAT YOUR PRISONER HUMANELY." Three decades later, Justin Volpe broke a code of conduct respected by dishonest and honest cops alike, as well as by the great majority of soldiers in Vietnam. By 2003 the Volpes and the Burges were running Abu Ghraib, Guantánamo, and the prison at Bagram Air Force Base, Afghanistan, with bad-guy brutality. I just can't imagine Sidney Rosenstock at Abu Ghraib.

In 1958, commenting on French torture of Algerian rebels and their French sympathizers, Jean-Paul Sartre contended that the torturers "do not look at themselves very closely." Their goal, he said, "is to make the prisoner feel that he does not belong to the same species: therefore they are undressed, they are beaten, they are mocked; soldiers come and go, proffering insults and threats with a nonchalance which they want to make as terrible as possible."

Under the new rules of American justice, an "enemy combatant"—whether he's Maher Arar or Badarzaman Badar (an Afghan who was released after three years in Gitmo and no trial)—is guilty until proven innocent. Since this juridical approach is more medieval (or 1950s French) than American, Ross's picture of the crusader fort in Syria aptly returns us to another era of spectacular barbarism. We can only imagine the hand-to-hand carnage of Christian-Muslim combat then and now, since the self-censoring U.S. media decline to publish or broadcast the unfiltered gore of modern conflict. This, once again, is why it's appropriate that we see virtually no people in Ross's photographs. Whether intentionally or not, he is underscoring the unpardonable embargo on graphic violence in post–9/11 America. Other than the Abu Ghraib snapshots and the amateur video of Saddam's hanging, the U.S. public rarely witnesses the consequences of what the new American authoritarianism has wrought. And the GIs billeted at Camp Victory in Iraq (see Ross's remarkable photograph of one of their tents at night, p. 123) can't watch the cascade of blood and gore routinely shown on Al Jazeera TV, even though they are surrounded by millions of hostile Arabs who can and do watch it.

In his essay in the *Nation* about Fernando Botero's Abu Ghraib paintings, which he calls "masterpieces of disturbatory art," Arthur Danto makes a risky declaration: "Photographs can only show what is visible; what Susan Sontag memorably called the 'pain of others' lies outside their reach. But it can be conveyed in painting…for the limits of photography are not the limits of painting." Danto was referring to the "notorious" Abu Ghraib snapshots, but he hadn't seen Ross's Cell 101 at Guantánamo or the segregation boxes at Abu Ghraib. He hadn't seen the row of metal-frame bunks in the Marine Corps Recruit Depot juxtaposed with the row of metal-frame beds in the Cuban mental institution and the rows of metal-frame beds at Los Prietos Boys' Camp in Santa Barbara.

Danto also hadn't benefited from what I consider Ross's most powerful photograph in this series: the communal room at the maximum security Pelican Bay State Prison in California. A better description might be the "communal pit," but it does remind me of ordinary public playground equipment, a school lunchroom, a gymnasium, even the promenade of Philip Johnson's New York State Theater at Lincoln Center. Stare at the Pelican Bay photograph for a while, and you begin to realize there's almost nothing civic, nothing uplifting, about either contemporary public architecture or the contemporary public mood.

So we're not surprised when Ross guides us, at the end of this book, to the lethal-injection room at another notorious prison, the Angola State Penitentiary in Louisiana. I think Danto is wrong; the "pain of others" is very much in evidence in this room, where the government makes believe it can kill people painlessly. This too is disturbatory art of great magnitude—inspired by Americans, working right here in America. If you feel guilty about what we've created, consider Ross's penultimate image, then think about calling the governor on the red phone and asking for a pardon.

Toddler classroom, Montessori Center School, Goleta, California

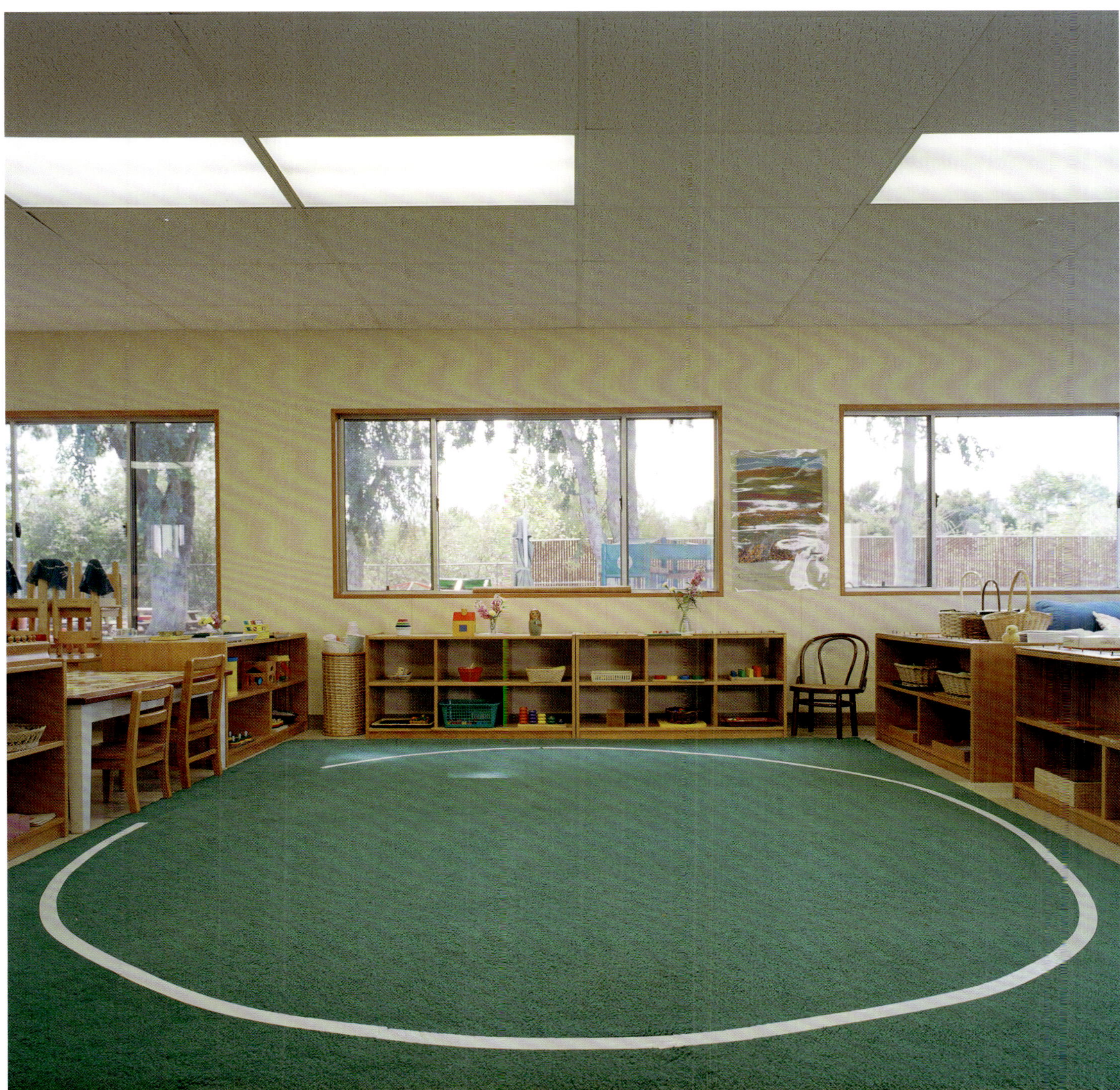

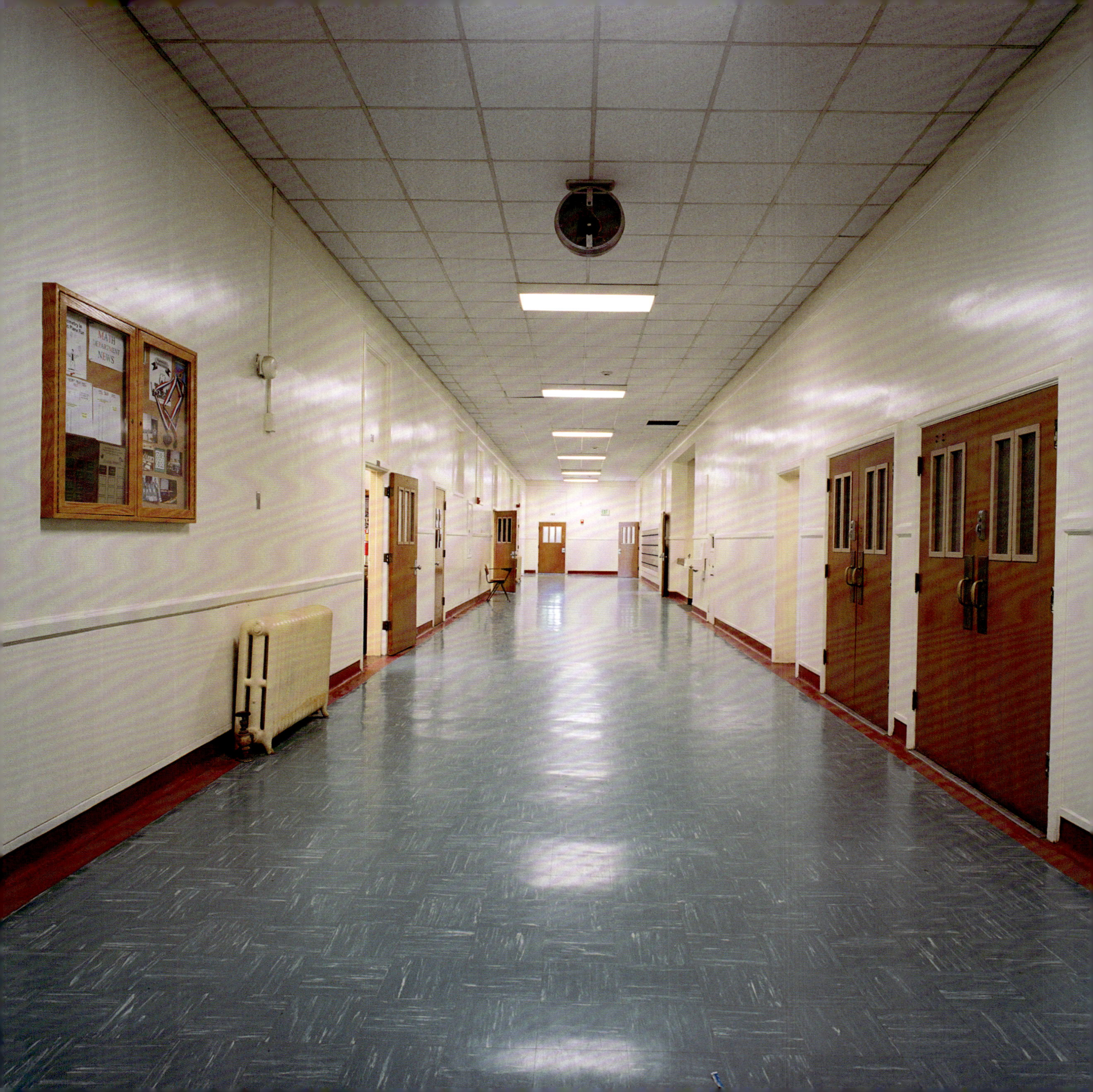
MATH
DEPARTMENT
NEWS

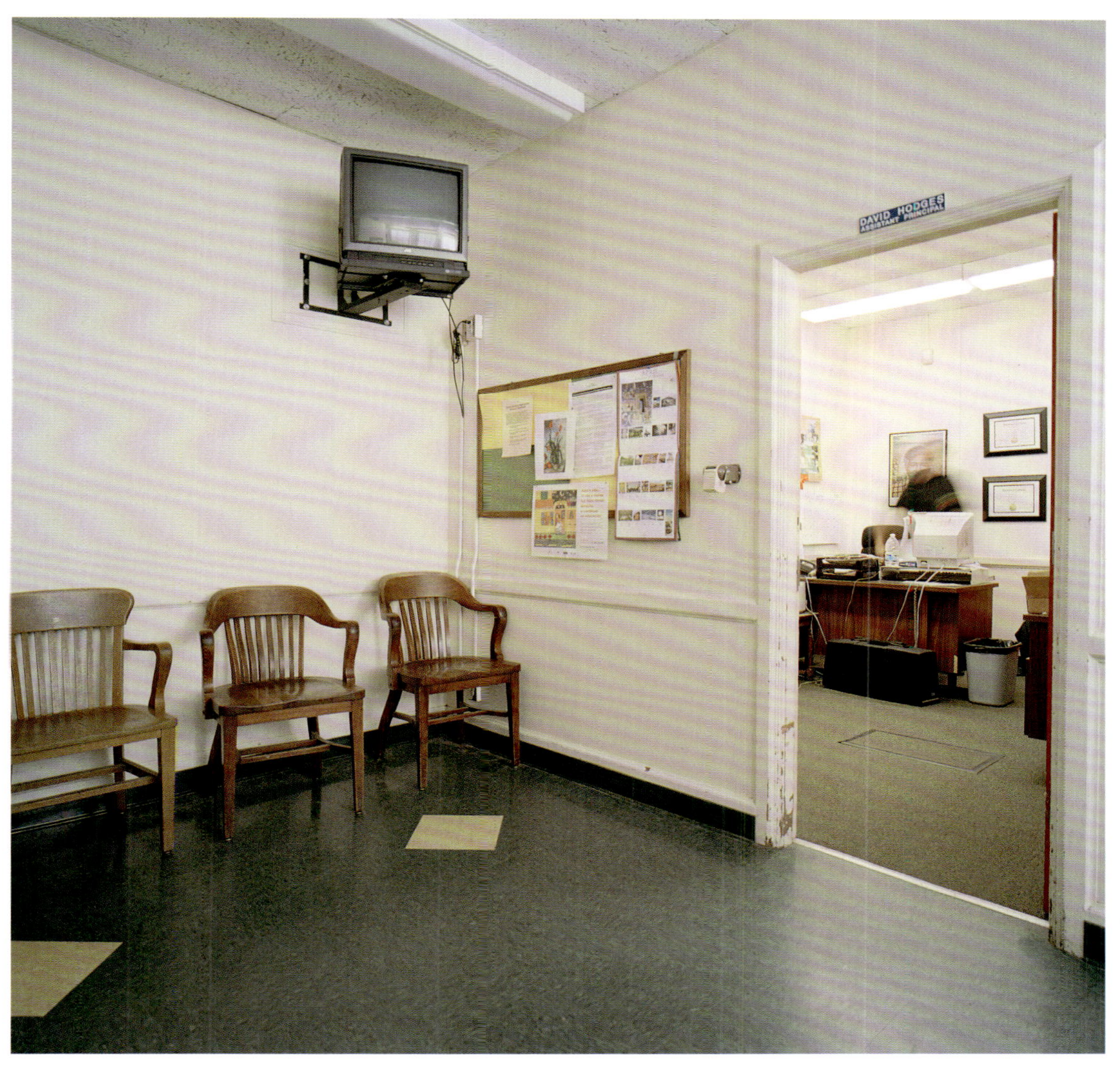

OPPOSITE: Second-floor corridor, Santa Barbara High School Santa Barbara, California

ABOVE: Office of Assistant Principal for Attendance and Discipline, Santa Barbara High School

Department of Motor Vehicles, Santa Barbara, California

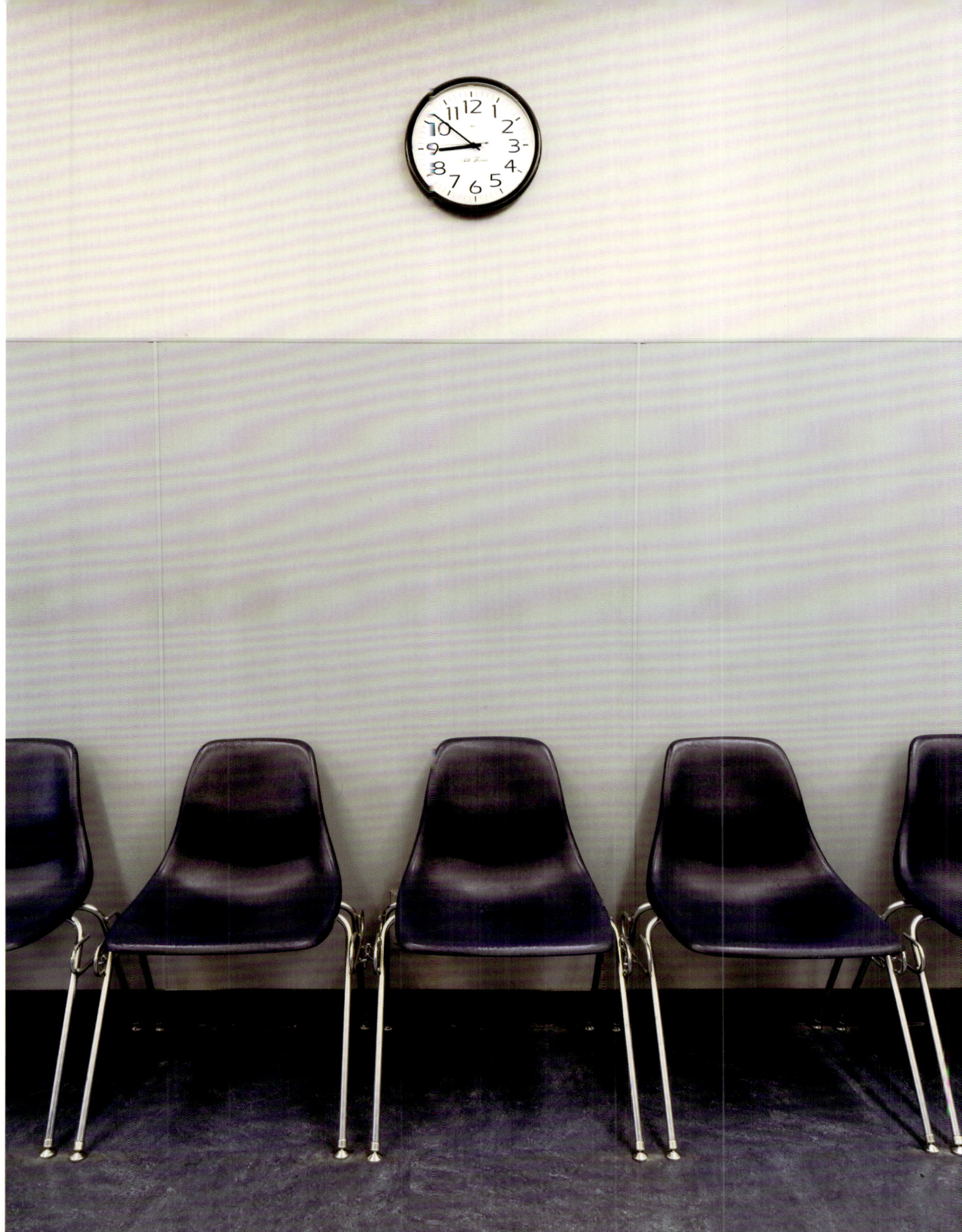

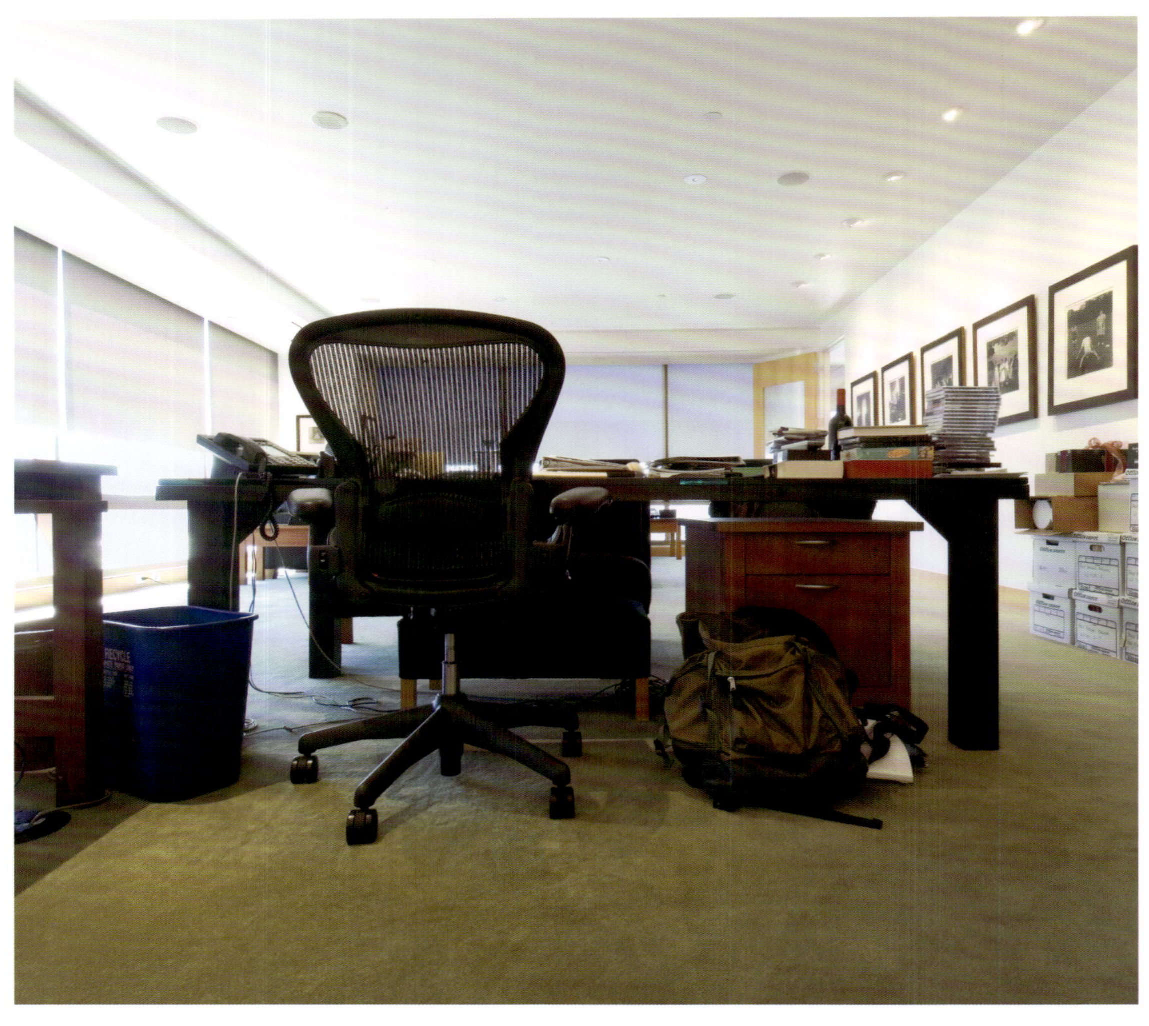

ABOVE: Movie executive's office, Burbank, California

OPPOSITE: Communications office in a bunker below the Imperial Palace, Ho Chi Minh City, Vietnam

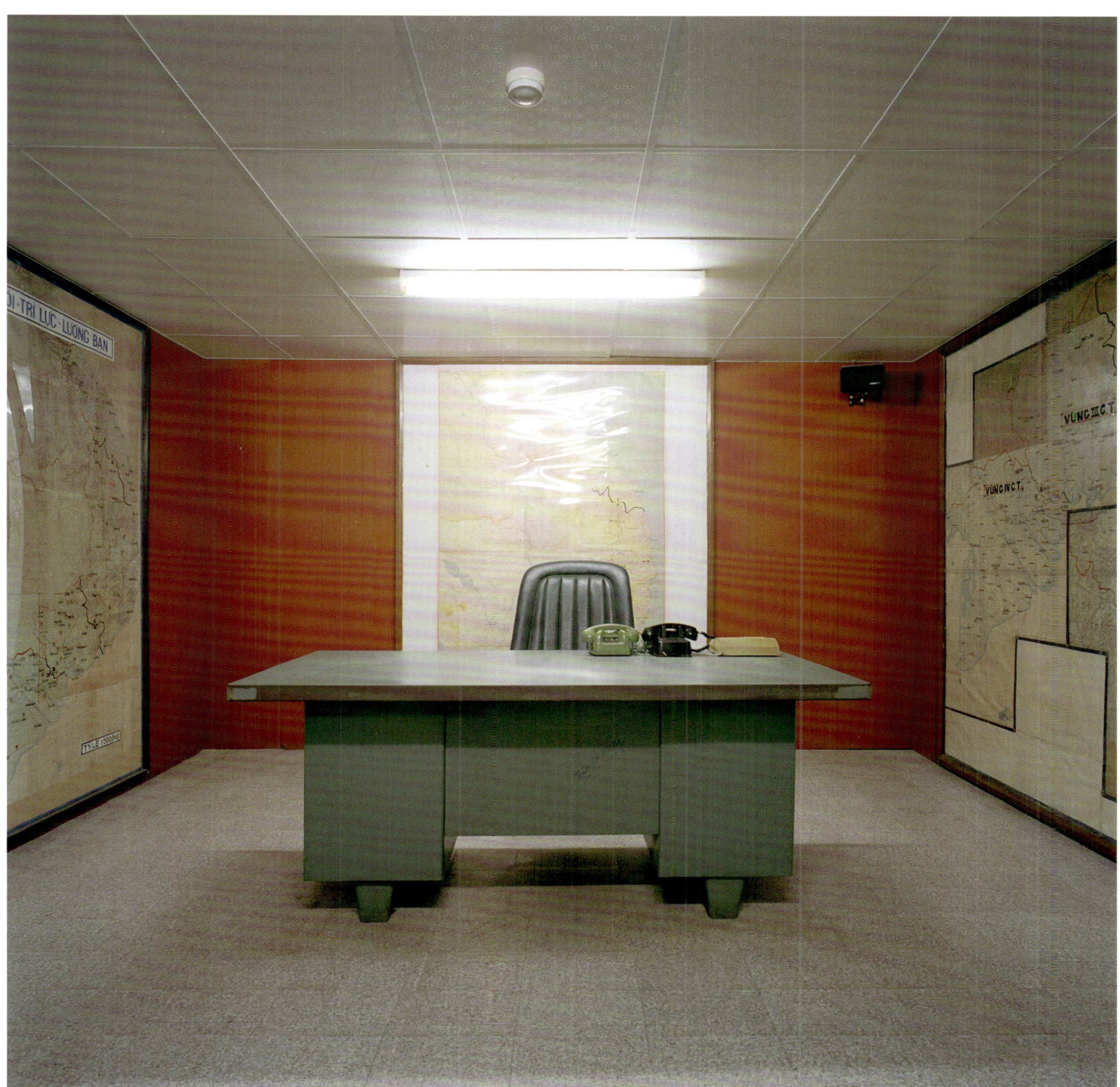
ỘI-TRÍ LỰC-LƯỢNG BẠN
VÙNG III C.T.
VÙNG IV C.T.

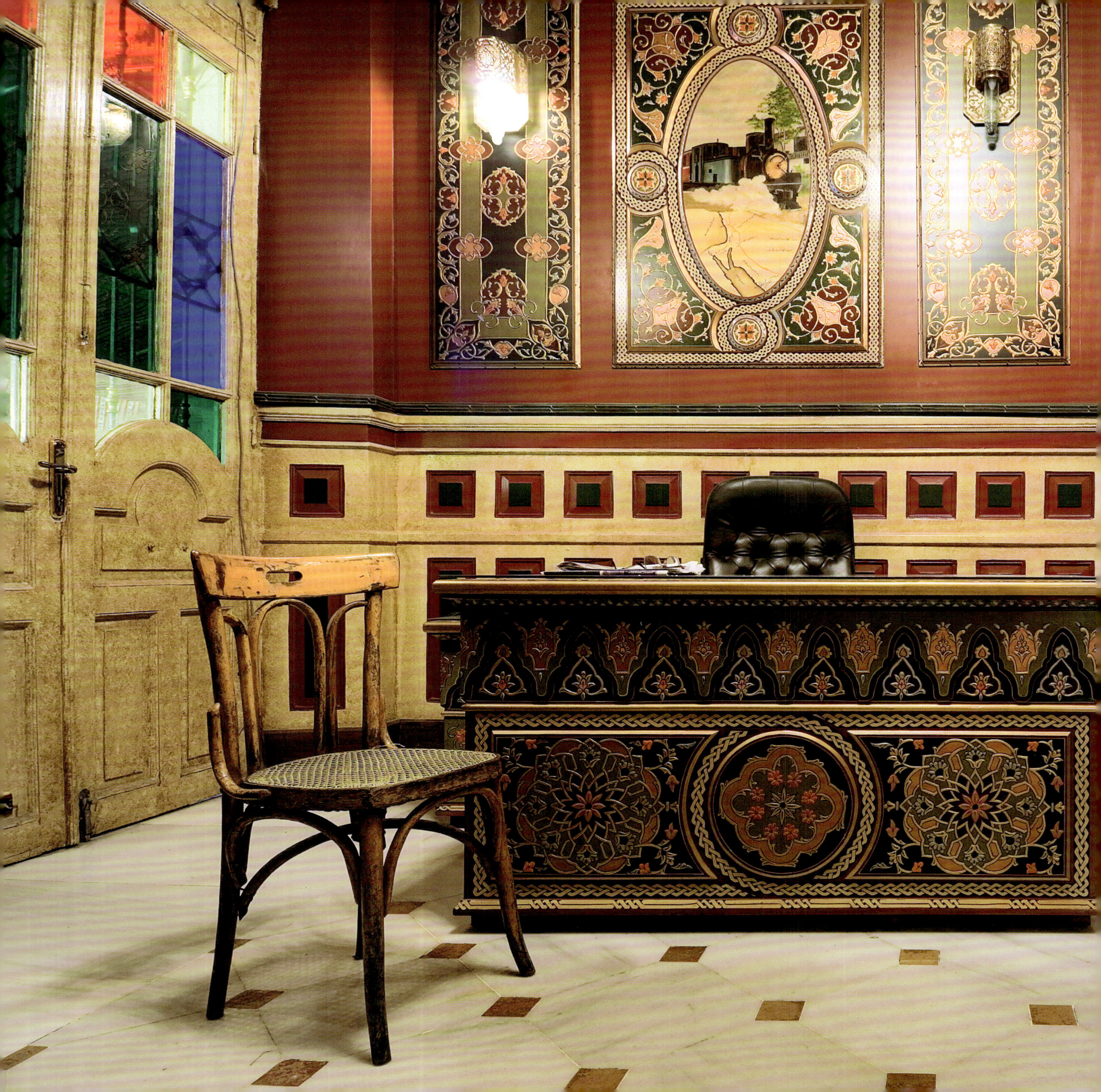

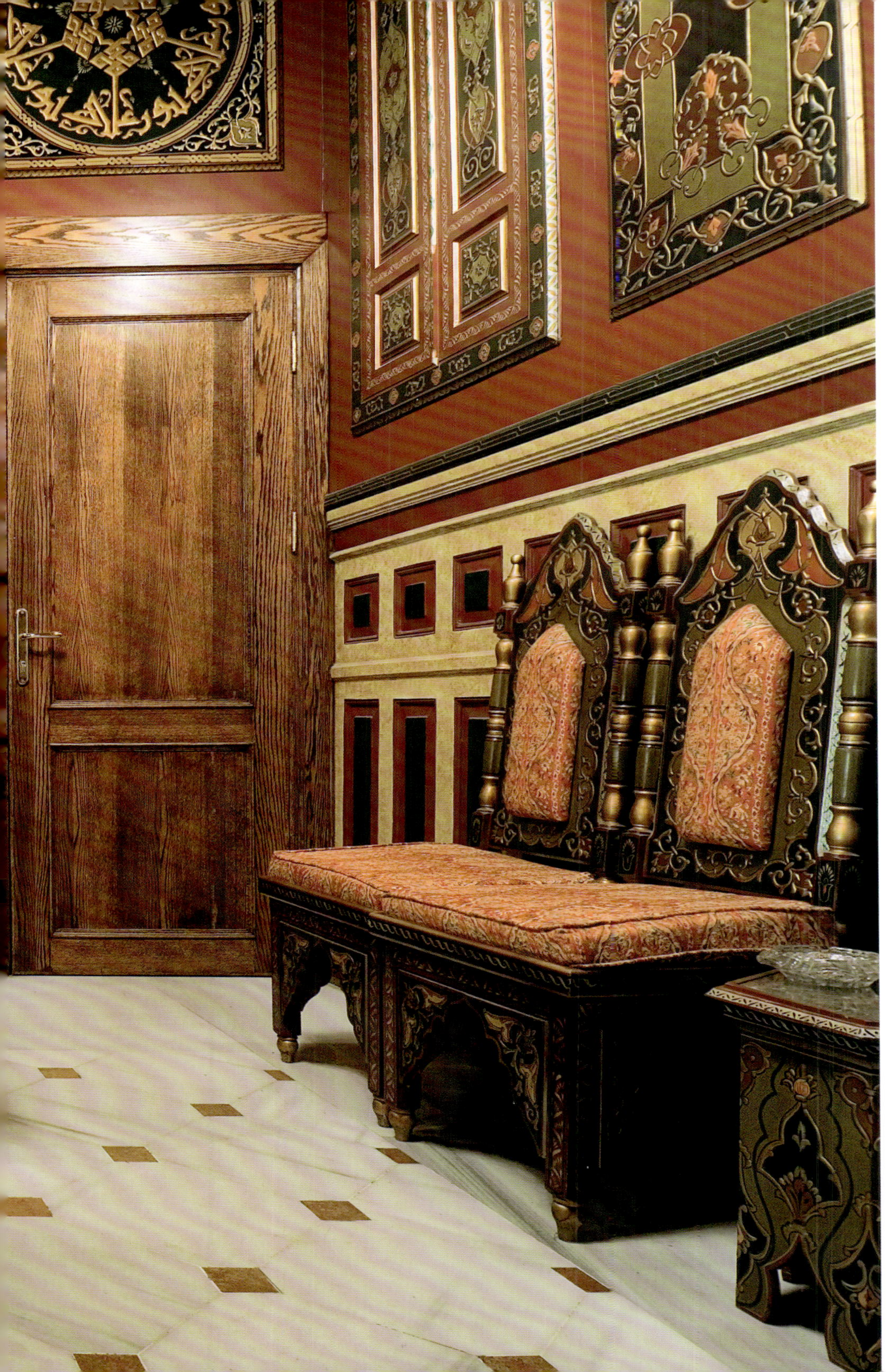

Contractor's office, Damascus, Syria, in a former train station for departures to Mecca

Mary Boone Gallery, New York

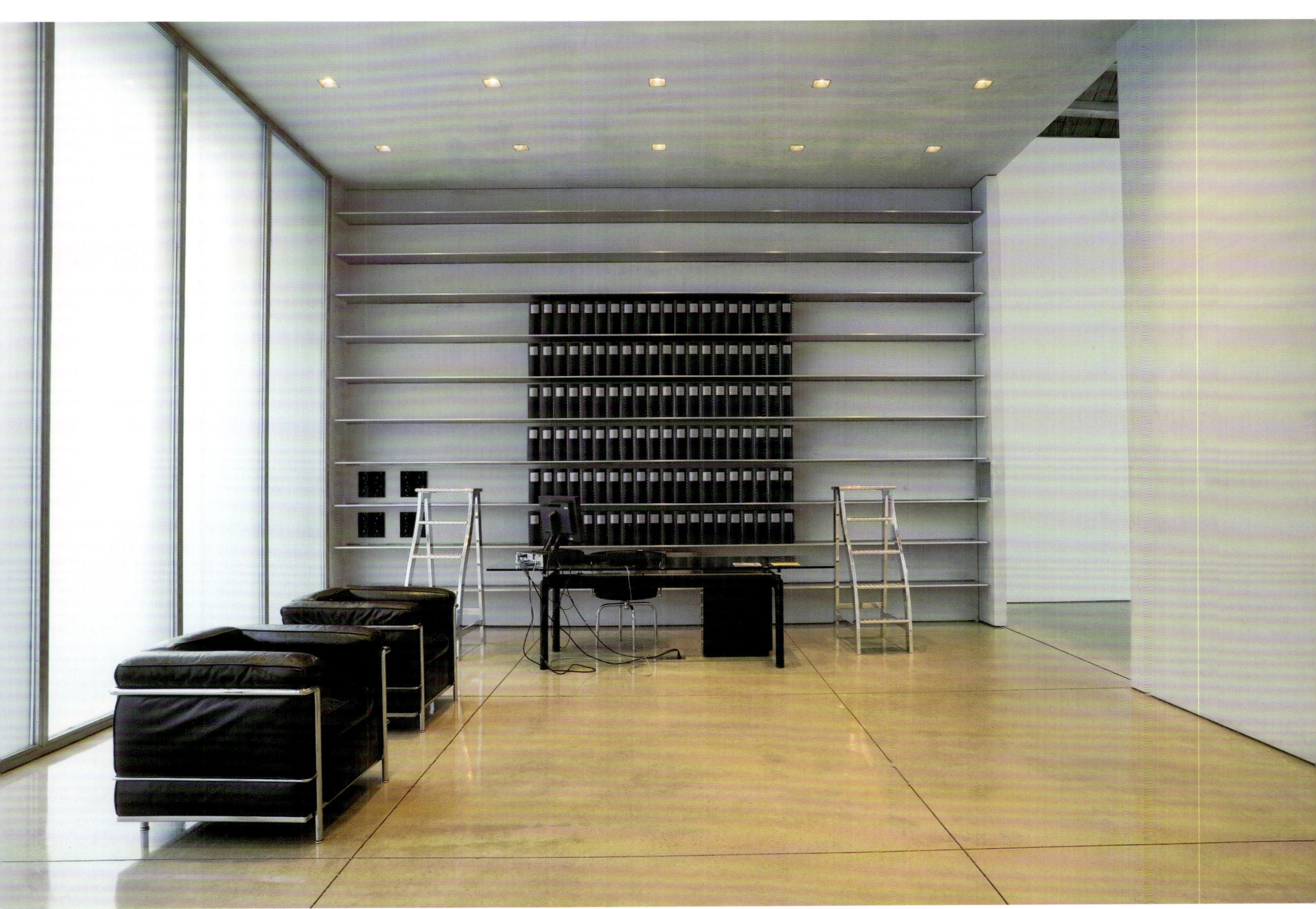

Lobby, Secret Service headquarters, Los Angeles

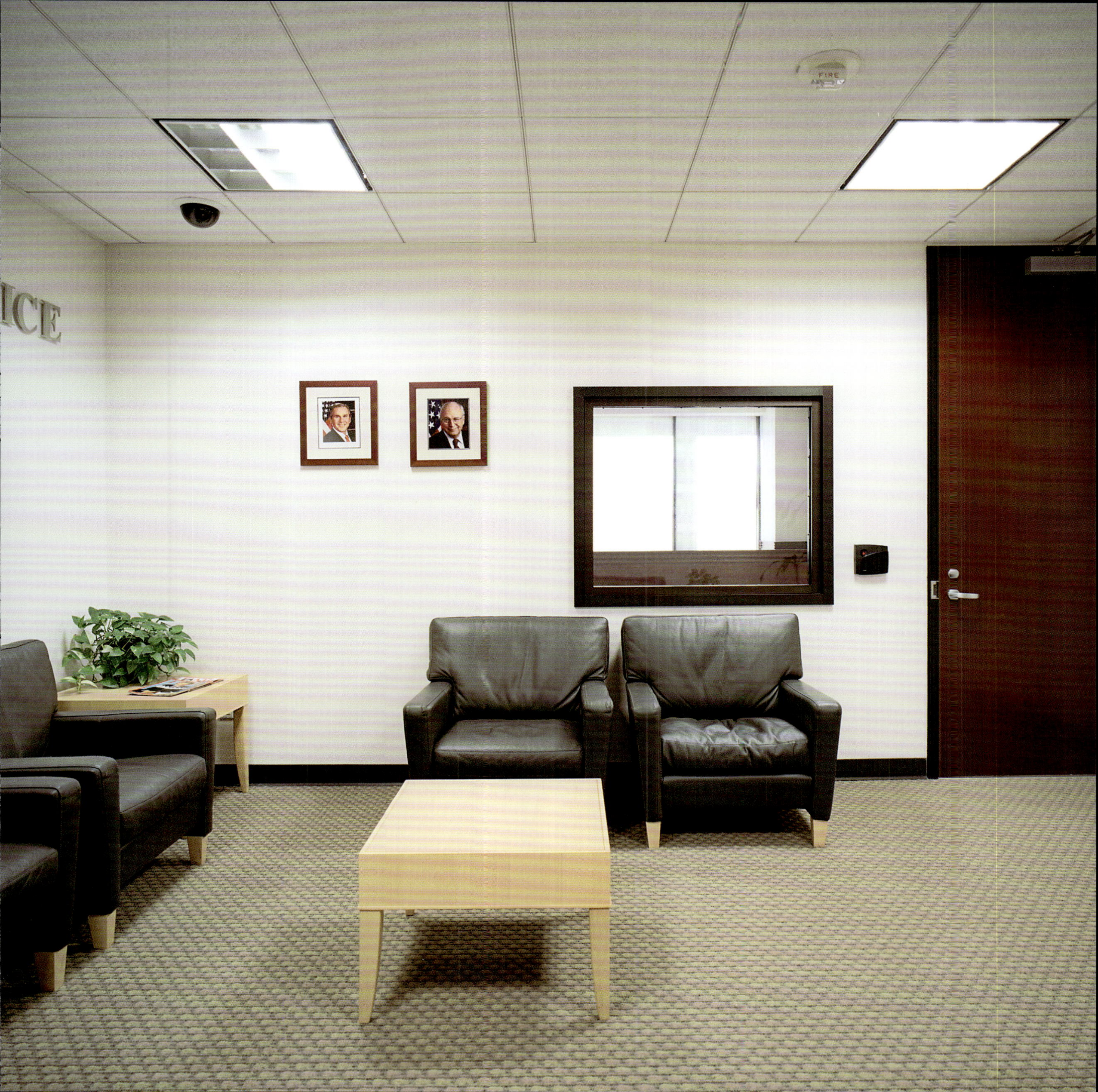
ICE
FIRE

Conference room, FBI headquarters, San Francisco

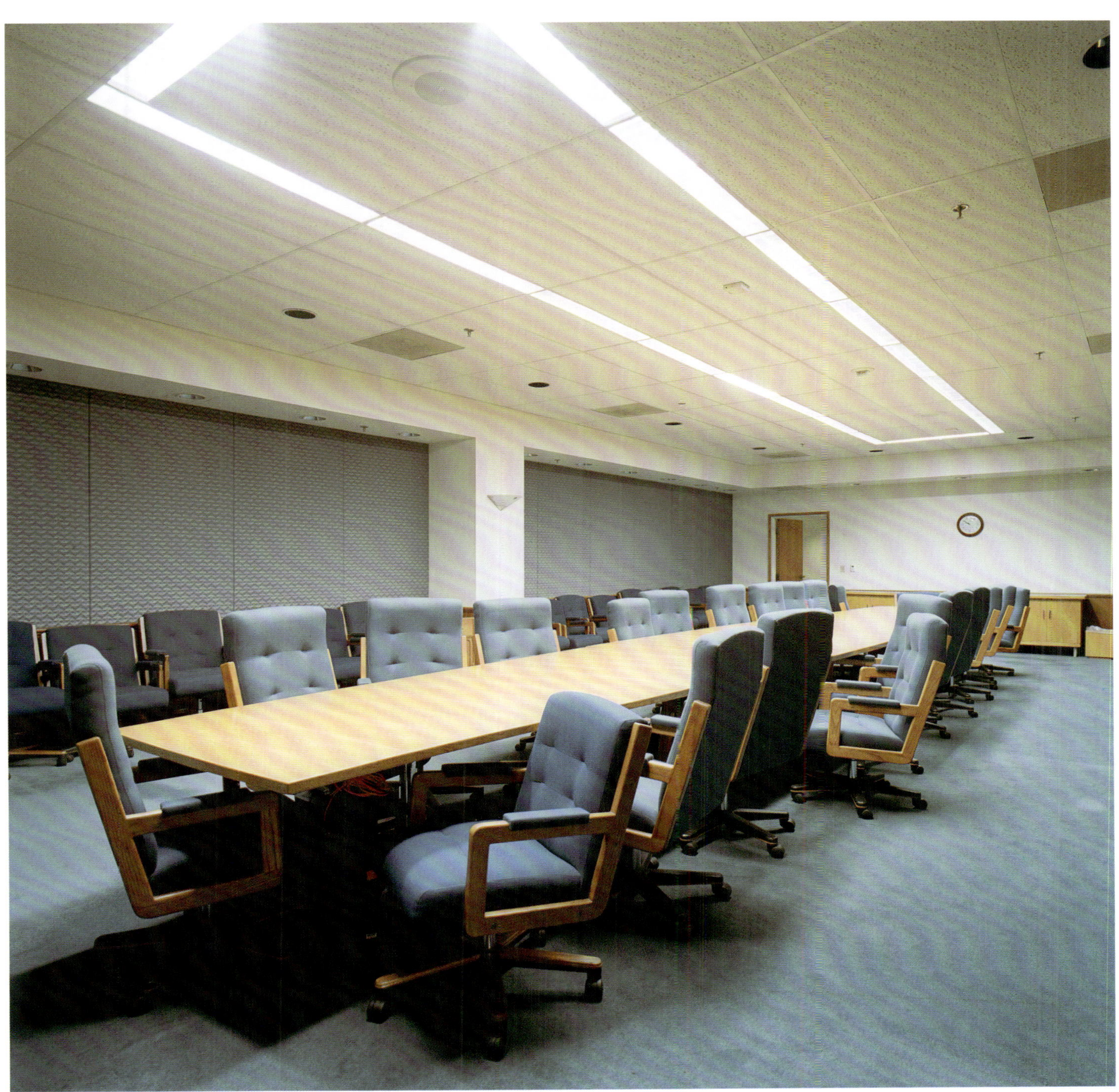

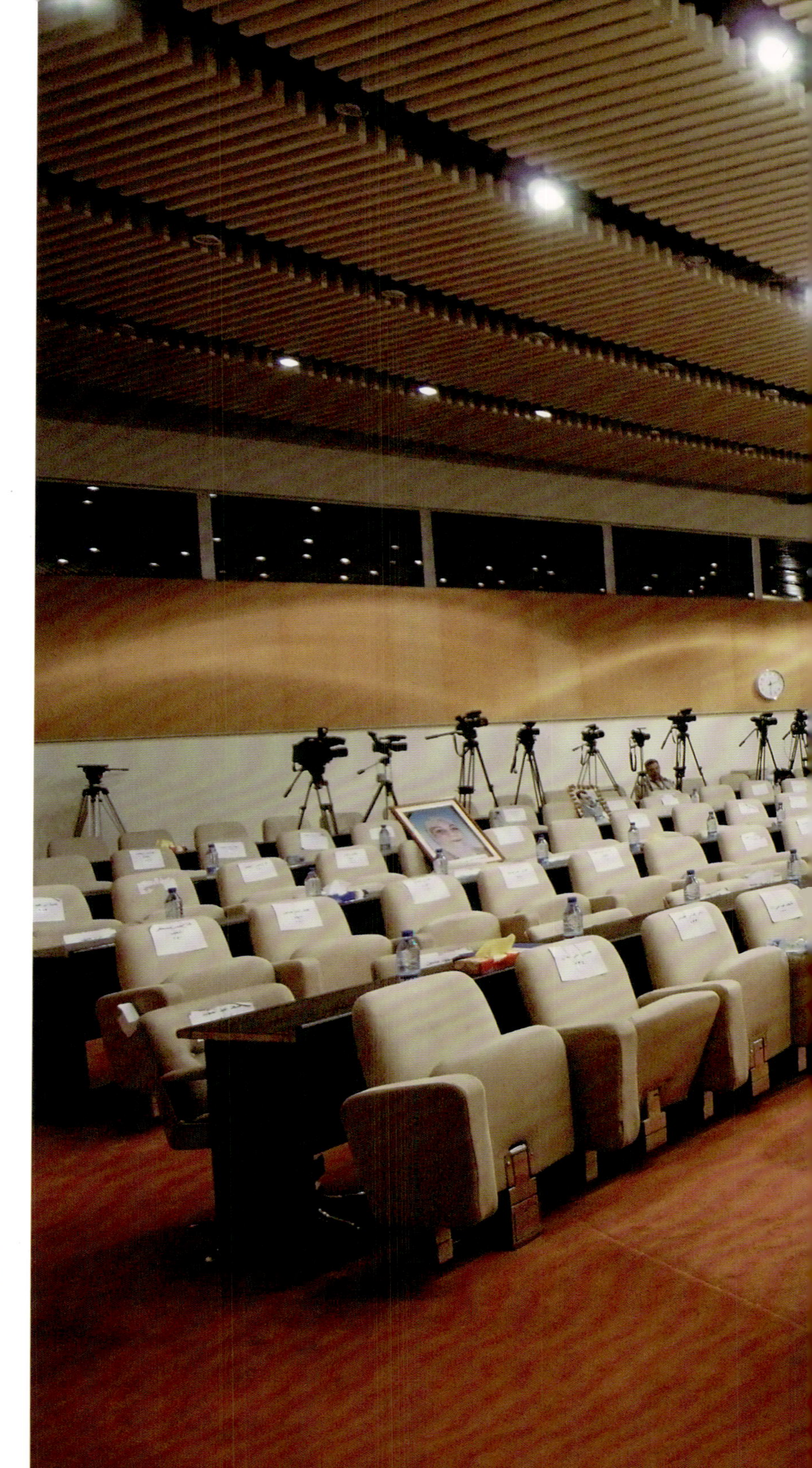

Iraqi National Assembly (also known as
Conference Room 4, Convention Center), Baghdad

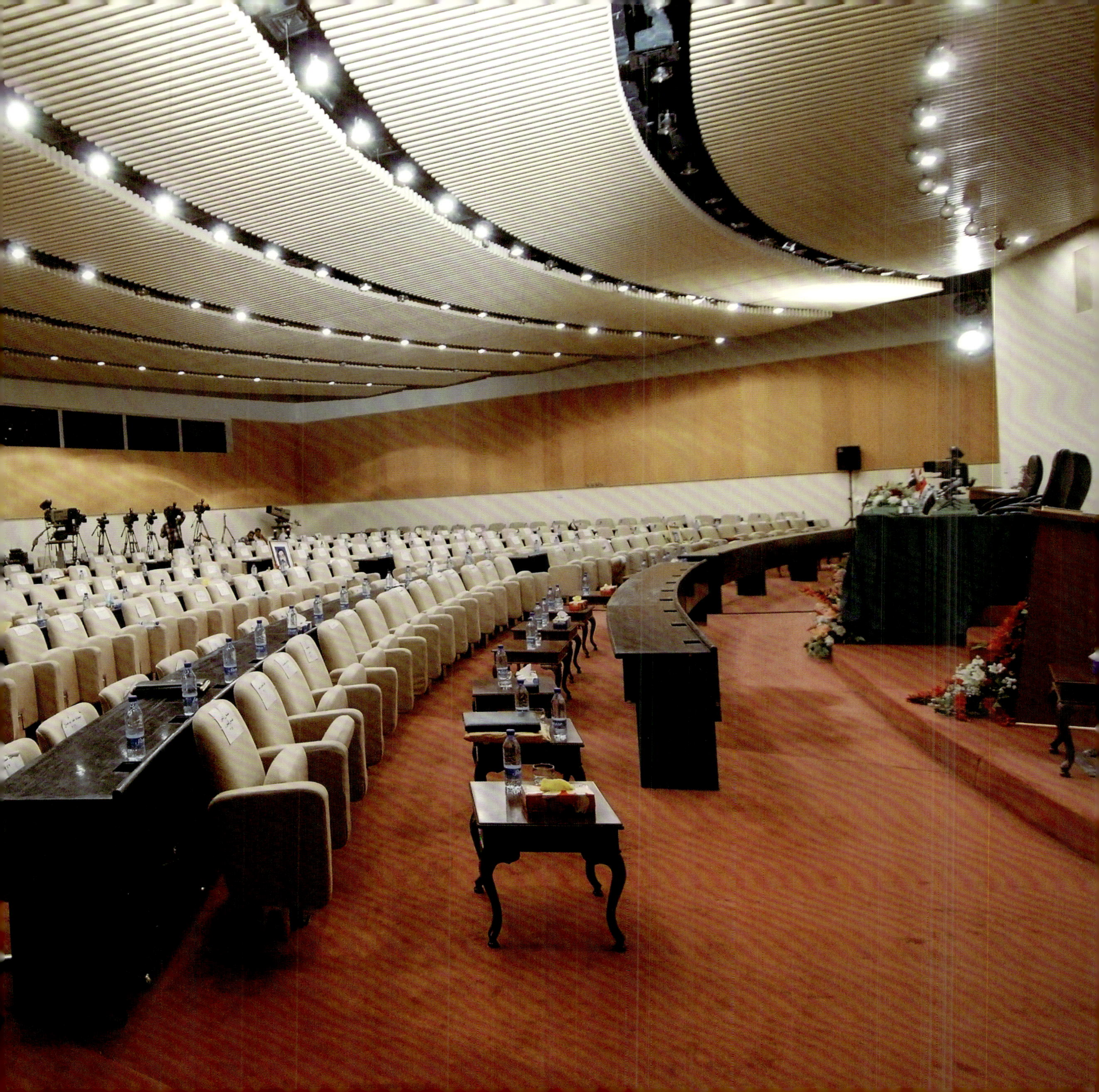

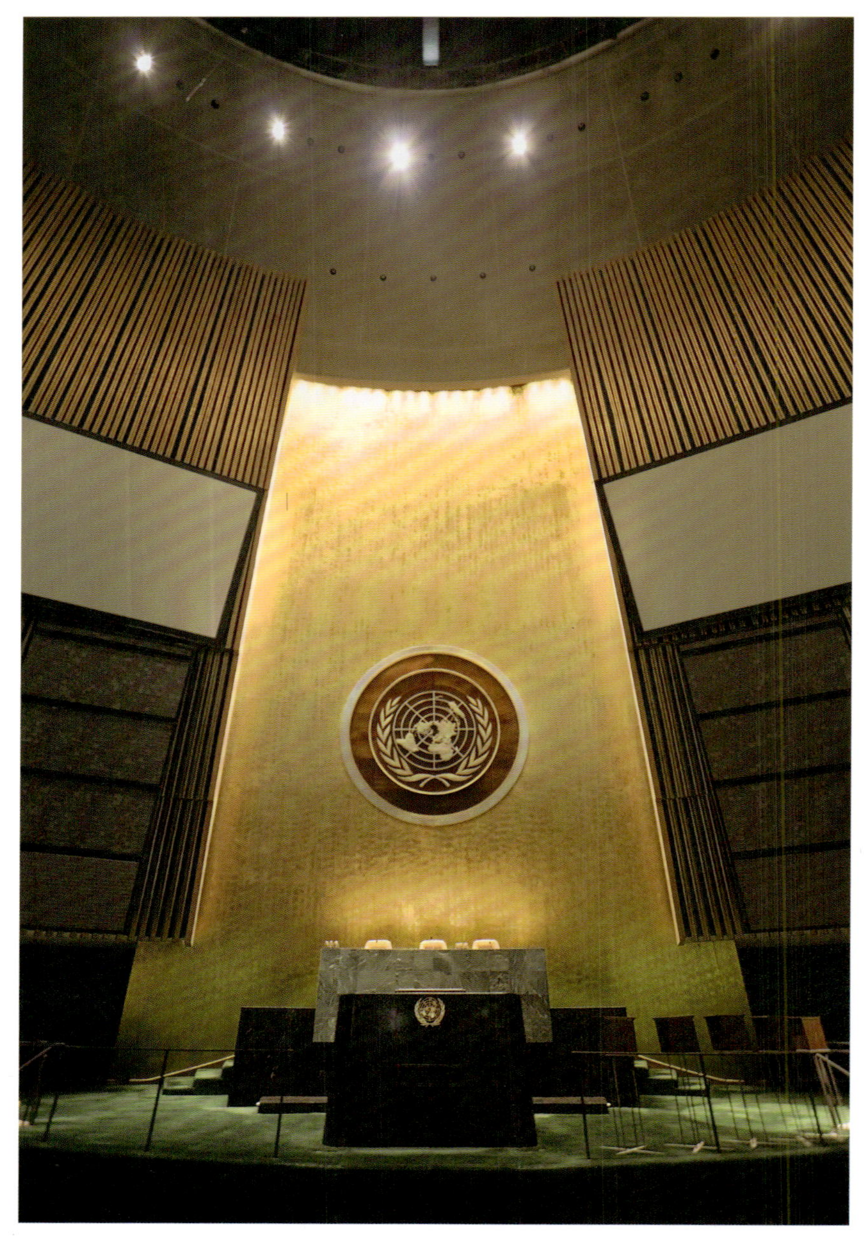

ABOVE AND OPPOSITE: United Nations General Assembly, New York

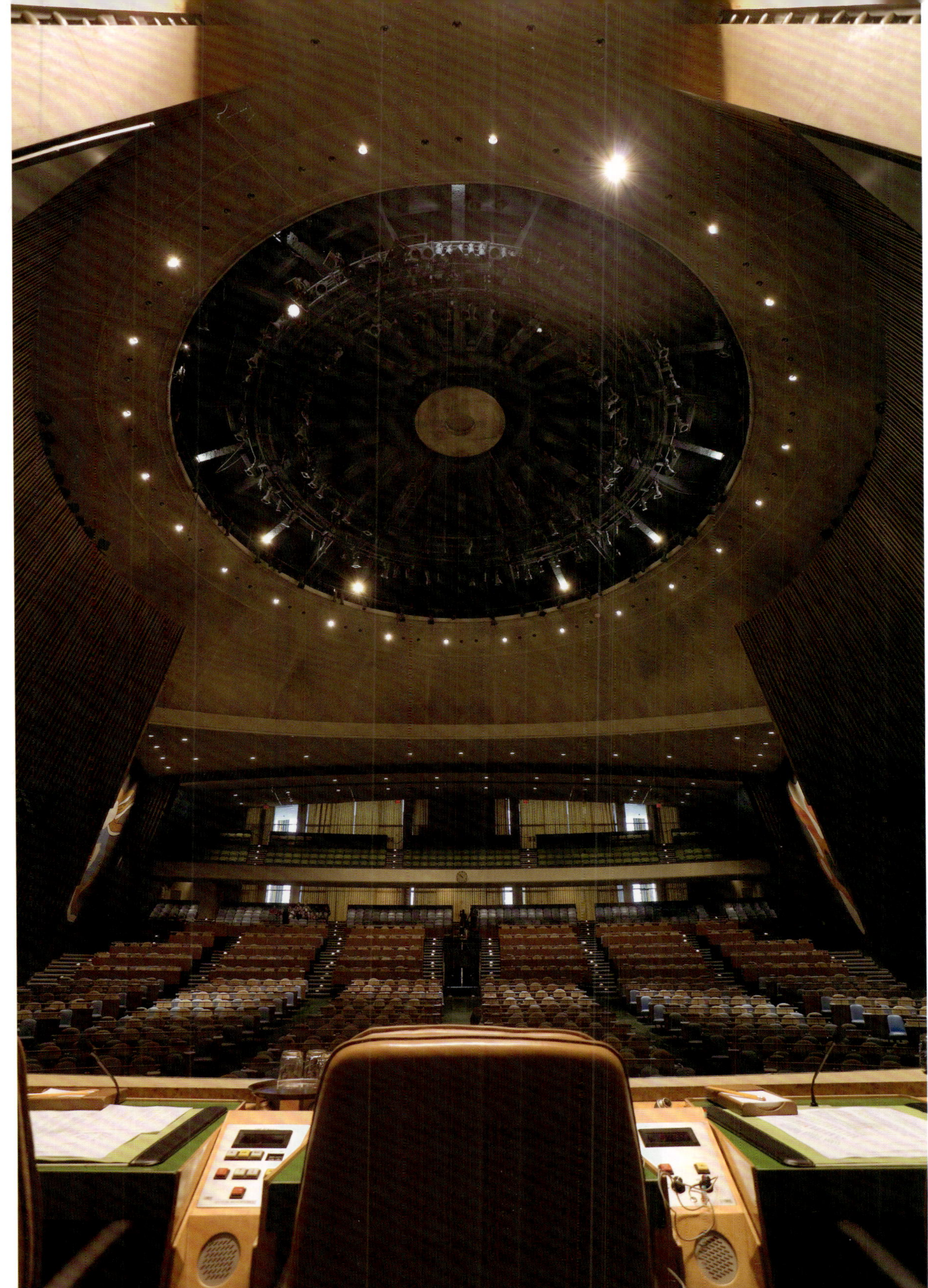

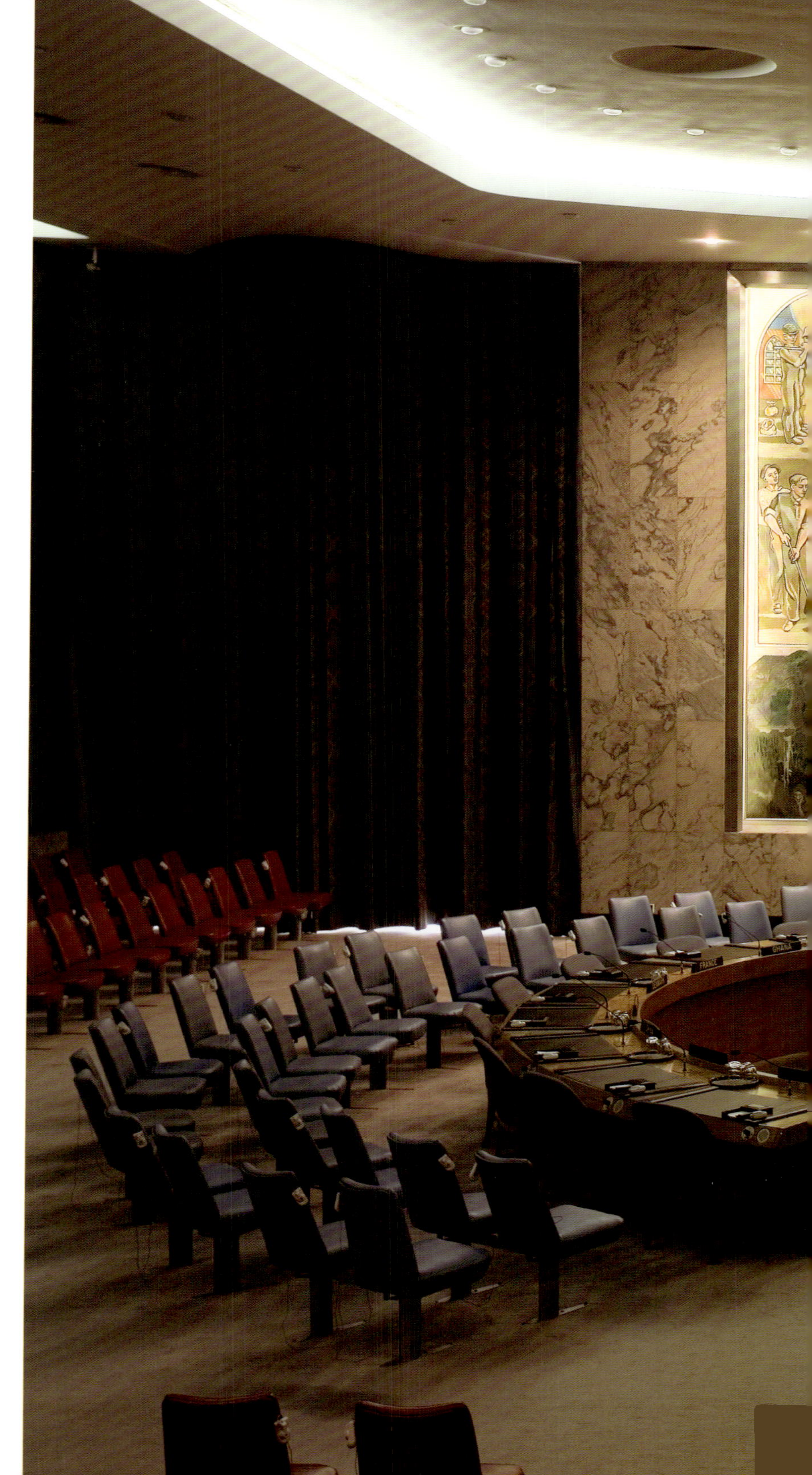

United Nations Security Council Chamber, New York

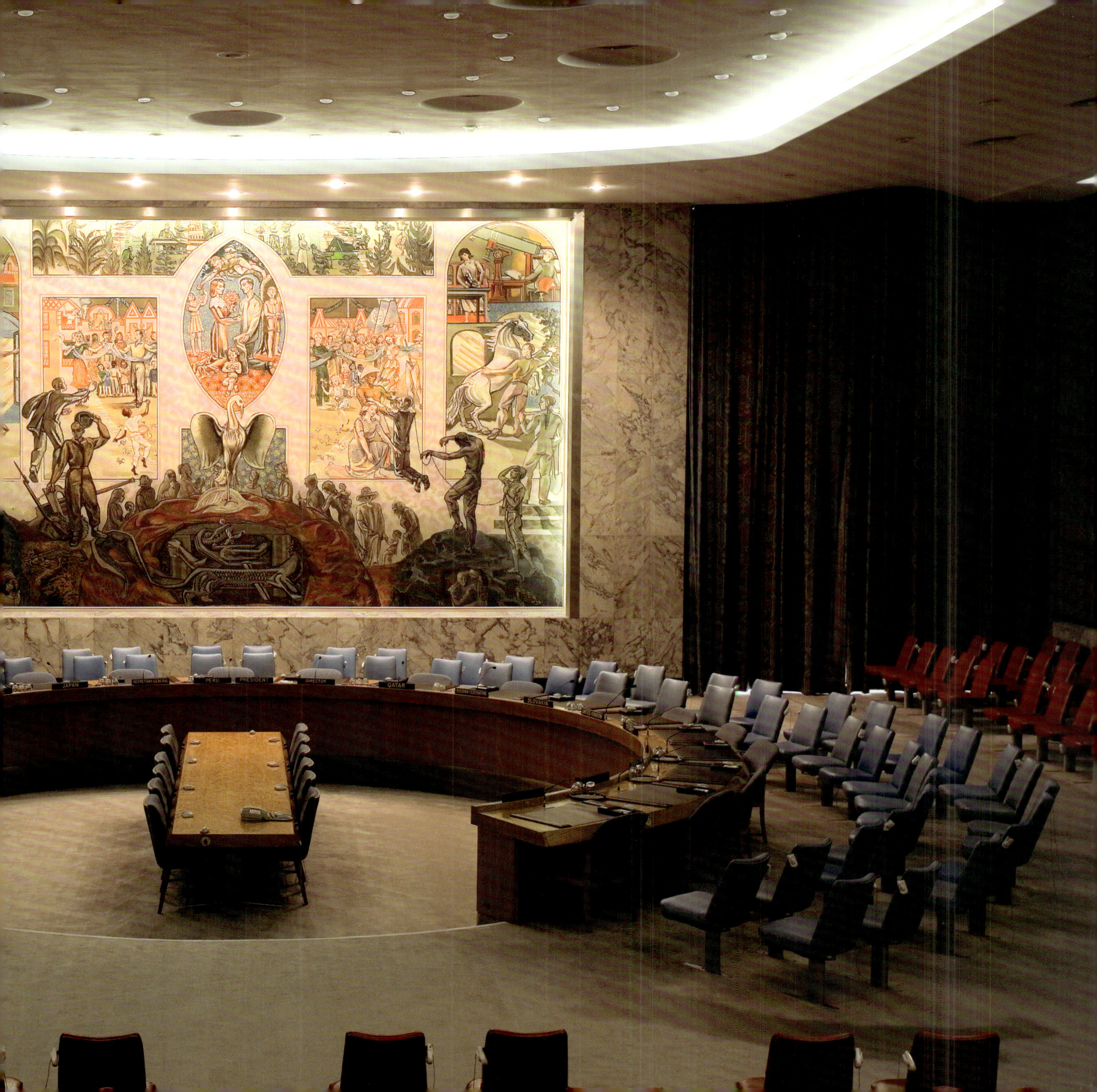
JAPAN
SECRETARY-GENERAL
PERU
PRESIDENT
DIRECTOR
QATAR
SLOVAKIA

Law Courts, Göteborg, Sweden

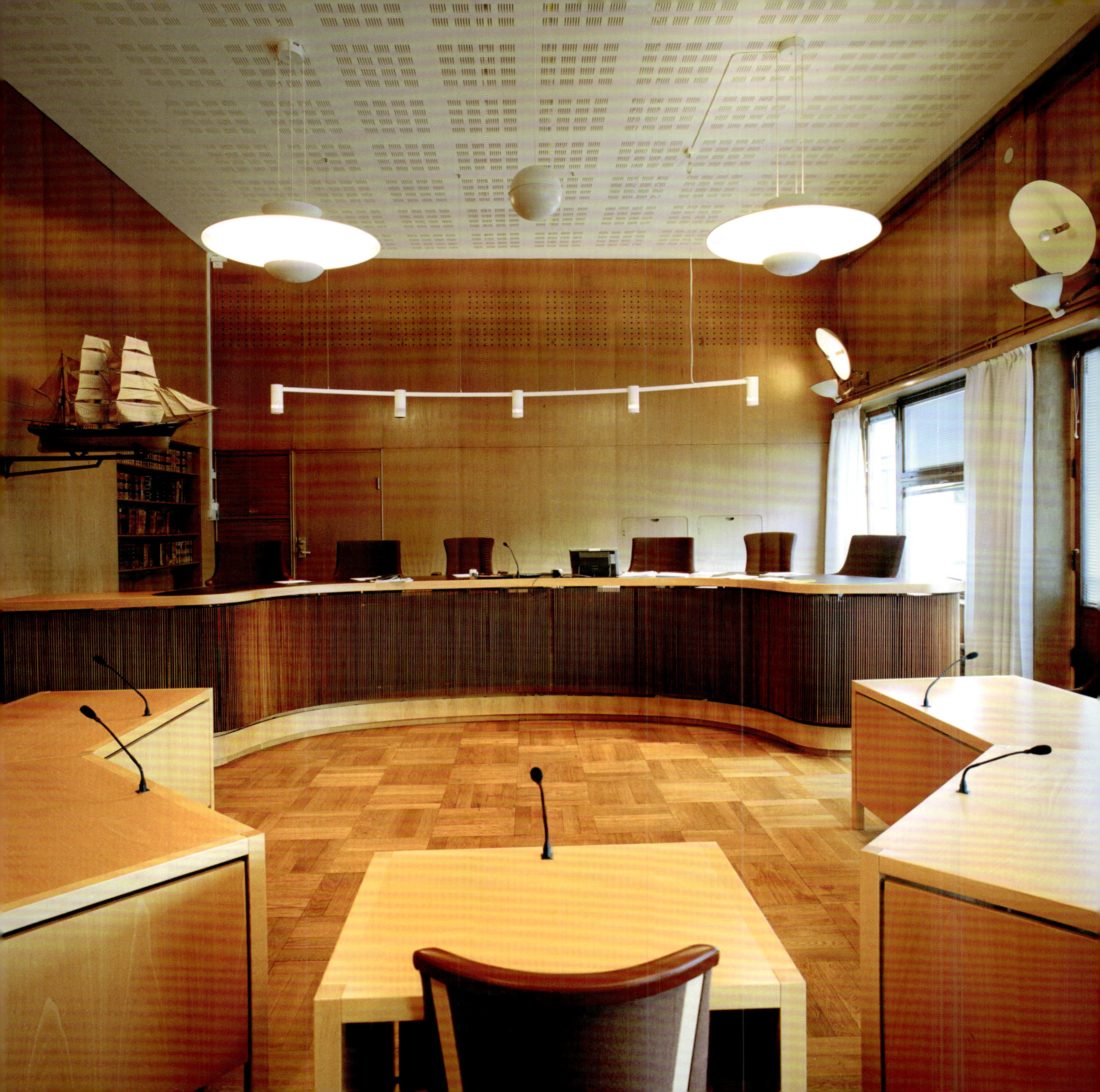

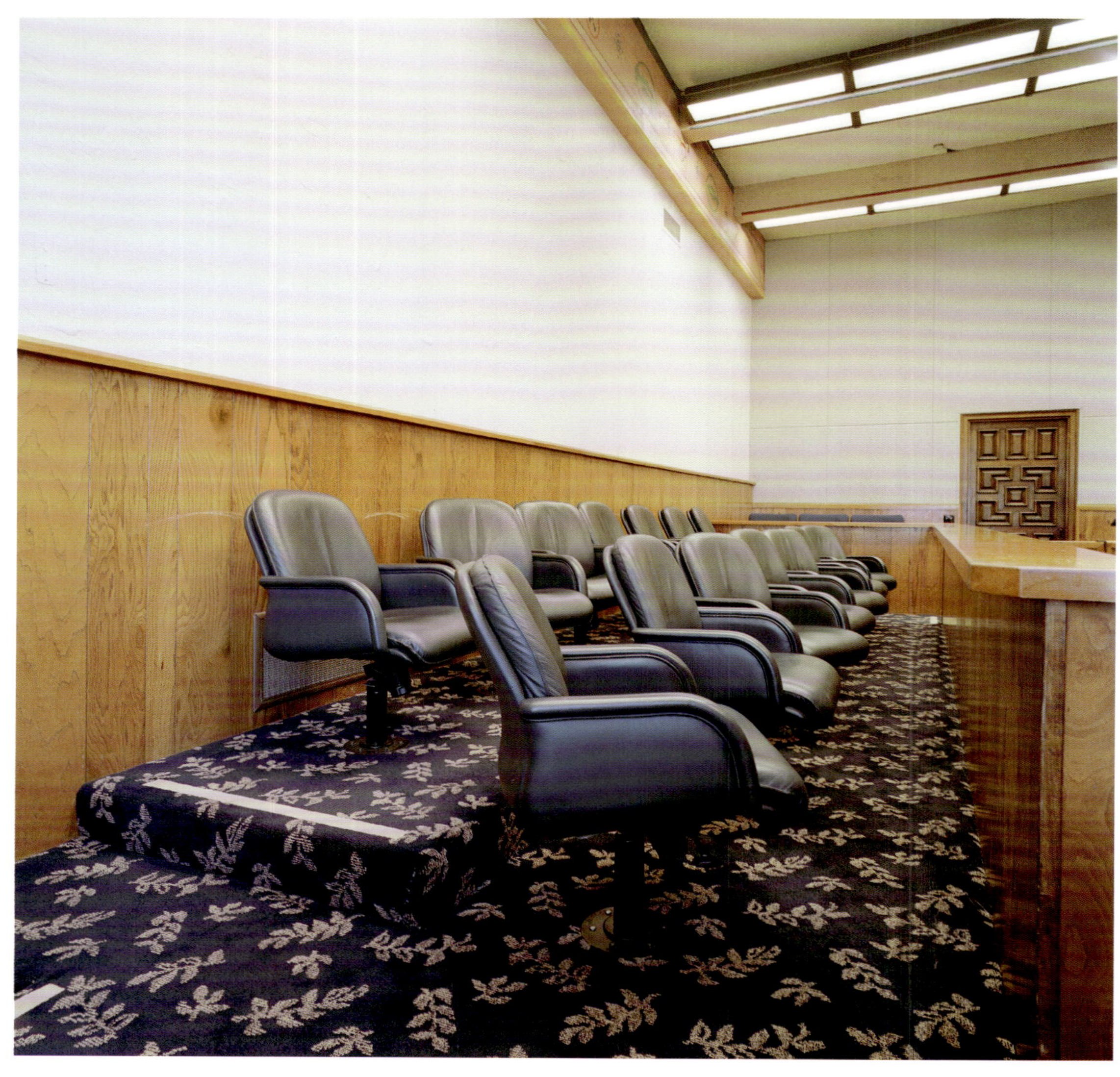

ABOVE: Jury box, Superior Court, Santa Barbara, California

OPPOSITE: Superior Court, Santa Barbara, California

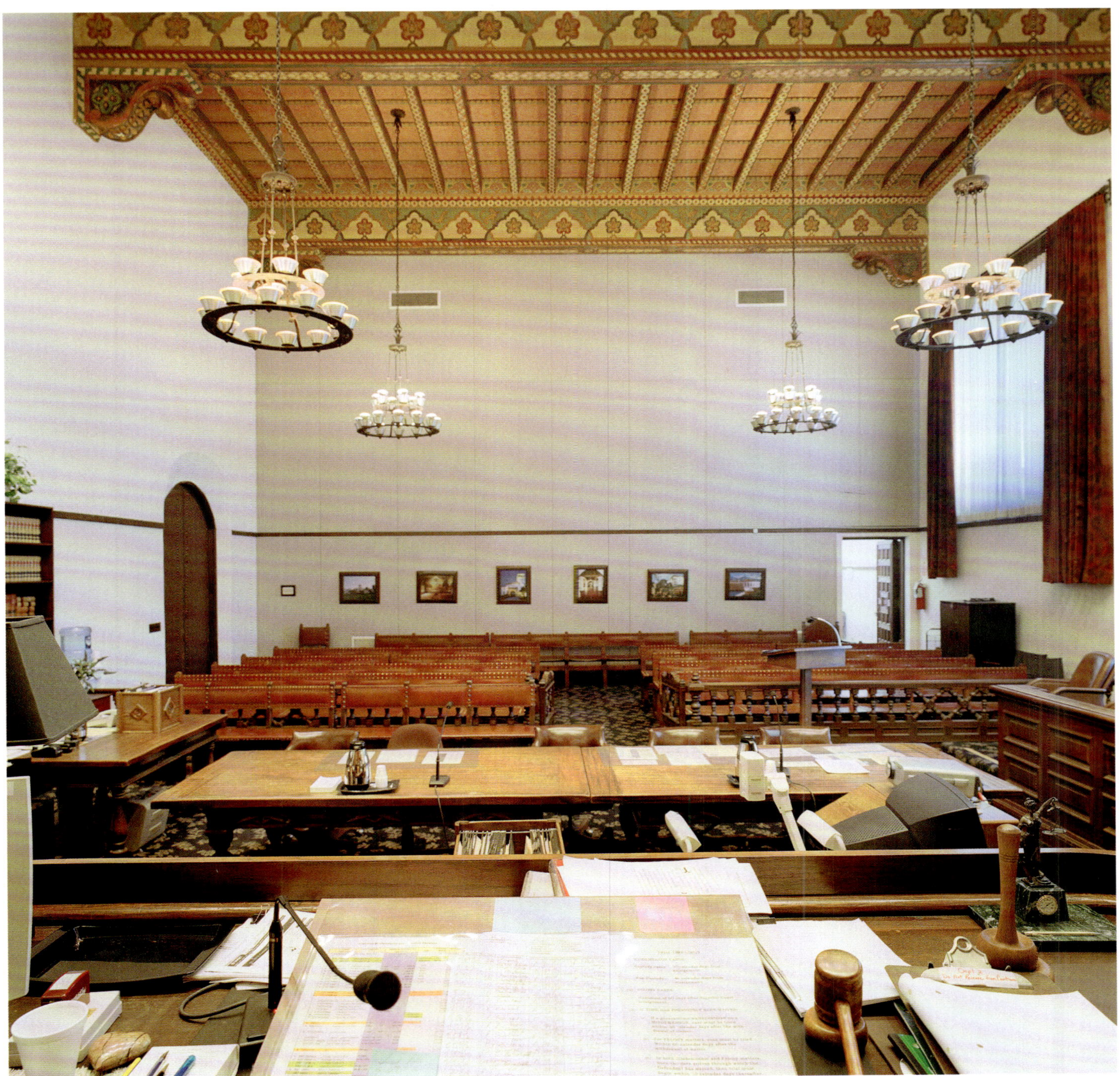

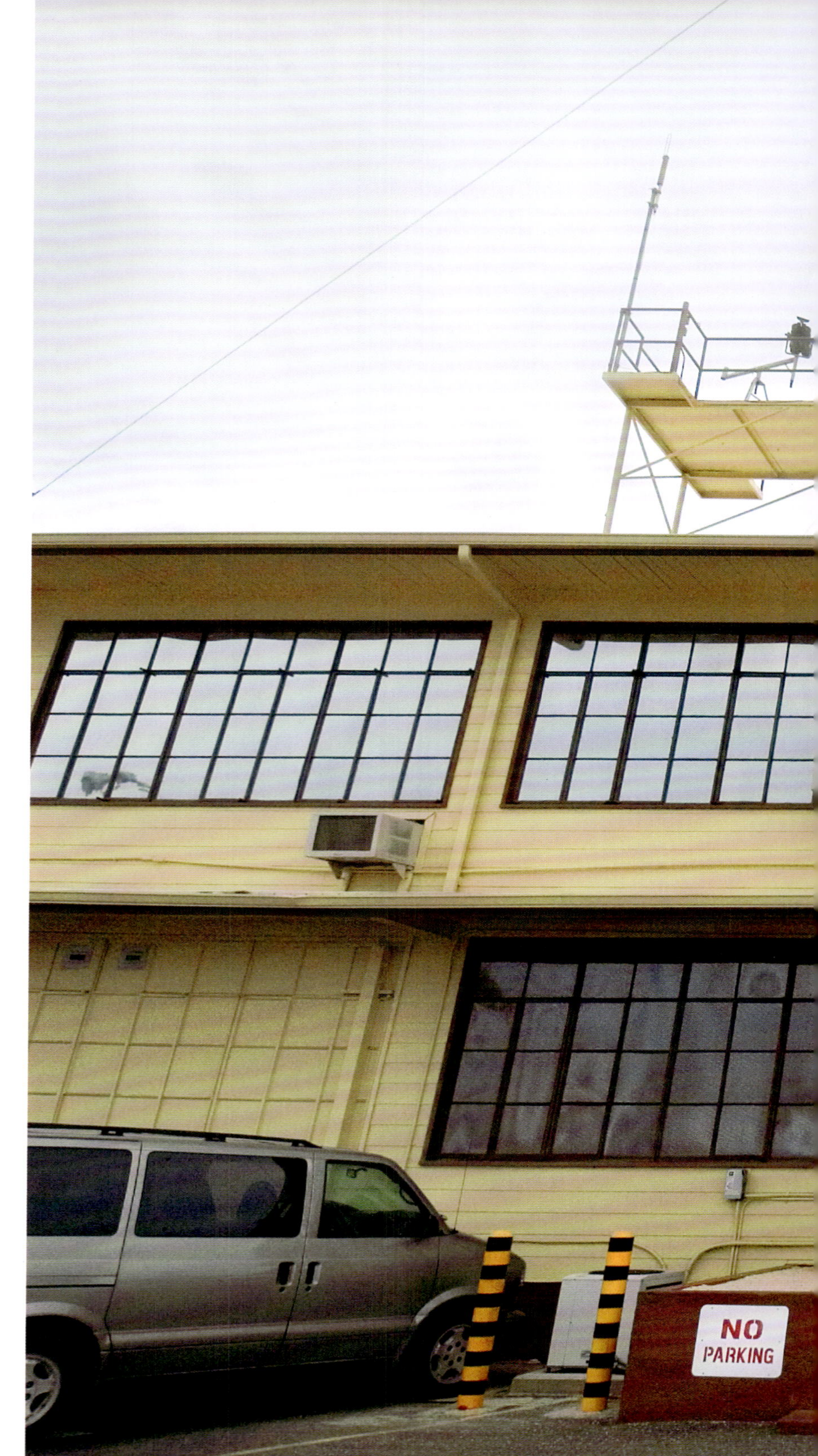

Military tribunal building, Guantánamo, Cuba

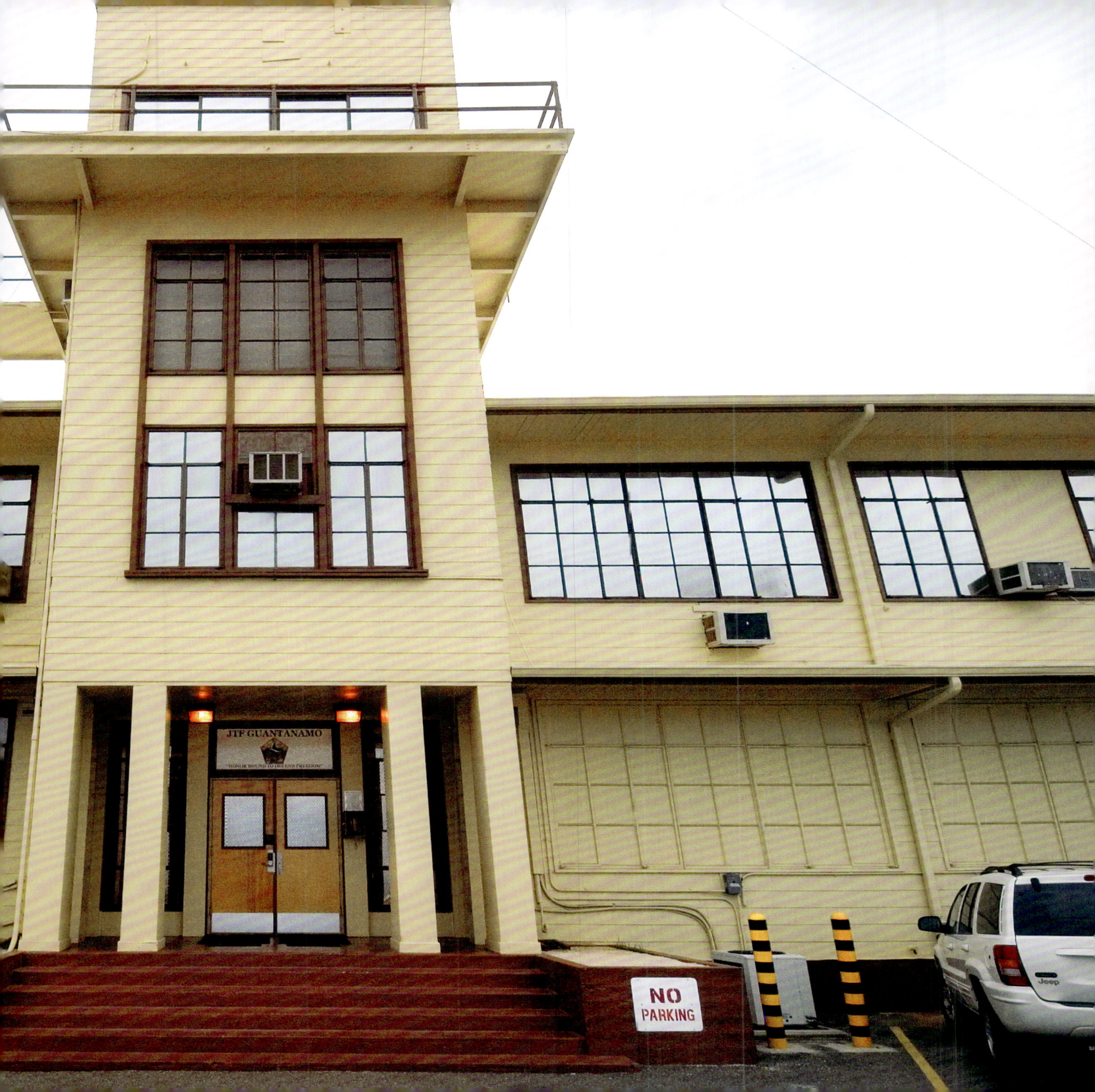
JTF GUANTANAMO
NO
PARKING

Los Prietos Boys' Camp, Santa Barbara, California

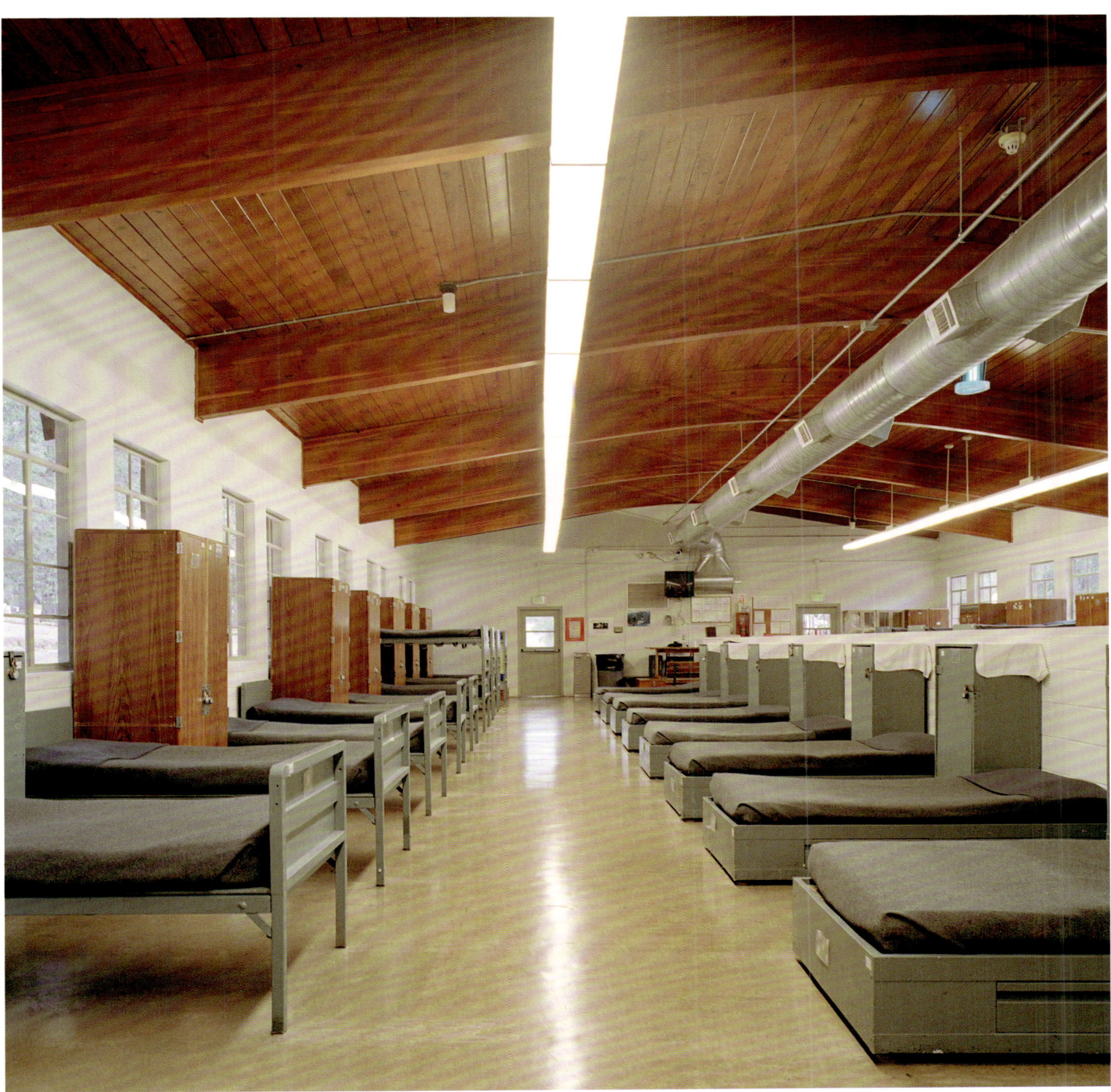

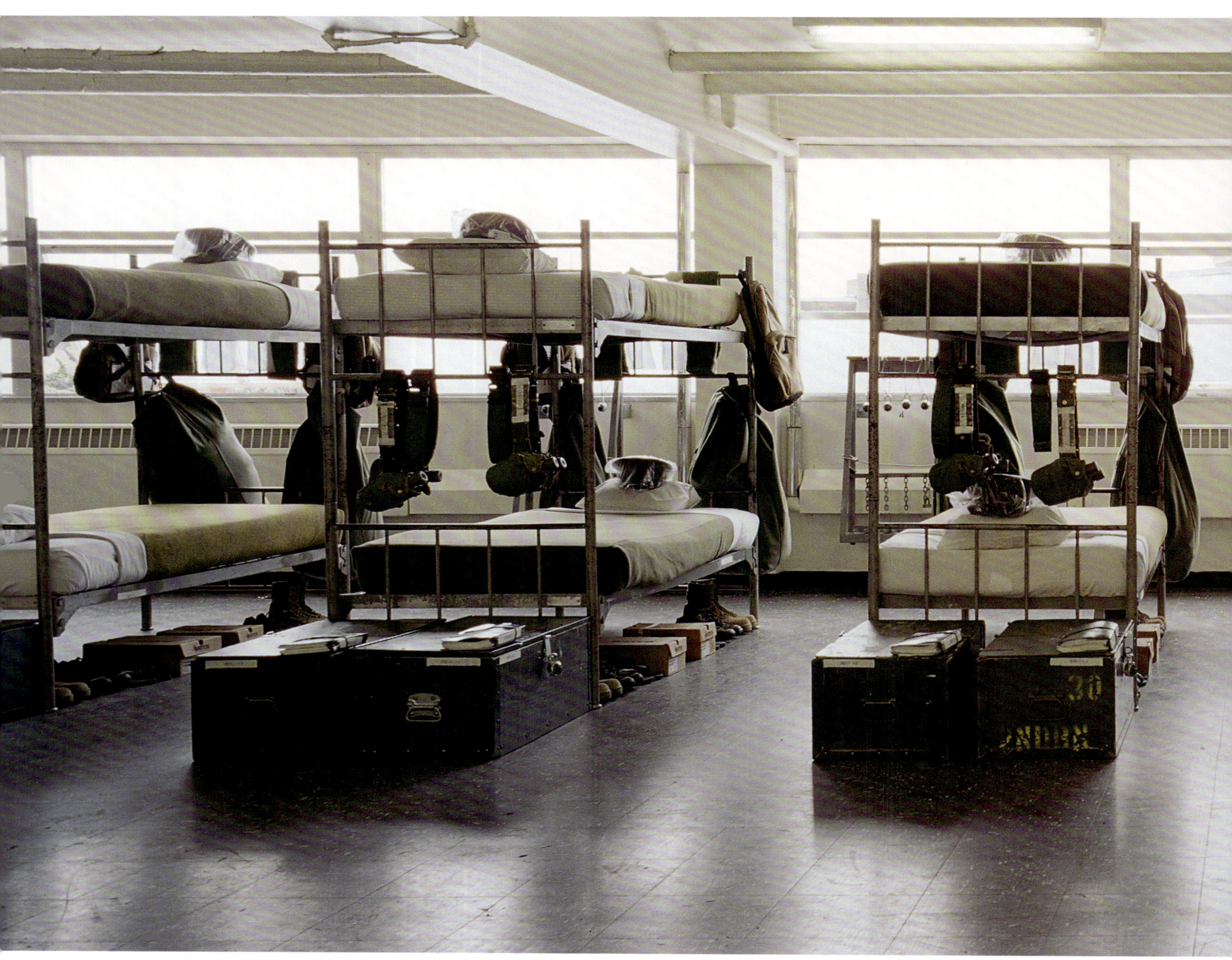

Marine Corps Recruit Depot, San Diego, California

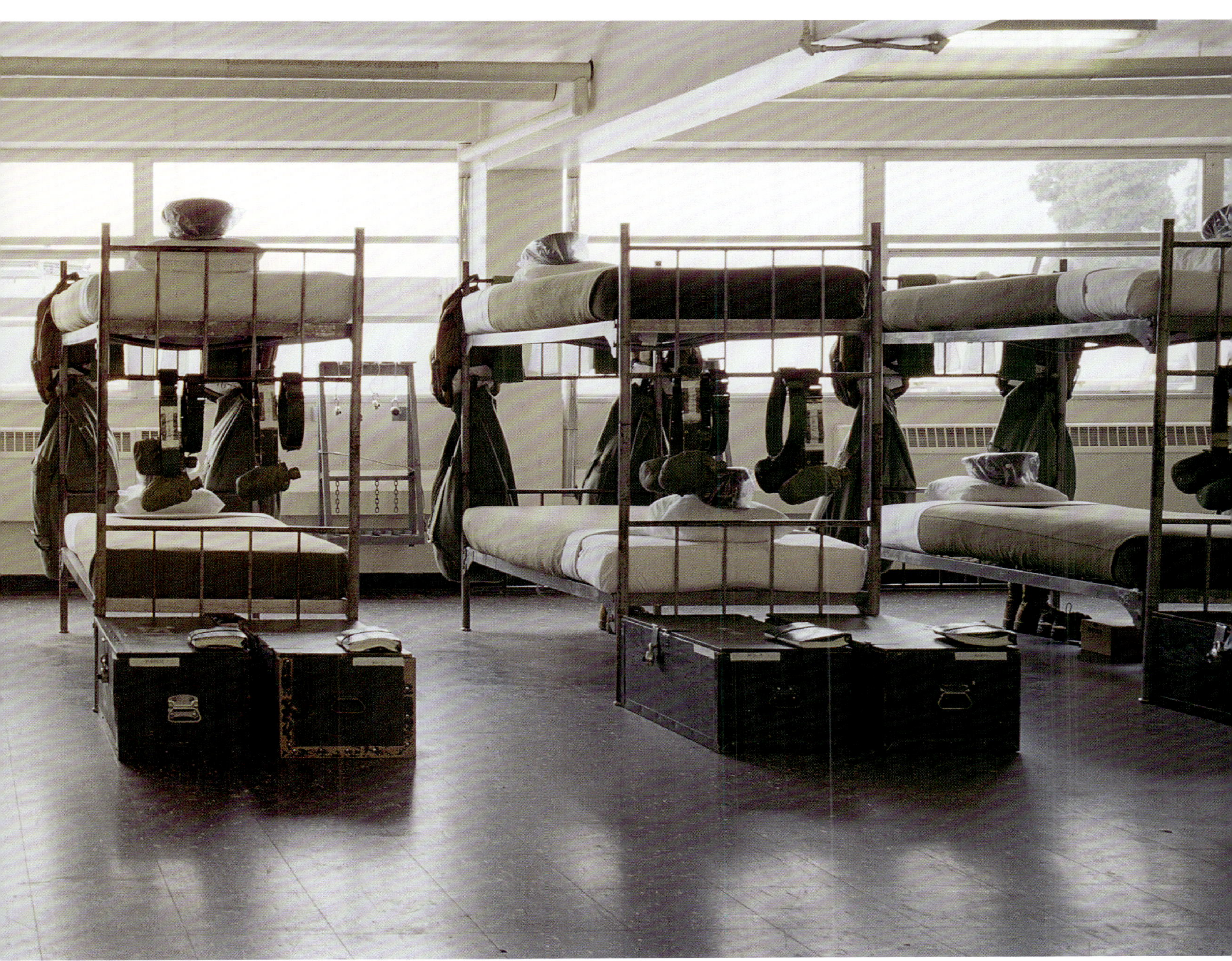

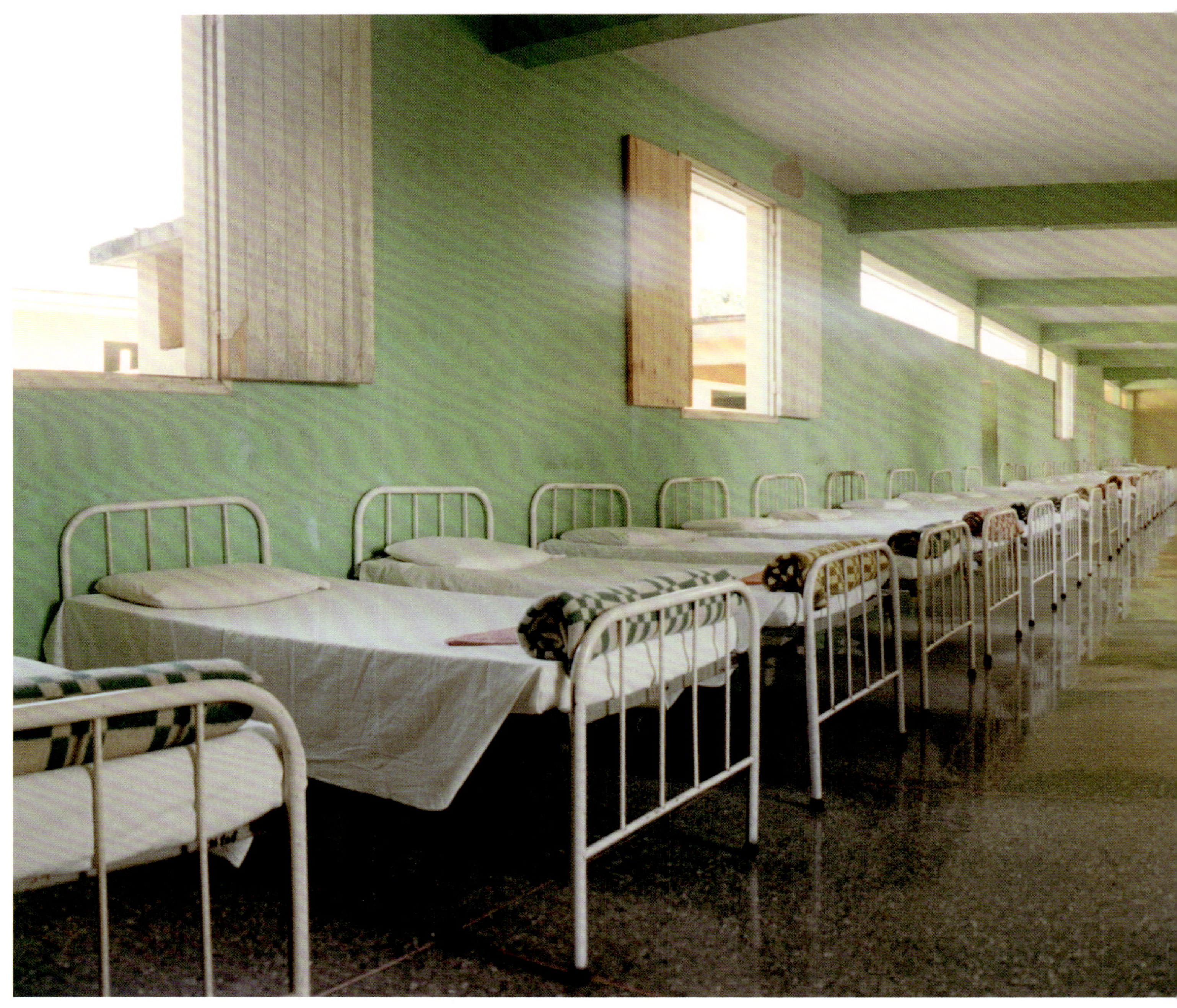

Dormitory, mental institution, outside Havana

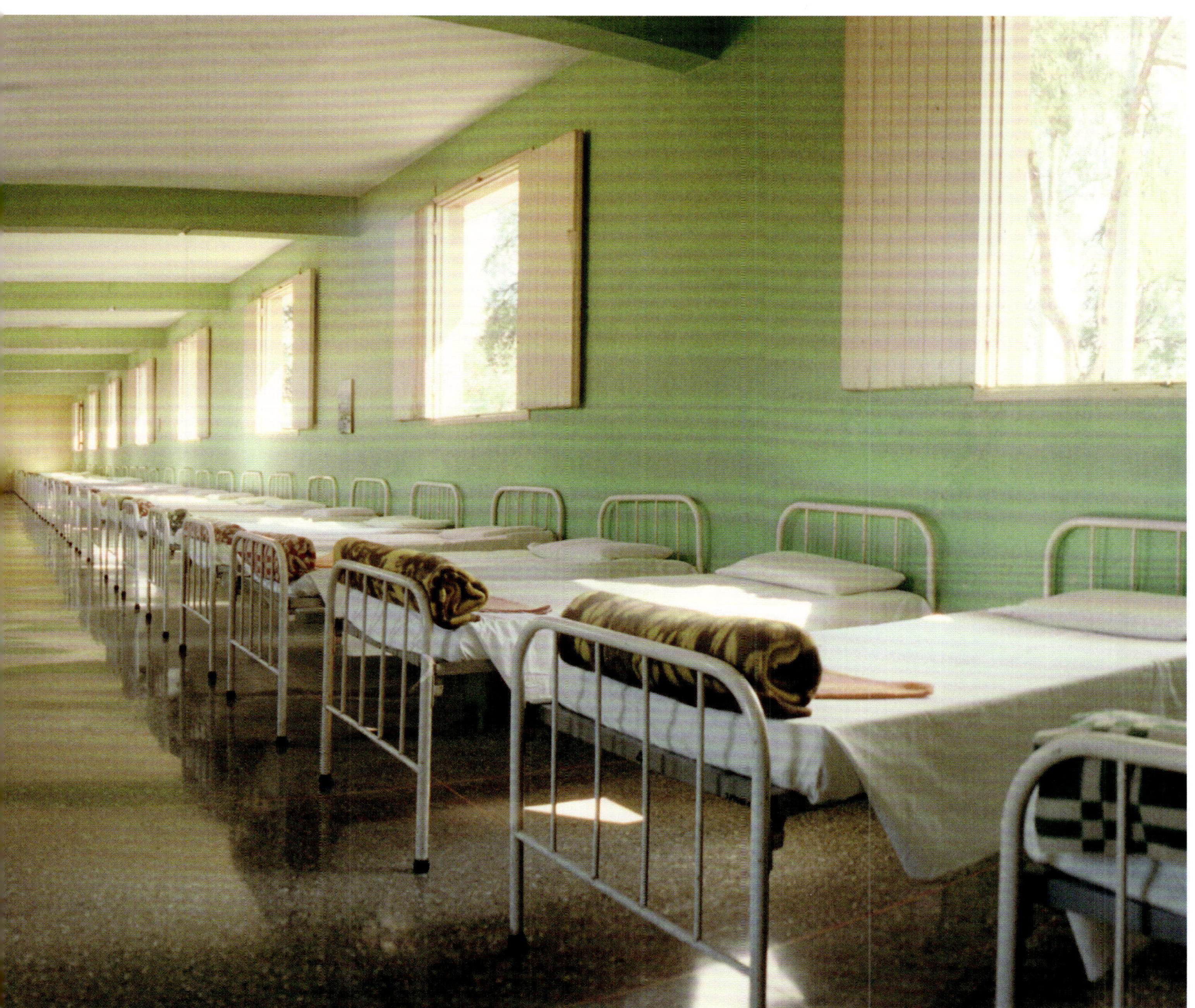

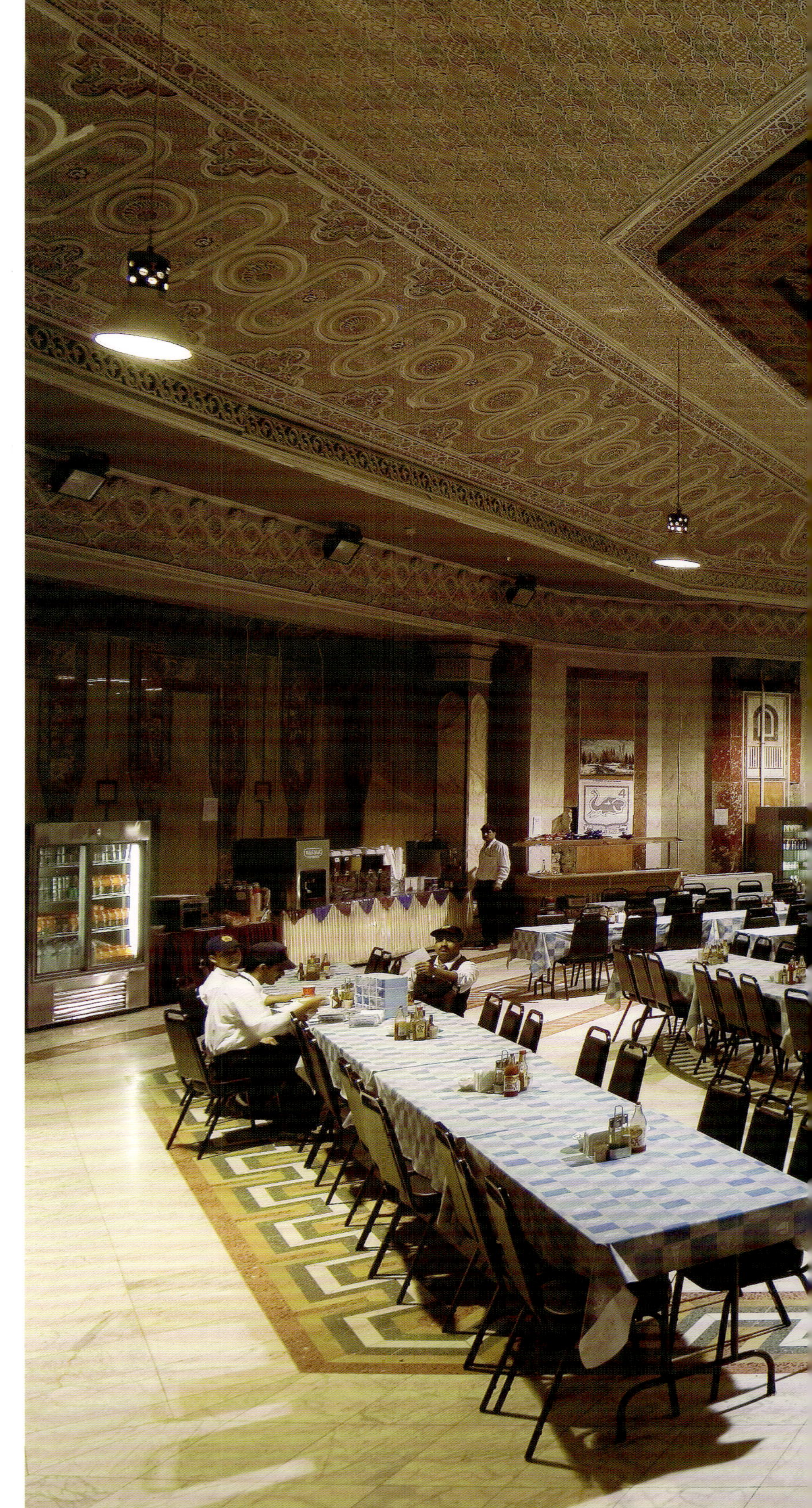

Dining room for the Fourth Brigade, Third Infantry Division headquarters (formerly Uday Hussein's palace), outskirts of Baghdad

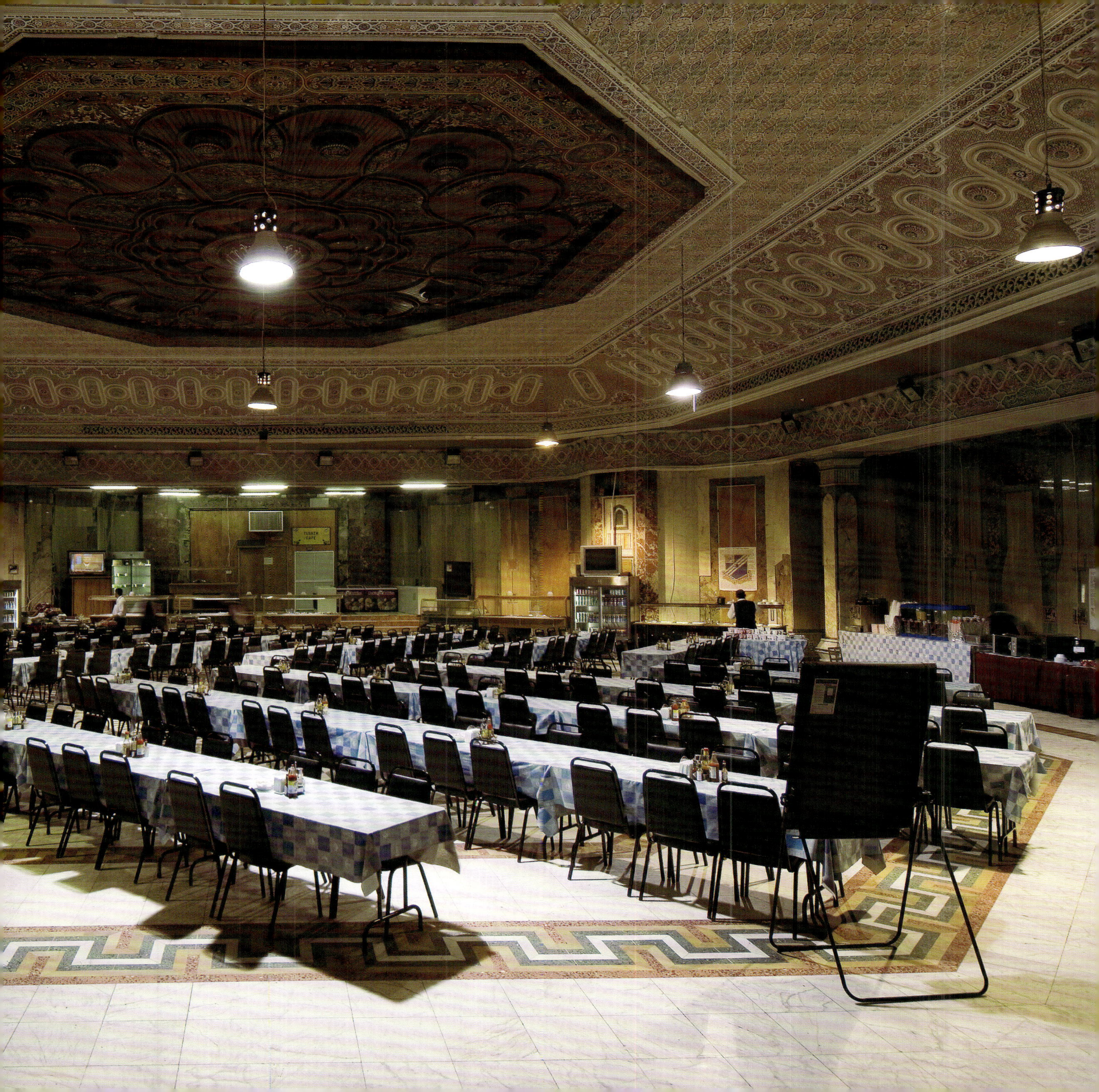

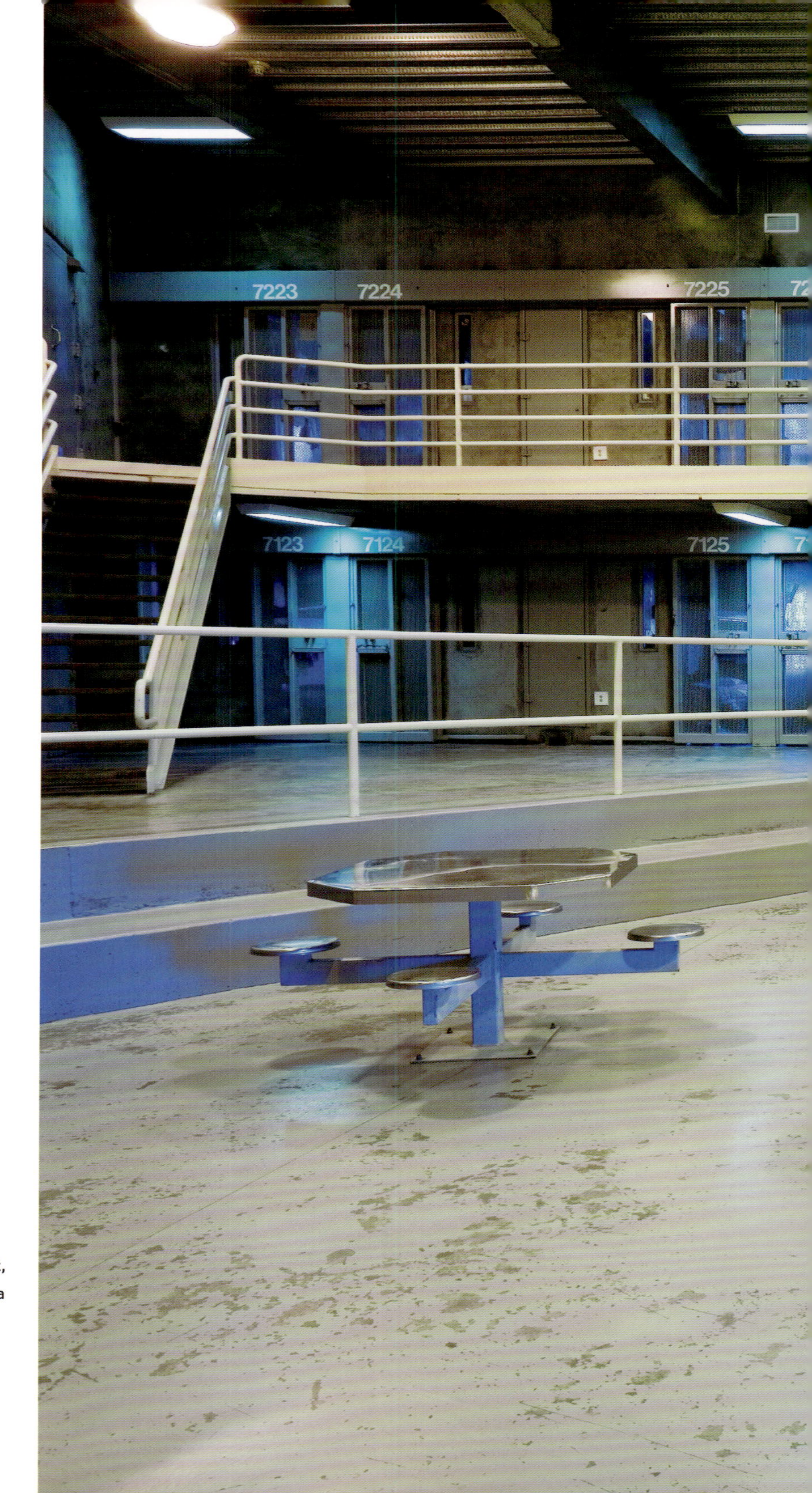

Communal room, Security Housing Unit,
Pelican Bay State Prison, Crescent City, California

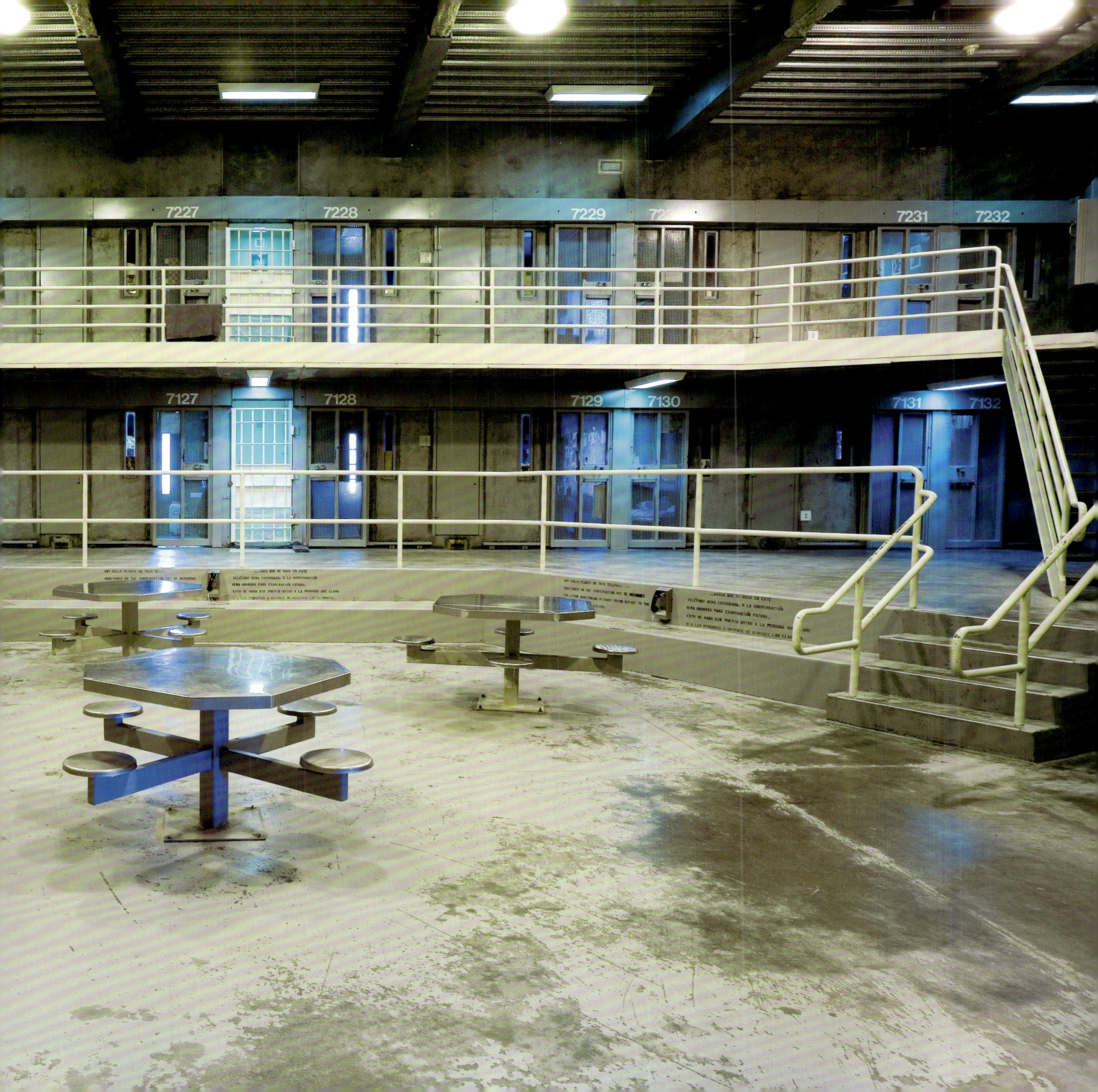
7227
7228
7229
7231
7232
7127
7128
7129
7130
7131
7132

CLOCKWISE FROM TOP LEFT:

"Communication with Others Room," Immigration and Customs Enforcement, Homeland Security, San Francisco

Confessional, Santa Barbara Mission, Santa Barbara, California

Communication area, Angola State Penitentiary, Angola, Louisiana

Four Seasons Hotel, Mexico City

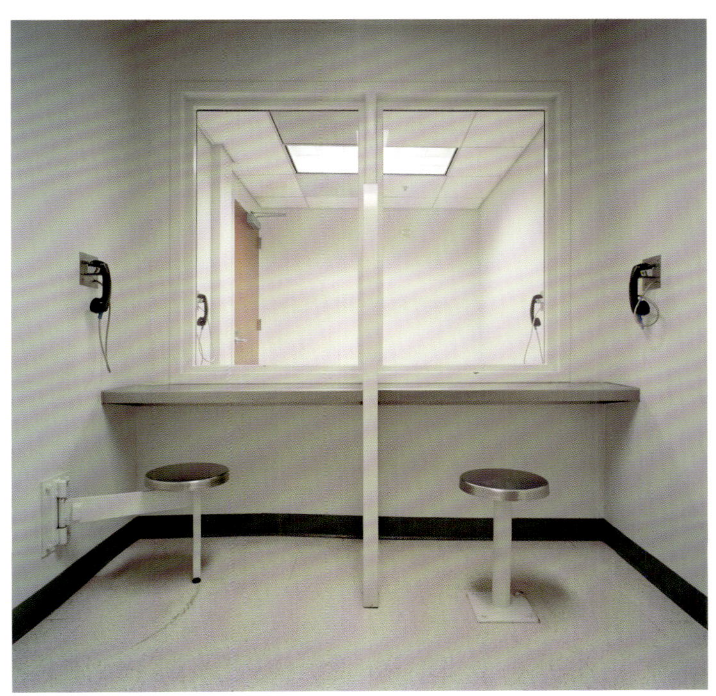

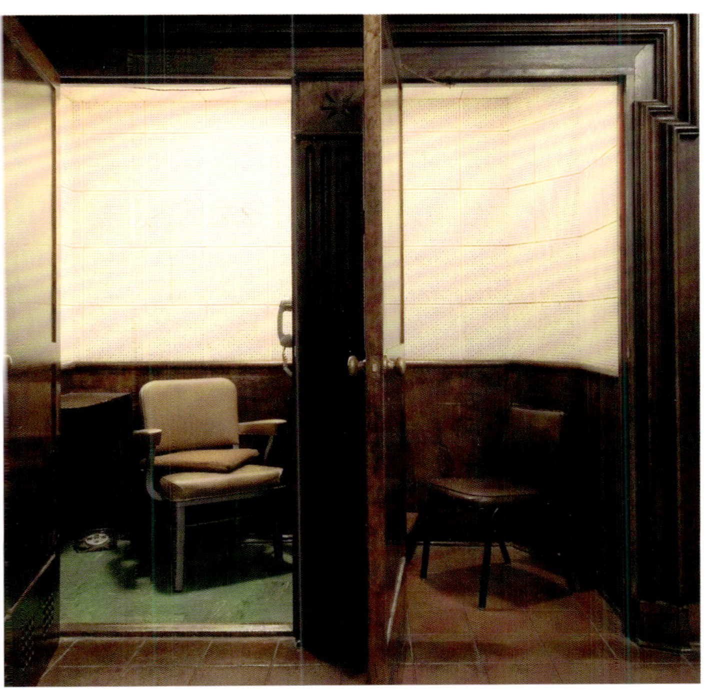

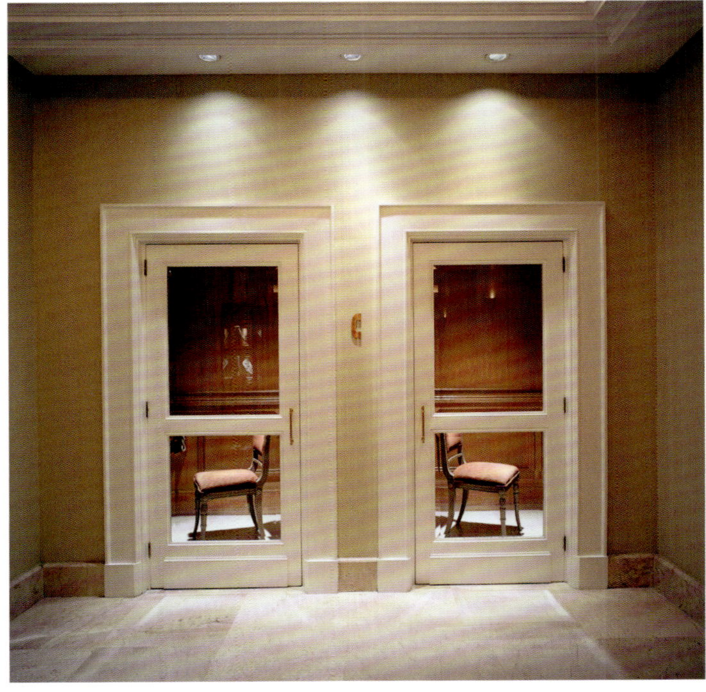

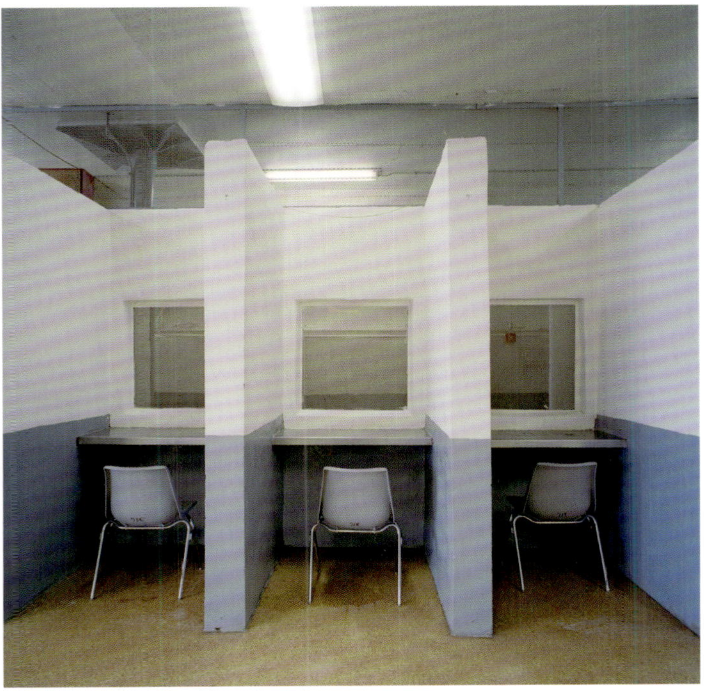

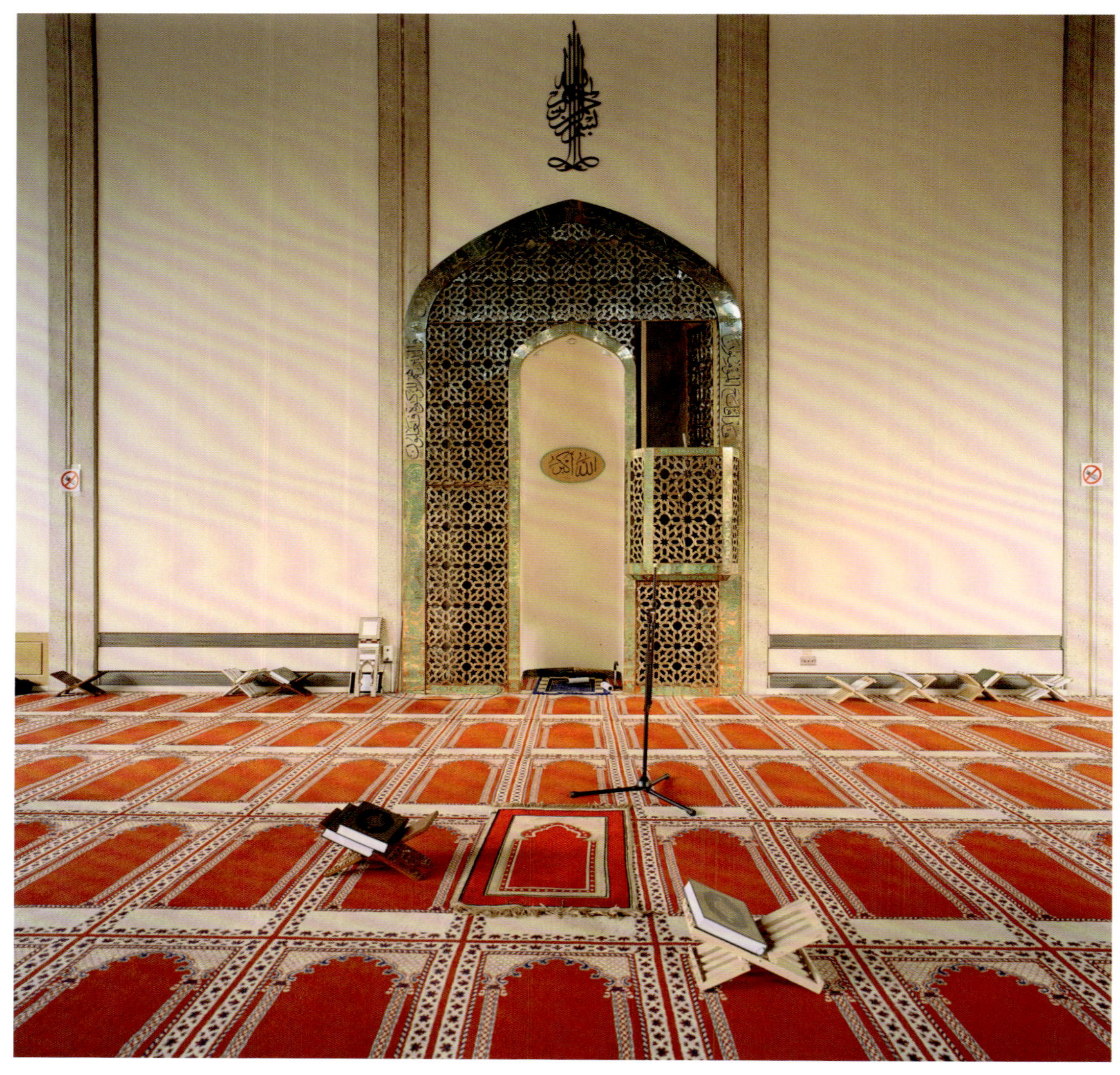

ABOVE: Central London Mosque

OPPOSITE: St. Kilda Church, St. Kilda, Scotland

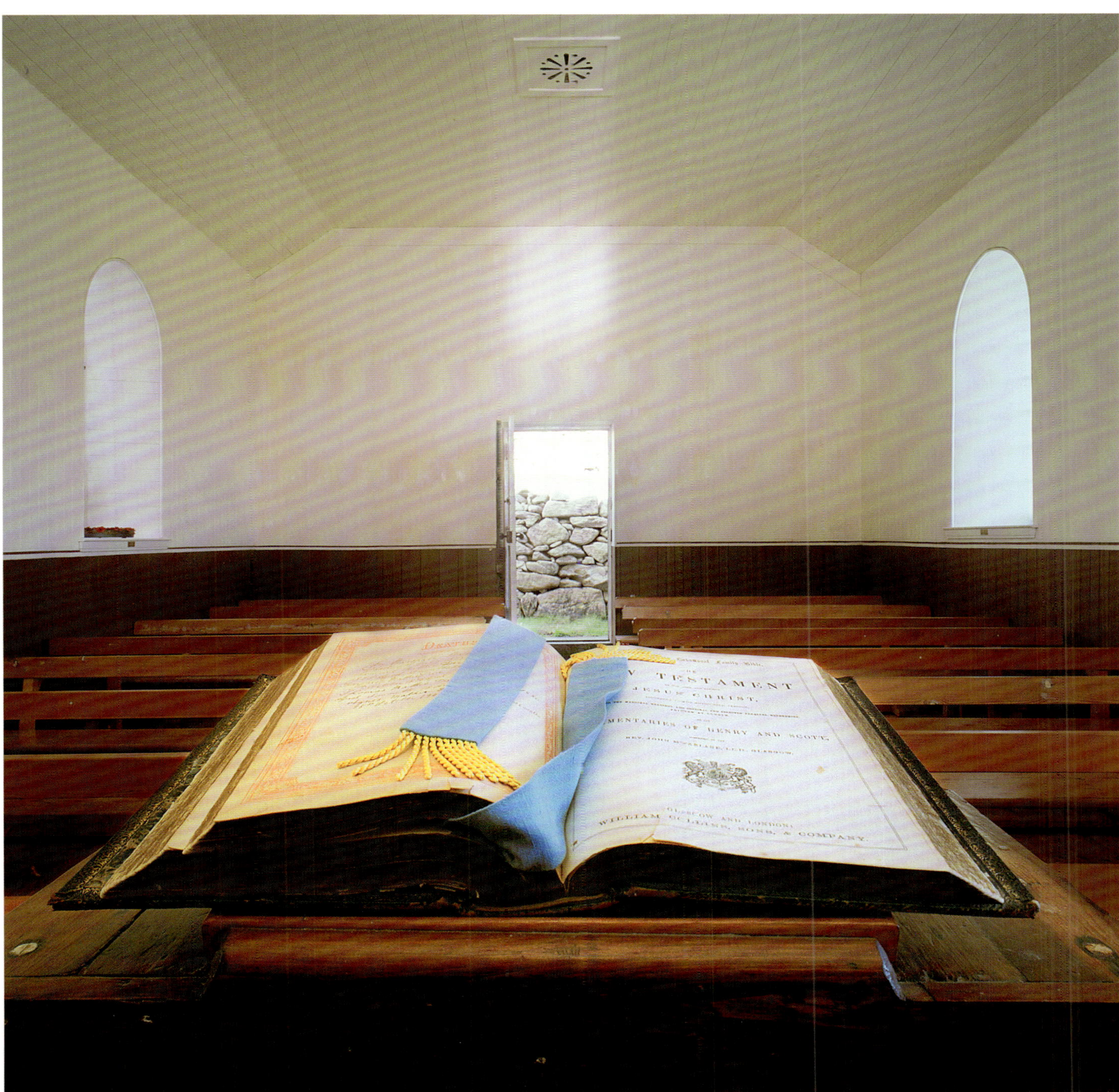
V TESTAMENT
JESUS CHRIST.
MENTARIES OF HENRY AND SCOTT,
WILLIAM COLLINS, SONS, & COMPANY.

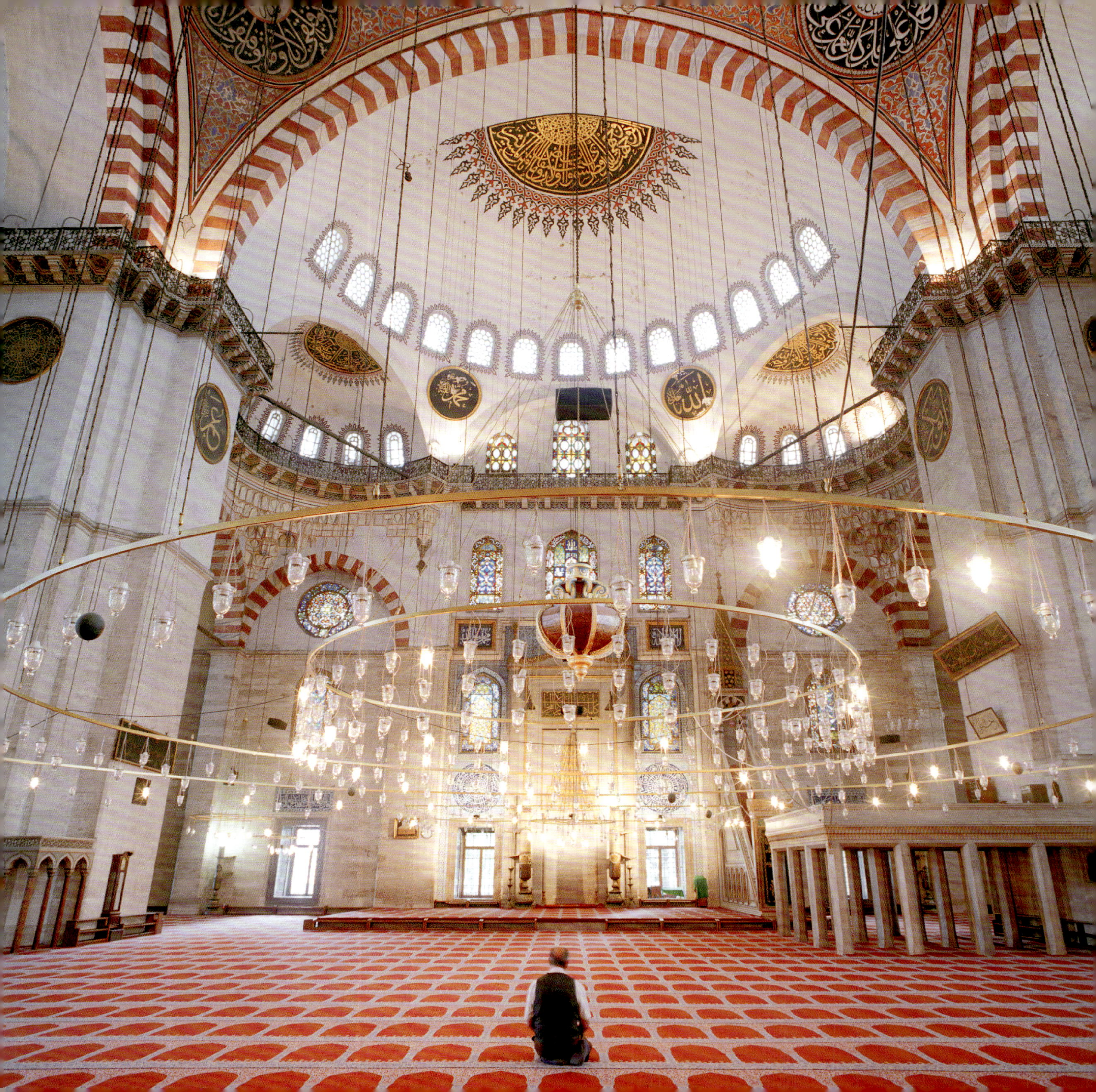

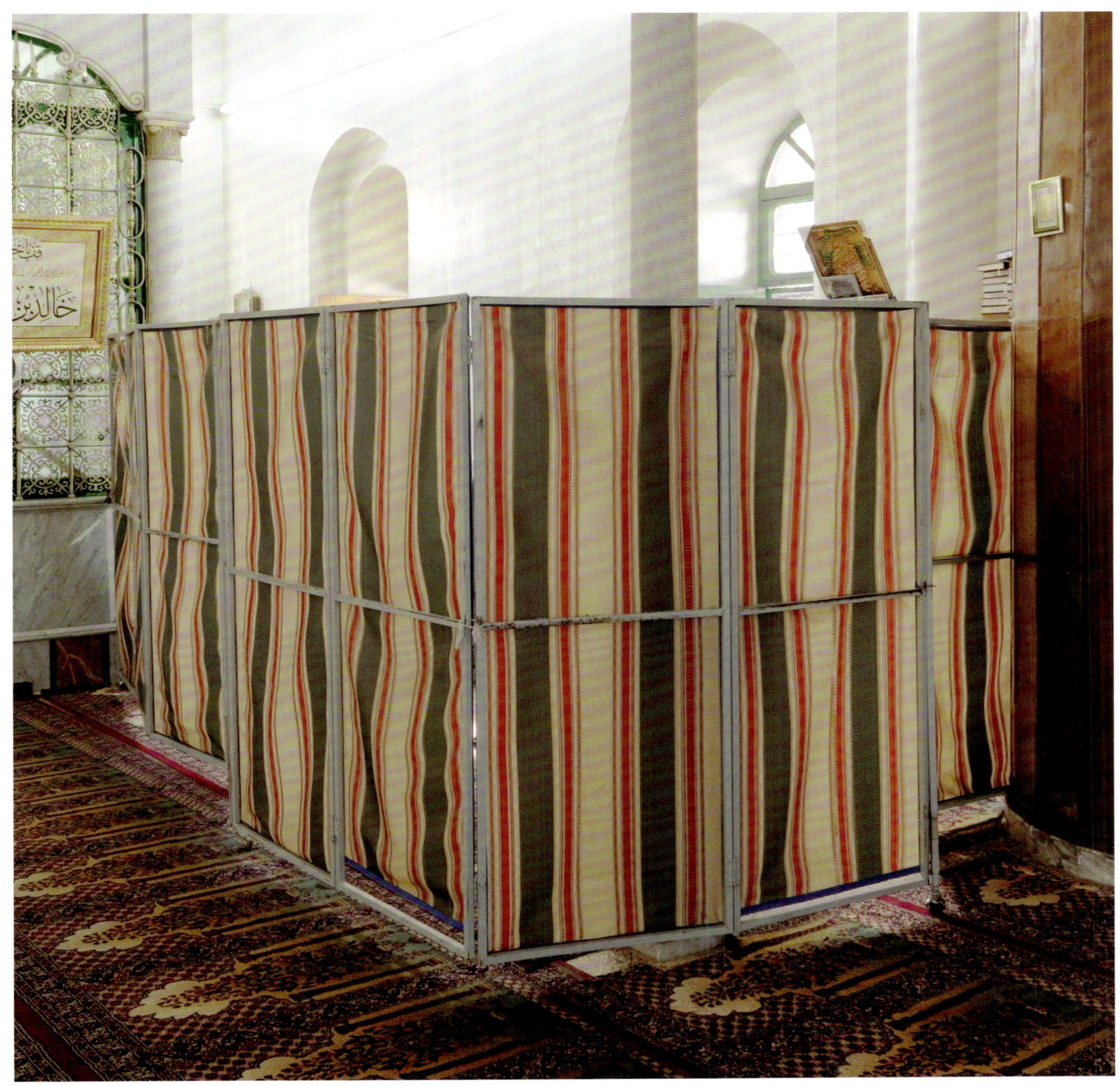

OPPOSITE: Blue Mosque, Istanbul, Turkey

ABOVE: Women's prayer area, Khaled ibn al-Walid Mosque, Homs, Syria

Confessional, Cathedral of Notre-Dame, Paris

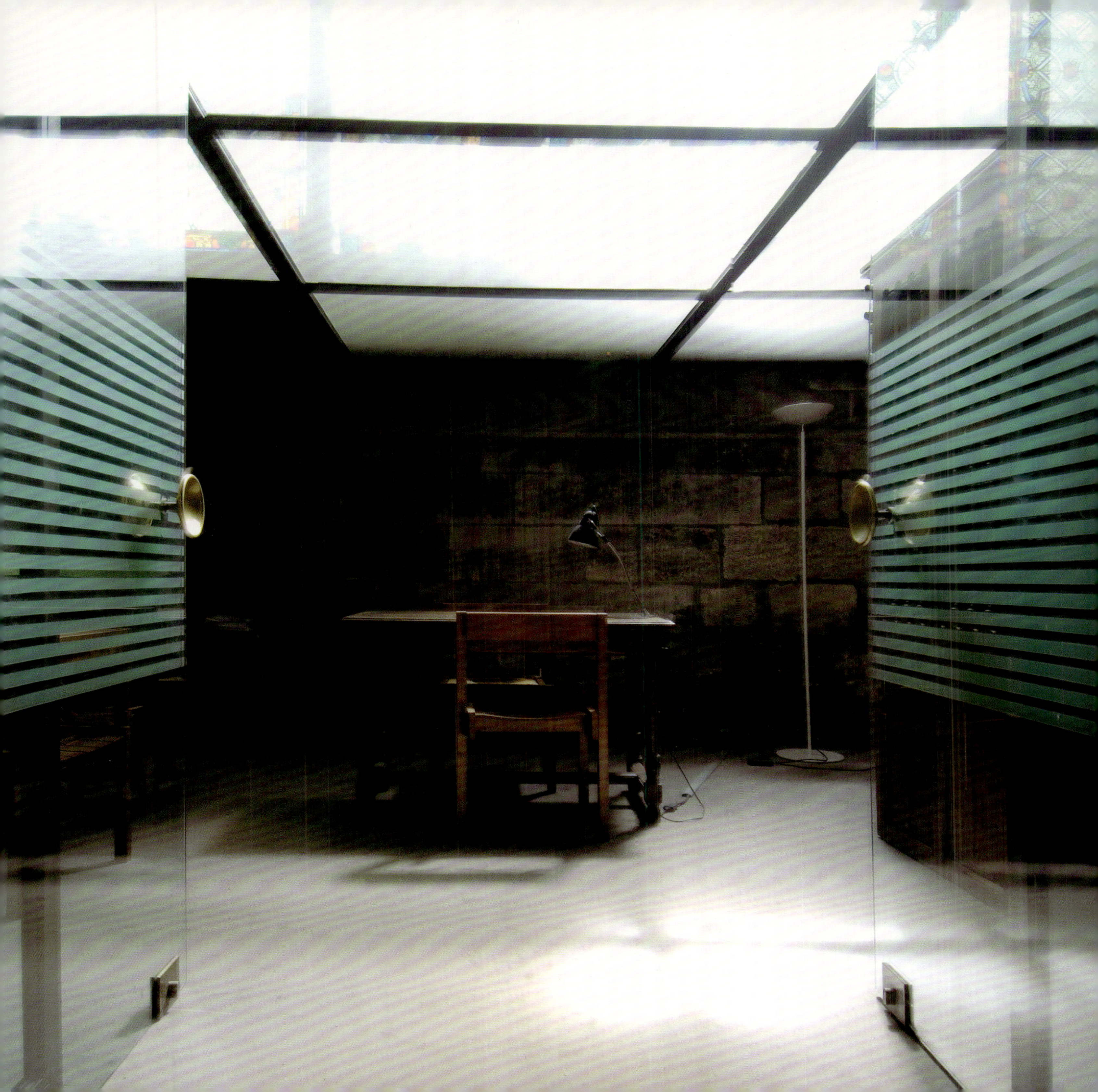

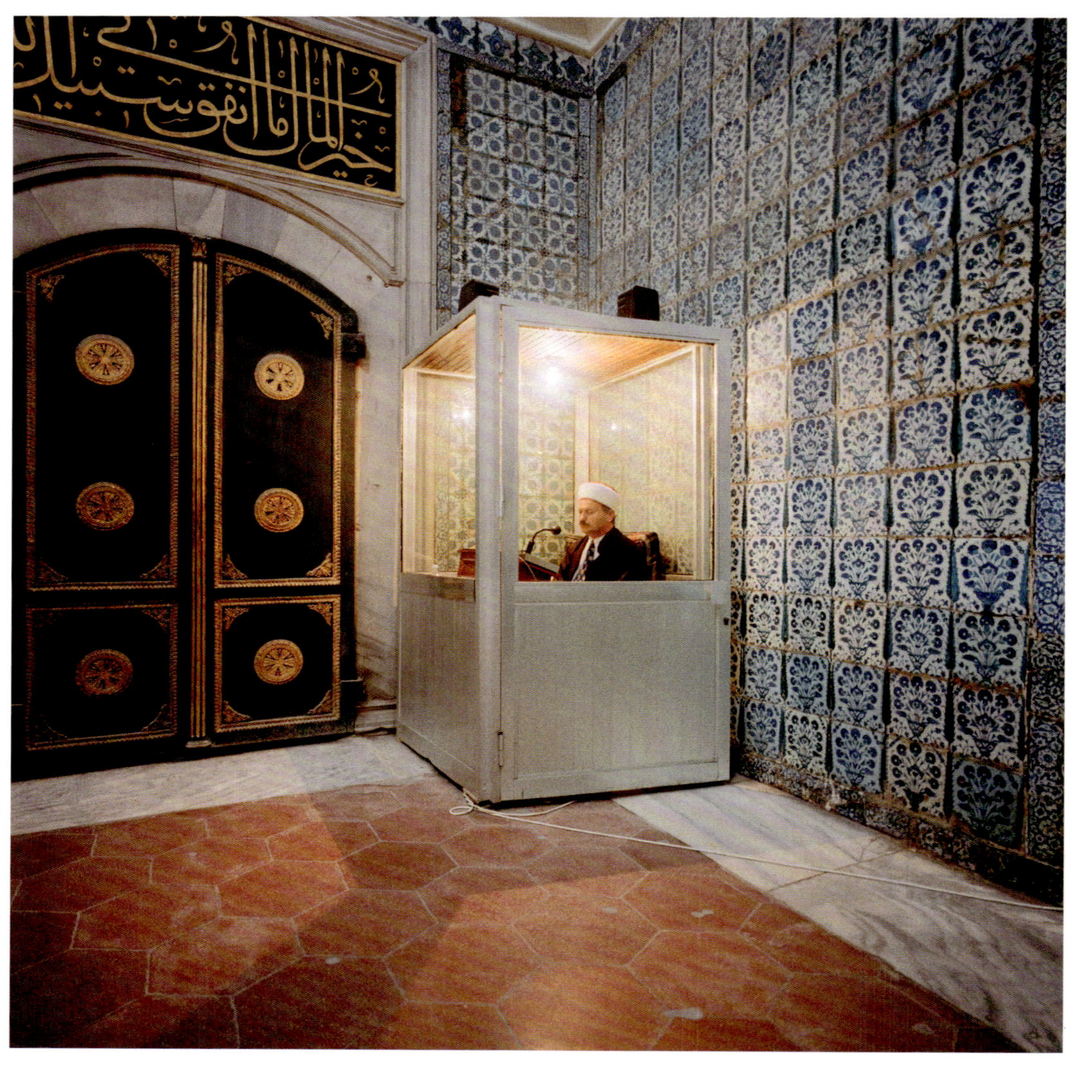

ABOVE: Topkapi Palace, Istanbul, Turkey

OPPOSITE: Guardhouse, Damascus, Syria

OVERLEAF: Segregation cells, Camp Remembrance, new Abu Ghraib prison, Abu Ghraib, Iraq

PAGES 64–65: Crusader fort, Craq du Chevalier, Syria

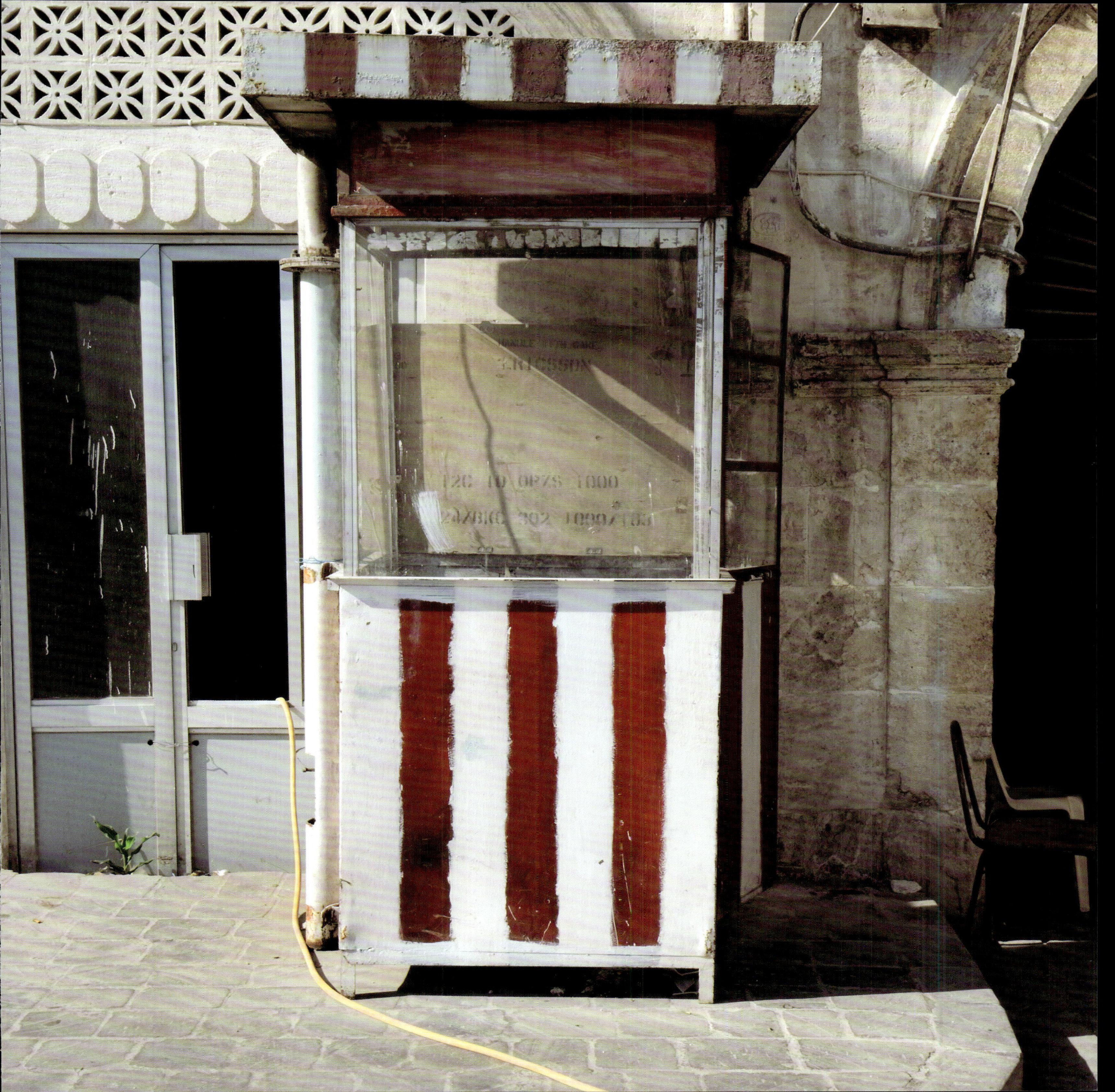

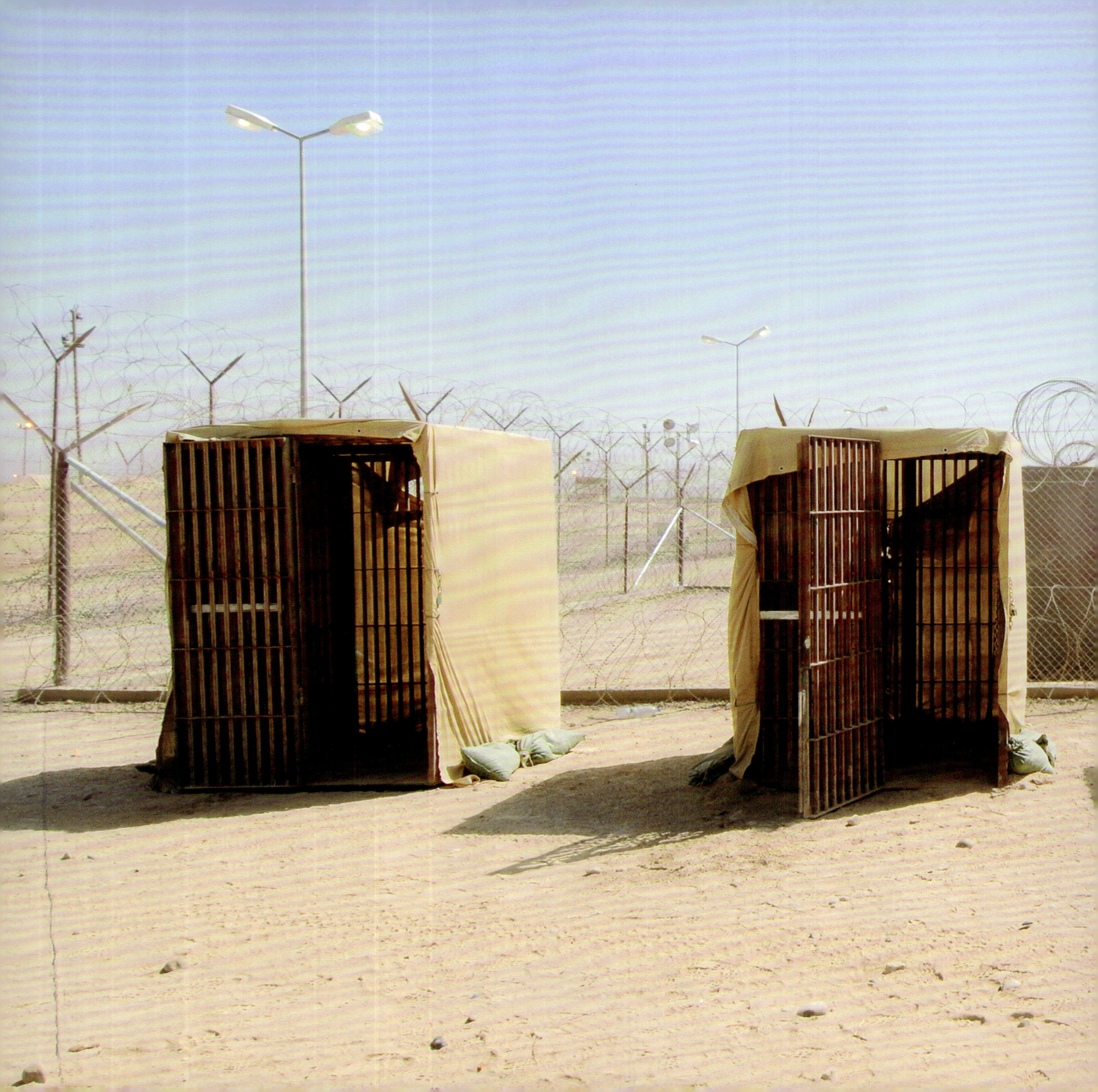

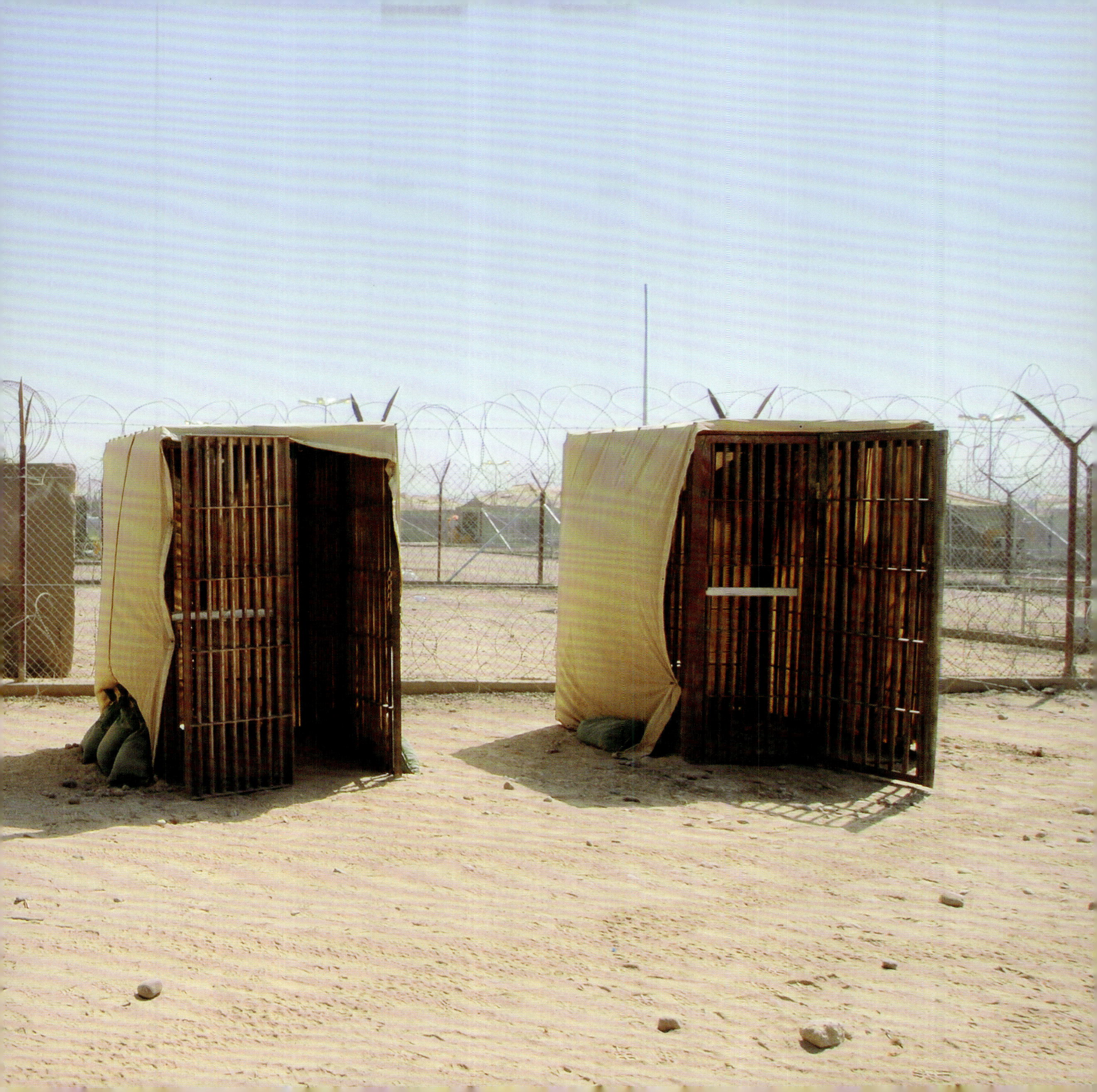

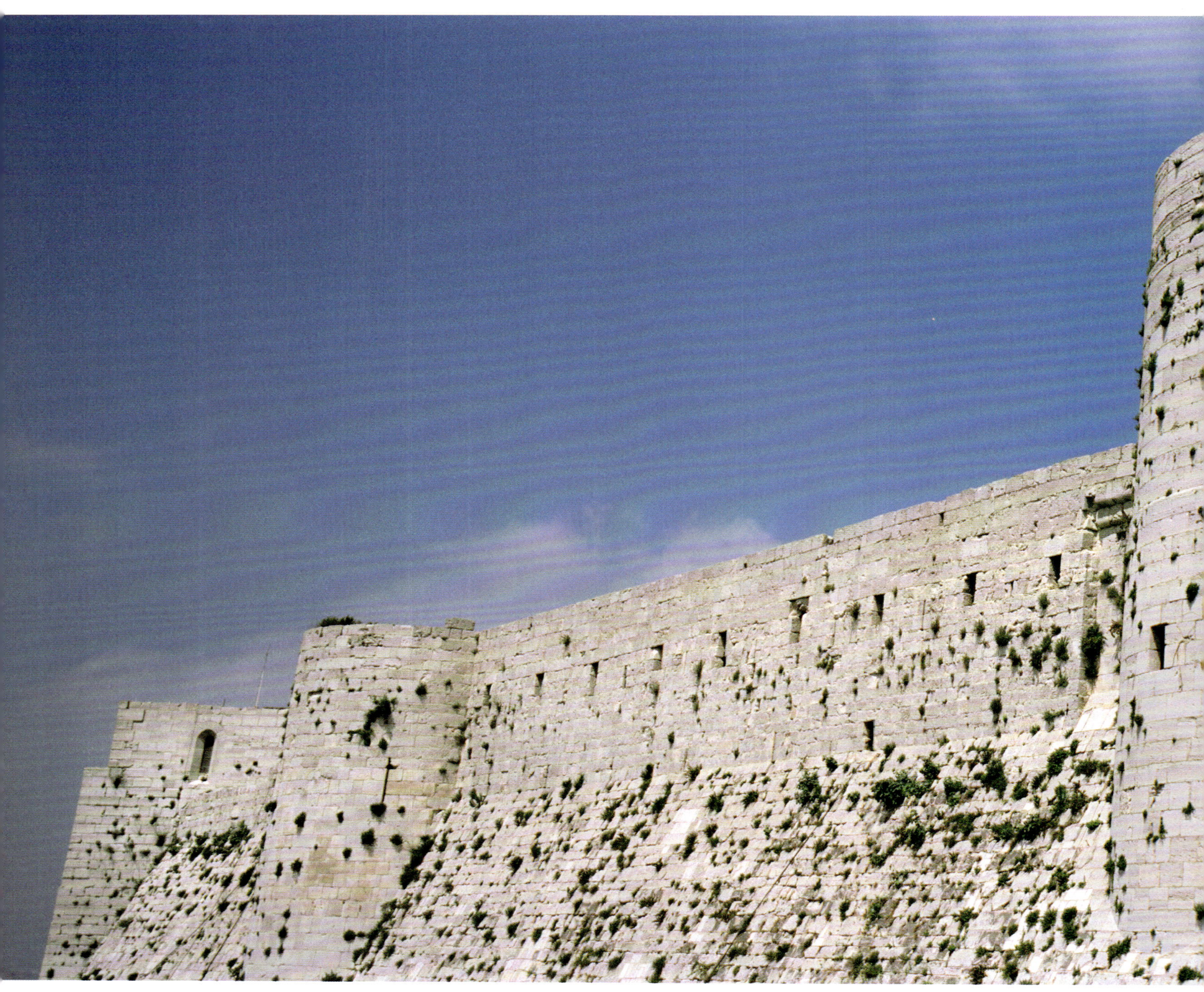

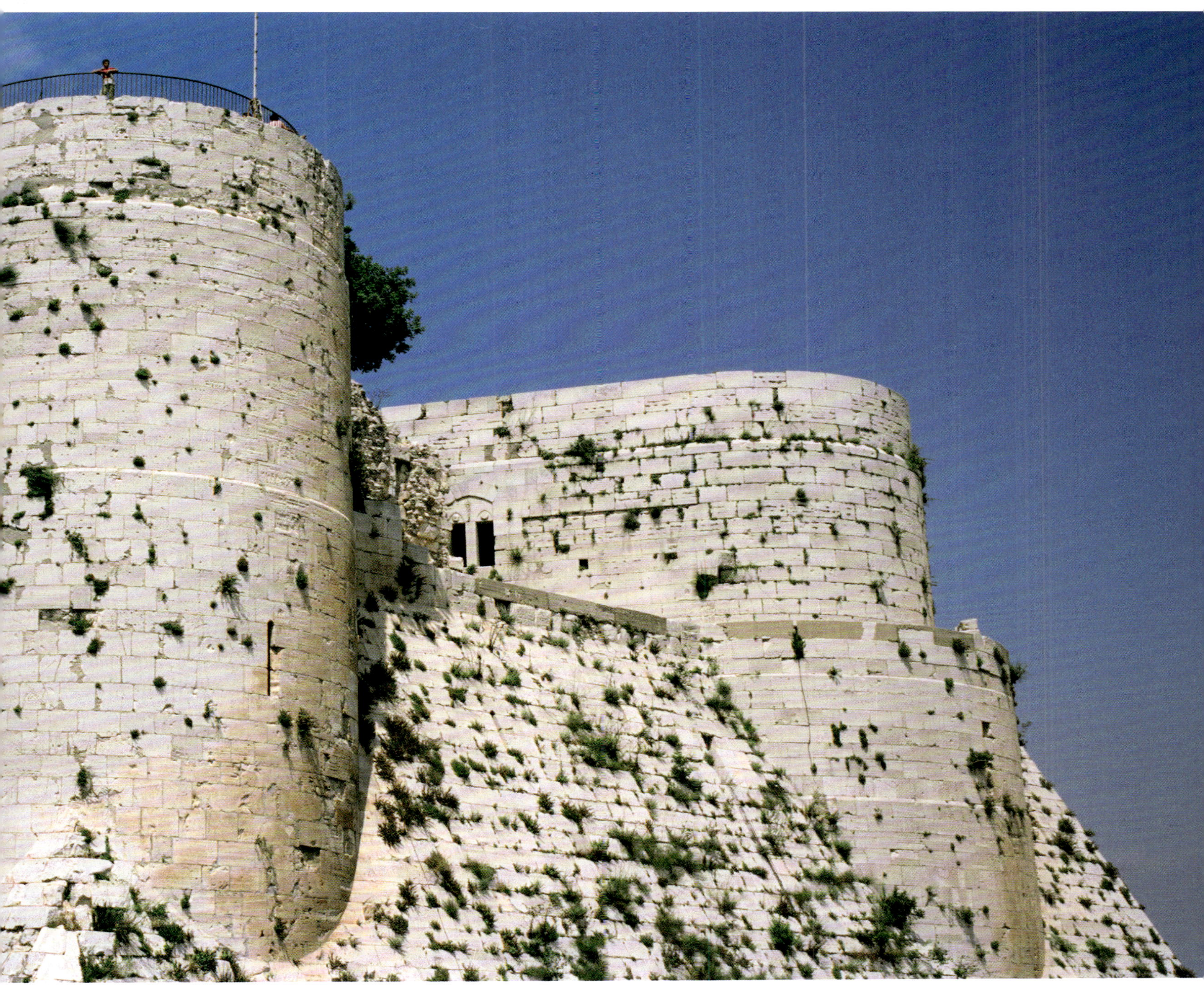

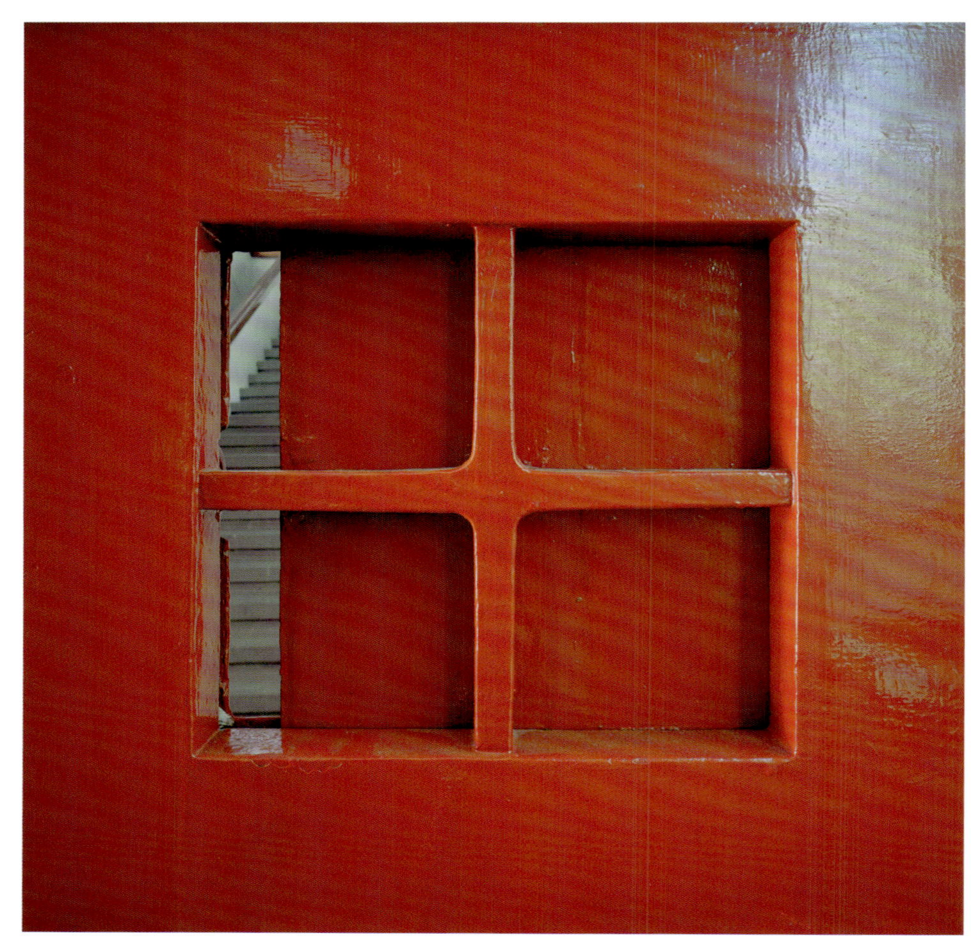

ABOVE AND OPPOSITE: Palacio de Lecumberri (former prison), Mexico City

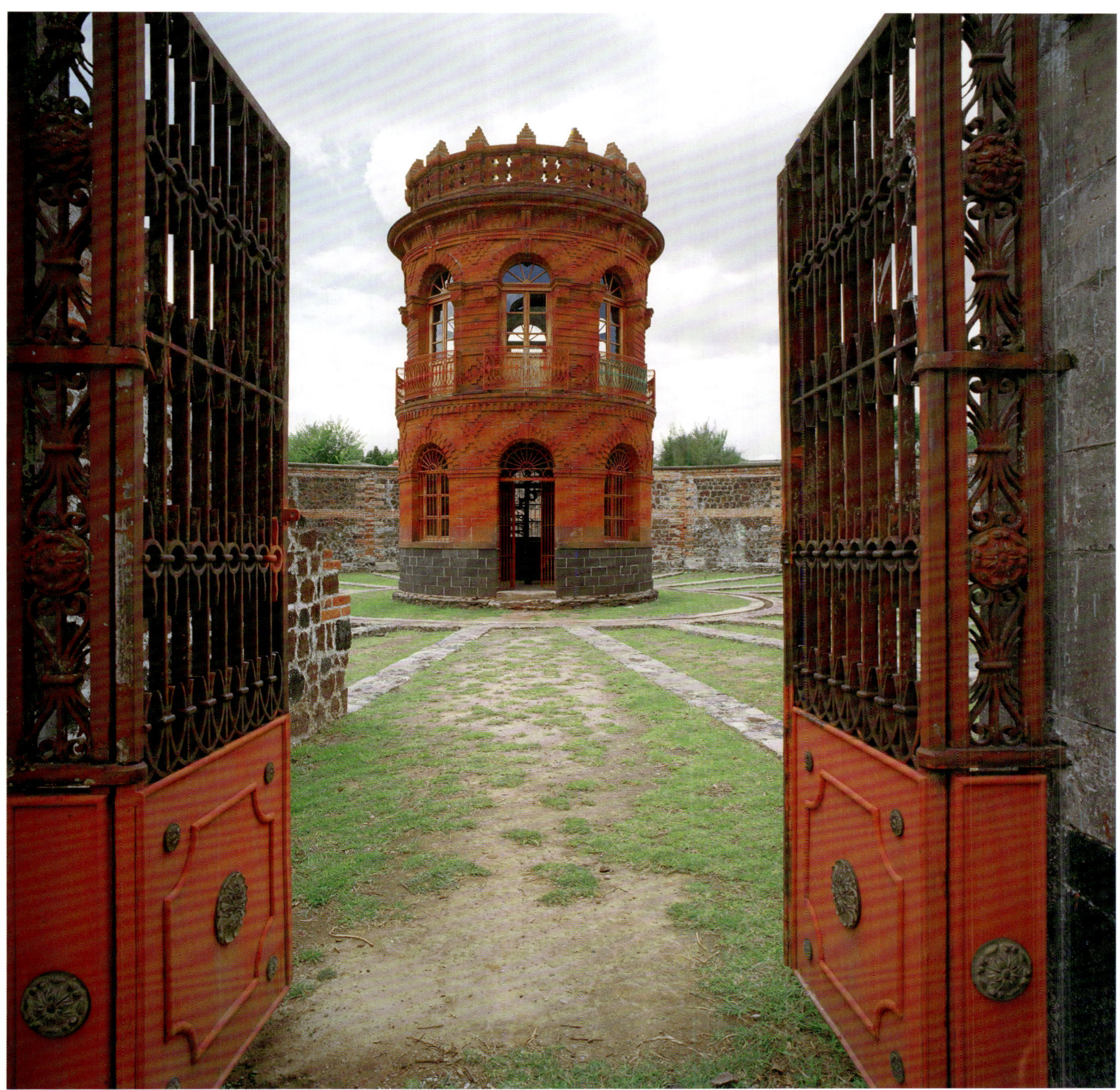

Chalk Farm tube station, Northern Line, London

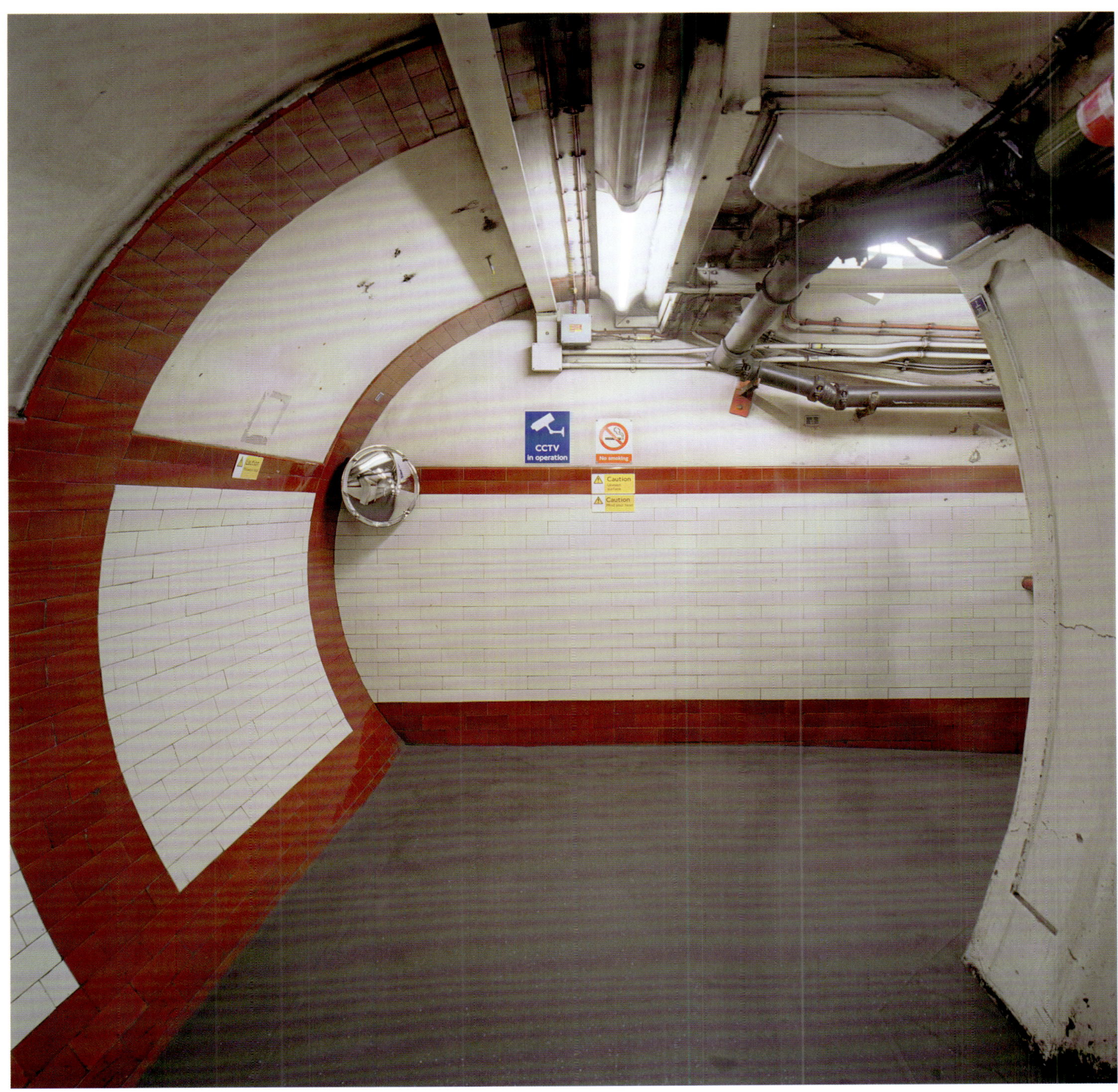

CCTV
in operation
No smoking
Caution
Caution

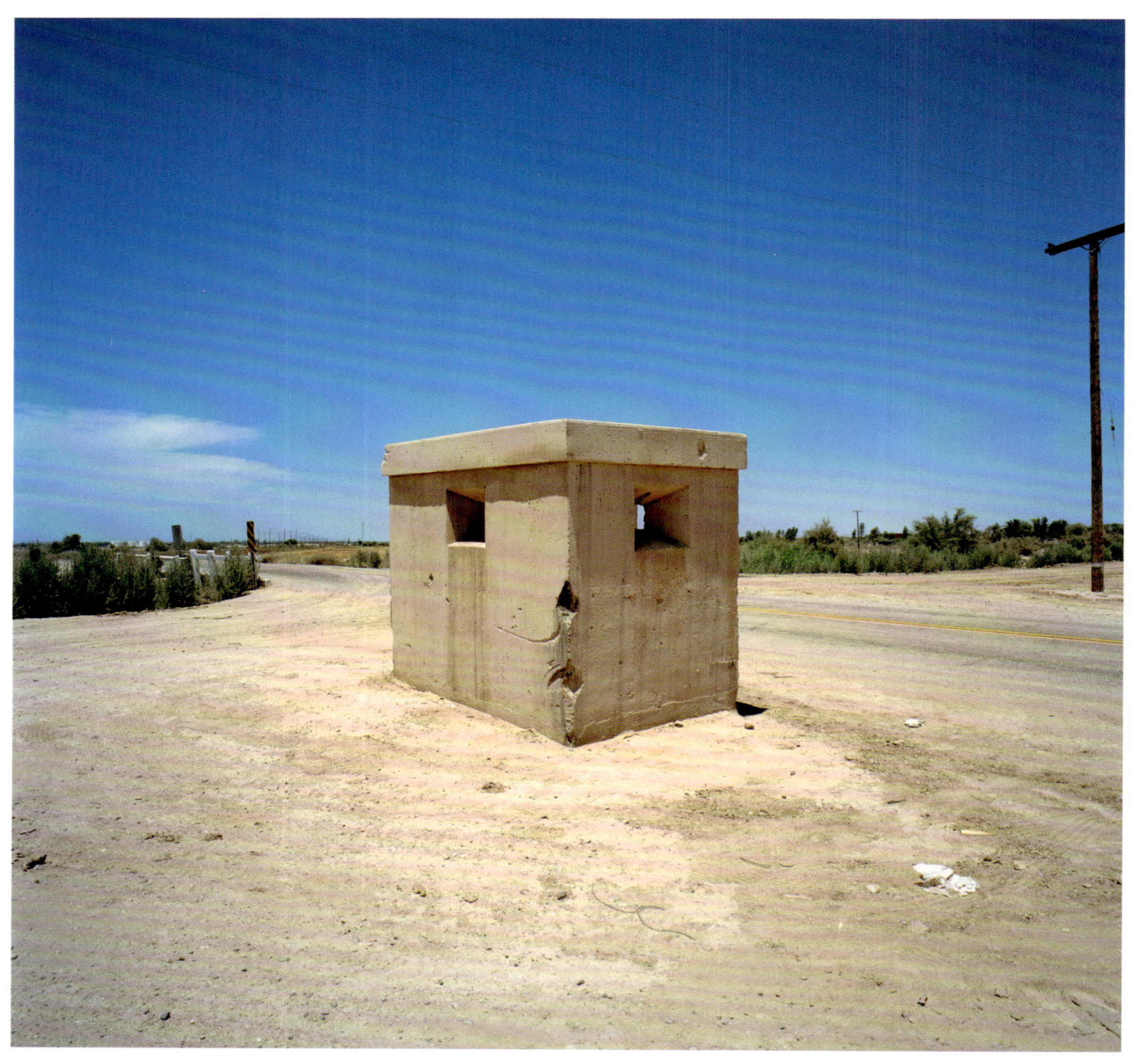

Guardhouse, abandoned Marine Corps post, Niland, California

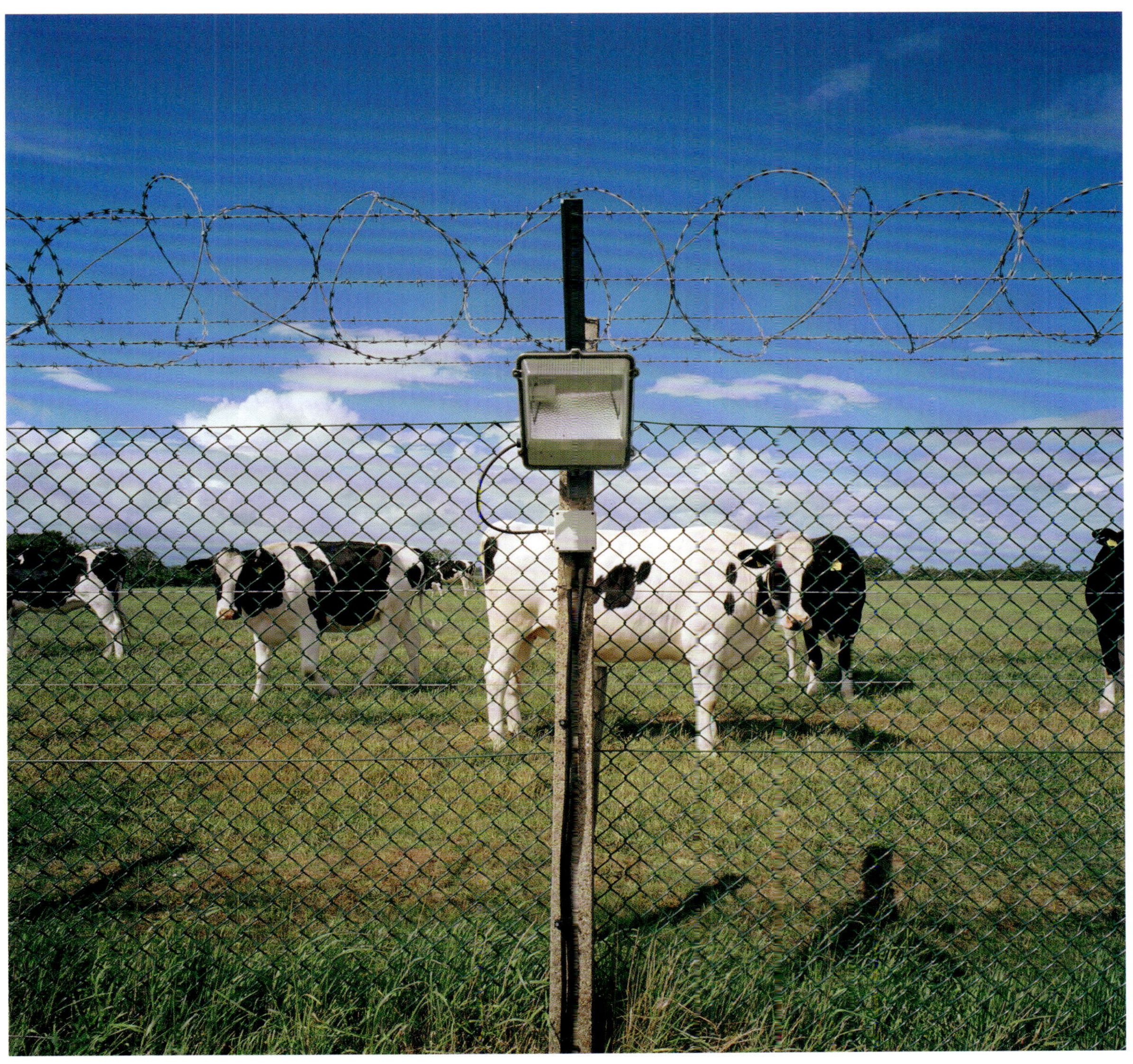

Inactive nuclear command center, Anstruther, Scotland

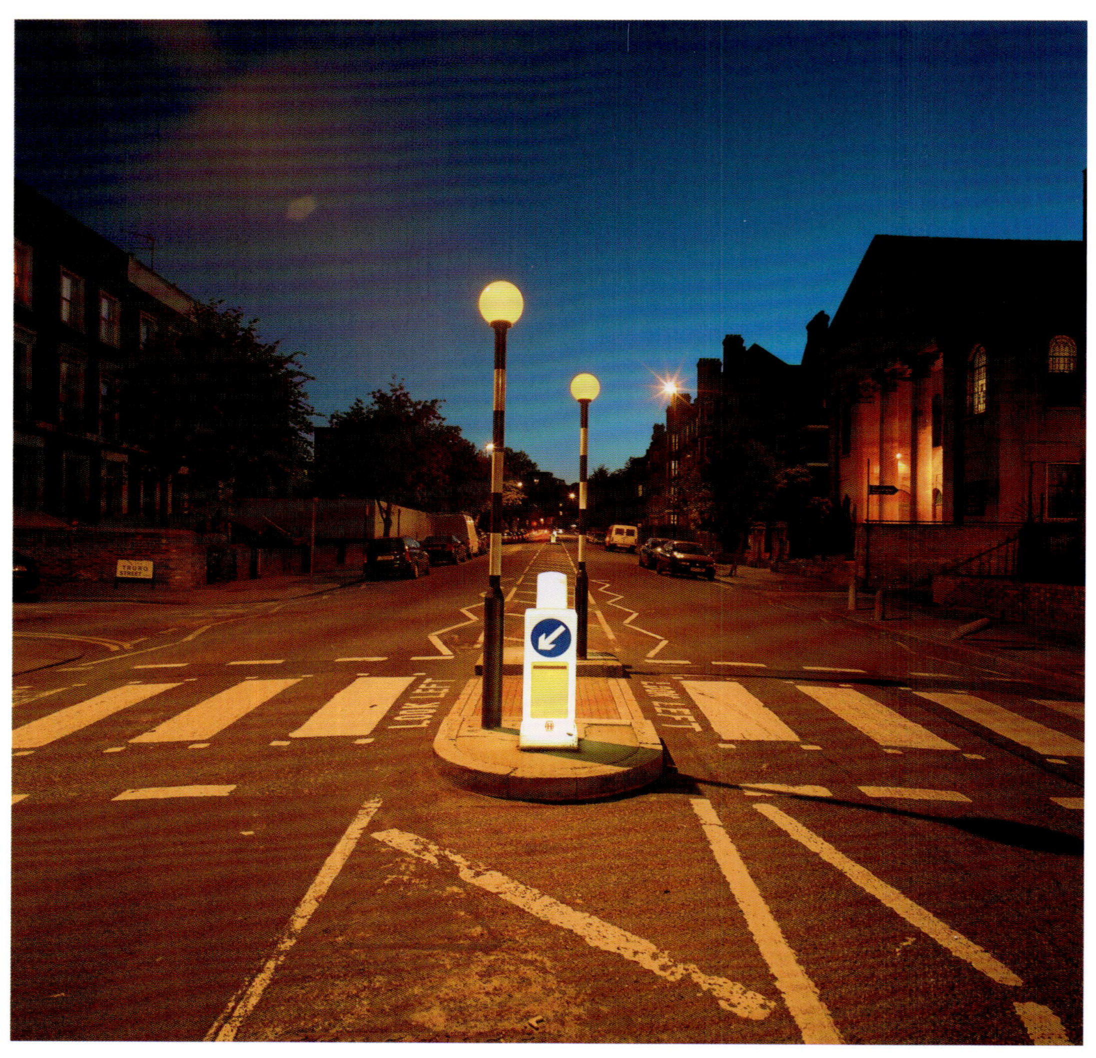

ABOVE: Prince of Wales Road, Chalk Farm, London

OPPOSITE: U.S. border inspection station, San Ysidro, California

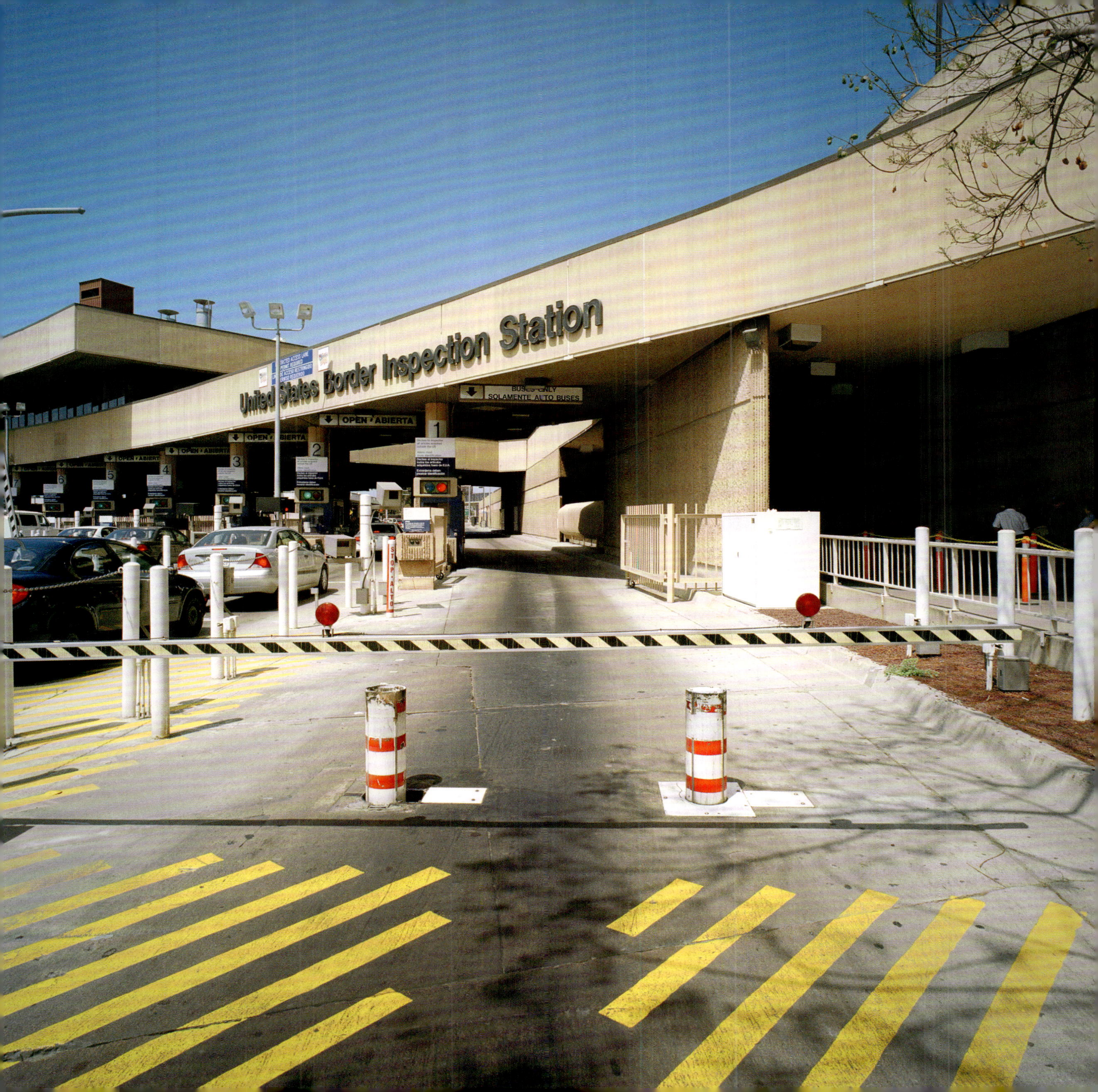
United States Border Inspection Station
BUSES ONLY
SOLAMENTE AUTO BUSES
OPEN ABIERTA
OPEN ABIERTA
OPEN ABIERTA
STOP ALTO

OPPOSITE: Air Force building, Ministry of Defense, Damascus, Syria

OVERLEAF: Border crossing from Jordan to Syria

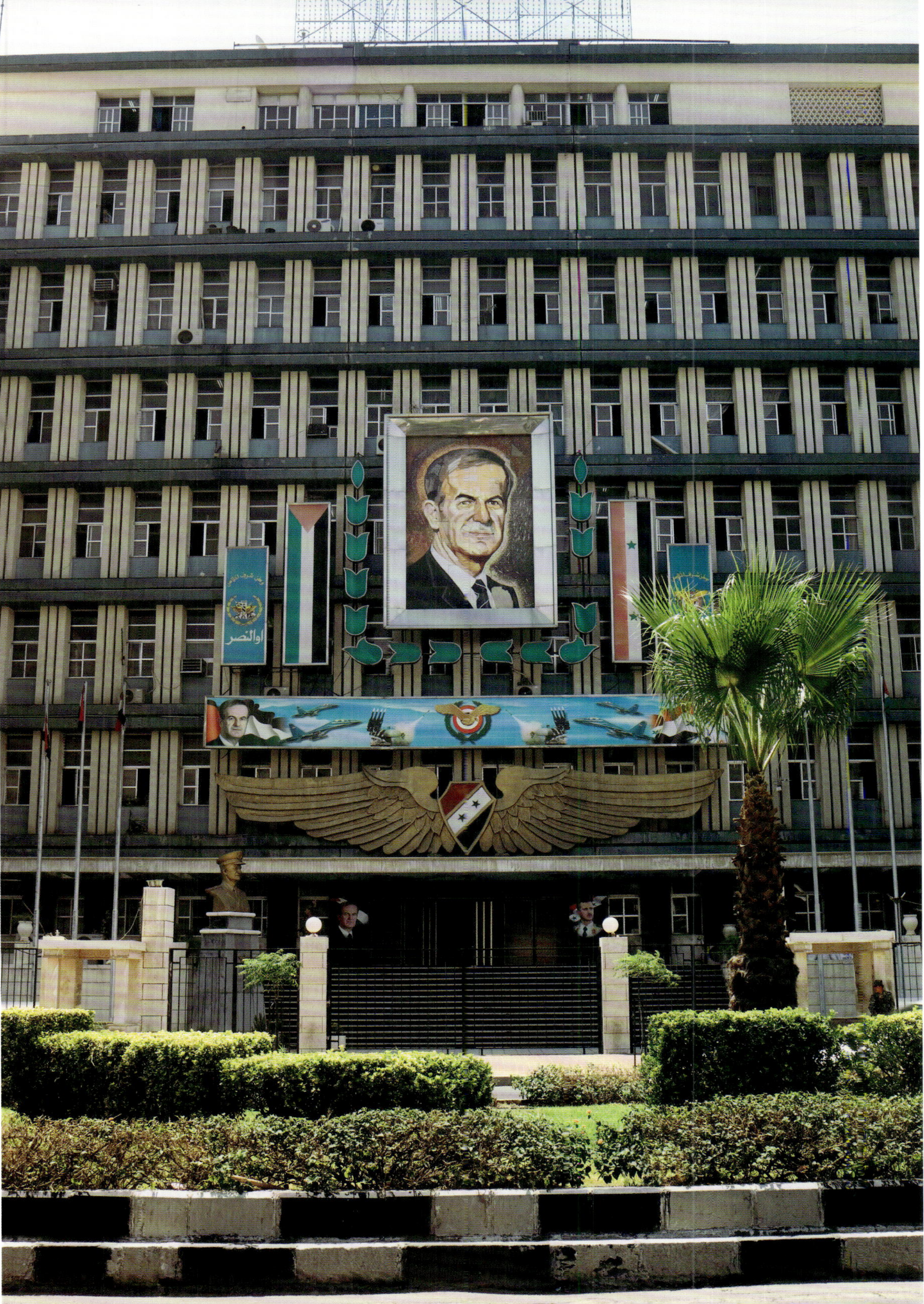
اوالنصر

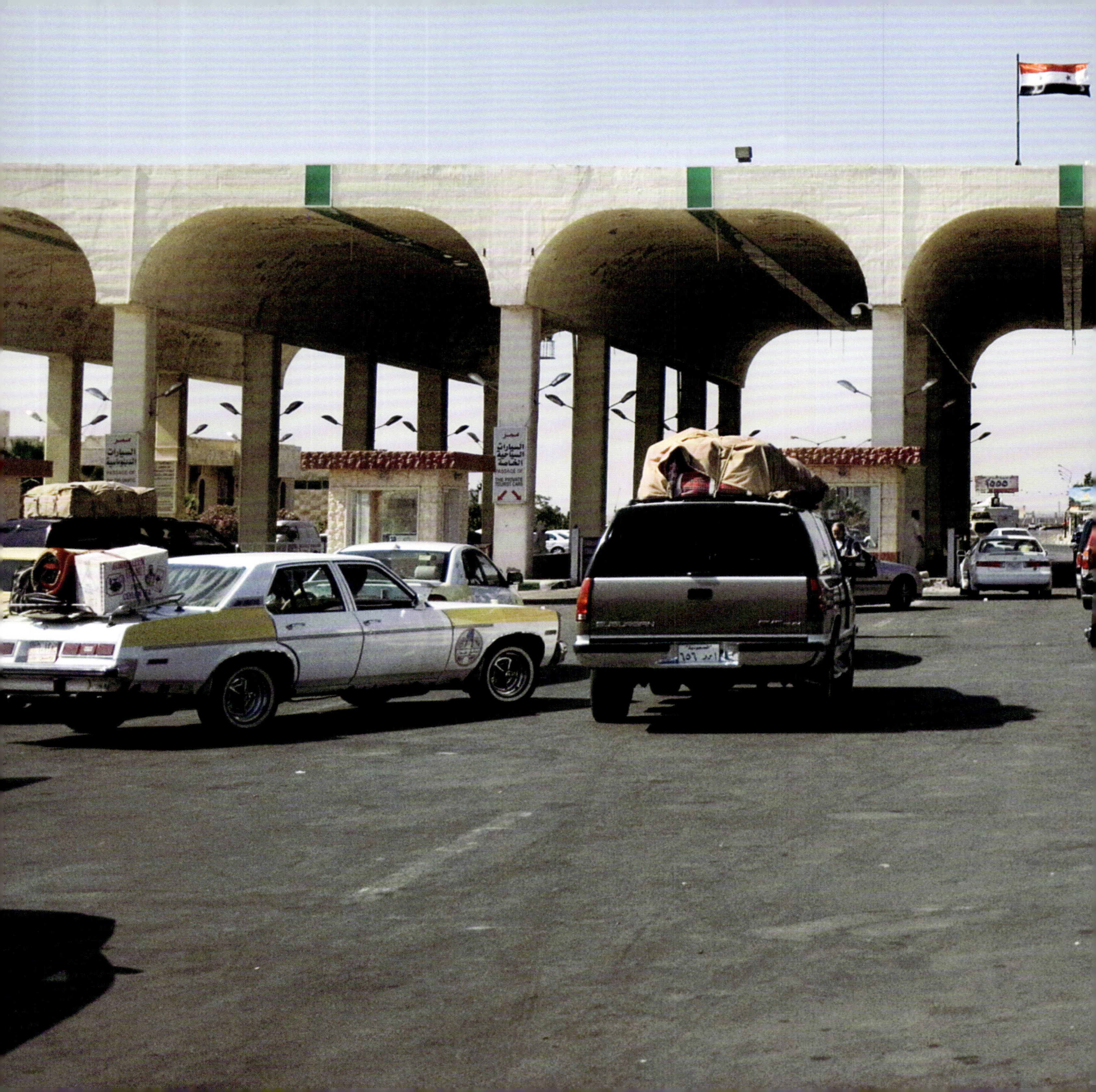
ممر
السيارات
السياحية
الخاصة

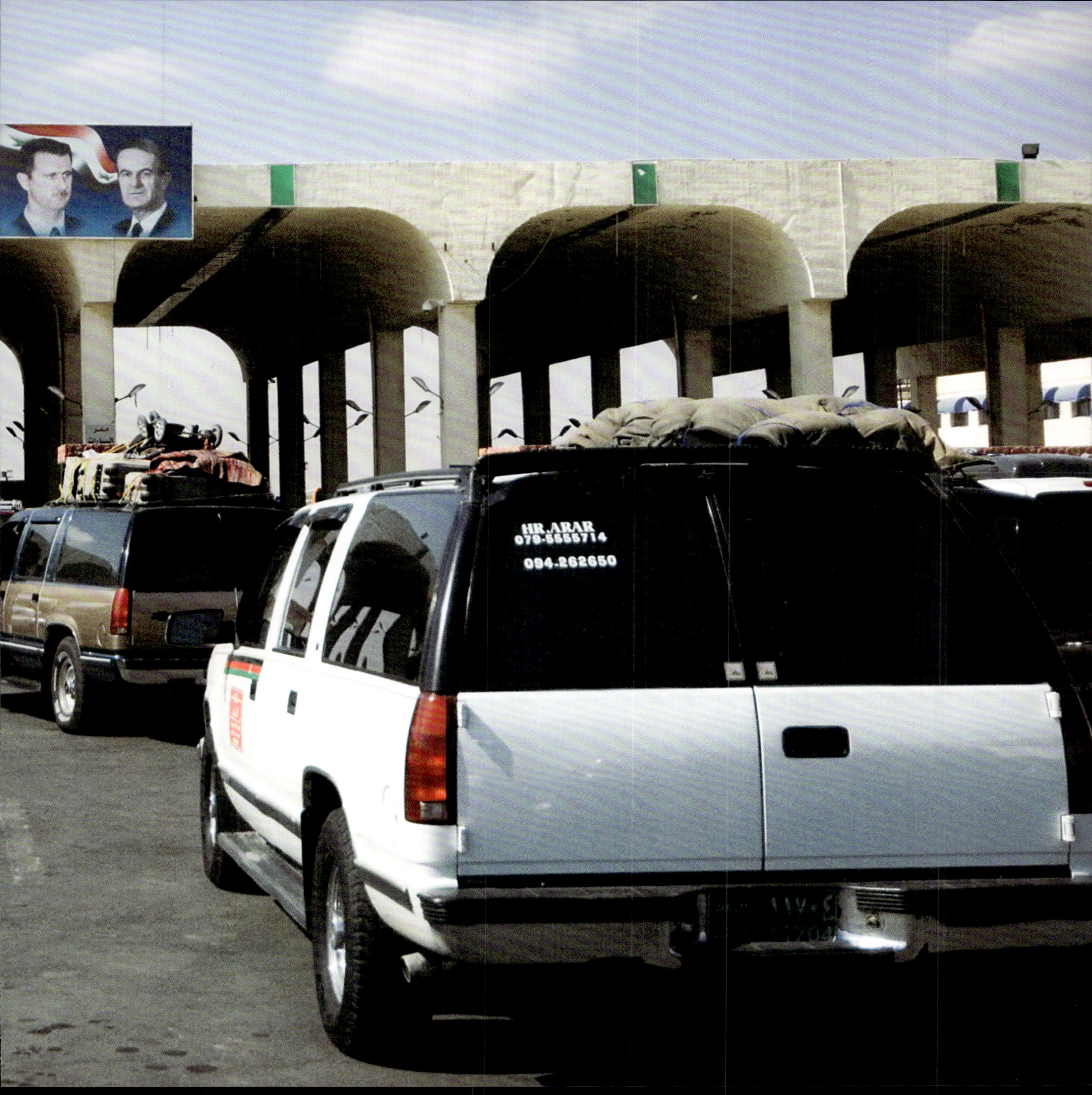
HR.ARAR
079-5555714
094.262650

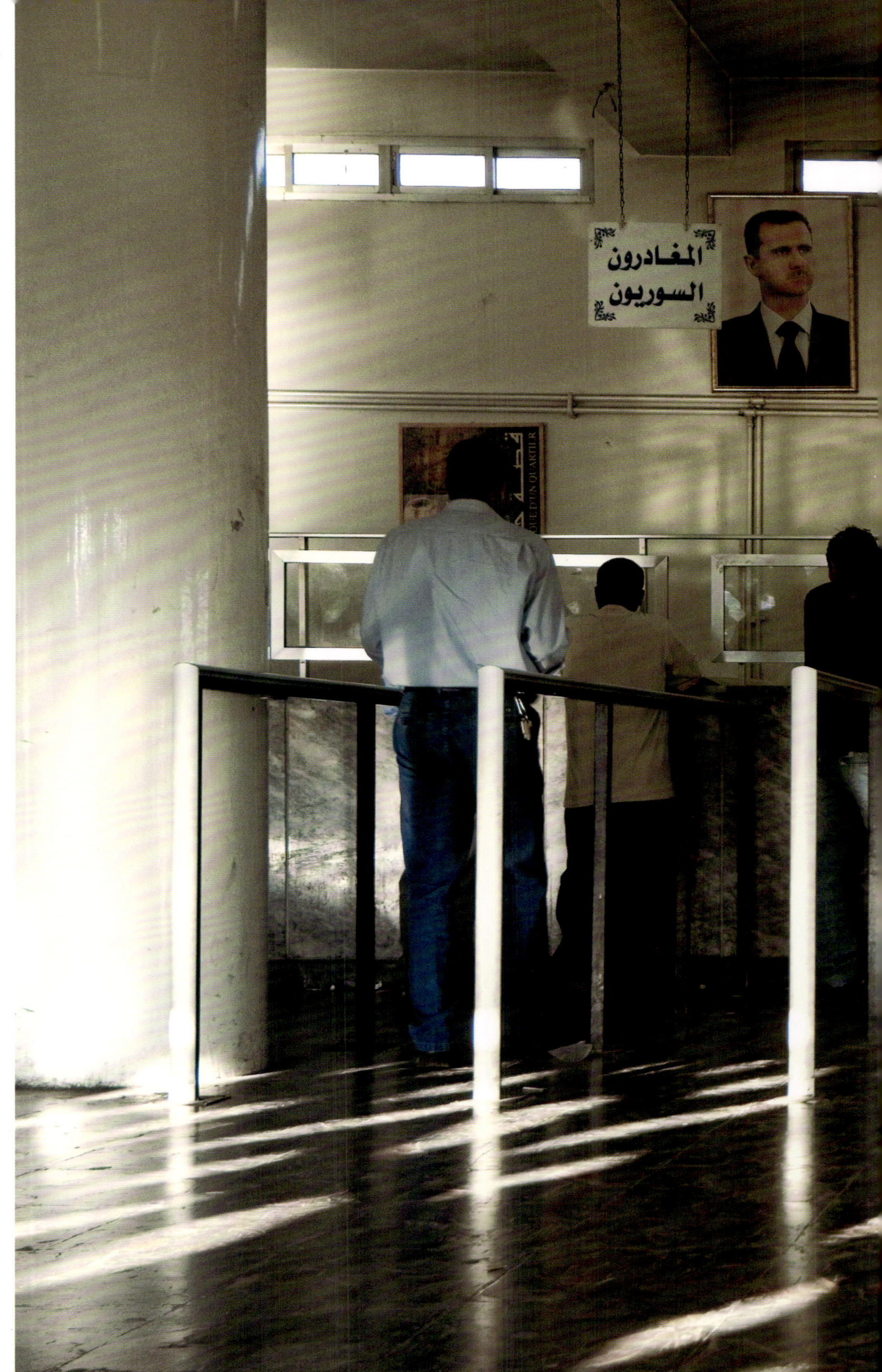

Border crossing from Syria to Lebanon

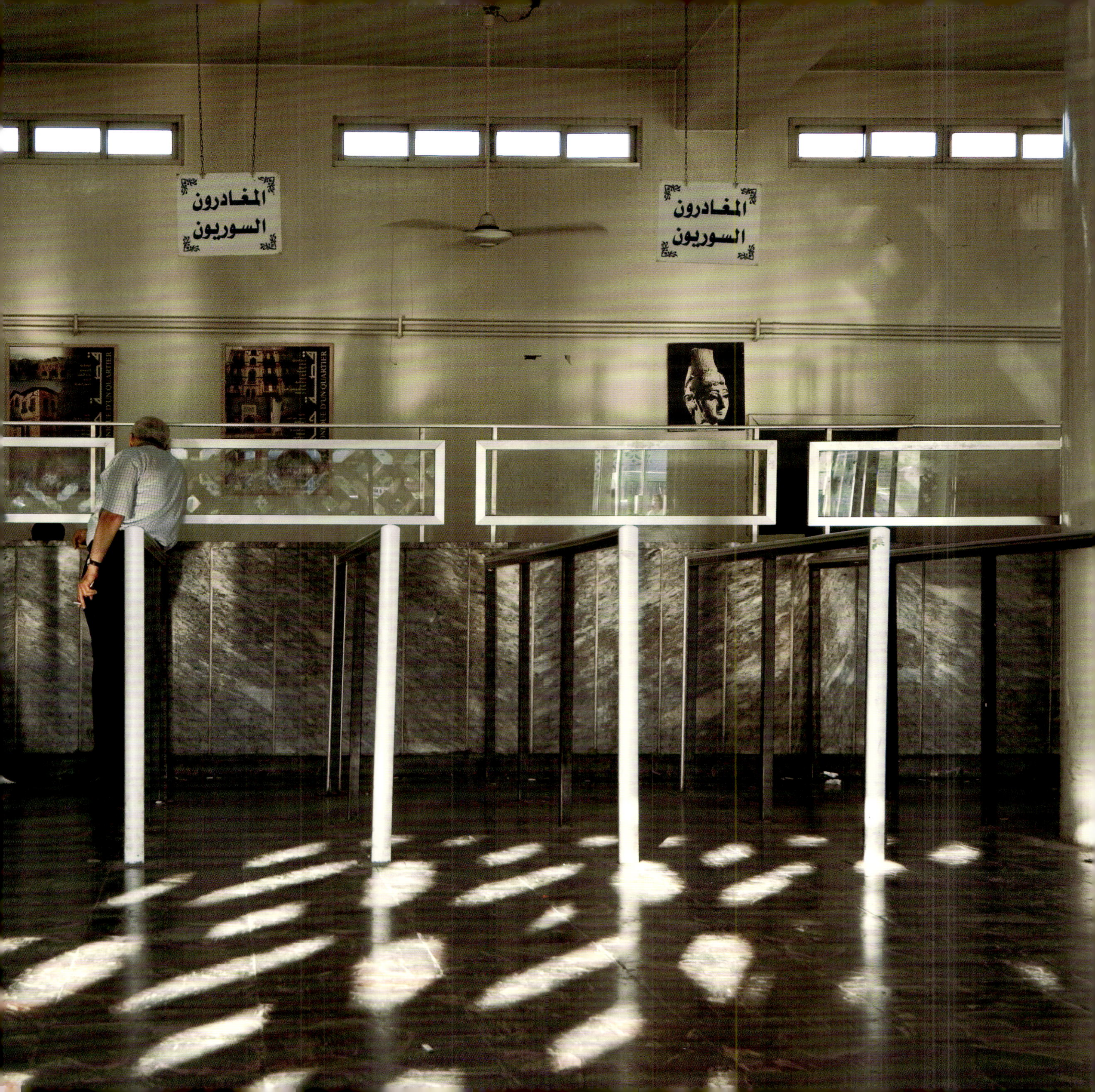
المغادرون
السوريون
المغادرون
السوريون

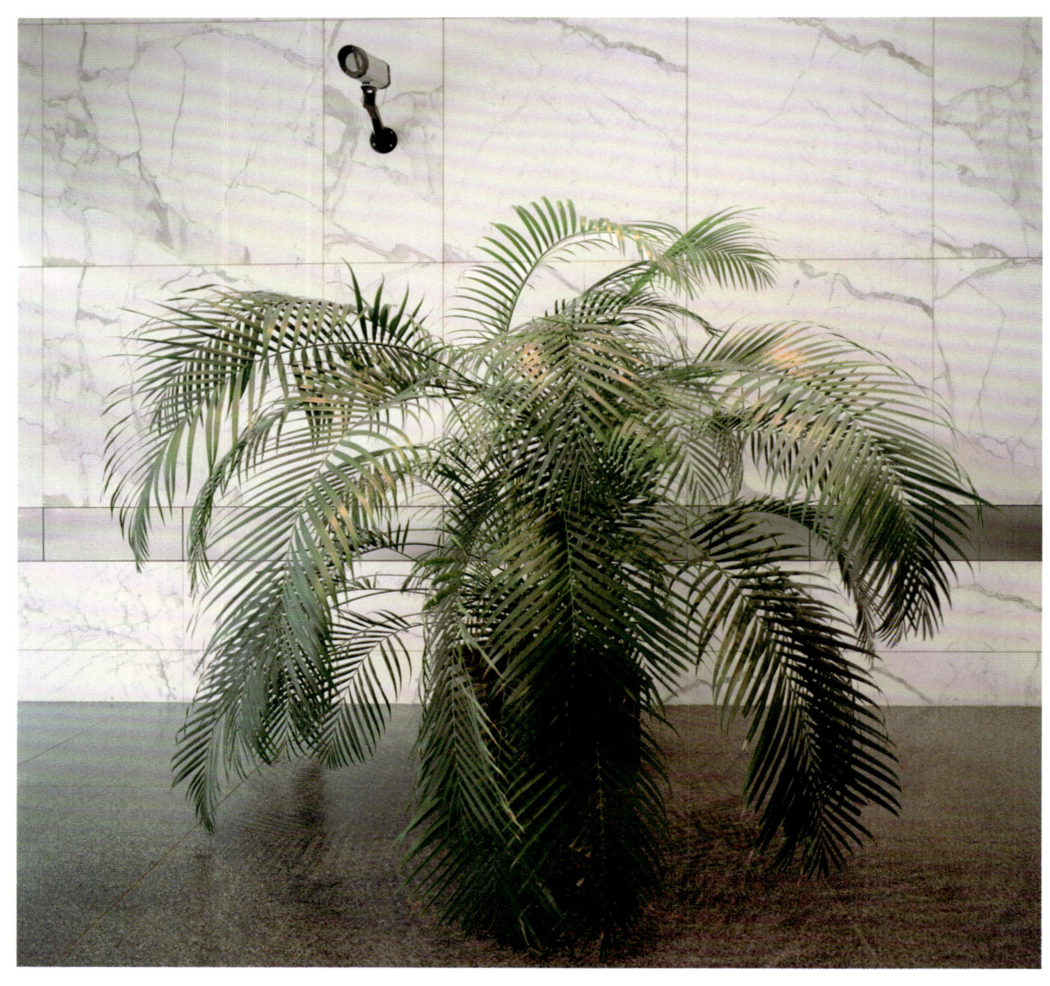

ABOVE AND OPPOSITE: DG Bank, Frankfurt

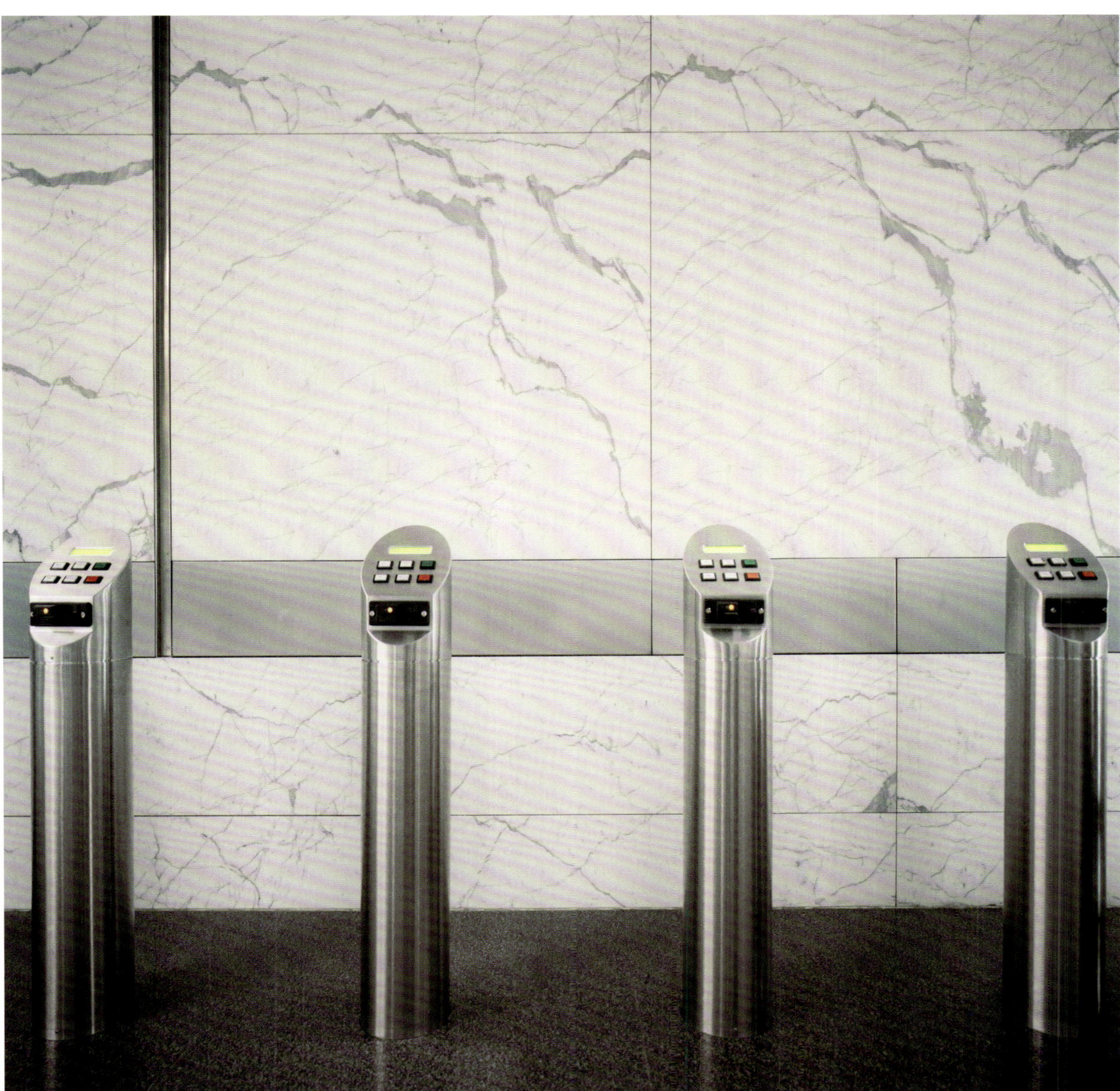

Exit from U.S. Customs and Border Protection, Los Angeles International Airport

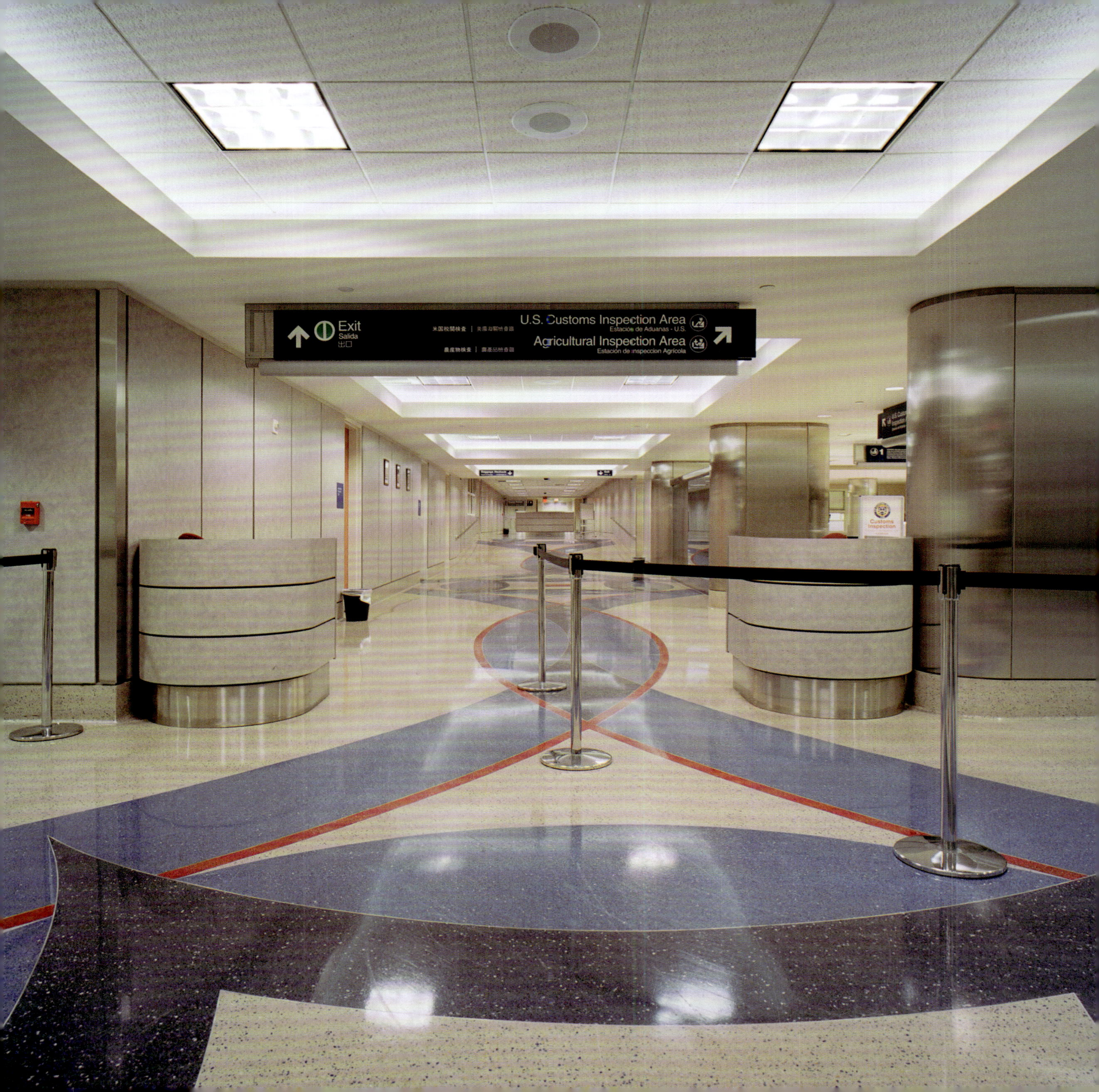
Exit
Salida
出口
U.S. Customs Inspection Area
Estación de Aduanas - U.S.
Agricultural Inspection Area
Estación de inspeccion Agrícola

New Scotland Yard, London

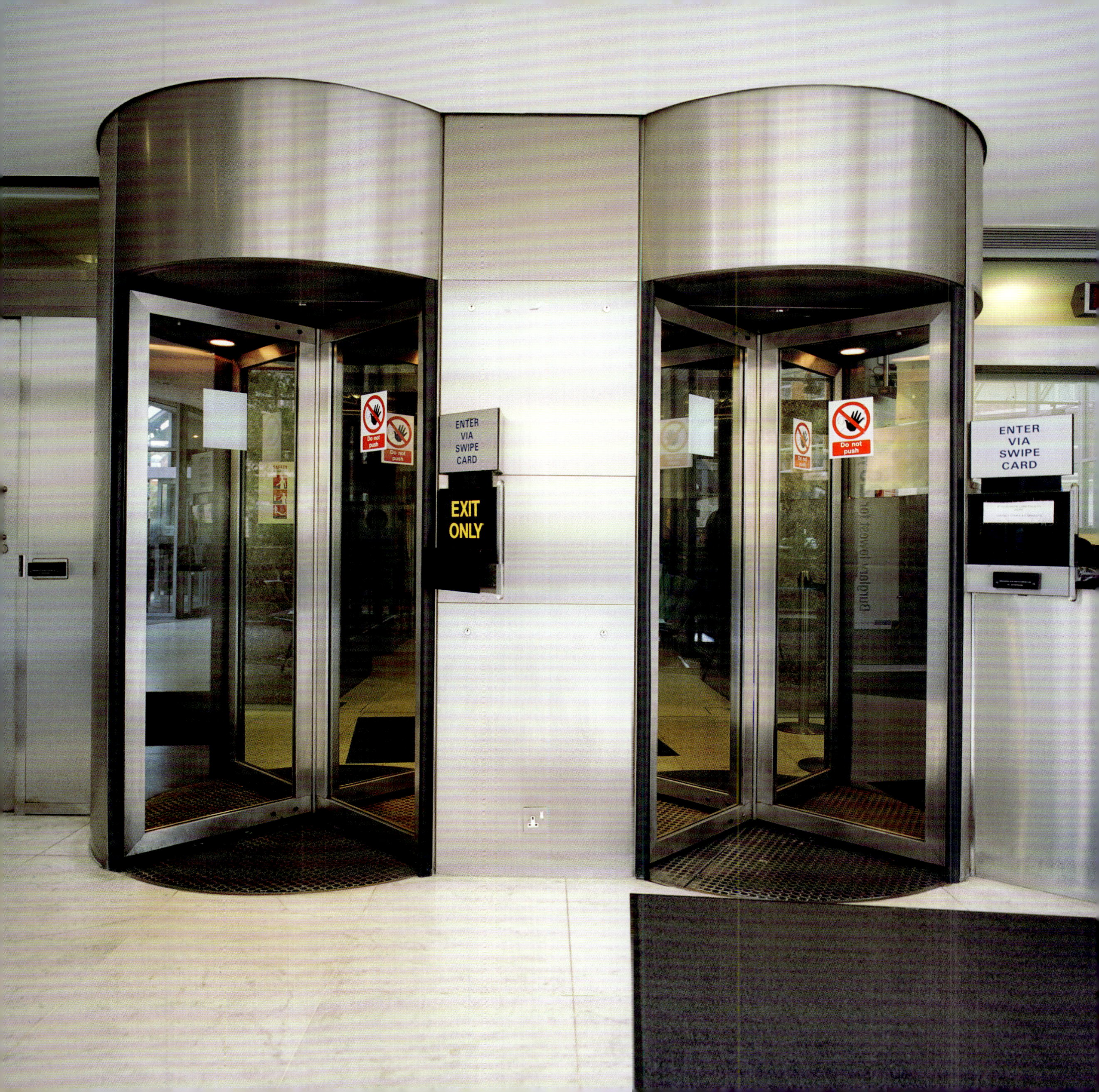

Do not push
Do not push
ENTER VIA SWIPE CARD
EXIT ONLY
Do not push
ENTER VIA SWIPE CARD

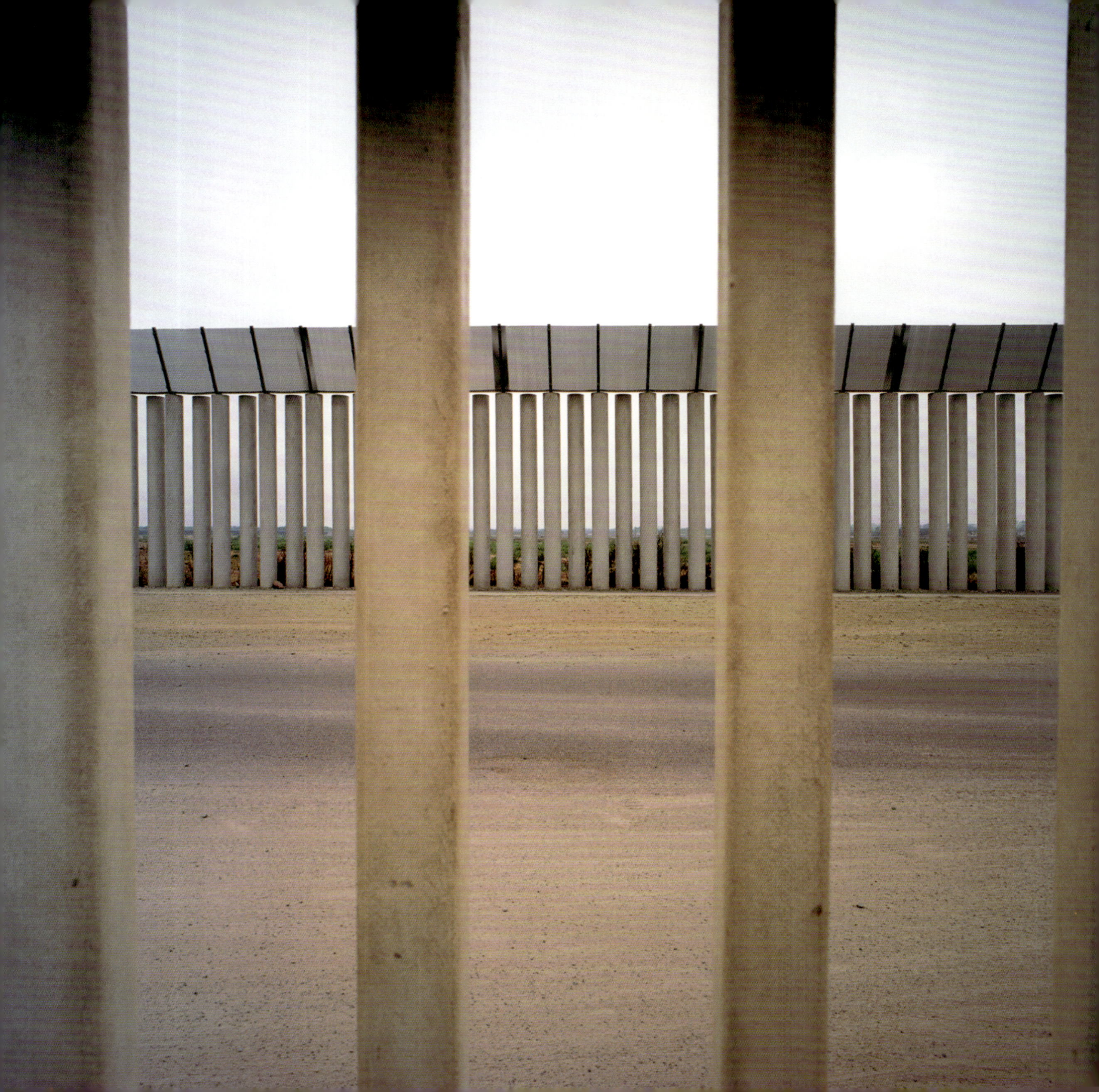

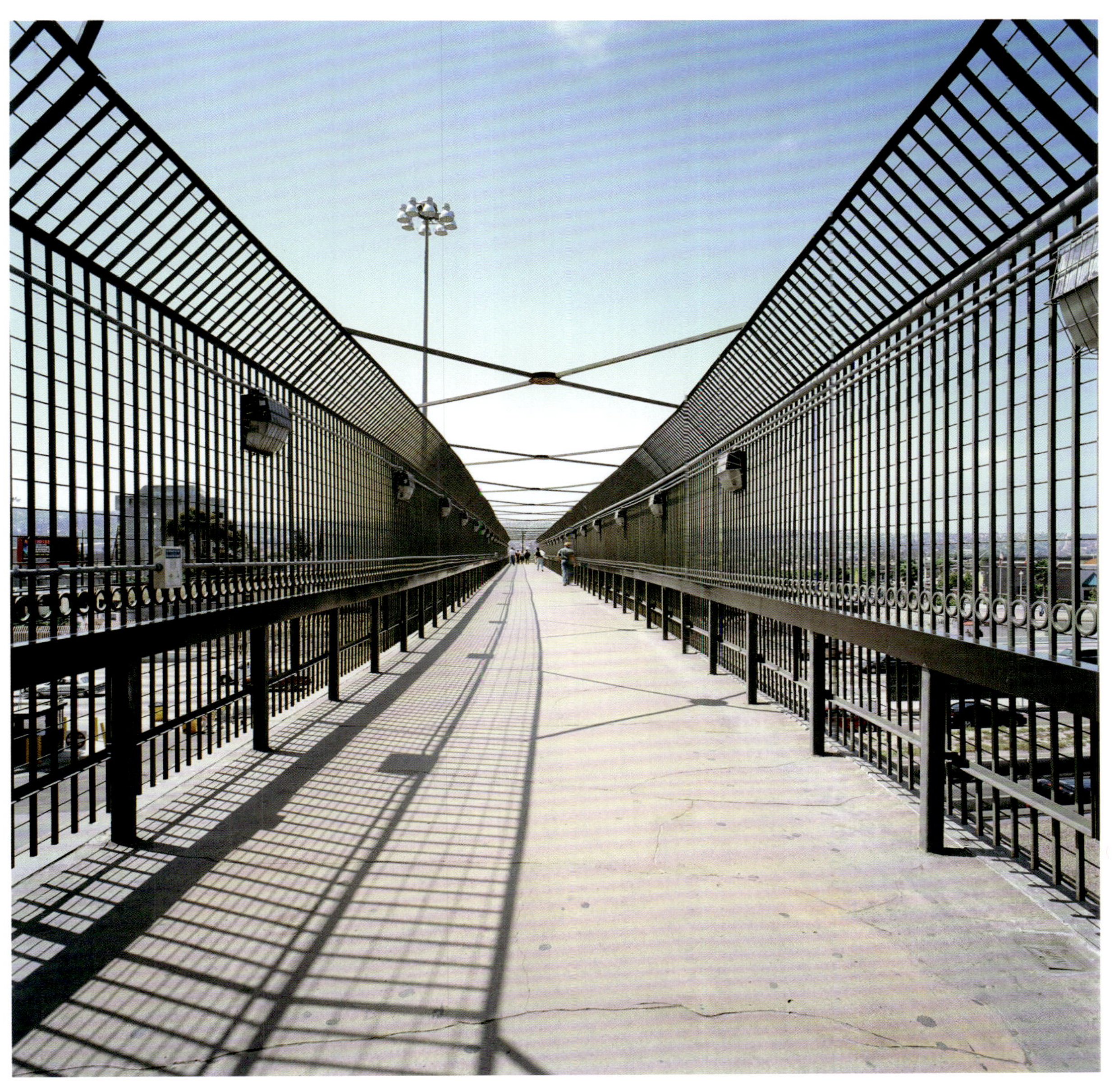

OPPOSITE: San Ysidro, California, seen from Tijuana, Mexico
ABOVE: Span over Tijuana, Mexico, and San Ysidro, California

U.S. Customs and Border Protection, San Ysidro, California

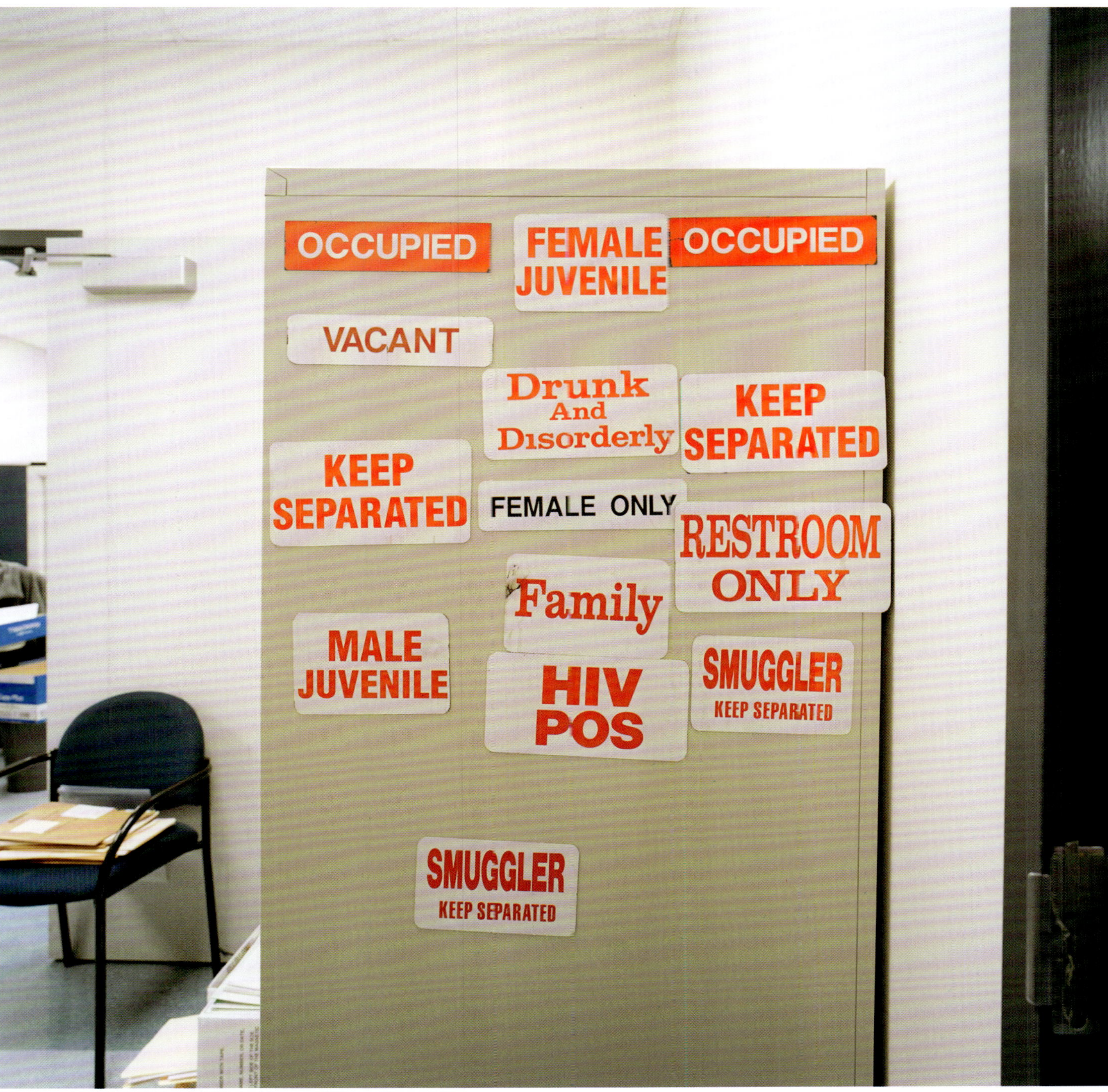
OCCUPIED
FEMALE JUVENILE
OCCUPIED
VACANT
Drunk And Disorderly
KEEP SEPARATED
KEEP SEPARATED
FEMALE ONLY
RESTROOM ONLY
Family
MALE JUVENILE
HIV POS
SMUGGLER KEEP SEPARATED
SMUGGLER KEEP SEPARATED

Seventieth Precinct house, New York Police Department, Brooklyn

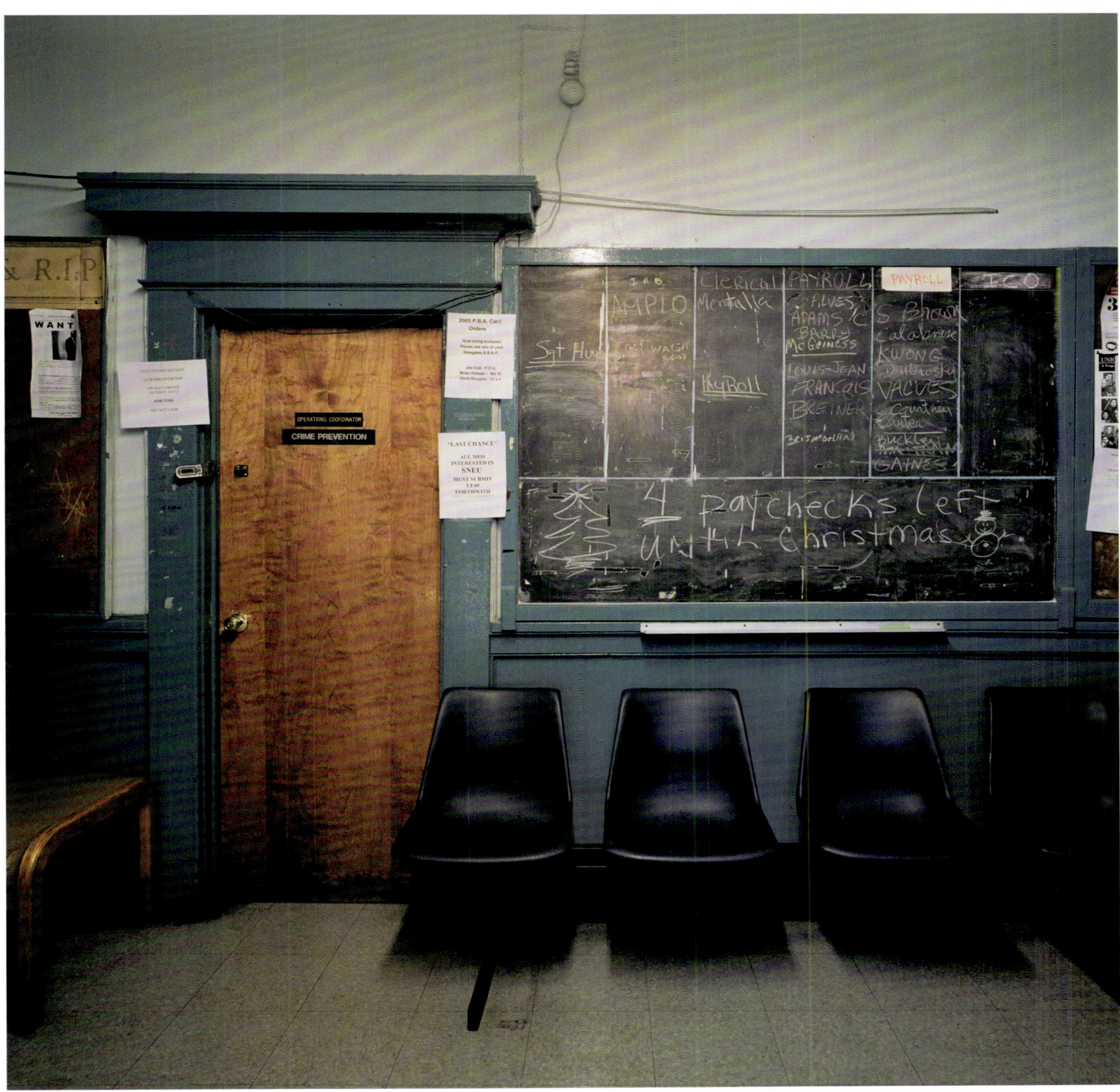
& R.I.P.
WANT
VOLUNTEERS NEEDED
TO WORK OVERTIME
ON HALLOWEEN
FOR TIME
SEE SGT LANE
OPERATIONS COORDINATOR
CRIME PREVENTION
2005 P.B.A. Card Orders
Now being accepted
Please see one of your Delegates A.S.A.P.
"LAST CHANCE"
ALL MOS INTERESTED IN
SNEU
MUST SUBMIT
UF49
FORTHWITH
Clerical
PAYROLL
PAYROLL
AMPLO
4 paychecks left until Christmas

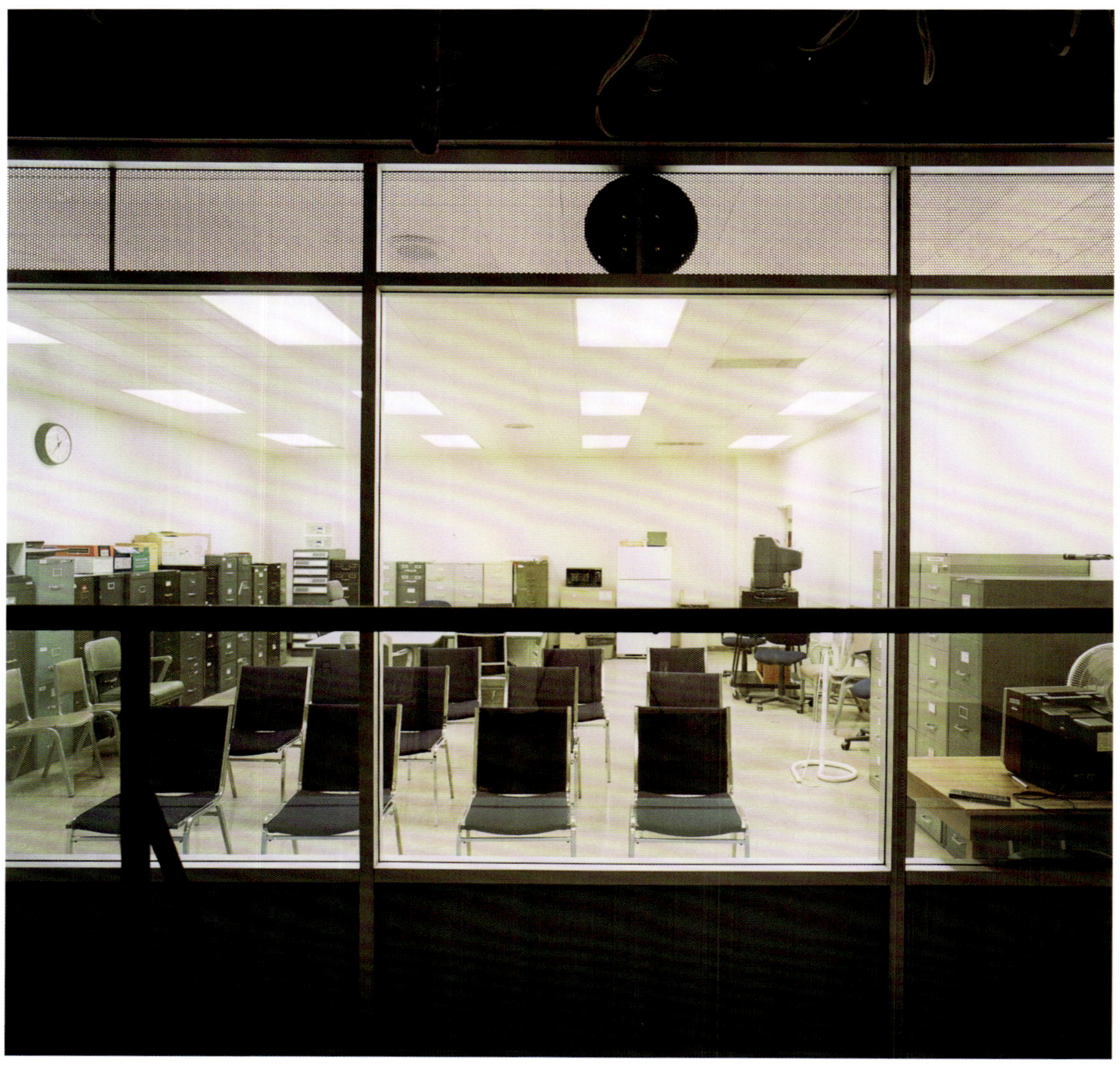

View from the line-up room, Oakland Police Department, Oakland, California

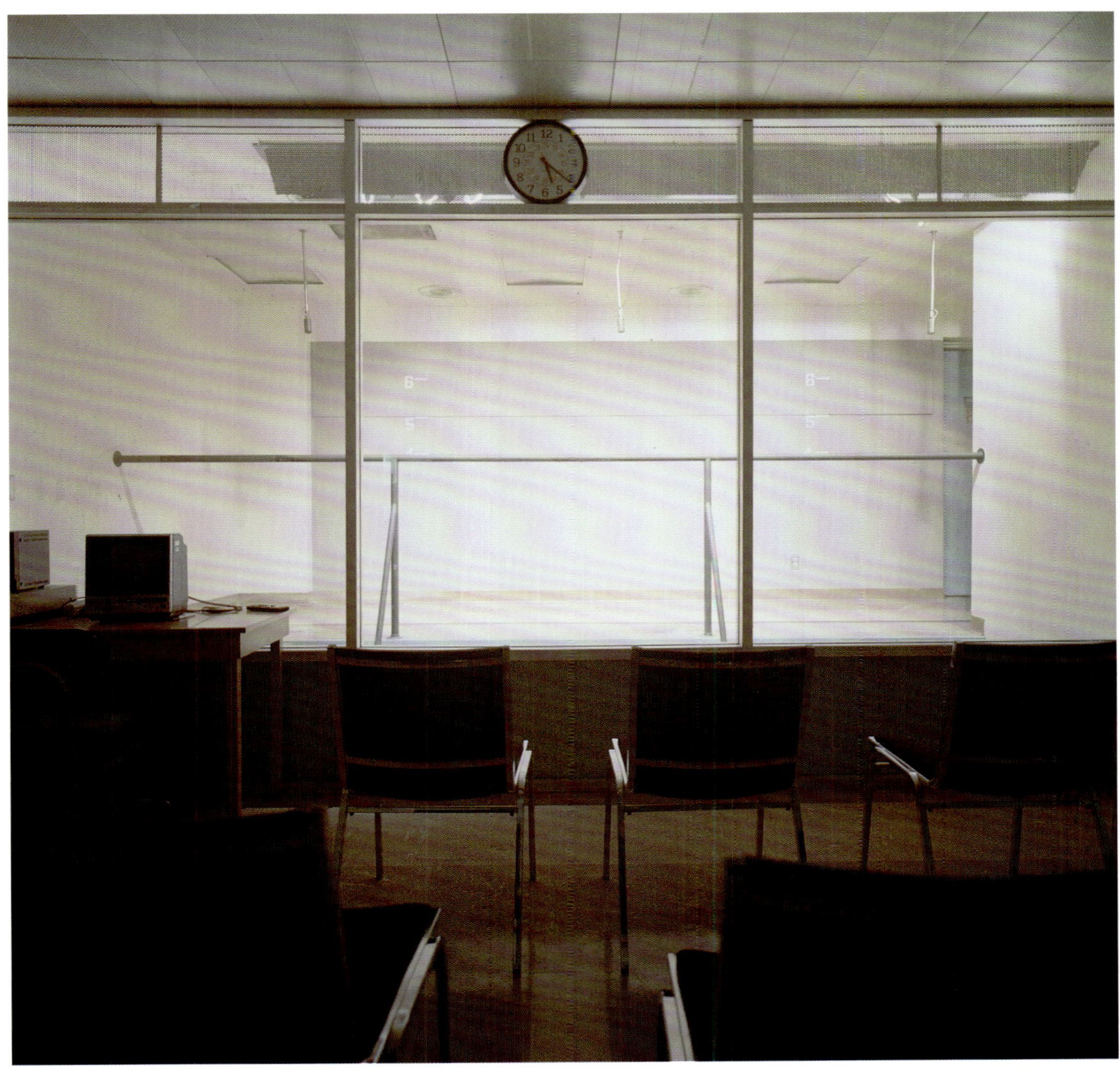

Line-up stage, Oakland Police Department, Oakland, California

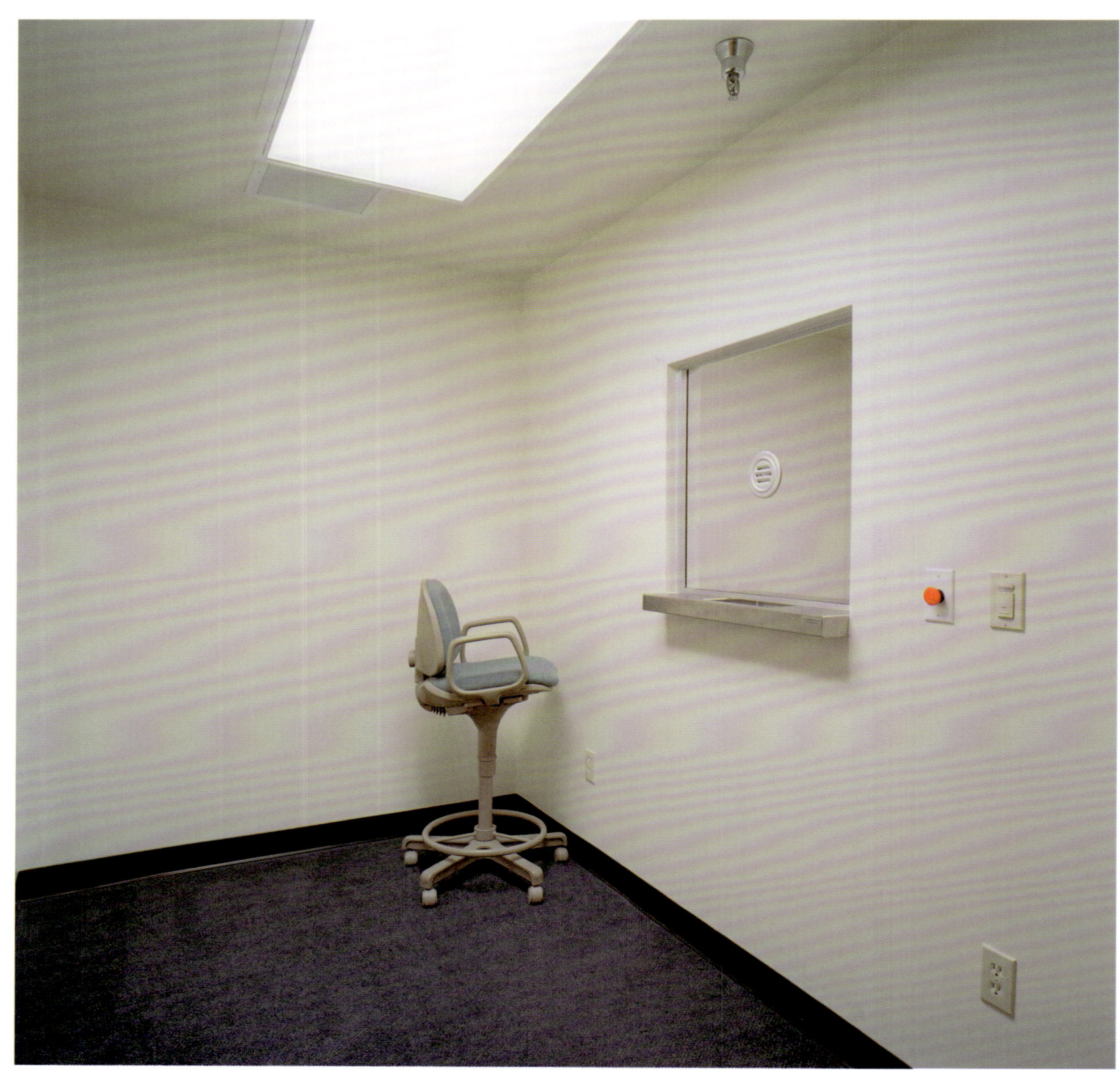

ABOVE AND OPPOSITE: Hard Interview Room, FBI headquarters, Los Angeles

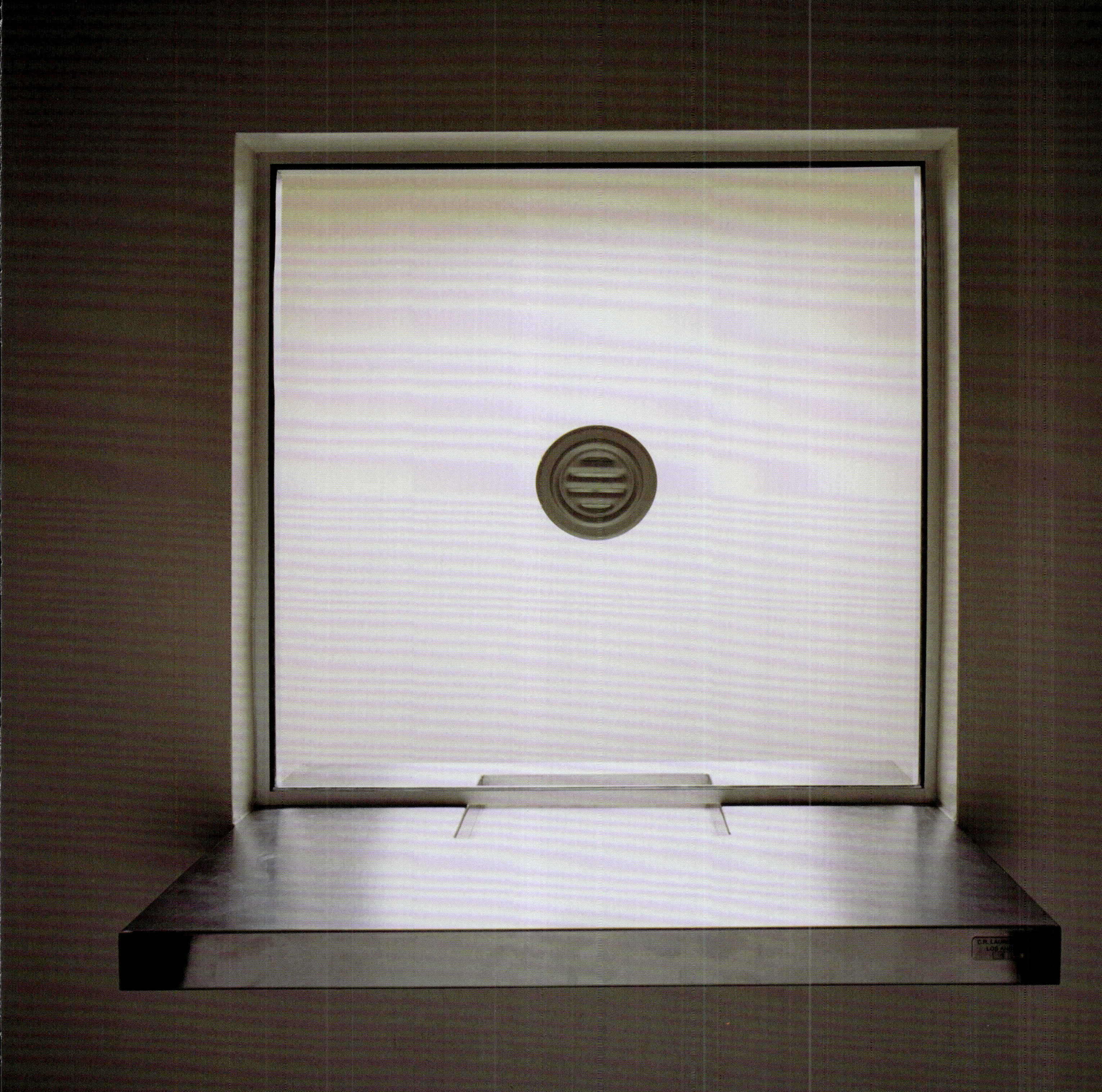

Grand Hyatt Hotel, Berlin

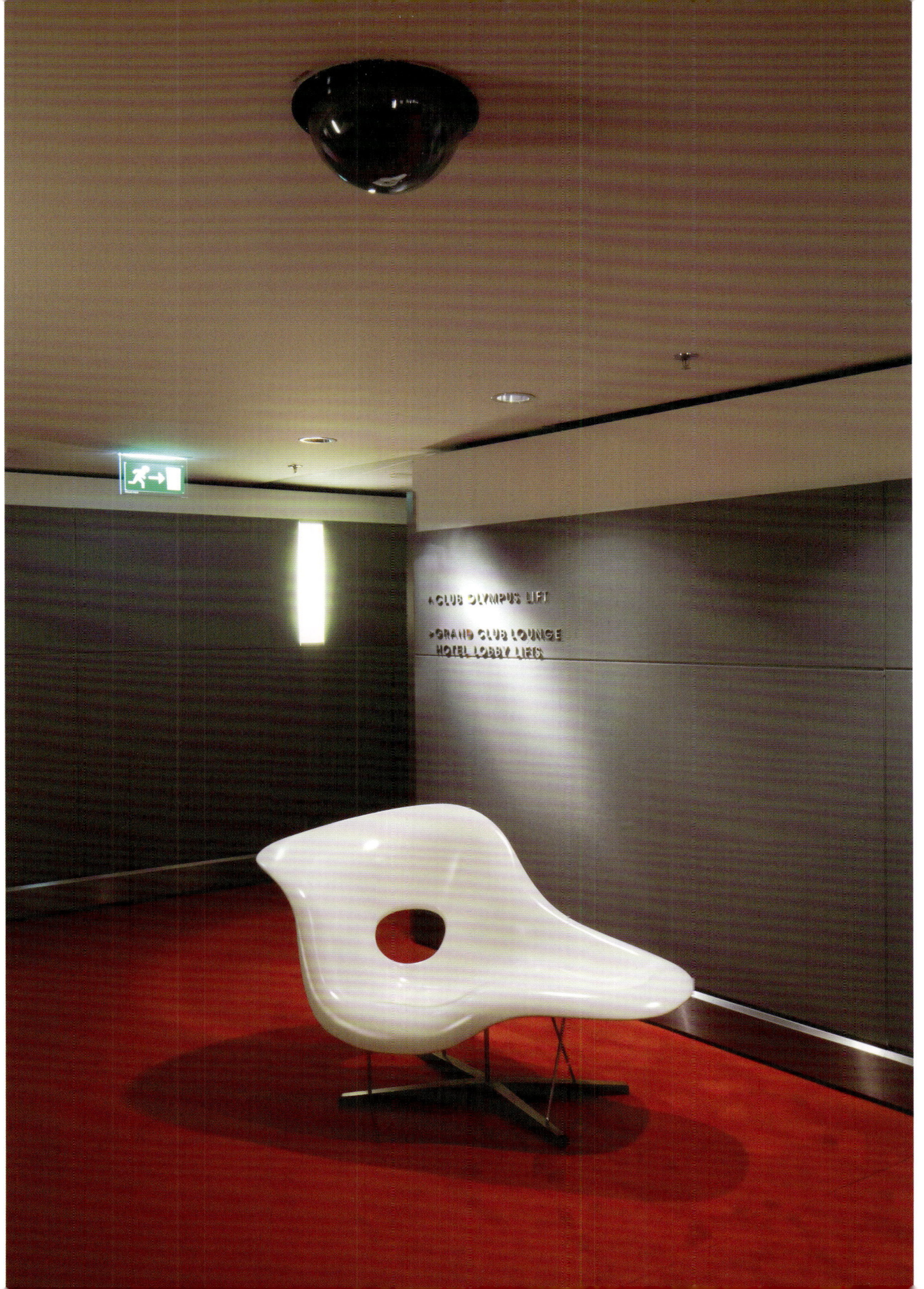
CLUB OLYMPUS LIFT
GRAND CLUB LOUNGE
HOTEL LOBBY LIFTS

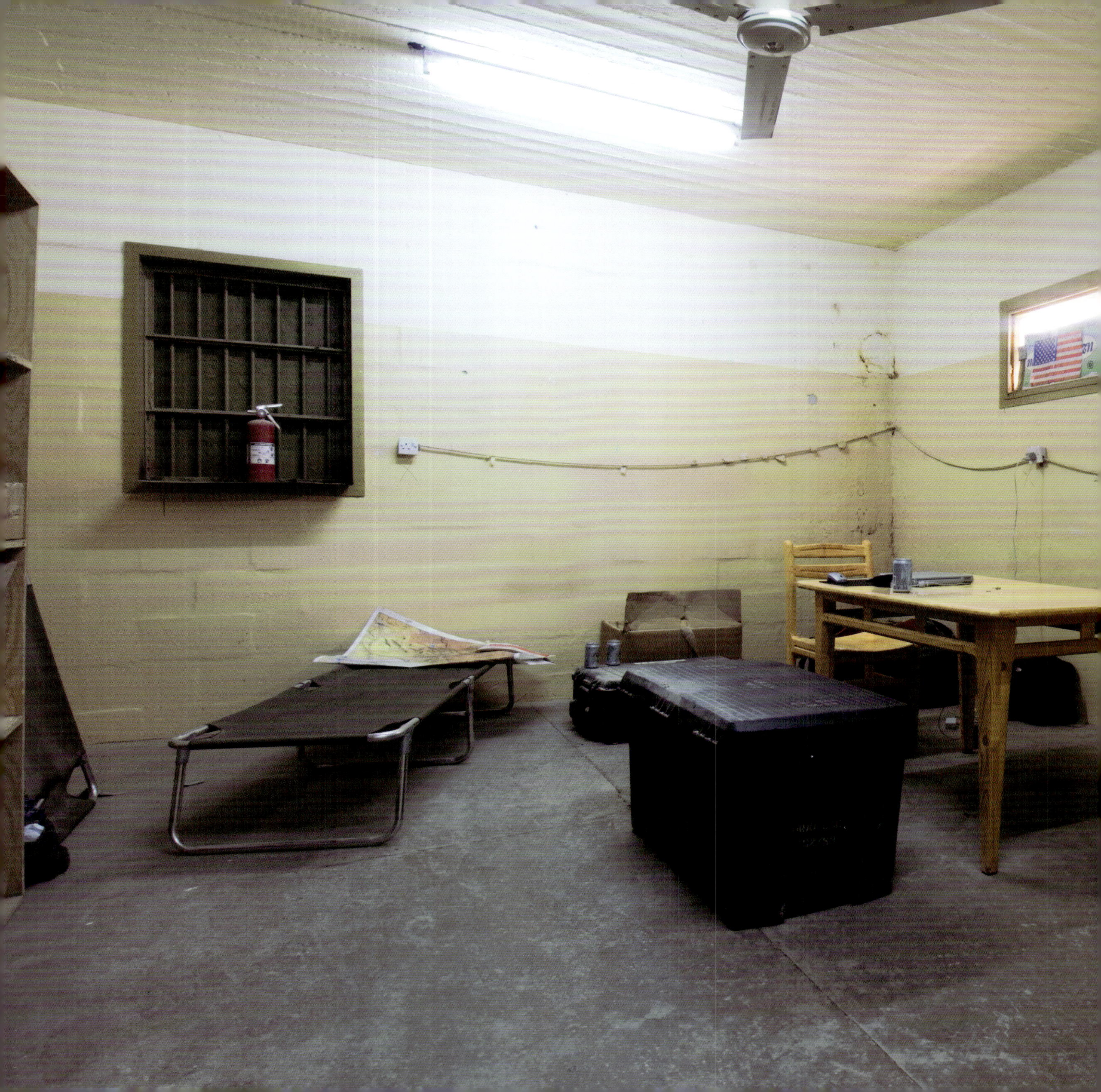

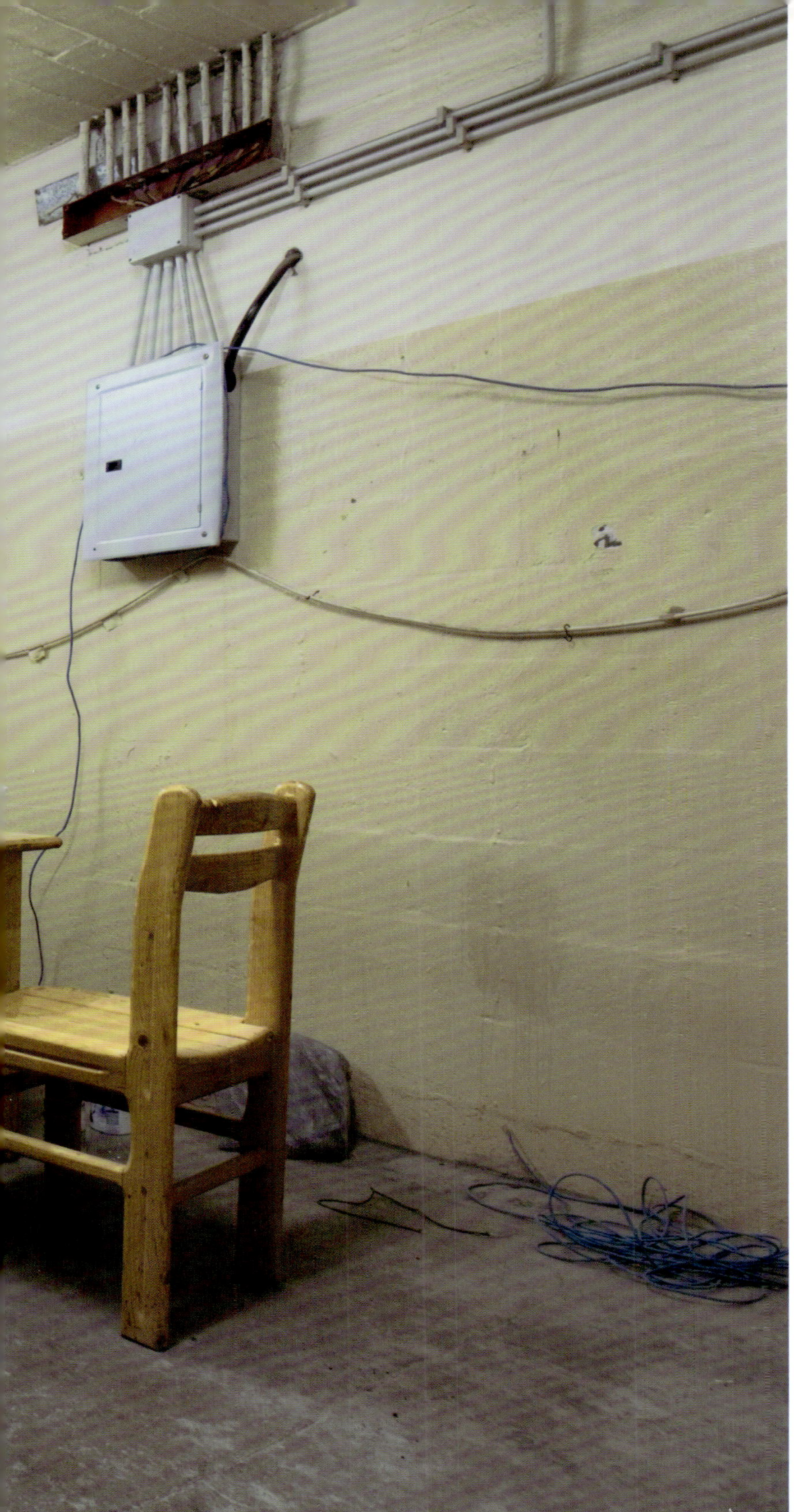

Interview room, Abu Ghraib prison ("hard site"), Abu Ghraib, Iraq

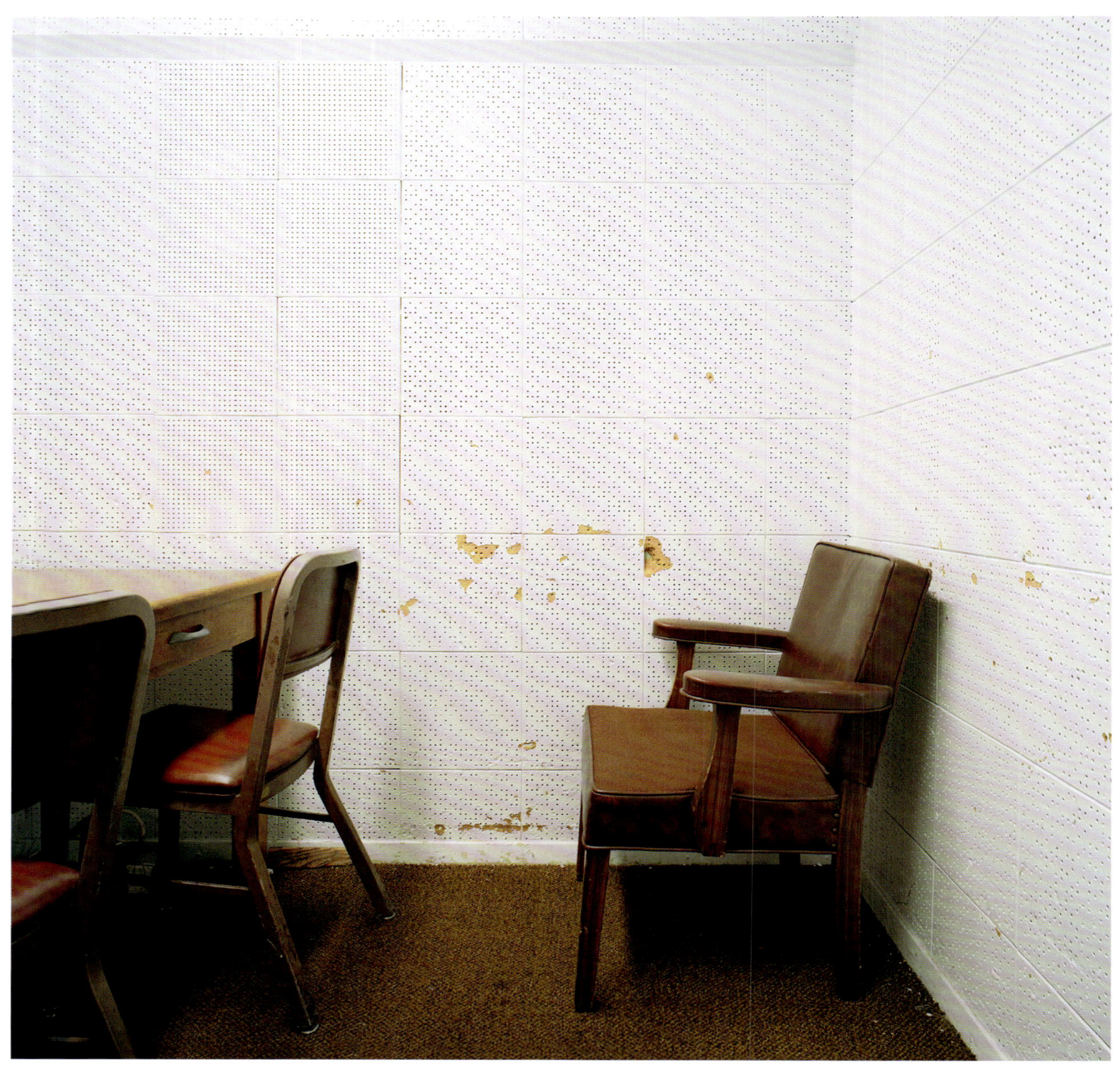

ABOVE: Interview room, Robbery and Homicide Division, Parker Center, Los Angeles Police Department headquarters
OPPOSITE: Interview room, Robbery and Homicide Division, Oakland Police Department, Oakland, California

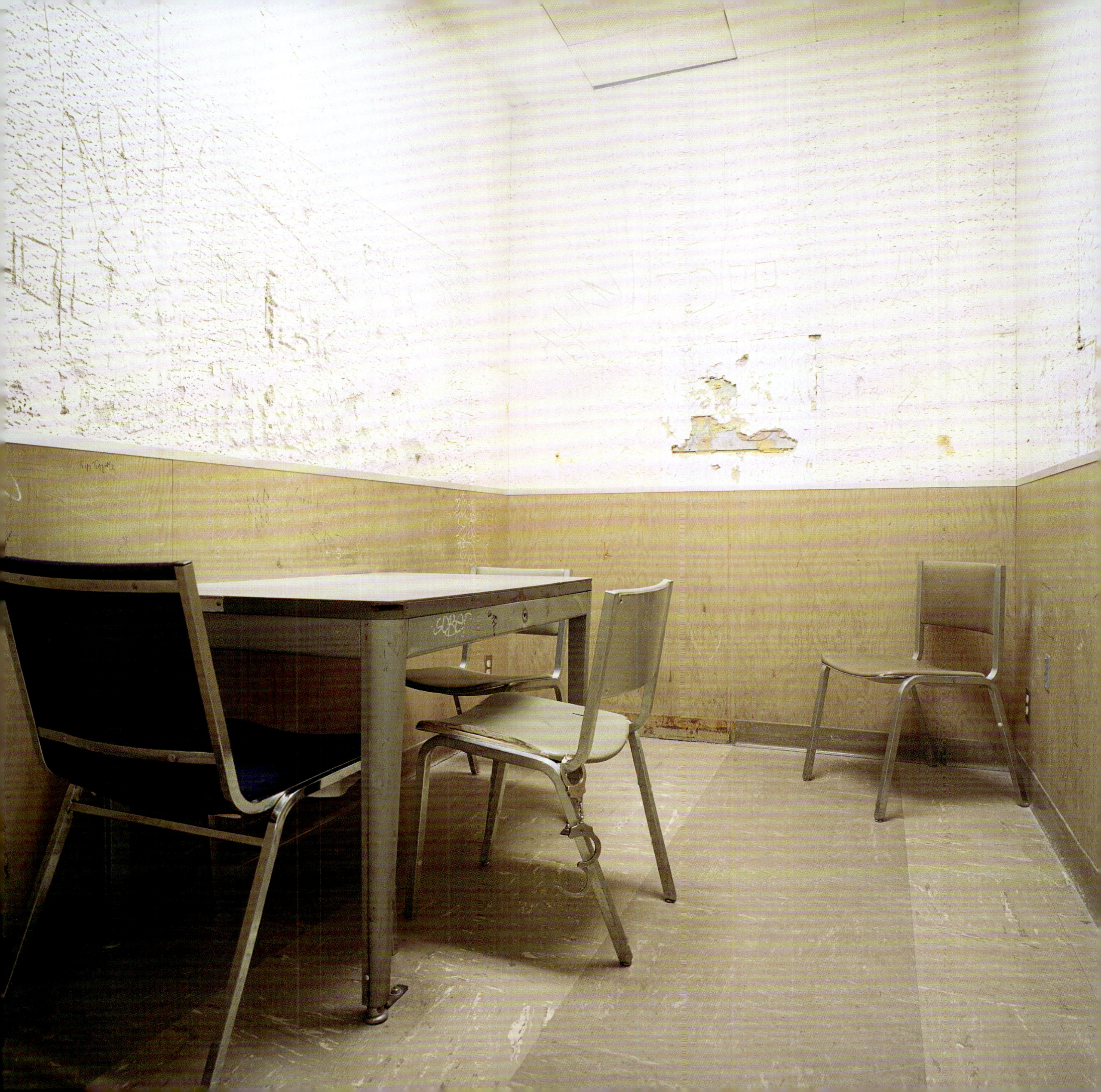

CLOCKWISE FROM TOP LEFT:

Interview room, Santa Barbara Police Department, Santa Barbara, California (top left and right)

Interview room, Secret Service headquarters, Los Angeles

Interrogation room, Delta Camp V, Guantánamo, Cuba

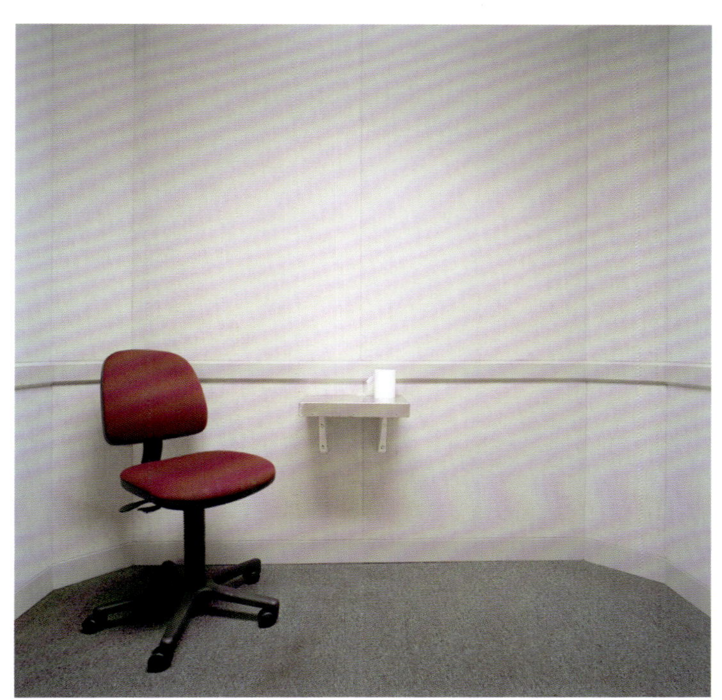

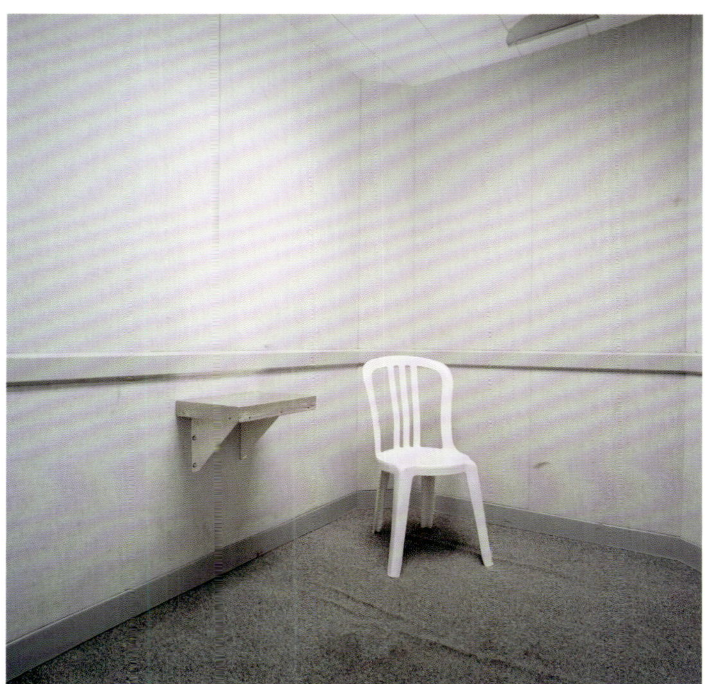

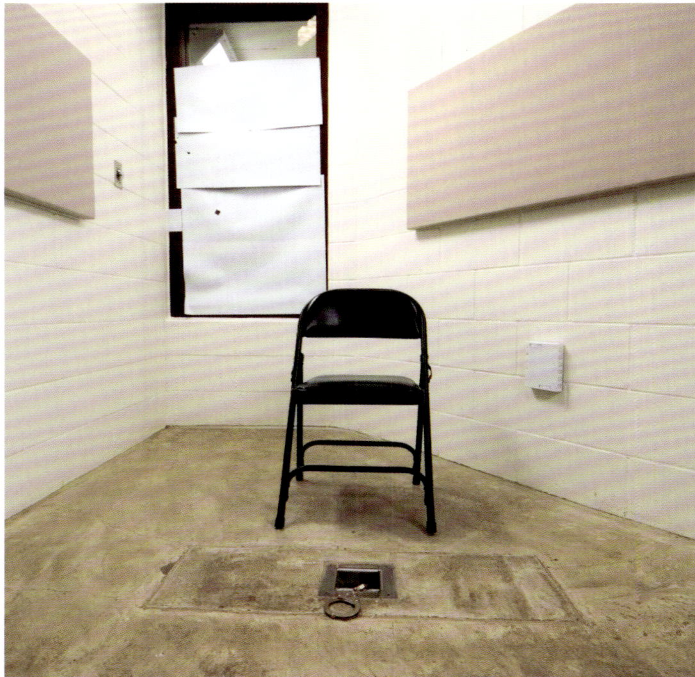

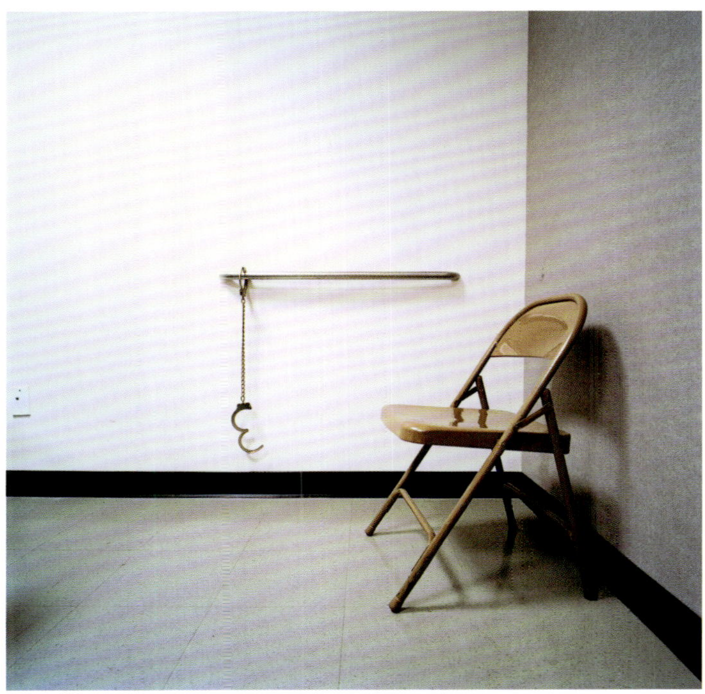

Booking bench, Los Angeles Police Department, Fifth and Wall Street station

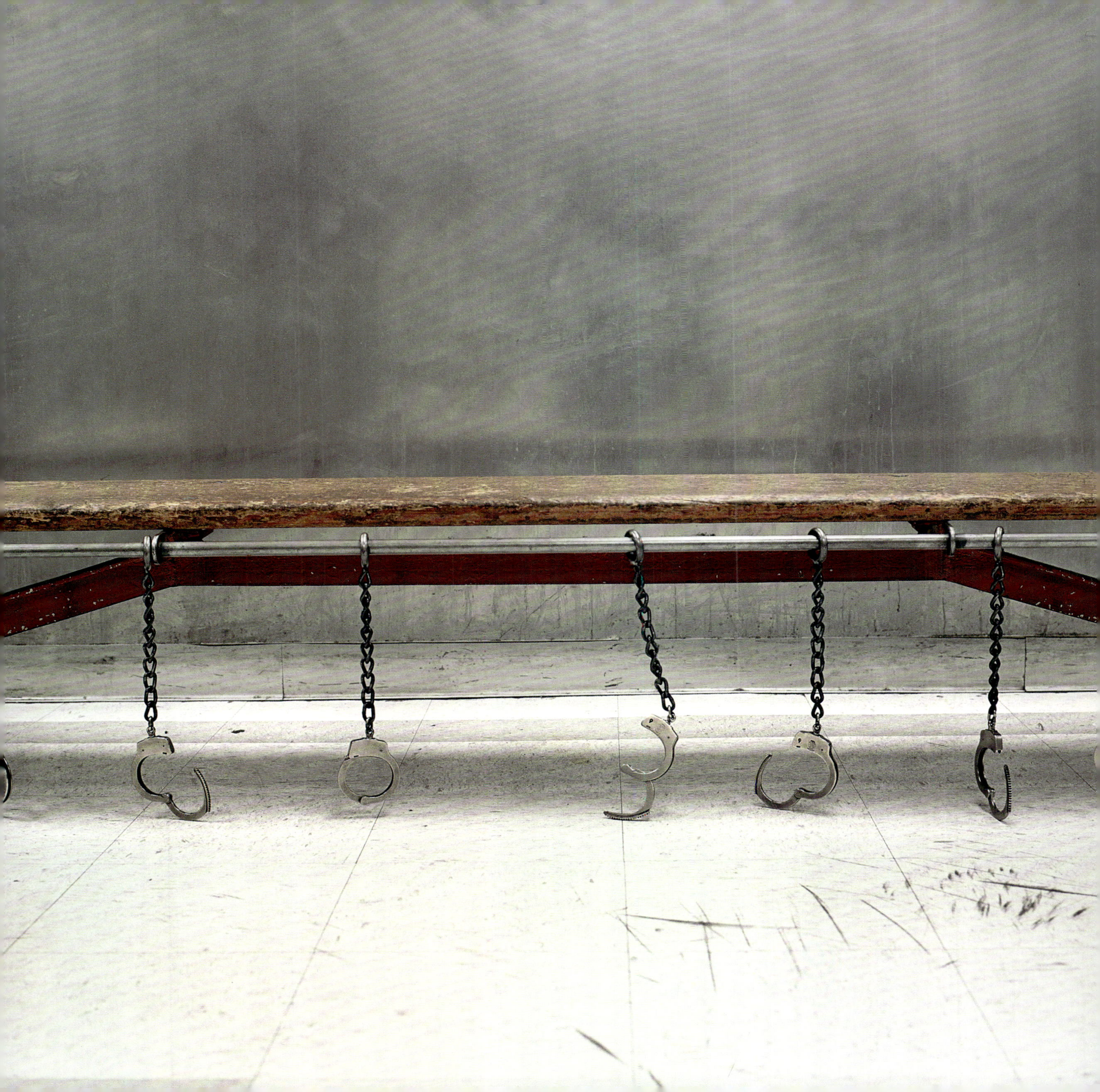

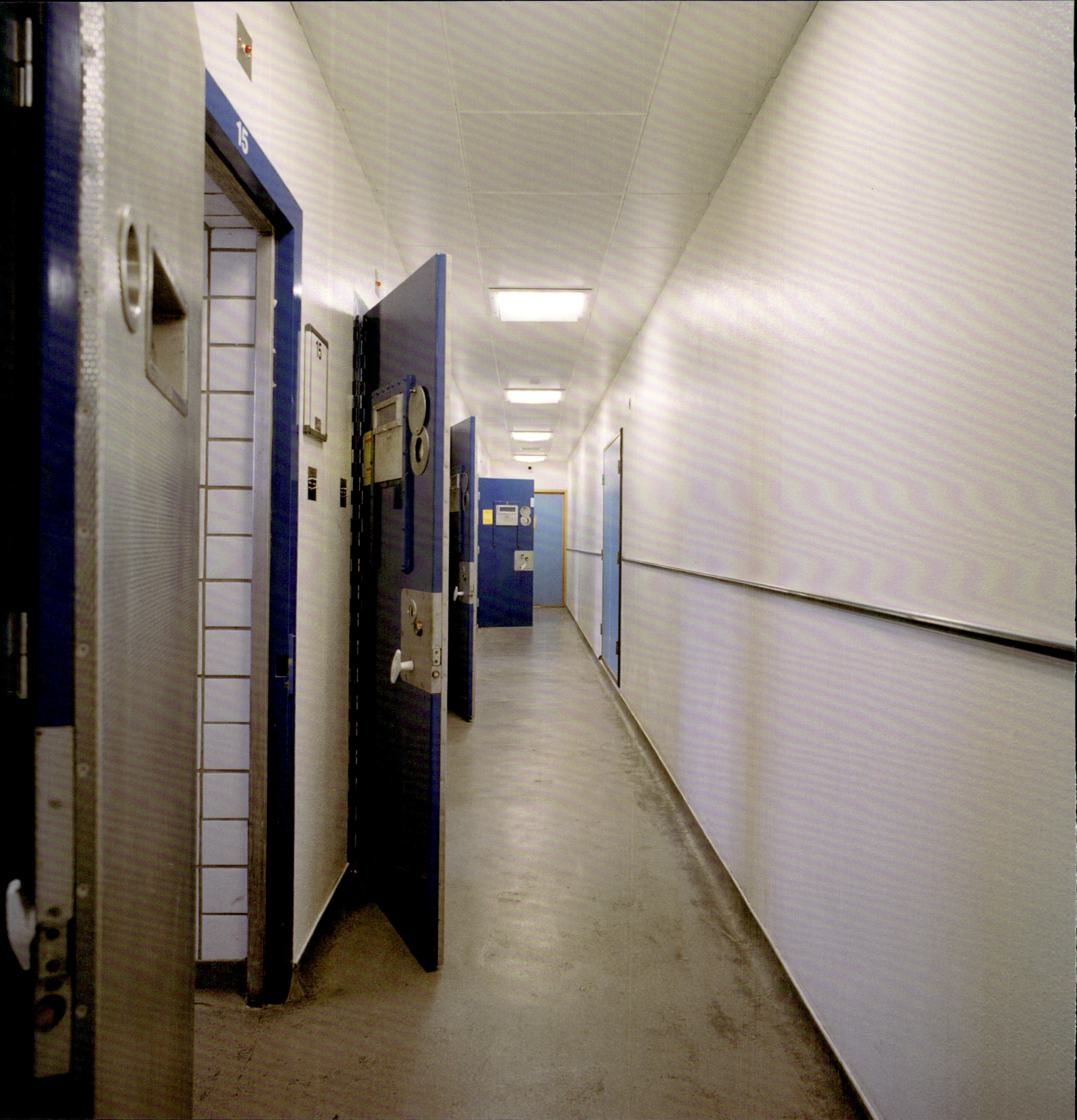
15
15

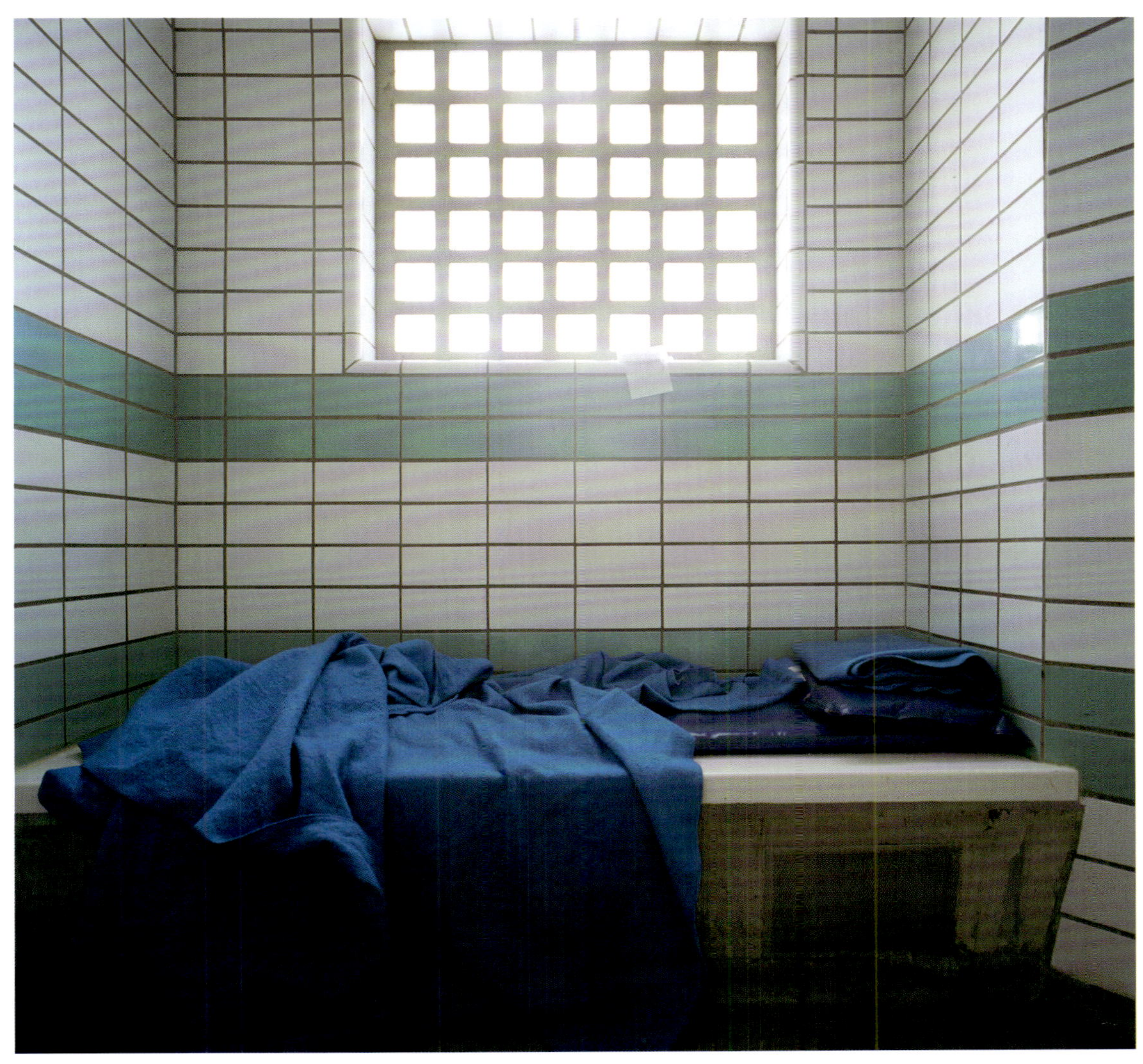

OPPOSITE AND ABOVE: Holding cells, Metropolitan Police, Collingwood Road, Hillingdon, London

Holding cell, Santa Barbara Police Department, Santa Barbara, California

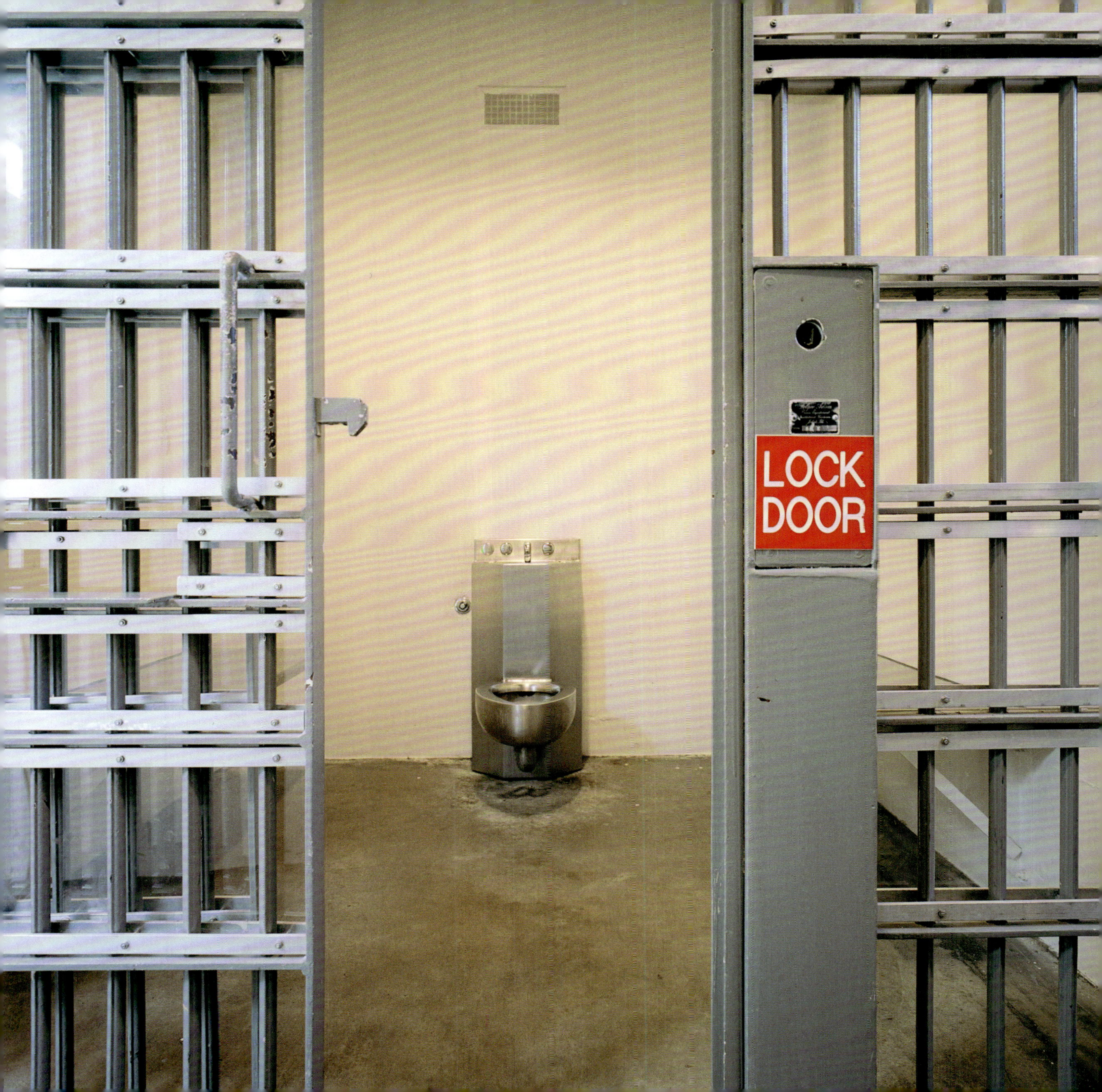
LOCK
DOOR

Holding cells, general population area, Security Housing Unit, Pelican Bay State Prison, Crescent City, California

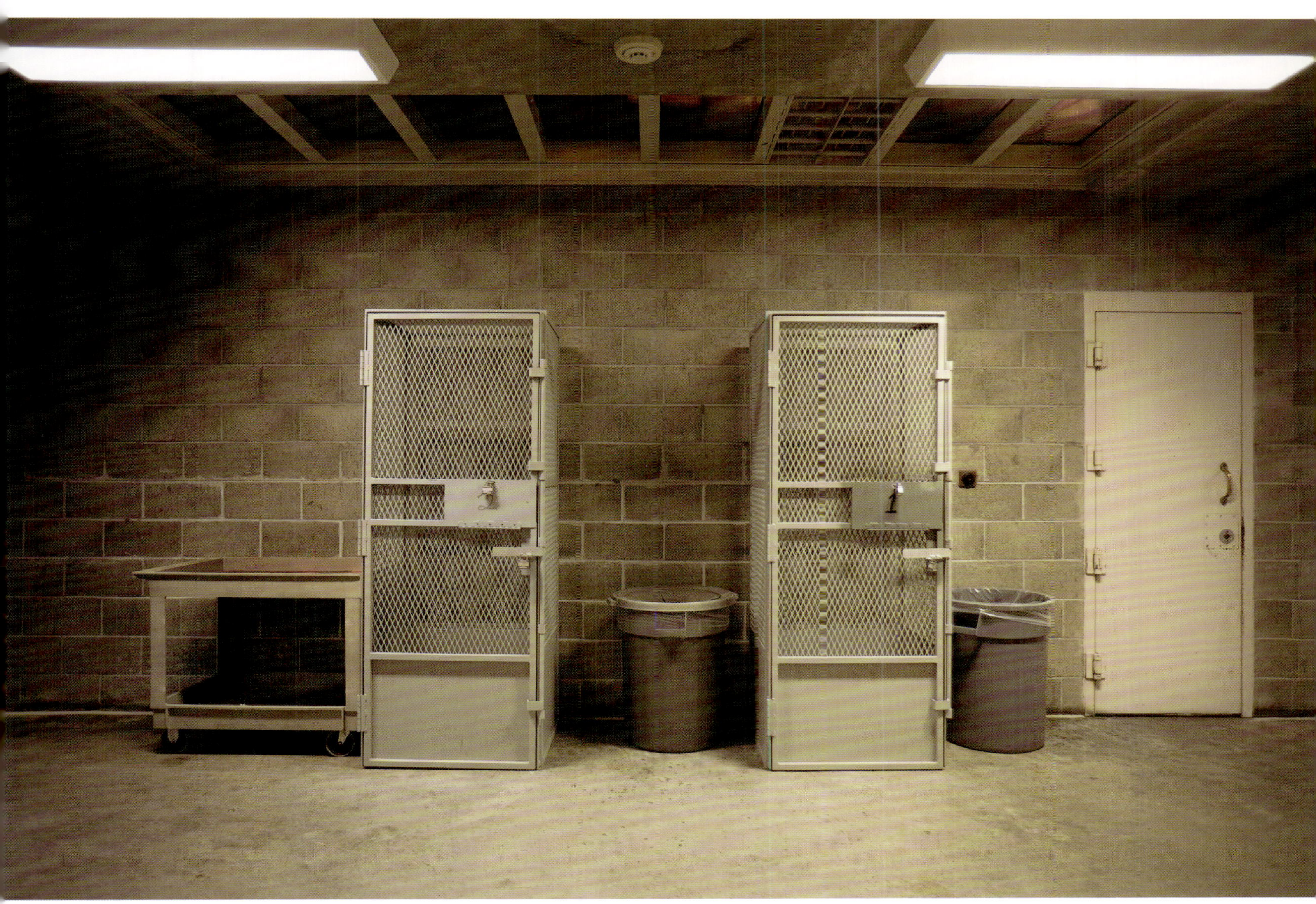
1

Isolation room ("rubber room"), U.S. Customs and Border Protection, San Ysidro, California

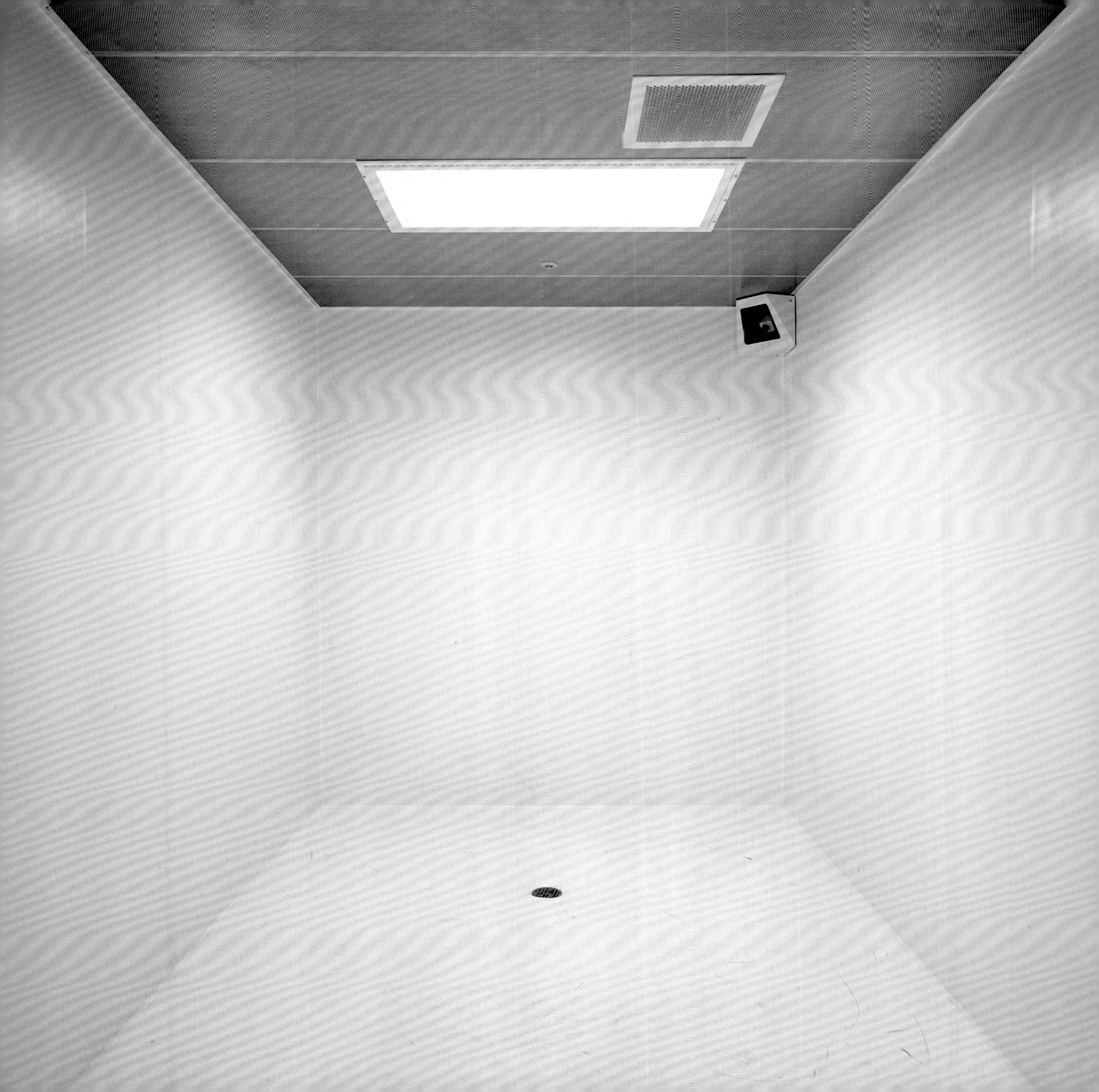

CLOCKWISE FROM TOP LEFT:

Isolation room ("rubber room"), exterior, Immigration and Customs Enforcement, Los Angeles

Isolation room, interior, Immigration and Customs Enforcement, Los Angeles

Secondary Inspection and Holding Area, Immigration and Customs Enforcement, San Francisco Airport

Holding cell, San Francisco Police Department, Northern Division, San Mateo, California

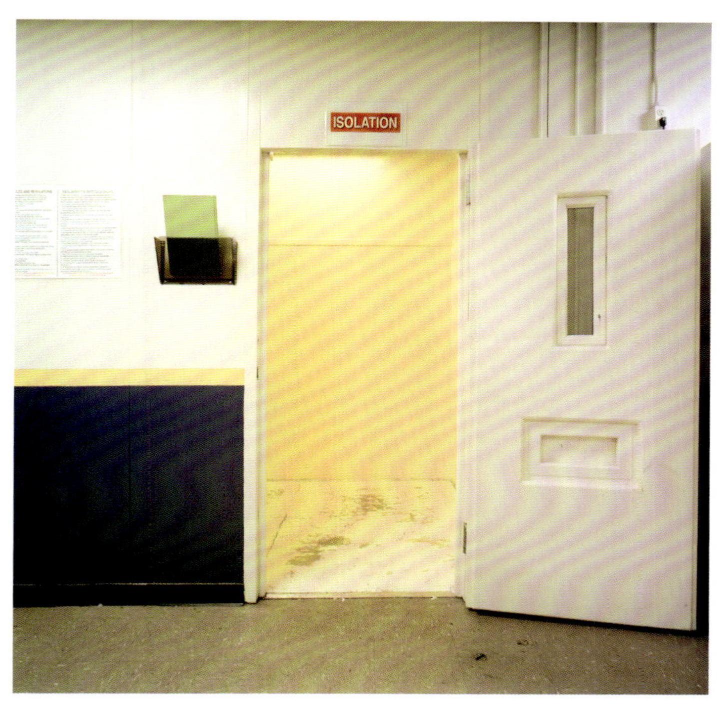
ISOLATION

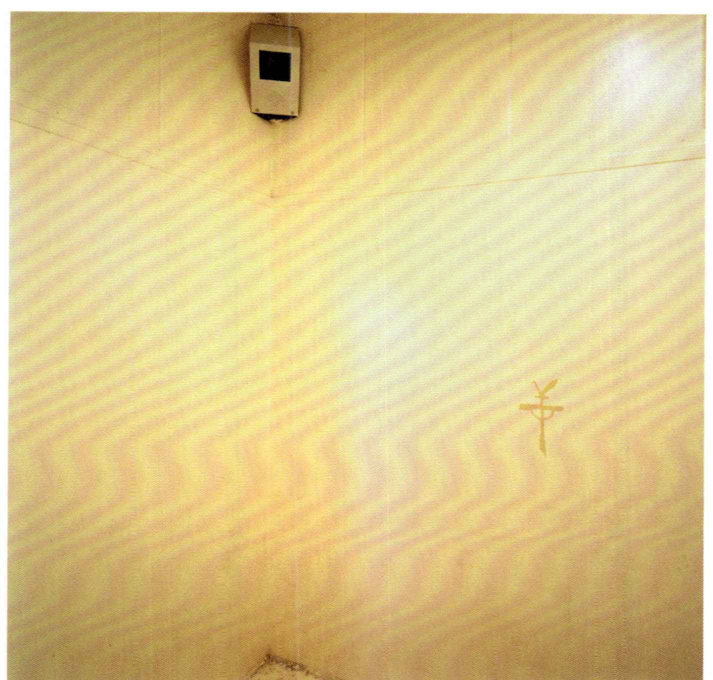

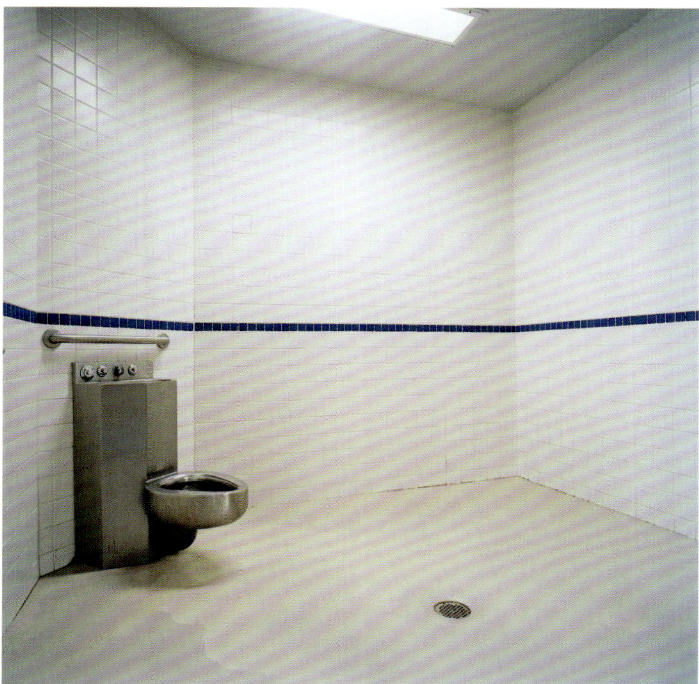

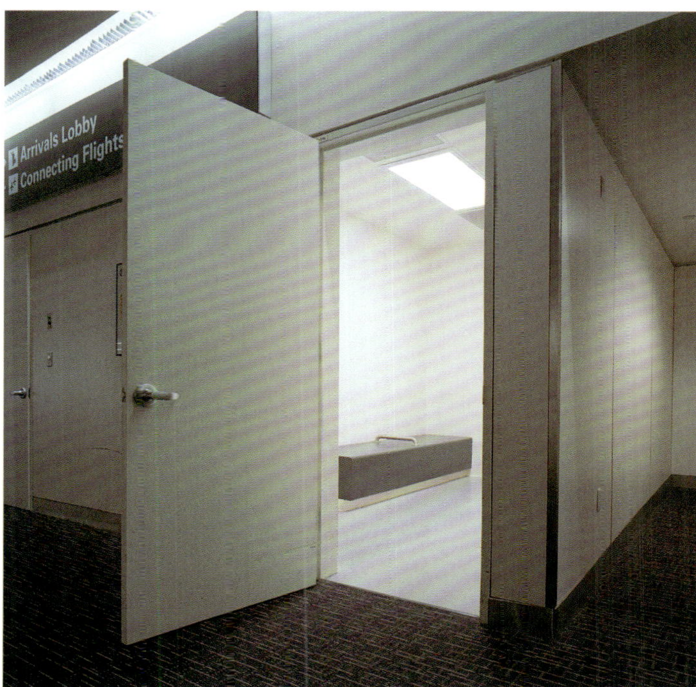
Arrivals Lobby
Connecting Flights

Secondary Inspection Room ("pat-down room"), U.S. Customs and Border Protection, Los Angeles International Airport

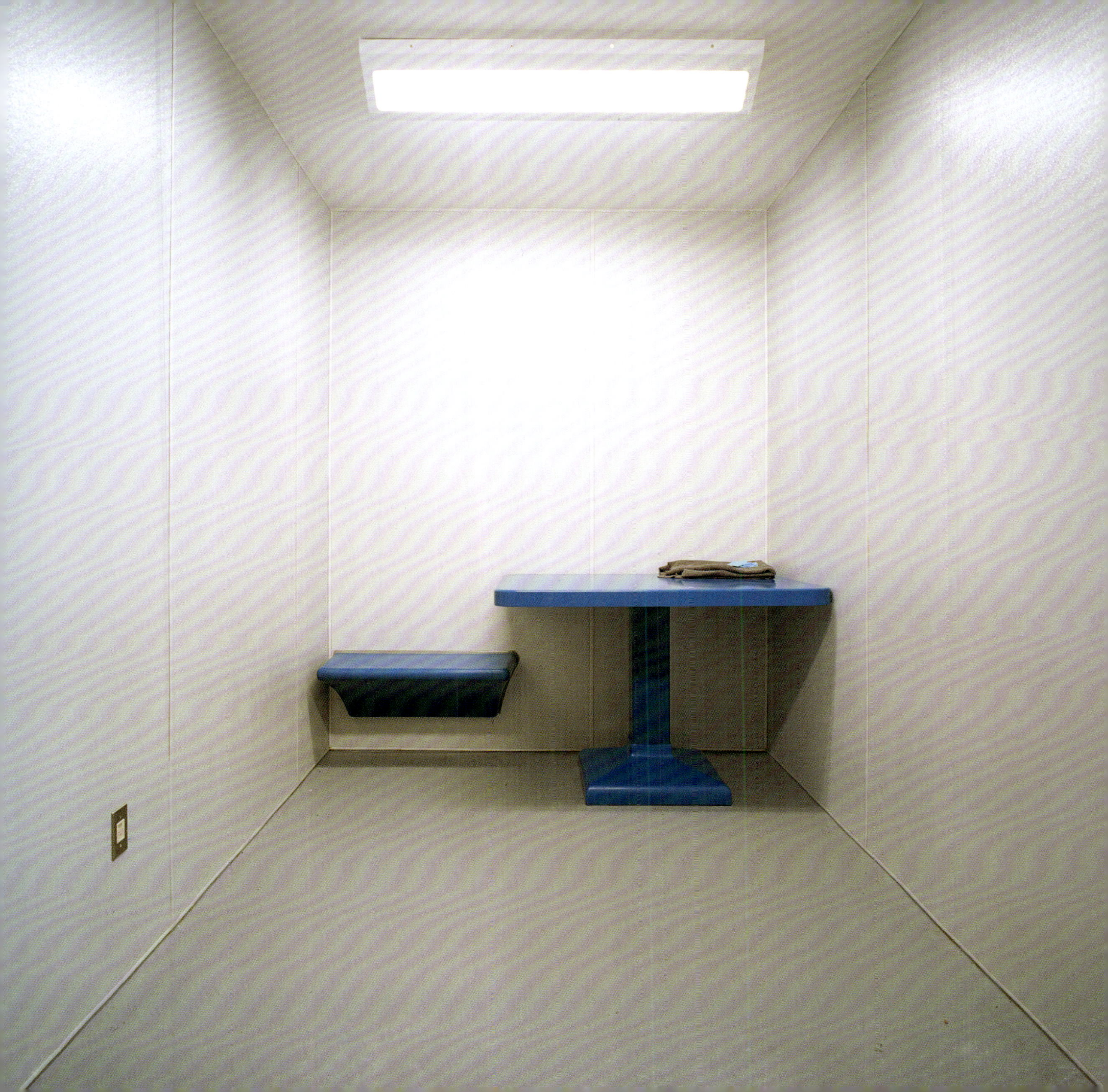

Outside courtroom, Central Criminal Court of Iraq, Baghdad

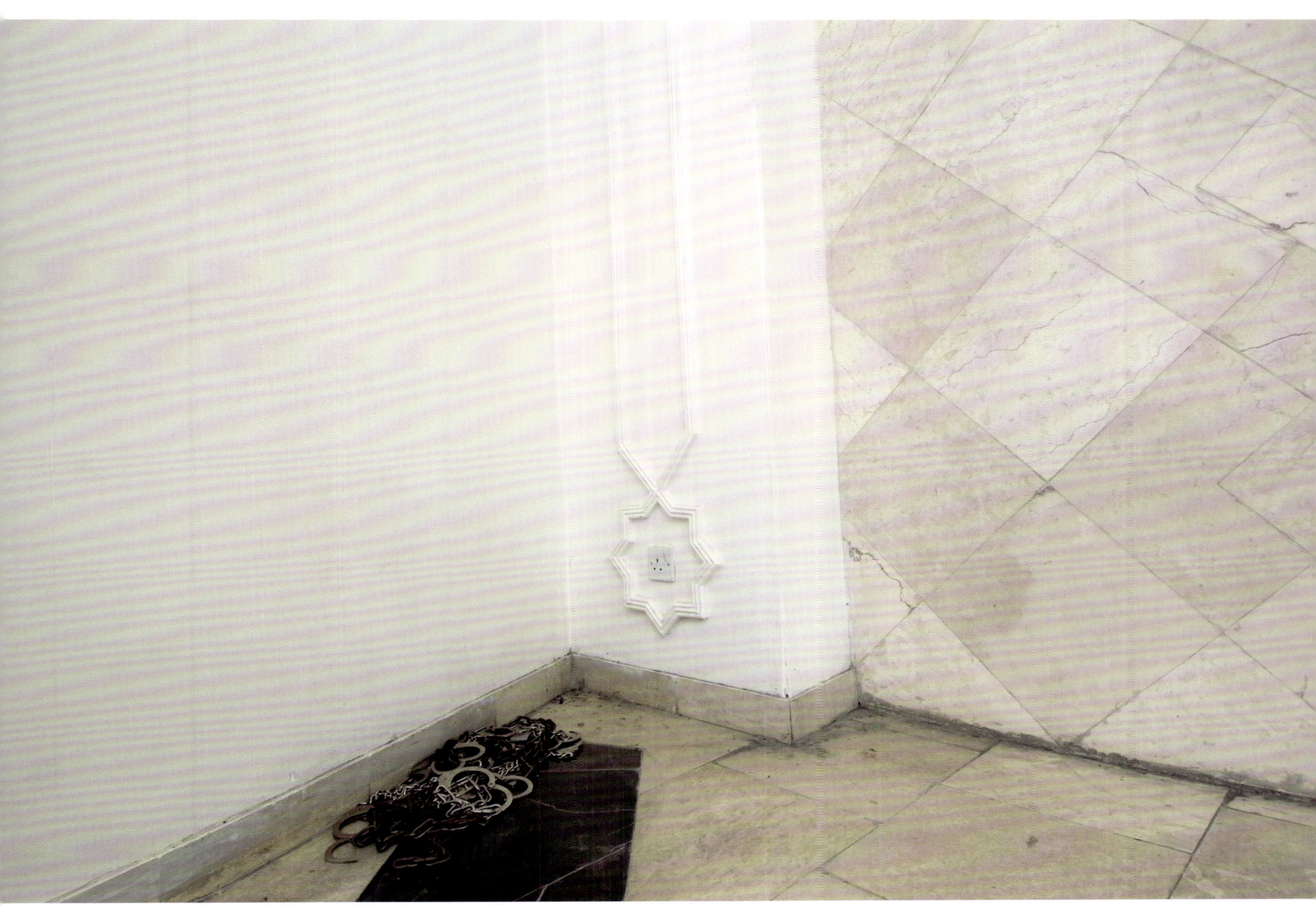

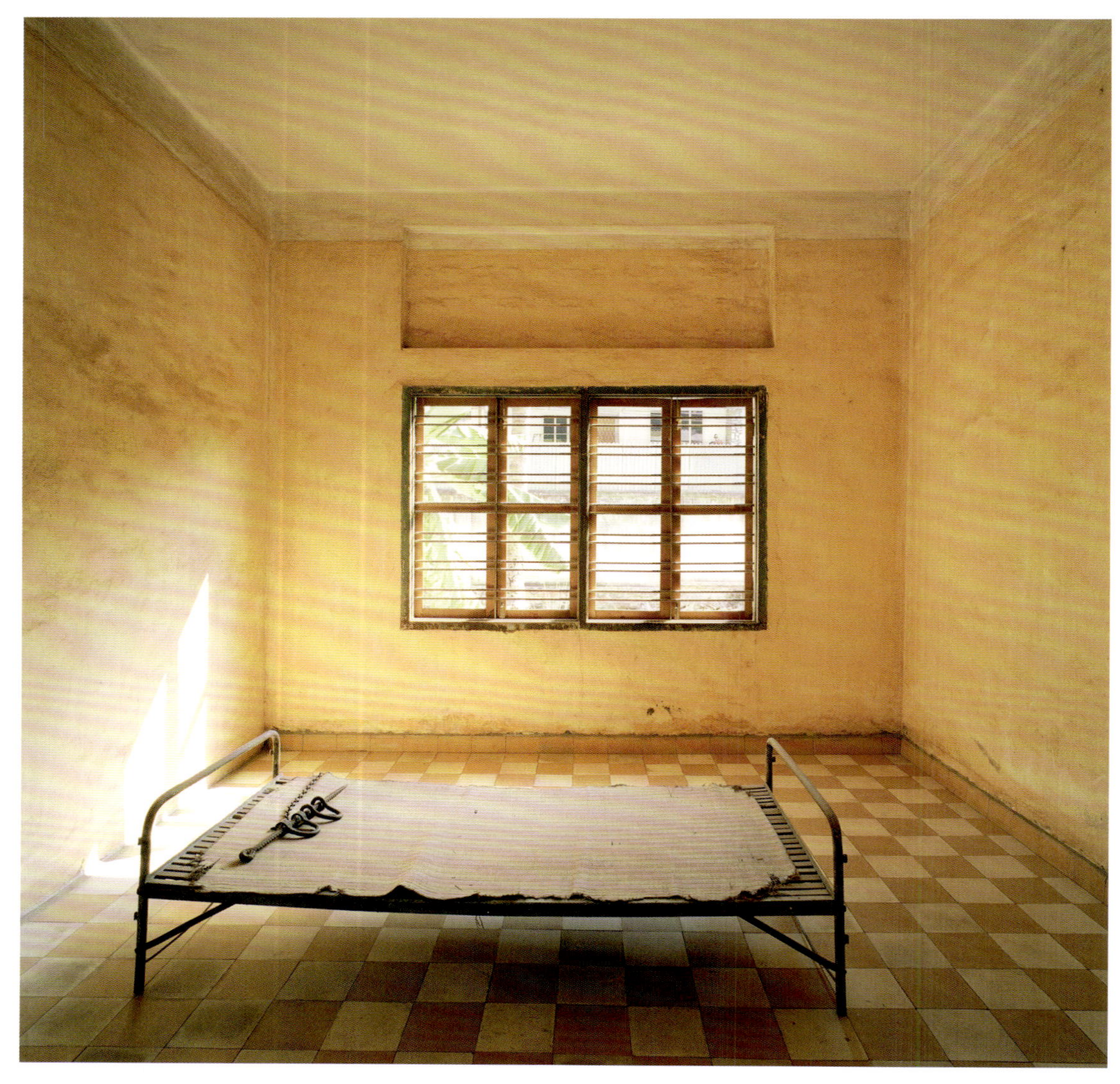

ABOVE: Holding cell, Khmer Rouge Prison 21 (no longer in use), Tsol Sleng, Phnom Penh, Cambodia
OPPOSITE: Cell, Eastern State Penitentiary Historic Site, Philadelphia

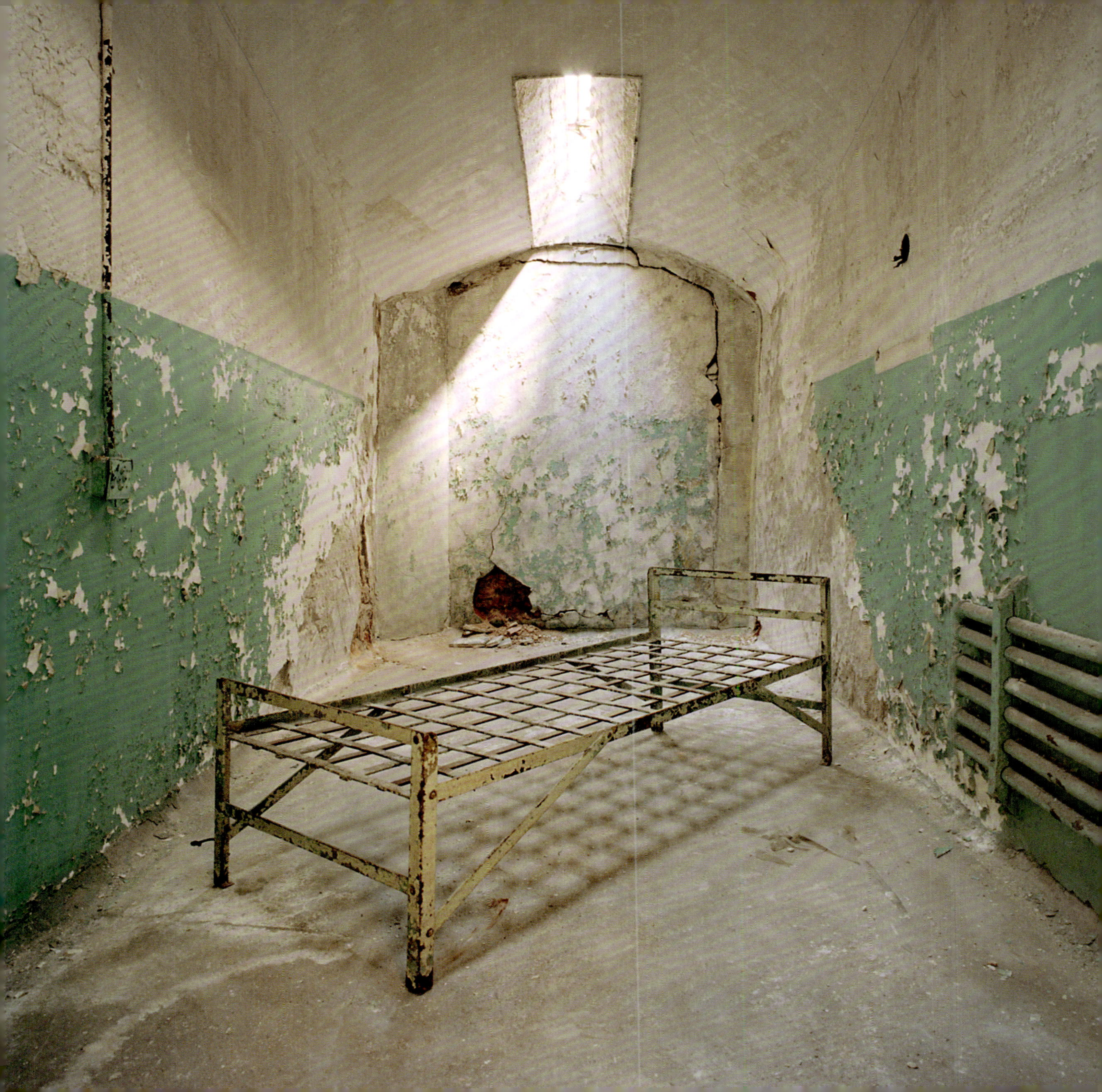

OPPOSITE: Troop billet, Camp Victory, outside Baghdad

OVERLEAF: Wall separating Green Zone (secure) and Red Zone (unsecure), Baghdad

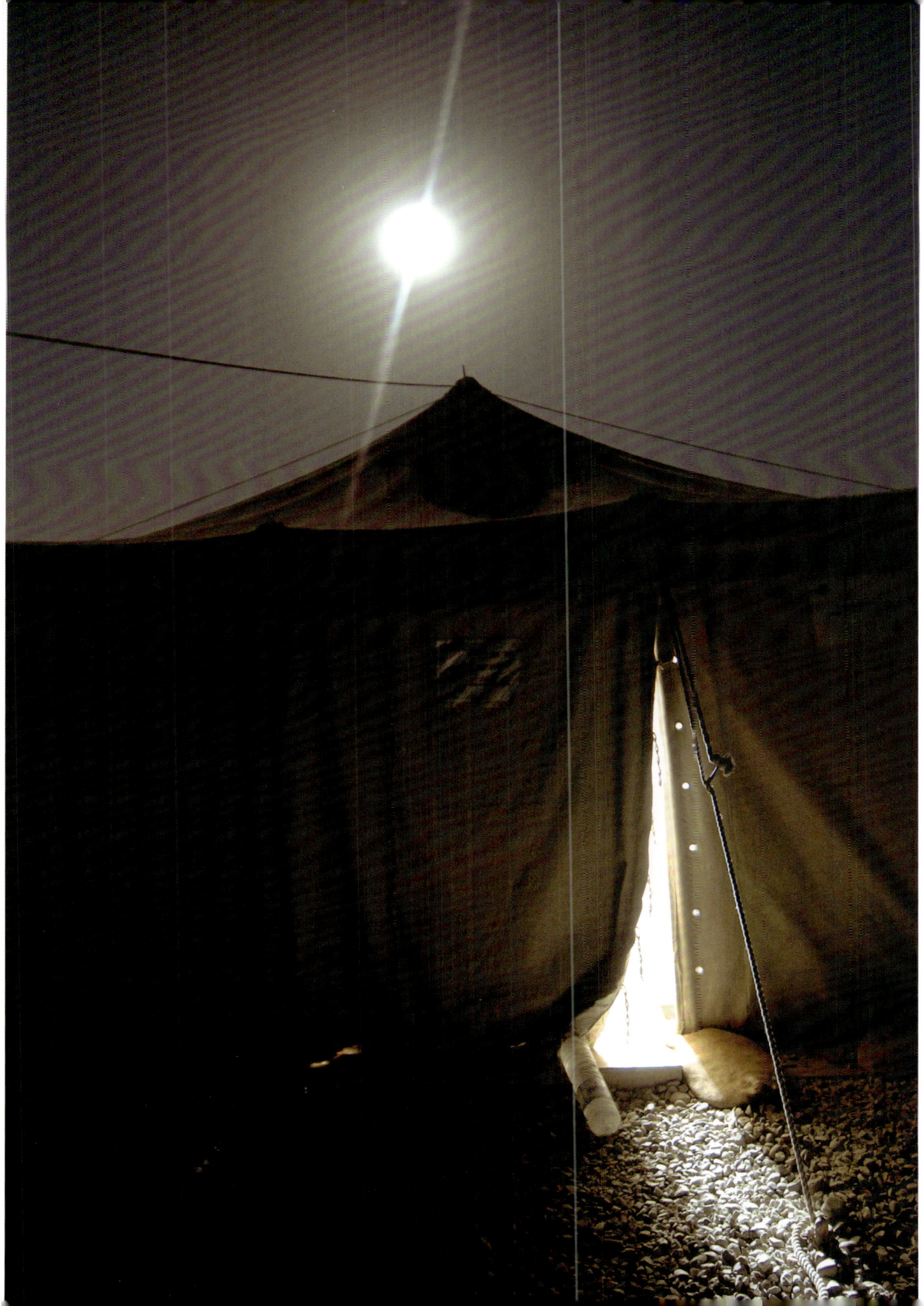

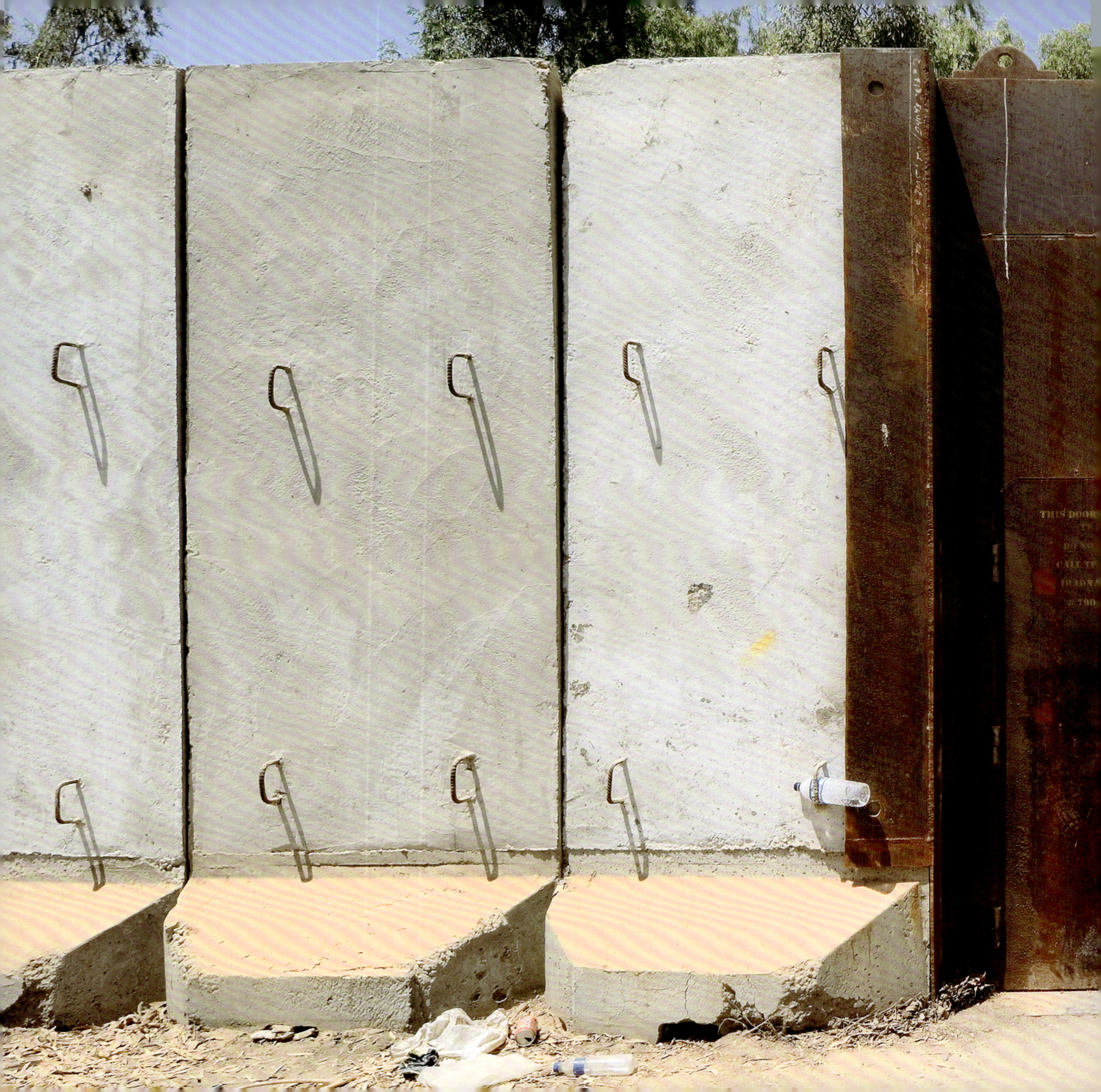
THIS DOOR

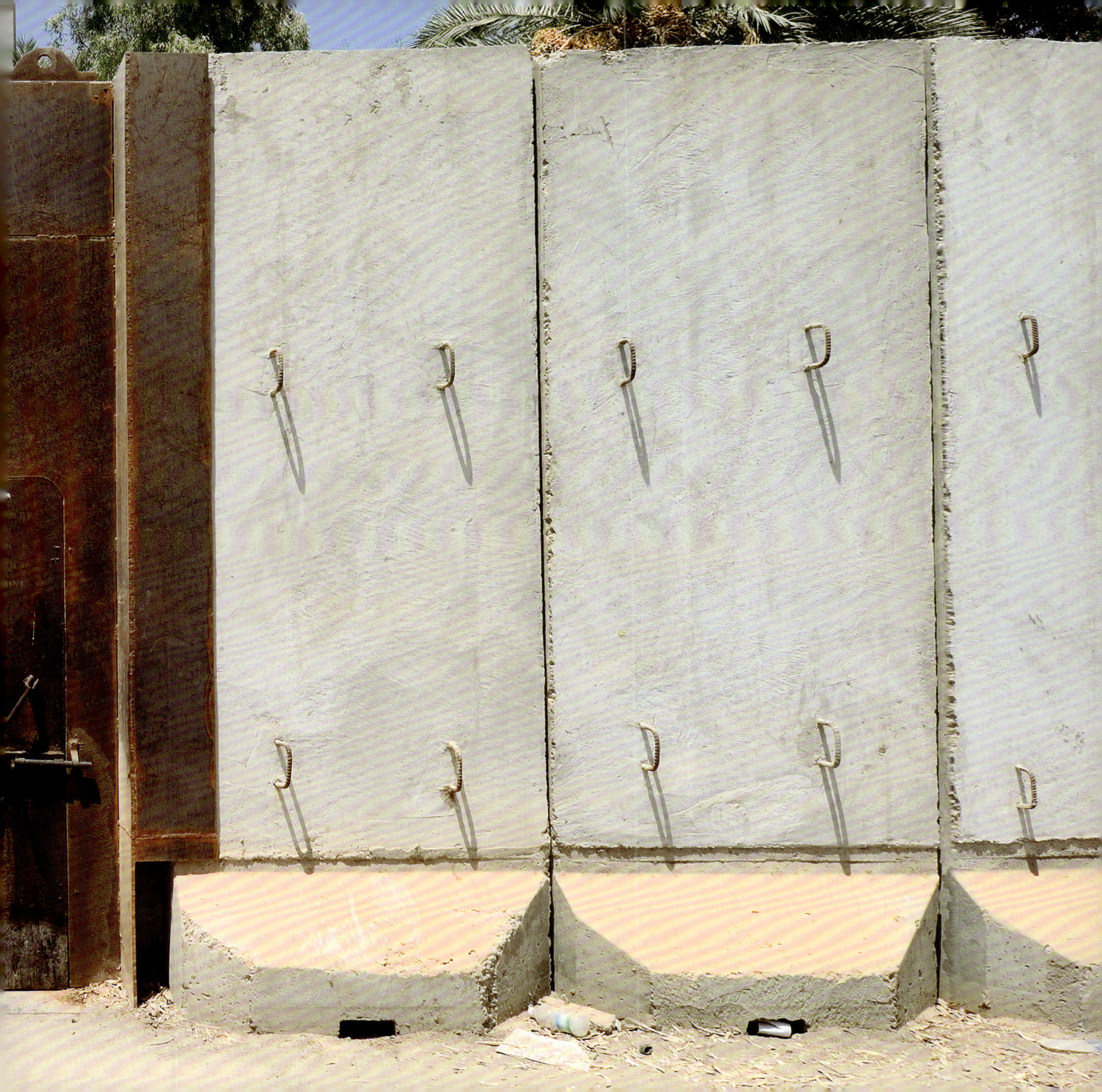

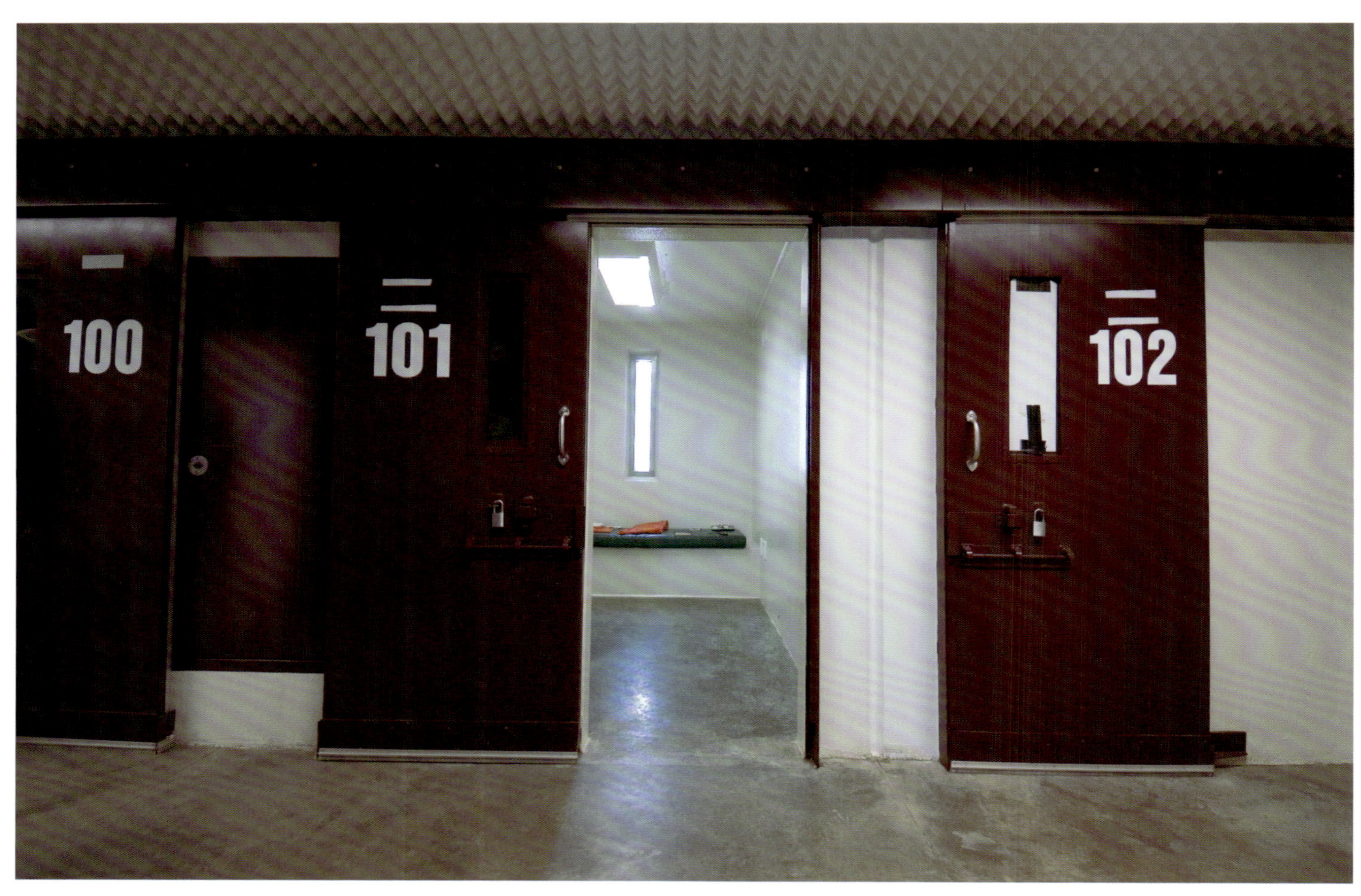

ABOVE AND OPPOSITE: Camp 5, Guantánamo, Cuba

OVERLEAF: Abandoned shower stalls, Camp X-Ray, Guantánamo, Cuba

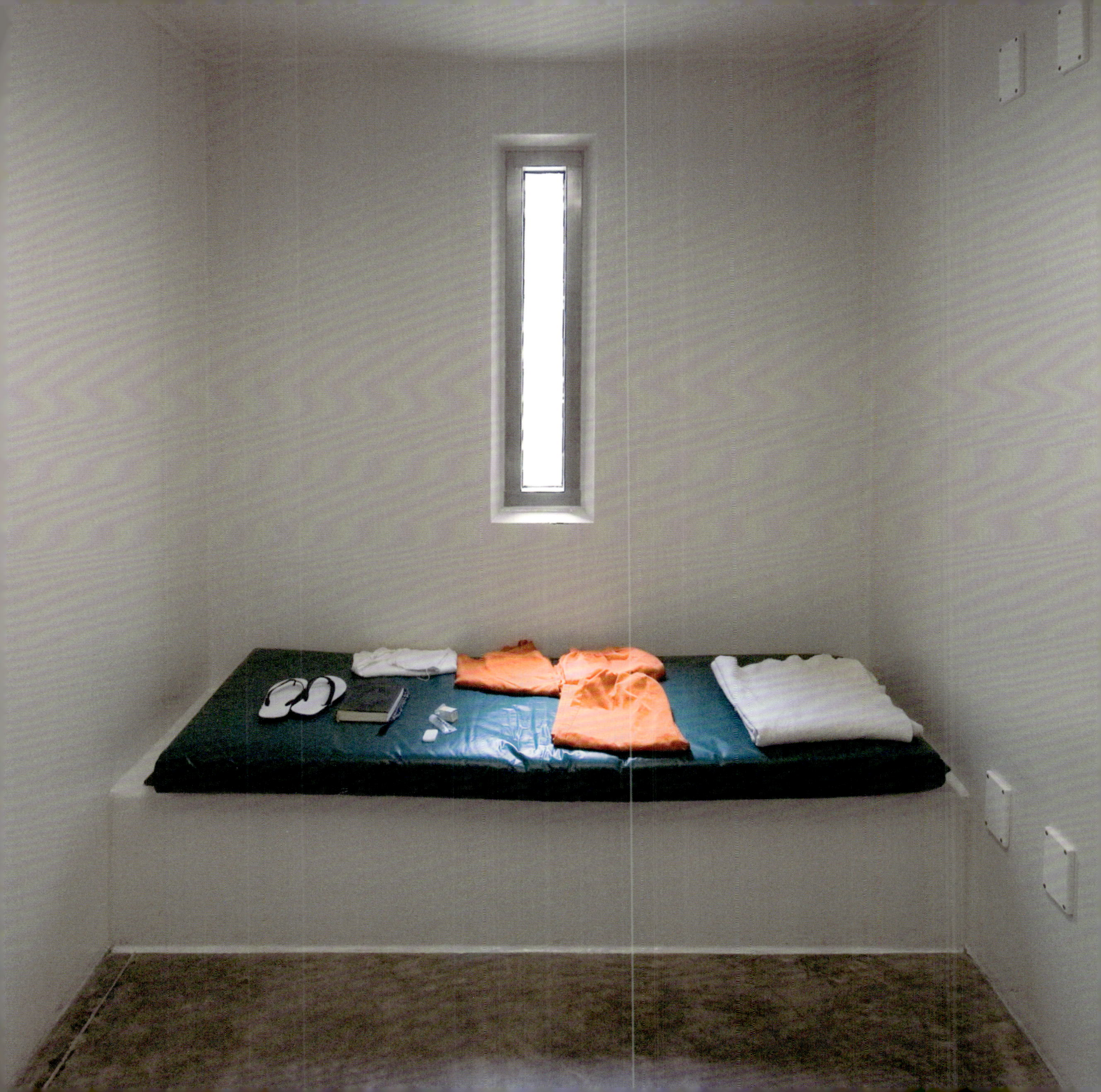

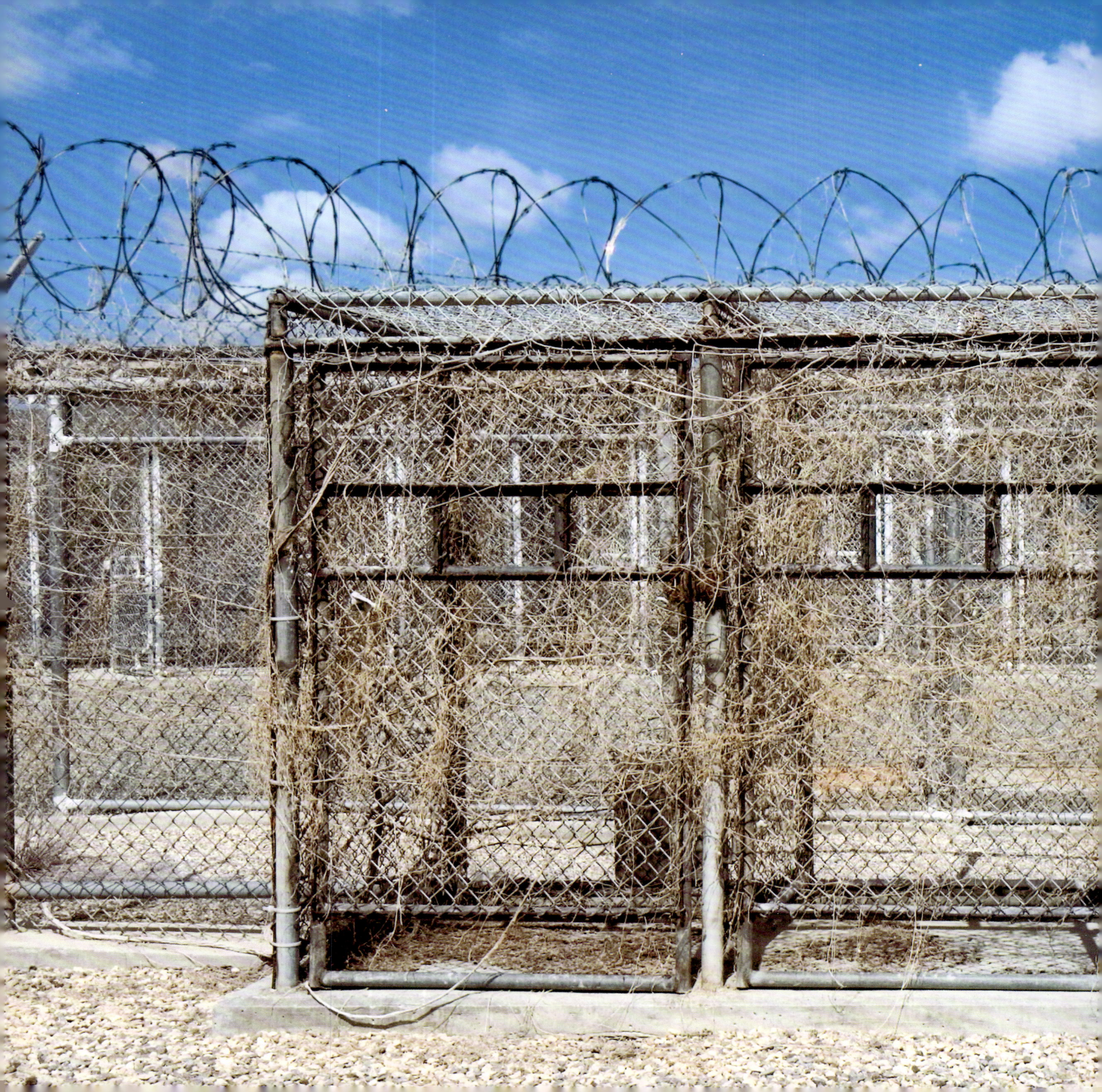

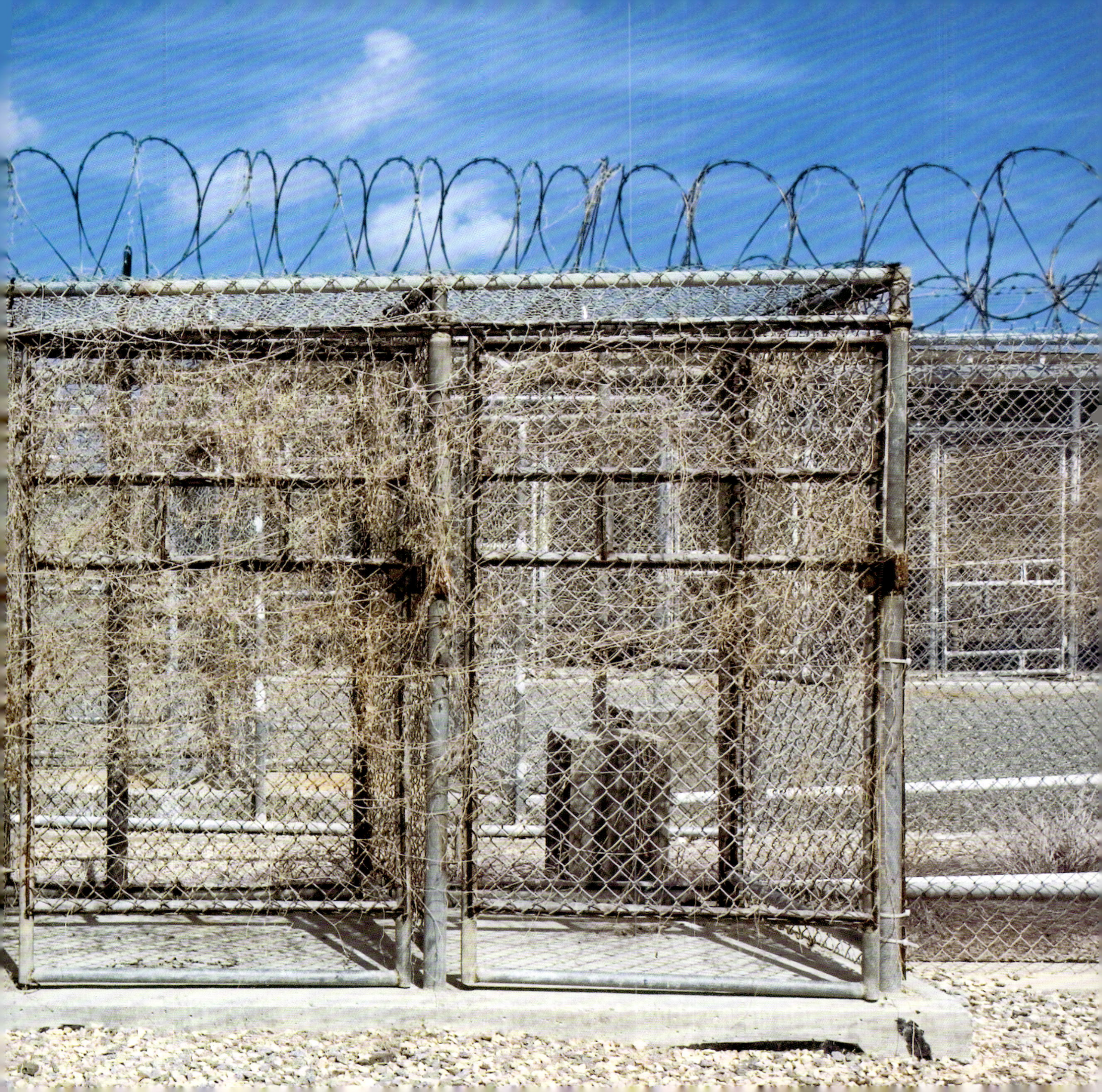

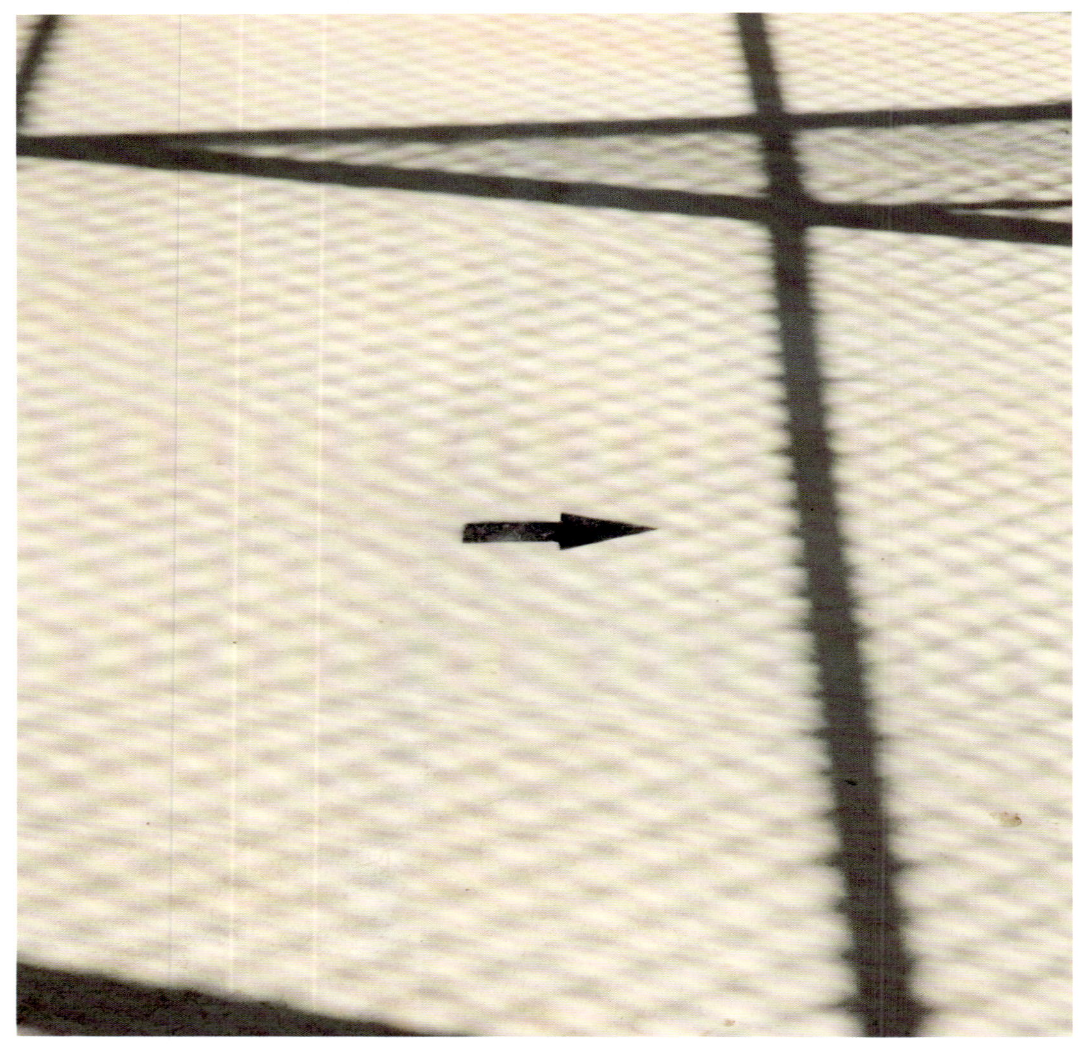

ABOVE: Arrow pointing to Mecca, exercise yard, Camp 3, Guantánamo, Cuba

OPPOSITE: Isolation exercise yard, Security Housing Unit, Pelican Bay State Prison, Crescent City, California

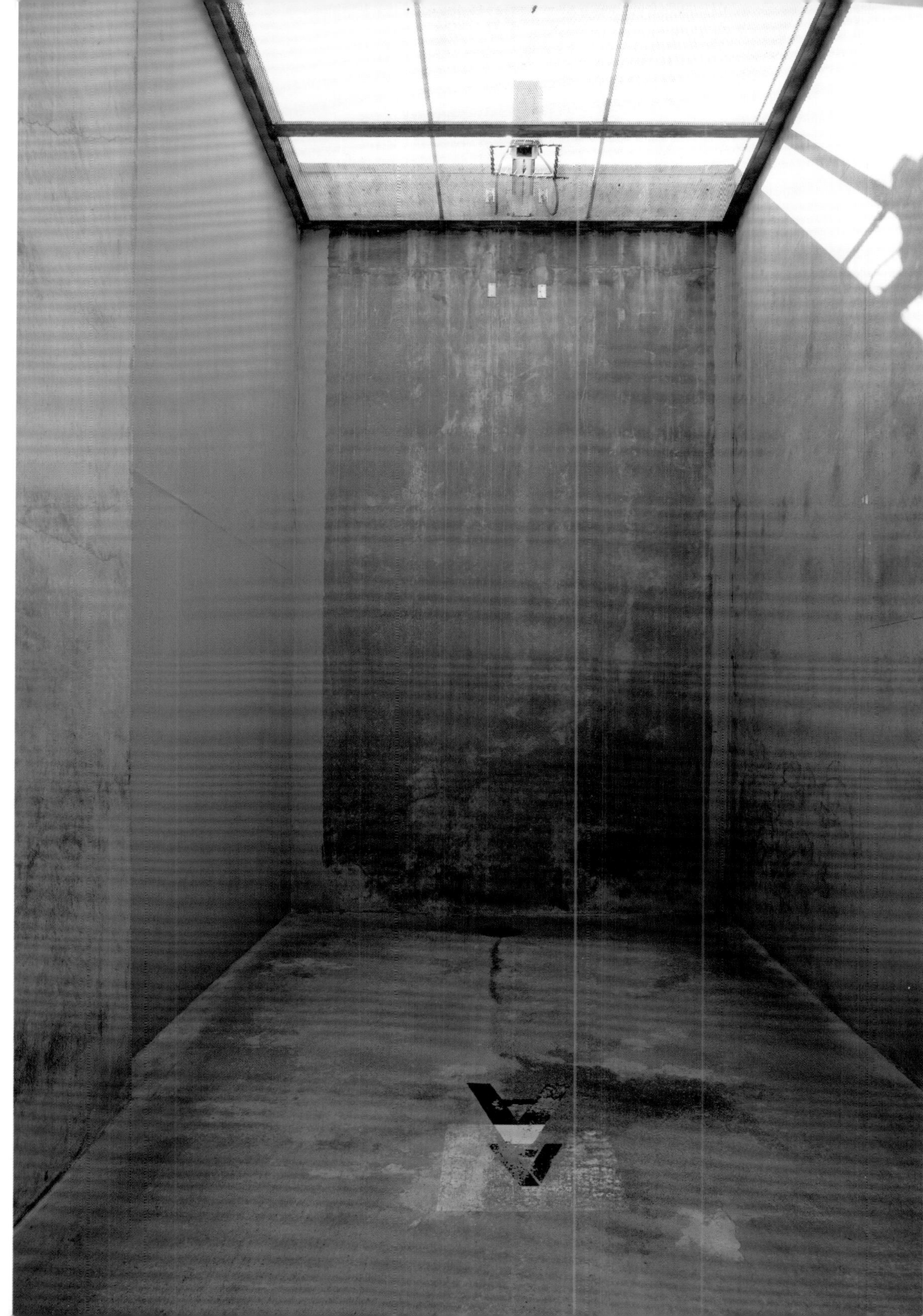

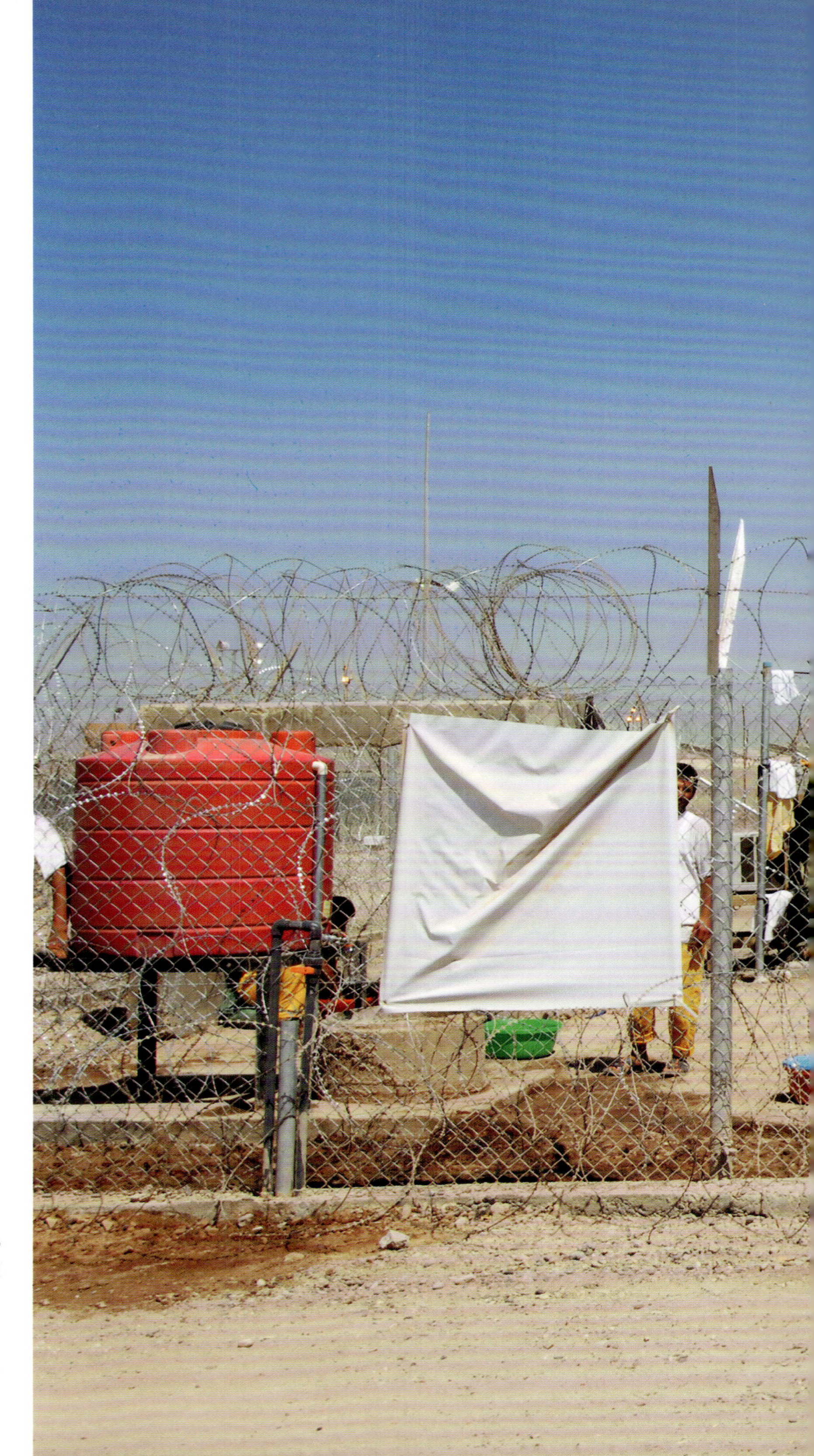

Detainee housing unit, Camp Remembrance,
new Abu Ghraib prison, Abu Ghraib, Iraq

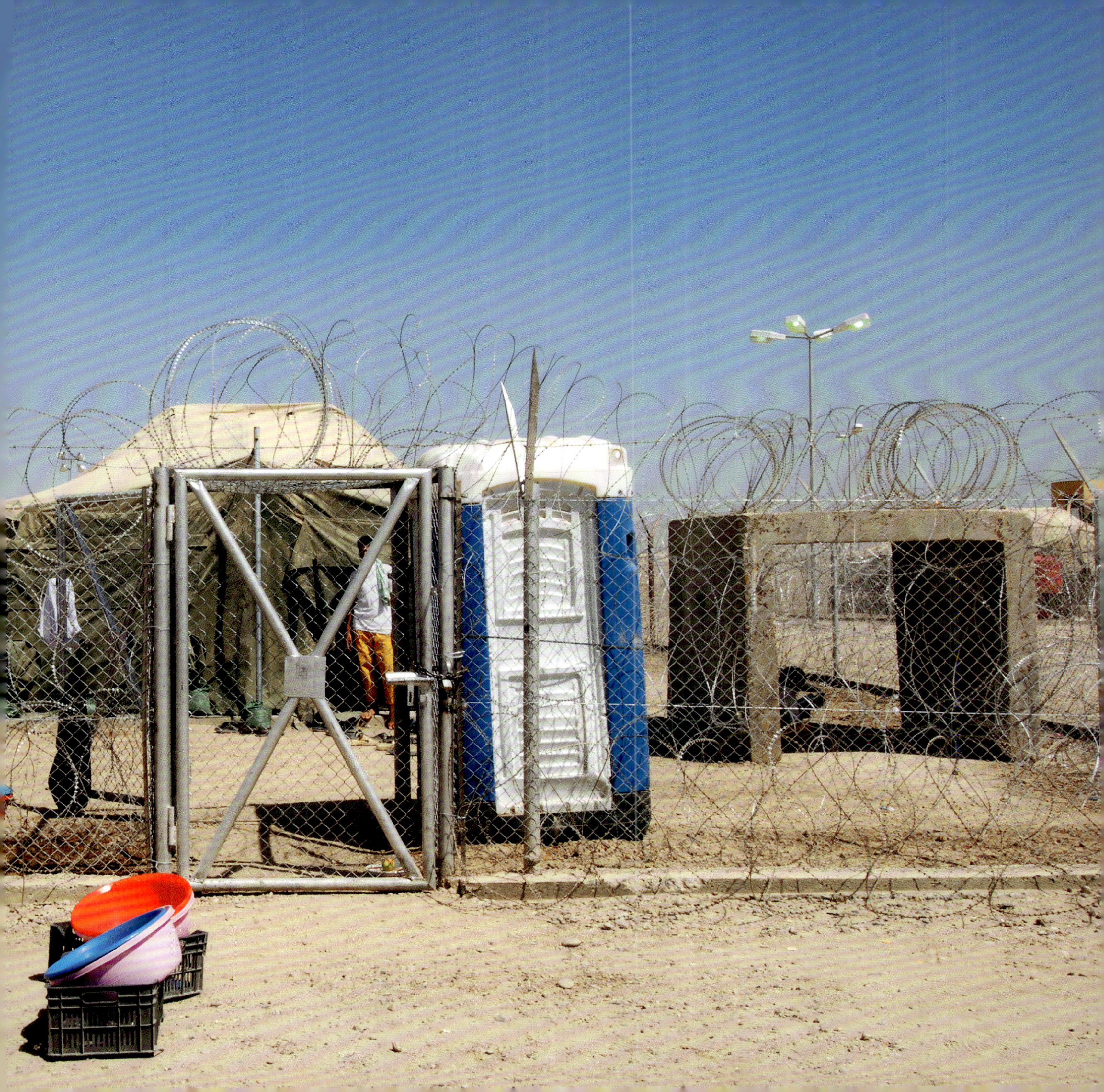

Clock and phones connected to the governor's office, Angola State Penitentiary, Angola, Louisiana

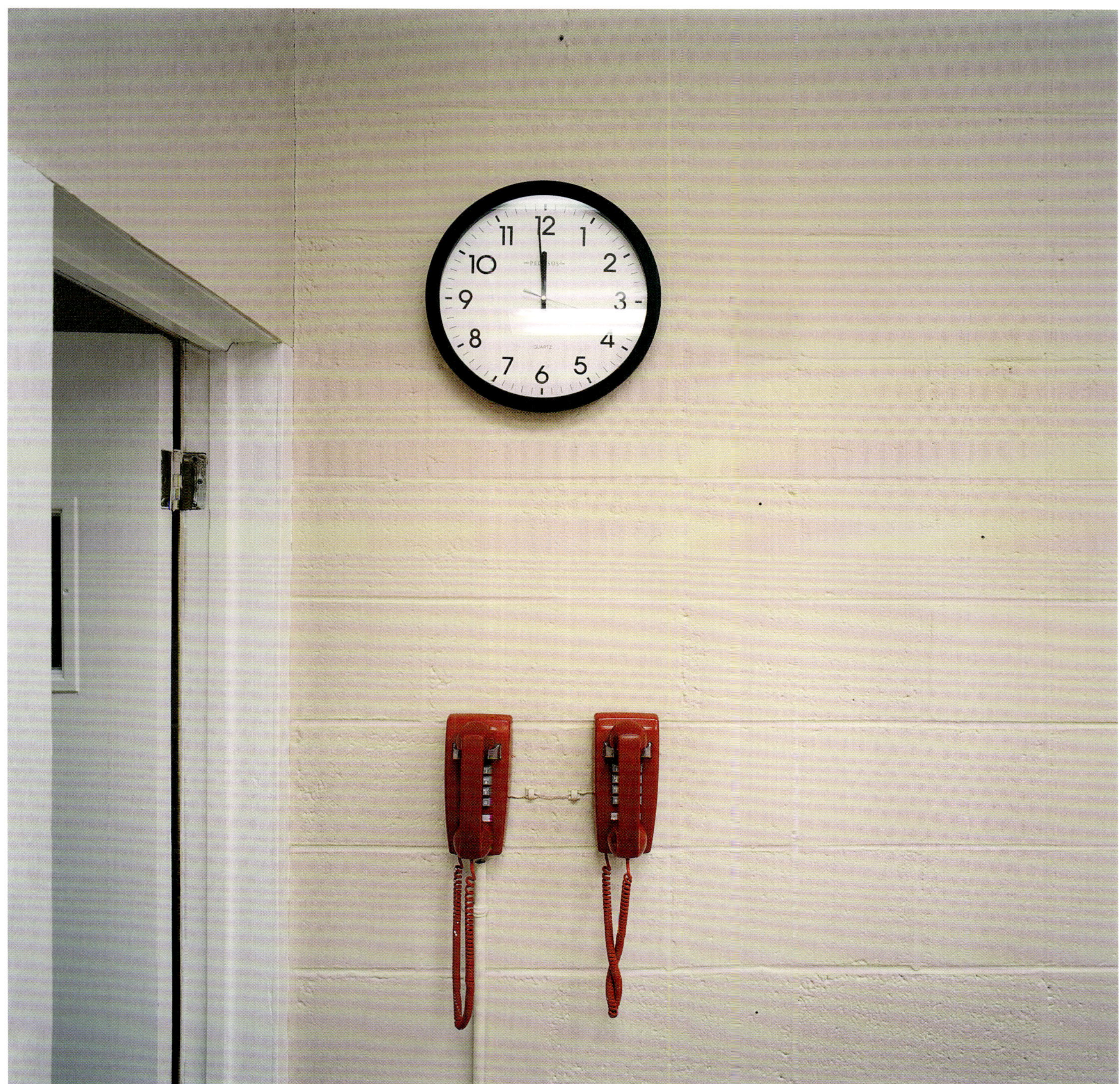

Lethal-injection room, Angola State Penitentiary, Angola, Louisiana

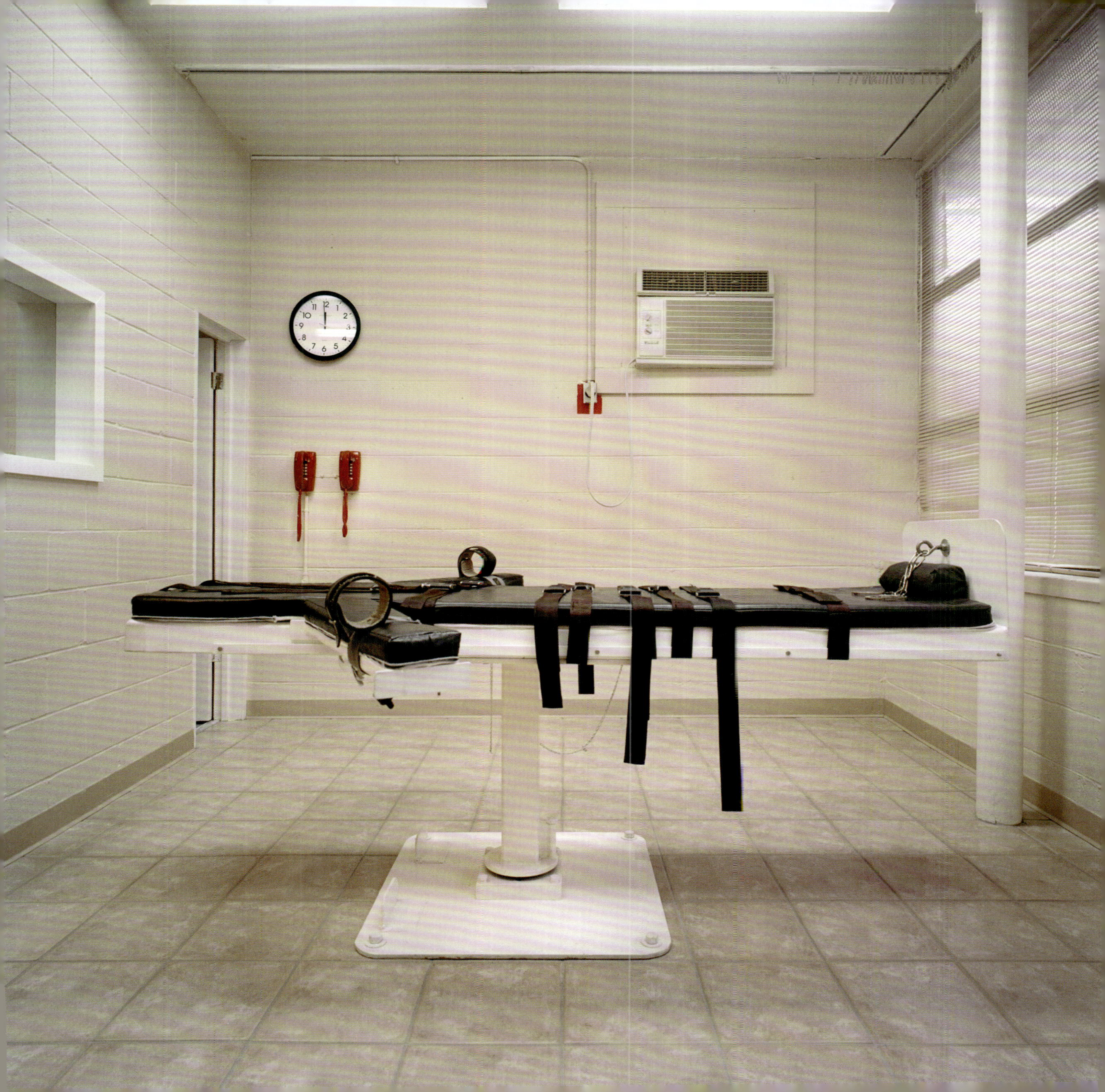

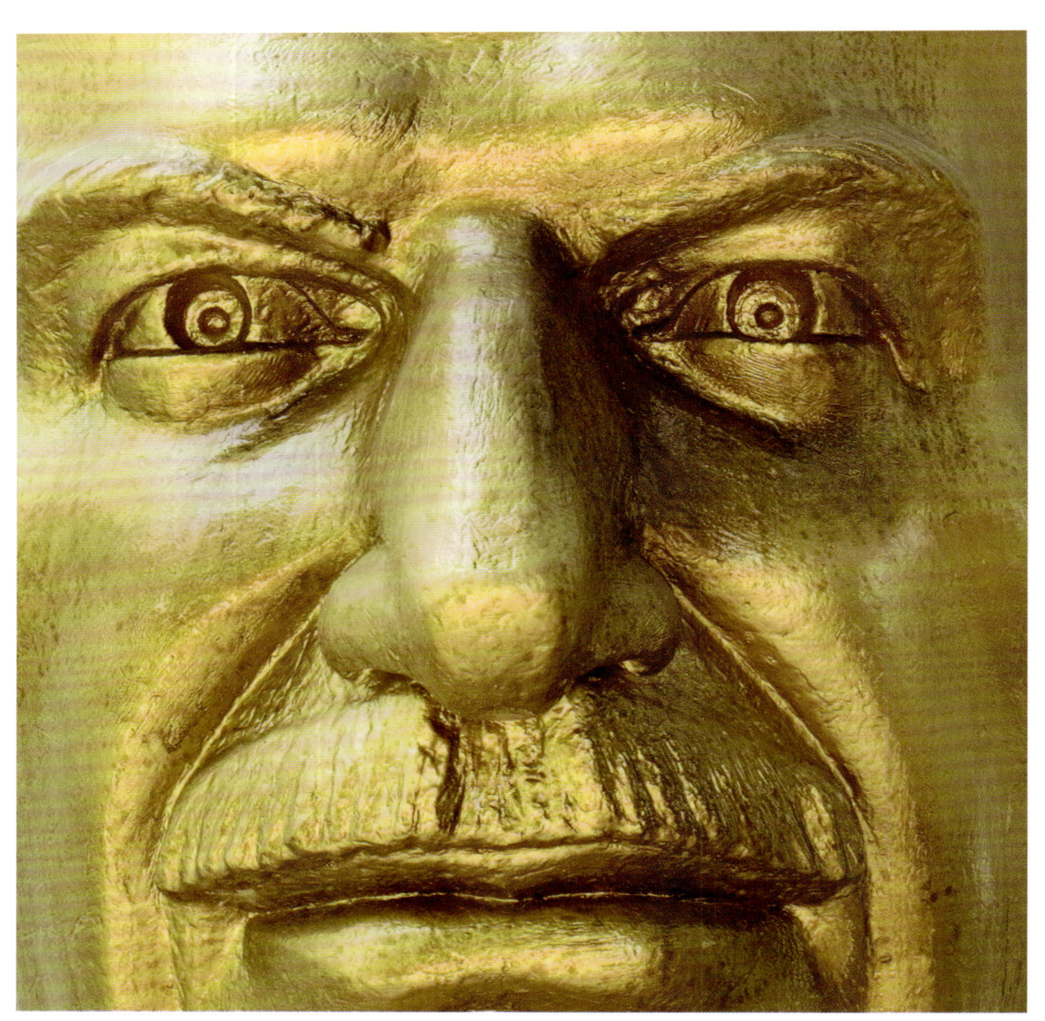

AFTERWORD

Richard Ross

Abu Ghraib, Iraq, August 2005

It is not particularly easy to get here. No rental cars on this stretch of road. Transport is via an armored Humvee, as part of a twenty-vehicle convoy. Prior to departure from Camp Victory, we all get the "what if" talk. "If we come under hostile fire; if a vehicle becomes disabled; if we take casualties." I listen with rapt attention. This is the same type of talk that I have heard a flight attendant give on countless flights to countless destinations. But for the first time I am not only paying attention I am straining to envision my actions in every one of these possible scenarios. As we move out, we project a physical space around us. Everyone local is aware that if you come close to a coalition convoy, you risk being stopped, or worse. On each vehicle there is a sign in Arabic: "Do not come closer than 500 feet or you will be shot." The soldiers in my vehicle ask, "Do you know how to fire a gun?" There are no pacifists on this portion of life's journey.

Sweat pours from my body, and it is not simply the heat. Nerves, twenty pounds of body armor, and a Kevlar helmet raise the temperature. The air conditioner goes at top blast but does little to stem the flow. The convoy is punctuated by three other Humvees, fuel trucks, and semis carrying lumber. As we travel, two Bradley Fighting Vehicles flank each of three overhead bridges and prevent traffic from approaching the convoy. Above us, two Apache helicopters oversee our bubble of protection as the convoy moves at a healthy forty-five-miles-per-hour clip along the road from Camp Victory toward Fallujah and my destination, Abu Ghraib. The bubble is a transitory assertion of authority, with anarchy before and madness trailing. While the convoy passes through an area, there is enough force from the front, rear, side, and above to exercise control over this moving target. I am not the prime focus of all this energy and expenditure—just a minor appendage to a military convoy, scheduled for a tantalizingly brief stop at the prison complex. After months of preparation and days of waiting, my actual working time at Abu Ghraib compresses to hours. I exit the Humvee and try to understand what it means to be here and what exactly I am seeing—not an easy task.

Physically, there are two distinct sides to Abu Ghraib; the "hard site" now administered by the Iraqis, and the new site, the sprawling Coalition Theater Internment Facility. The line between them is blurry, and the Iraqi side is administered, in part, by a warden from Missouri. The American side is the

Statue of Hafez al-Assad, Military Museum, Damascus, Syria

area for detainees. These are people who are not yet tried and convicted, nor are they acquitted. They simply wait. Within the new American-built camp are four distinct sectors, named Liberty, Redemption, Redemption South, and the newest, Remembrance. These camps are separated by wire into smaller subdivisions of single tents. Each tent has a portable toilet and a small air conditioner standing next to it. This is a demanding environment, visually and conceptually. There is not a blade of grass in sight. No bird flies through the air, and not even an insect interrupts the stillness—there are just silent men in cages.

The most dominant feature of this landscape is not visible. It is the pervasive heat, which becomes a separate element, a tangible obstacle to any but the most essential activity. Today it is 118.5 degrees.

I am unsure how many detainees are inside the canvas tents hiding from the August sun, but outside each tent two or three of them stare at me as I mount my camera on a tripod. I exist for them only as a nameless, silent, unexplained figure who breaks the routine of their day for a passing moment. These detainees await hearings by the Combined Review and Release Board. As my escort rattles off statistics citing the amount of calories as well as the number of medical, dental, and ophthalmologic visits each detainee gets, I am acutely aware that there are individuals in this facility—over four thousand of them. Each has hopes and beliefs, each is a person somehow put on this square of hell in the middle of the desert.

The way to liberty and redemption is paved by degrees of cooperation. I have seen the same construct used at Guantánamo. Both are environments with infinite architectural nuances. Cells, interview rooms, interrogation rooms, have a certain familiarity around the globe, and every prison has its segregation cells, isolation areas, "the pit," and "the hole." Architecture is not necessarily an innocent act of creativity. A confessional in a Catholic church and an interview room at Los Angeles Police Department headquarters share the same intimate dimensions. They are both uncomfortably tight spaces constructed to force people together, to extract a confession in exchange for some form of redemption.

At the front of Camp Redemption stand four ominous monoliths—"seg cells." These are the isolation units, separated from the rest of the camp, where uncooperative detainees are placed for various rule violations. These four cells are icons of authority, standing as a harsh reminder to detainees as to who is in control. Detainees are held here for infractions such as talking between compounds, failing to obey, and fighting. The isolation cells are directly in the guards' line of vision, so any detainee placed here is never out of sight.

I am not an official inspecting the camps, and so I am given only a circumscribed view of them. Still, it is impossible not to be startled by what I see. The camps are a vast area punctuated with rows of chain-link fence and concertina wire. Green floodlights bathe the grid of the compound twenty-four hours a day, so there is an omnipresent eerie glow. There is a marked disparity between the patrolling military police (MPs)—formally uniformed in long-sleeved camouflage fatigues, body armor, and helmets—and

Shelter under the Imperial Palace, Ho Chi Minh City, Vietnam

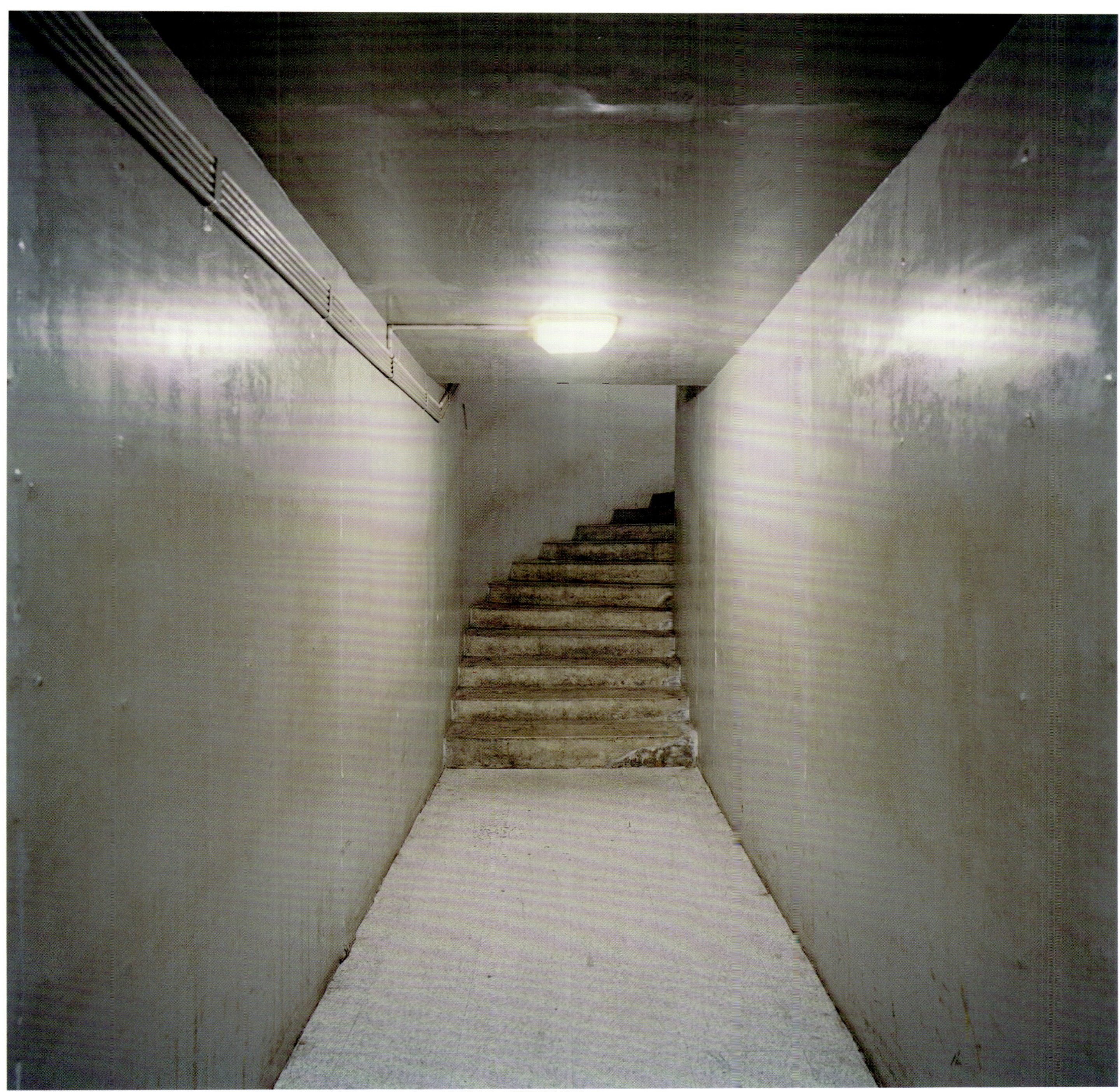

the prisoners, with their casual flip-flops, orange pants, and dingy white T-shirts. Most American troops in Iraq serve rotations of nine to twelve months; detainees have a much less defined tenure.

I wait in the guard shack at the entrance to Camp Remembrance for permission to photograph the seg cells. Even though I have already been allowed to photograph the other side of Abu Ghraib, Saddam's death chamber, there is a heated discussion between the public assistance officers (PAOs) and the MPs, who ask, "Who authorized this visit?" The majors keep me standing there while they debate whether I am cleared to photograph the seg cells right outside the door, the pictures that for me are the signature images of my entire project.

I have shed so much sweat and replaced it with so much water that I do not notice that my electrolytes are so out of whack that the simple act of standing up has become compromised; I'm teetering. A soldier gives me a cold Gatorade, and the imbalance disappears in one gulp—that helps. My time at Abu Ghraib is limited, and the convoy is forming to return to Baghdad. If I had the strength, my anxiety would be higher, but I am simply too tired and too drained by the heat. Almost comatose, I am virtually oblivious to the discussion. The images I want are right in front of me, and the decision to allow me to shoot them, after I have come from across the world, depends on the outcome of this conversation.

While I am drifting, waiting in the guard post, I read a brass plaque that bears the names of the first responders who lost their lives in the 9/11 attack on the World Trade Center. "Remembrance" seems a curious name for a detention camp in Iraq, since the attackers were primarily Saudi nationals. The plaque offers the possibility of rewriting history by linking the current detainees to the terrorists' actions four years past. Victors write their own histories, and lapses of attention allow them great latitude.

An accord is reached. A lieutenant gets her "ass-chewing," and I get five minutes to shoot as the convoy is preparing to go back to Baghdad. I finish with sixty seconds to spare before the Humvee returns to get me.

I remind myself that the people held here are prisoners or detainees, not necessarily convicts. Such nuances of language are important. At Abu Ghraib, as well as Guantánamo, there are detainees who have not been convicted. At Guantánamo, they are being indefinitely detained. At Abu Ghraib they have to appear before a board within six months, but once that occurs, they can be released, turned over to the Iraqis for trial, or put back into holding for another period of six months. At the "hard site," many are convicted by the Central Criminal Court of Iraq; hence, they are called convicts. At Guantánamo, no such rules exist; detainees are in limbo, purgatory—they are nowhere men. Time stretches infinitely, governed by the caprice of the American rules. José Padilla is to the United States what Josef K. was to Kafka, a citizen held under a set of rules that keep changing. This fictionalized nightmare becomes our reality, our legacy.

I grew up in the golden age of America—no metal detectors to get into school, no warnings on bleach bottles not to drink, no warnings on coffee cups that the contents are hot. It was a simpler time. Now I am going through a mass of images and asking the questions: What is the relationship between

words such as *power*, *authority*, *tyranny*, *architecture*, *morality*, and *hierarchy*? How did we evolve from my childhood paradise of Brooklyn to the horrors of this new world?

"How did you gain access?" Since *Architecture of Authority* is rooted in a kind of plea for honesty and transparency in my government, I should reciprocate by explaining how I went about photographing these images. As Rick MacArthur points out in his essay, I was born in New York, where "No" is just a starting point. So my persistence has played a part. But I also found that once the original barriers were breached, few people wanted to be left out of the project. When I received clearance from the Secret Service, I was able to get to the FBI, then ICE (Immigration and Customs Enforcement), and so on. Many people did not need major introductions or credentials. They were just willing to share their world with someone who showed genuine interest in it.

Luck, sympathy, and coincidence helped too. The Secret Service headquarters in LA was headed by Tony Chapas, who wanted to make his office accessible and relatively "nonsecret" so that the general population would understand its function. It didn't hurt that his wife had taken a class with the art historian Dave Hickey, who wrote the foreword to an earlier book of mine. And so the world spins. Guantánamo did not welcome an artist or a professor, so I wore the hat of a journalist and did a piece for *La Repubblica*, from Milan. Once in Guantánamo, I bought anyone and everyone beers (Red Stripe) when we went to lunch or dinner, and they gave me contacts for Iraq. I never lied; I always shared my concern and commitment with anyone who would listen. I always respected the people working for the military or government agencies. I believe it was refreshing for the people I was contacting to deal with someone who was neither patronizing nor adversarial. Rather, I tried to approach the project as research. Most people were disarmed by my interest in photographing architecture rather than people. They felt this was more benign.

More detailed information about each image in the book can be found on the Web site www.richardross.net.

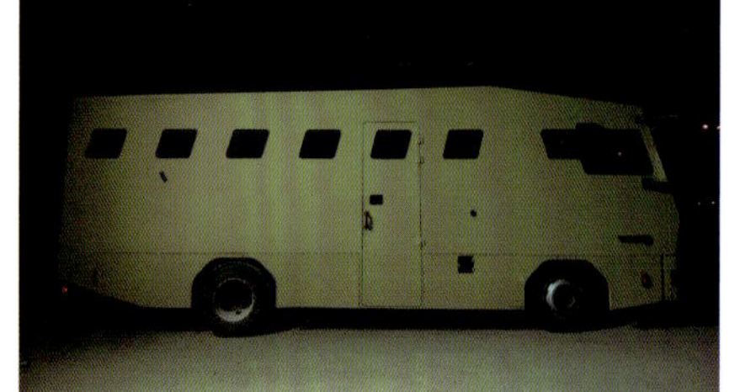

Rhino Runner (armored bus), on Route Irish, between Baghdad International Airport and the Green Zone

ACKNOWLEDGMENTS

Nothing of note is done in my life without the tacit agreement, blessing, and support of Cissy, Leela, and Nick, who tolerate, travel with, assist, cajole, and humor me.

The supporting cast of characters in the studio includes, at various times: Teja Ream, Michelle Yap, Ben Foxworthy, Nikki Kurtz, Betsy Filson, Heather Phillips, Hunter Howatt-Nab, Jonathon Cecil, Isabella Re Snyder, Joel Sherman, Margo Sturer, Michael Schmidt, and Atsuo Baba. All work long hours for a demanding and difficult ringmaster.

The book would not have been possible without the support and intelligent criticism (both intellectual and visual) of Laura Lindgren, the best of designers, and Nancy Grubb, my spirited, supportive, and challenging editor.

Julien Robson, curator of the Speed Art Museum in Louisville, Kentucky; Stephen Foster, director of the Hansard Gallery in Southampton, England; Meg Linton, director of the Ben Maltz Gallery at Otis College of Art and Design; and Randy Sommer, codirector of ACME gallery, both in LA; and Karen Sinsheimer, curator of the Santa Barbara Museum of Art, have long surpassed their professional roles and become friends and sounding boards for any and all ideas.

Thanks also go to: Craig Hitzelburger, the travel agent who booked me tickets out of Beirut with shells flying overhead; Margaret Cota, teacher at Montessori Center School; Richard Konoske of SAMYS; and Dinh Q. Lê, a friend who opened up his Vietnam for me.

To Andy Davis, who keeps me sane.

To Haytham Abed and Khaled Malas, who helped me out of war zones, into hotels, and pointed me in the right direction in Syria.

To Gary Fowlie, who was instrumental in allowing me access to the United Nations.

There were many people in the military who were curious but tolerated my unusual point of view. It is impossible to name them all in this space, but the most instrumental were Staff Master Sergeant Anne Proctor in Baghdad and Major Jeff Weir, JTF, Guantánamo, who were helpful beyond measure.

On the civilian side of law enforcement and administration: Tony Chapa, special agent in charge, U.S. Secret Service, Los Angeles, and Jonathan Weis, special agent, head, FBI Joint Terrorism Task Force, San Francisco, were critical to the project. Adel Hussain Joda, Abbas Radhi, and Sheik Hammoudi of the Iraqi Transitional Government showed me an Iraqi point of view.

Part of my work involved an investigation of how the media portray authority. That portion was aided by Sam Bender, *Law and Order CI*; Bruce Berman, Village Road Show Pictures; Steven Boccho, *NYPD*–20th Century Fox; Tom Pollock of Montecito Pictures; and finally Dick Wolfe.